PETER HART

AT CLOSE RANGE

LIFE AND DEATH IN AN ARTILLERY REGIMENT, 1939–45

PROFILE BOOKS

This paperback edition first published in 2022

First published in Great Britain in 2020 by
Profile Books Ltd
29 Cloth Fair
London
EC1A 7JQ

www.profilebooks.com

Copyright © Peter Hart, 2020

1 3 5 7 9 10 8 6 4 2

Typeset in Garamond by MacGuru Ltd
Printed and bound in Great Britain by
CPI Group (UK) Ltd, Croydon CR0 4YY

A CIP catalogue record for this book is available from the British Library.

ISBN 978 1 78816 166 4
eISBN 978 1 78283 505 9

'A British Band of Brothers'

Major Gordon Corrigan, 2018

CONTENTS

MAPS

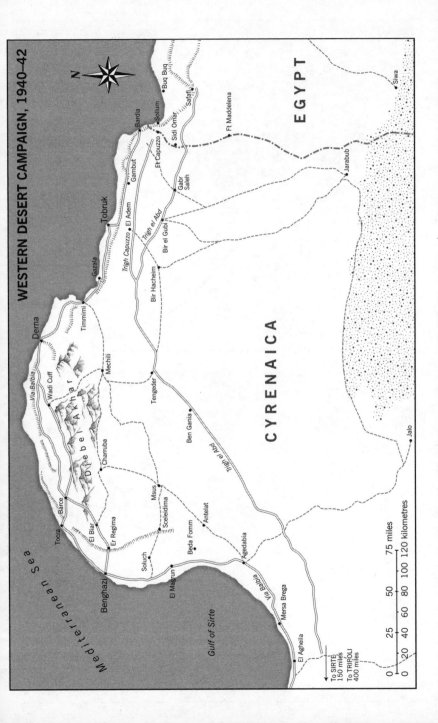

WESTERN DESERT CAMPAIGN, 1940–42

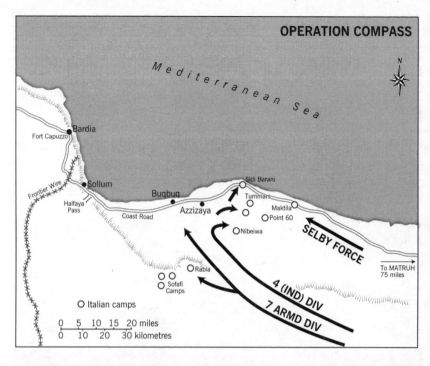

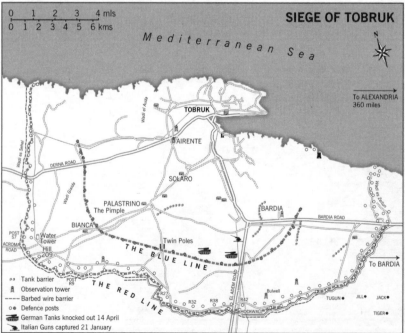

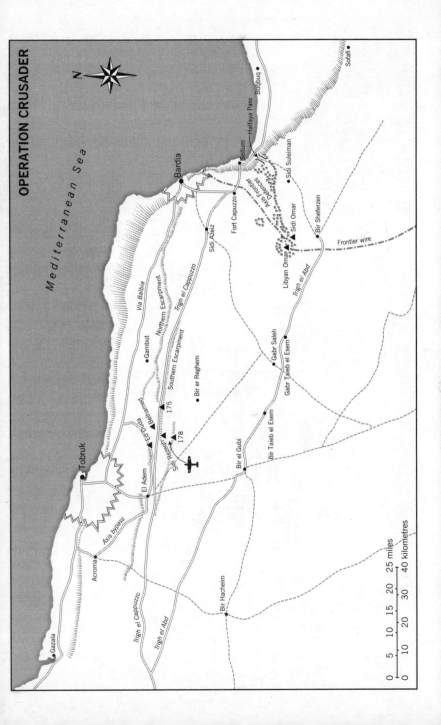

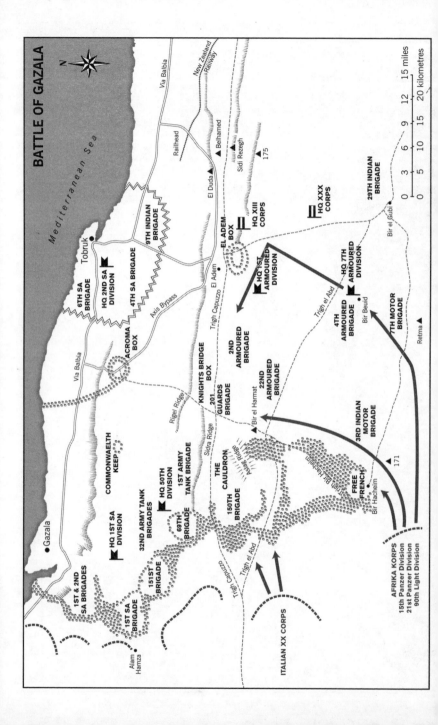

BATTLE OF GAZALA

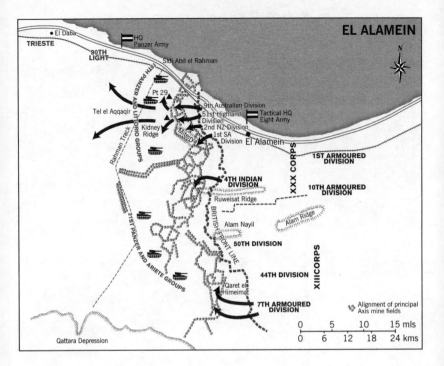

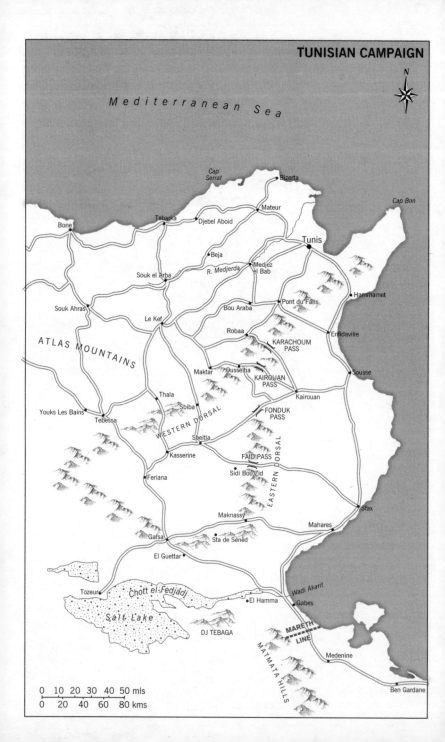

ADVANCE OF CANADIAN FORCES AND SOUTH NOTTS HUSSARS

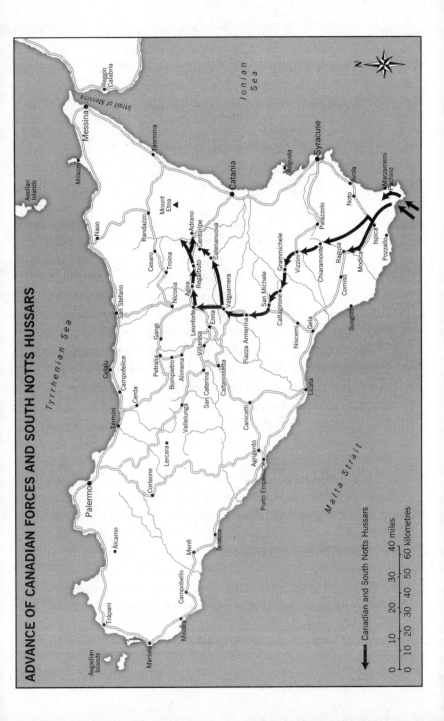

Canadian and South Notts Hussars

PREFACE

THIS BOOK COVERS THE ADVENTURES of just one regiment of the Royal Artillery during the Second World War. What matters here is the men who fought the battles: not the grand strategy, the operational theories, the tactical minutiae – all fascinating enough in themselves – but the heart of this book is the experiences of the soldiers, from the traumatic excitement of action to the banalities of life as a soldier at war. The men that sweated over their guns, mastered the abstruse technicalities of gunnery, cursed the diving Stukas, sheltered from German counter-battery fire, flinched at the howl of the nebelwerfer and faced tanks over open sights. These men are the real story. Most of my generation thought little or nothing about Second World War veterans as we were growing up. They were 'everyman' – the middle-aged chaps we saw on our streets, at football matches and in the local pubs. Our own parents and uncles. I myself was obsessed with the Great War: it seemed so much more interesting; far more remote; such a tragic waste. There seemed nothing special about the numerous Second World War veterans that surrounded us – or so I believed as a callow youth.

I was wrong.

In the late 1980s, as one of the oral historians with the Imperial War Museum Sound Archive, I began interviewing Second World War veterans. I soon found that they too had a great history to tell, one just as fascinating, just as exciting as those from the Great War. But they were younger – in their sixties or seventies – not in their nineties. Their voices were vigorous, their memories vivid, their grip of details still firm. I managed to interview some fifty veterans from just one artillery regiment: the South Nottinghamshire Hussars. By combining their memories, I could examine battles from multiple angles: blending their stories together, much as a director edits a film.

It allowed me to get 'up, close and personal' to the essence of their experience in a manner rarely found other than in fiction. To vicariously share veterans' hopes and fears; the deafening explosions of the shells, the screams of the wounded; the pleasure of good comradeship and the despair at friends lost for ever. It was a pleasure and an honour to meet men like Ray Ellis, Bob Foulds, Harold Harper, George Pearson, John Walker and all the others – ordinary young men from Nottingham who had to face up to the challenges of war service with 107th (South Notts Hussars) Regiment, Royal Artillery in September 1939. Taken from their families, exposed to the rough camaraderie of military life, they were taught their various trades as gunners, signallers, drivers, cooks, NCOs and officers, then thrust into the North African desert campaign in 1940. We chart their endless hours of training initially on first 18-pounder and then 25-pounder guns, their first experiences of battle, the prolonged privations during the Siege of Tobruk in 1941, then the slaughter and despair as they were overrun by German tanks during the Battle of Knightsbridge in June 1942. The unit soon reformed as 107 Battery, part of the 7th Medium Regiment, Royal Artillery. The survivors of the carnage at Knightsbridge were joined by men from all over the country, often conscripts, but all keen to build a new spirit and ready for the challenges of mastering their powerful new 5.5-inch medium guns. A whole raft of new characters joins our story: Reg Cutter, David Elliott and Ken Giles among them. Their guns would blaze out again to great effect during the Battle of El Alamein in October 1942, then time and time again in the battles to finally clear the Germans out of North Africa in 1943. They fought alongside the Canadian Corps throughout the Battle of Sicily, until they finished up firing across the Straits of Messina in support of the Eighth Army landings on the Italian mainland on 3 September 1943. Then it was back to England. Here the 107 Battery left 7th Medium Regiment to merge with the 16th Medium Regiment, thereby creating – like a phoenix rising from the ashes – a new 107th (South Notts Hussars) Regiment. Soon they were in the thick of it again when they landed in Normandy in July 1944. In the fighting to take Caen, they fired some 20,000 shells, usually in a counter-battery role attempting to silence the German guns that were holding up the advance. In the summer of 1944, the British artillery was once again the war-winning force it had been at the end of the Great War – the massed guns grinding down German resistance in conjunction with airpower. After the capture of Caen the regiment had one of its more gruesome successes in the war, when shells were poured into the Falaise Gap through which the Germans were retreating in August. The advance was then rapid, until they took part in the clearance of the Channel ports in September 1944. Next was the drive to free the port of Antwerp as a logistics hub. After crossing the Leopold Canal, the 107 Regiment RA provided covering fire during the hazardous missions to capture South Beveland and Walcheren Island at the end of October. Already, they had fired some 70,000 shells – around 4,400 100lb shells per gun. Then the Allies pressed towards Germany. The fighting was hard, as counter-battery fire, bombing raids and strafing attacks all made their presence felt. One of the most tragic losses of men was caused by bombs jettisoned from a crippled Allied aircraft. This was no cakewalk to victory. After crossing the Meuse and then the Rhine in March 1945, the advance continued deep into

Germany – and then 'suddenly' it was VE Day and on 8 May 1945 hostilities ceased. During the period of occupation in Germany, the men suffered a much-resented return to spit and polish, as the regiment gradually faded away under a phased demobilisation programme. At last those that had survived could return to their homes, their families and their friends. Their war was over.

The book is limited firstly to those that survived and left their memories, whether on my tape recorder, or in printed form. Our story is therefore not academically 'balanced'. There are not many quotes from the older generation of NCOs and officers, nor from the miners of 426 Battery who suffered the early deaths common to their trade. Wartime incidents cannot be covered if no witnesses left usable accounts. Let us not regret what we have lost, or could never have, but instead concentrate on the treasures that exist in these pages: not thanks to the author, but thanks to the unstinting efforts of the veterans themselves in making the IWM recordings – totalling in all some 356 hours. They also created the South Notts Hussars museum at Bullwell Barracks, still managed to this day by the next generation of dedicated volunteers.

Their collective story allows us to sense how our country responded to the stress of war. Not everything went well. There were disasters. Some men let themselves down under the terrible pressure. Many were killed, dreadfully wounded, or all but lost their minds. Several were taken prisoner. Few were totally unscathed by their experiences. But in the end, most endured and did their duty as best they could in what – in the end – proved a victorious battle. When collected together their voices are the distillation of what the British soldier endured in the war against fascism. As the military historian Major Gordon Corrigan recently remarked, 'This is a British Band of Brothers'. The phrase has been hijacked somewhat by the Americans in recent years, but it is worth recalling its origins in Shakespeare's version of the powerful call to arms made by Henry V in his speech before the Battle of Agincourt:

> *We few, we happy few, we band of brothers;*
> *For he to-day that sheds his blood with me*
> *Shall be my brother; be he ne'er so vile,*
> *This day shall gentle his condition*

The speech also includes the poignant line:

> *Old men forget; yet all shall be forgot*

But we must try not to forget. The old veterans themselves rarely forgot their wartime exploits. They were sometimes ignored by their families: as typified by 'Leave it out, Uncle Albert!' the response from Del and Roderick Trotter whenever their uncle tried to tell them his war stories in the popular comedy *Only Fools and Horses*. Only when they were dead did the veterans' surviving relatives and friends attempt to defuse any slight residual guilt with the cliché, 'He never liked to talk about it!' They *did* talk about it – mainly to those that understood and shared the horrors of war. Most maintained close friendships with their old wartime comrades for the rest of their lives, through the regimental association and Royal British Legion.

Does it matter that this book is centred on what some might consider a relatively obscure regiment? Not really. These men stand as representatives of all British soldiers in that five-year battle to save the world from Nazism. Sometimes we forget what was at stake in the Second World War. We are so used to modern wars, launched without a formal declaration of hostilities, sometimes with cloudy motives, and with our forces wielding armaments futuristic in comparison to those of their opponents. But eighty years ago, British troops fought to stop

Hitler and his evil creed of Nazism; they may have seemed 'ordinary', yet these men were anything but ordinary. We owe them all a huge debt of gratitude.

1

AS BAD AS IT GETS

AFTER ENDURING THE LONG SIEGE of Tobruk in 1941, the men of 107th (South Notts Hussars) Regiment, Royal Horse Artillery were desert veterans – confident they could cope with anything the Germans could throw at them. They had faced screaming dive-bombing Stukas, heavy shellfire, mass panzer attacks and had survived relatively unscathed. But on 6 June 1942 everything changed: they were trapped with their 25-pounder guns in shallow gun pits scratched out in the stony ground in the Cauldron, a saucer-shaped depression deep in the Libyan desert. Surrounded by overwhelming German forces, they had been ordered to fight 'to the last round'. Among them was an ordinary Nottinghamshire lad, Sergeant Ray Ellis of A Troop, 425 Battery.

> They brought in their artillery and we heard it open up. You think, 'Oh, bloody hell!' Then that started to fall among us. Then we took cover. That's when you get in your slit trench and you hide behind any little rock you can find. If you press flat, you could probably get your body under the ground, but the hams of my bottom were probably just sticking above the surface! They called in their air force as well, and it was absolutely devastating. The noise, the bombs were crashing

down, the shells at the same time – all on to the area round the guns.[1]

Then the German tanks began to rumble forwards. Now they had no choice but to get out of their shallow trenches and man their 25-pounder guns.

> You're very excited, not afraid, you're involved; it's before and after that you're afraid. In the actual battle you're trying to get things done quickly. If a high-explosive 25-pounder shell hits the track of a tank, it is going to blow the track off and the tank will slew and stop. That means you can put another one into it, bang one in the back of him – and he'll explode and brew up. Horrible: black smoke, red flame – an awful sight. By this time, you can see something coming over from the left getting close to you, so you whip the gun round to have a go at him. Sometimes the shell will hit the tank, explode – and the tank would keep coming. It's probably given everyone in the tank a headache, but it didn't stop the tank, or kill them all – and they could keep coming. But you're not just firing at one tank, you've got tanks all over the place! You think, 'I'd better have a go at him – he's getting a bit close!' To be honest, all you're looking at are the few tanks that are coming near your gun. All you're thinking about is knocking out any tanks that look dangerous to you – not saving the British Empire![2]

Soon they came under extremely heavy fire.

> The air was just alive with red-hot steel. I remember hitting a Mark IV tank and it slewed round and burst into flames. The next thing I was in the air – as if someone had picked me up and thrown me in the air – spinning in the air! We'd had a direct hit on the gun. I dropped, 'WHHOOMPH', on to the ground. I lay there a second or two dazed and then, before I picked myself up, I went up spinning in the air again and

dropped again. This time I think I was unconscious for a short time.[3]

A German 88mm gun had dropped two shells right into their gun pit. Ellis slowly regained his scrambled senses; only to be confronted by a scene of horror.

> I can remember kneeling and hearing the battle going on in a dazed sort of way. I stayed like that for quite a long time. Then it went quiet again and I realised the tanks had been fought off. I looked round and my gun was upside down and the crew were draped on the floor all round. I thought I must be wounded but I couldn't feel anything. My shirt and body were all black, my clothes were all bloodstained, and I was in a hell of a state. I staggered round to look at the crew – some were obviously dead – and as I went round, I realised that I was the only one to have survived – the whole crew had been killed. My next thought was for self-preservation – a very strong instinct – 'Get your head down, Ray!'[4]

Still stunned, he found a small hole in the ground and began to scrabble away, trying to dig down and piling up small stones all around the edge – desperate for any cover no matter how scant. Then he saw a shell burst right over the No. 1 gun section close by. Against all his natural instincts for self-preservation, Ellis found himself propelled forward to rejoin the battle.

> The crew just fell to the ground and nobody moved. It occurred to me that with two guns out of action that was half the strength of the troop gone and the next time they put in an attack, this could mean they would get through. With a great deal of reluctance I got out of my hole and went over to No. 1 gun. The gun was in a parlous state: the shield was all riddled, at least one of the tyres was flat, but it was workable. Other people must have noticed because from somewhere men started to

appear – they were signallers, or specialists, or drivers, but they helped to man the gun. These men were not gunners, but you could tell them what to do.[5]

His makeshift gun team was still under heavy fire as the German tanks drew closer. Death was all around him; but Ellis himself seemed to have a charmed life.

As one man was mown down, then somebody else appeared. It eventually got to the point where they were not just South Notts Hussars, they were strangers. I remember a man from the Royal Corps of Signals coming on to the gun position in the late afternoon. This man caught a burst of machine-gun fire right in the bottom part of his body, he jumped in the air – an instinctive muscle movement – then fell to the ground. I looked at this lad and he was frightened – his eyes were terrified. I crouched down to try and trying to console him with all the noise going on round, 'You're all right lad, you're all right, don't worry you're not badly wounded, we'll soon have you away. I reckon you've got a Blighty!' Trying to ease his fear. While I was talking, I noticed the sand was settling on his eyes. He was dead. He died in my arms.[6]

By around 18.00, the situation was beyond desperate. His battered gun was in a terrible state, and they were fast running out of ammunition. But still Ellis fought on.

I was left with just one man on the gun, everyone else had been killed. He was a complete stranger; I don't know who he was or where he'd come from. He wasn't a South Notts Hussar. He was standing on the right of the gun opening and closing the breech. I was loading, pulling the gun round, aiming at a tank then running and getting on the seat, aiming it and firing it. I'd just fired a shell and I'd gone back behind the gun, got hold of the trail arm, when I heard a machine gun which sounded

4

as if it was a few inches behind me – it sounded so close! This man was just splattered against the inside of the gun shield. I looked behind and I could see the tank within 20 to 30 yards behind me – with the machine gun still smoking. I tensed myself and waited for this burst of fire – which never came. I shall never know whether the gunner had compassion, ran out of ammunition, saw something that distracted him – I like to think he had compassion![7]

After all his terrible experiences that day, Ray Ellis was in a state of shock. The guns had finally fallen silent and their war was over.

I was very, very thirsty and I walked over to Peter Birkin's armoured vehicle. In it were the bodies of the driver and Jim Hardy. He had been cut in two, but his water bottle was sort of hanging there. I got my knife, cut his webbing, took the water bottle and drank this lukewarm water from old Jim's bottle. I looked down at his lifeless face and I just burst into tears – reaction I suppose – seeing an old pal from the day I joined the regiment.[8]

Many more had died; most of the rest, including Ray Ellis, were taken prisoner. It was 6 June 1942; the worst day in the history of the South Notts Hussars. The men that survived never forgot it.

2

GROWING PAINS

We did realise that war was highly likely – and that the country ought to prepare for it – *we* ought to prepare for it! The sooner we got in there, did a bit of training and got established in something that might help, the better.[1]

Charles Westlake

MANY OF THEIR FATHERS HAD FOUGHT in the Great War. Few of those 'old' soldiers really believed that they had fought in the 'war to end wars'; but they had a reasonable hope that the devastation inflicted by a widespread European conflict might perhaps skip a generation. Surely their children would not have to face the shells, the chattering machine guns and the terrors of industrial warfare? It was not to be. The rise of Hitler and his Nazi Party created a nascent threat from Germany, which, coupled with the economic tribulations of the Great Depression, formed a grim backdrop to the lives of youngsters growing up in the 1930s. Attacks on civilians from the skies during the Spanish Civil War had made it apparent that in any future war, massed bombing would bring a new terror. Soldiers' families would no longer be safe 'back home'. Nor was Germany the only threat: Italy was intent on carving out an African empire, while Japan was an increasing menace in the Far East. The British were also under pressure from within, as national resistance movements began to gain traction across the empire. Truly they were living through 'interesting times'. Of course, they did not *know* there was going to be a war, and most hoped that it could be avoided; but there was an underlying sense of unease.

Life was very different then. Nottingham was a relatively well-ordered society divided into distinct strata which seemed to 'know their place'. Beneath the surface tensions simmered, triggered by extreme variations in personal wealth, the dreadful impact of the endemic unemployment, low wages and poor-quality standards of housing. Echoes of the 1926 General Strike still lingered in the mining communities dotted all around the county. The officers and men who would fight side by side in the Western Desert in 1942 had little in common when back at home in England; few would have had the opportunity, or inclination, to mingle socially. The officers included the wealthy scions of the local aristocracy, colliery owners and textile magnates. Most of the men were a mixture of coalminers, clerks, commercial travellers and various types of industrial labourers.

Recruits seeking to join the army had two main avenues open to them: they could join the professional regular army; or they could join the Territorial Army (TA). There was a wide choice of TA units, including infantry battalions of the Sherwood Foresters, the cavalry squadrons of the Sherwood Rangers, Royal Engineers, Royal Signals or Royal Army Medical Corps units, and the Royal Artillery, as represented by the South Nottinghamshire Hussars.

The South Notts Hussars had been raised as a yeomanry cavalry regiment back in 1794, in response to the threat posed by revolutionary France. Drawn from the local gentry and farmers, they were a home defence unit, and not called into action until they acted as enforcers to put down the Luddite riots of 1811. The control of various forms of civil disturbance – rowdy political demonstrations, riots and outbreaks of looting – was their *raison d'être* until the advent of a properly constituted police force in the mid nineteenth century. With the decline of agriculture and the increasing domination of the coalmines, commerce and industry, the composition of the yeomanry gradually changed, with more and more recruits originating in Nottingham and its satellite coalfield villages. In 1900, a squadron of volunteers was sent out to fight with the Imperial Yeomanry during the Boer War in South Africa, where they suffered several casualties – their introduction to warfare. In 1908, the ramshackle organisation of disparate, militia, volunteer and yeomanry units was standardised and turned to proper purpose by the creation of the Territorial Force by the Secretary of State for War, Richard Haldane. The new territorial units would be raised and administered by County Territorial Associations, their finance and training being under the central control of the War Office. From this time recruits to the South Notts Hussars would sign on for military training with drill nights and weekend training sessions, augmented by a two-week annual camp. The territorials were primarily intended for a home defence role, but provision was established for voluntary service overseas in the event of war. Shortly afterwards the regiment moved into spacious new accommodation at the purpose-built Derby Road Drill Hall.

On the outbreak of the Great War in August 1914, the South Notts Hussars were swiftly mobilised. The majority of the men volunteered for imperial service overseas and became the 1/1st South Notts Hussars, which was assigned to the 2nd Mounted Division and initially fought in a dismounted capacity during the ill-fated Gallipoli campaign of 1915. They then served as the divisional cavalry with the 10th (Irish) Division on the Salonika Front, before participating with the Desert Mounted Corps in the Palestine campaign. From June 1917 the gradual obsolescence of the cavalry resulted in their amalgamation with the Warwickshire Yeomanry to form the B Battalion, Machine Gun Corps. Their deployment to France was delayed when, on 27 May 1918, their troopship, the *Leasowe Castle,* was sunk off the North African coast with a heavy loss of life. Once the unit had rebuilt, it was redesignated as the 100th Battalion, MGC, and spent the last months of the war fighting as infantry on the Western Front.

The British Army had changed during the Great War. The approach that finally delivered victory for the Allies was based on a complex mixture of interlocking 'All Arms' tactics and firepower. Although there was still a role for cavalry, it was fast diminishing, and with the development of more powerful tanks and armoured cars in the immediate postwar years it was evident that this would not be reversed. In sharp contrast, the role of the Royal Artillery had been massive, underpinning every offensive with a sophisticated range of barrages that came to dominate the battlefields of the Western Front. The writing was on the wall, and many cavalry units would find themselves given new roles. In 1921 the Territorial Force was renamed as the Territorial Army, and in March 1922 the South Notts Hussars Yeomanry became the 107th Field Brigade, Royal Artillery, composed of 425 and 426 Batteries, each equipped with four 18-pounder guns.

The more traditional and hidebound officers were, as might be expected, resistant to the change, particularly as their local rivals, the Sherwood Rangers, retained a 'cavalry' horsed role for a few more years. Despite vehement protests and detailed submissions based on the relative seniority of the various regiments on the Army List, the War Office was immovable. The South Notts Hussars were required to make the best of their conversion to artillery, their only consolation being the retention of their traditional acorn and oakleaf cap badges instead of the Royal Artillery crown and gun badge emblazoned with the proud motto '*Ubique*' (Everywhere). This privilege would be controversial in later years.

Notwithstanding the change in status, the regiment continued its tradition of recruiting officers for the 'Hussars' from the families of prominent local landowners and businessmen. The same names cropped up across the history of the regiment: thus, the Seely family would provide two generations of senior officers to the South Notts Hussars. Lieutenant Colonel Frank Seely commanded the regiment at Gallipoli, while his son, Major William Seely, would rise to command them in the early years of the Second World War. Another example was the Barber family, who were wealthy colliery owners. Major Philip Barber had served with the South Notts Hussars in both the Boer War and the Great War, while his son William Barber, after preliminary training with the Officer Training Cadets (OTC) at Eton, would follow in his father's footsteps in 1924.

> I joined 426 Battery – it was just automatic you just joined. I was a very junior subaltern. They were nearly all miners. They wanted to join – that was one of the things my father always said, 'They make the best soldiers in the world.' They're born fighters: they're always fighting against their employers for a start; they're almost always fighting against conditions down the pit.[2]
>
> William Barber

His cousin, Colin Barber, had also joined 426 Battery.

Another wealthy young recruit was Bob Hingston, the son of a Nottingham lace manufacturer. Educated at Lancing School, Hingston had been a somewhat sickly child and by no means a natural soldier. Indeed, he had found his OTC infantry training a dull experience.

I grew up as a boy during the First World War and I read quite a
lot afterwards of all the ghastly casualties on the Western Front.
Both my brothers went into the regular army, but I had a horror
of war – I was almost a pacifist. The OTC hadn't helped!
Then 1936 came along, and it looked pretty obvious; there was
another war coming. Quite suddenly, out of the blue, Colonel
Holden of the South Notts Hussars wrote to me asking if I
would care to join. I agonised over it, absolutely agonised,
'God, this is the moment, I must do something, there's a war
coming, I must get ready for it!' And then, 'Oh, my God, join
that army, no I can't face it!'[3]

Bob Hingston

In the end, encouraged by his brother, who was already in the
army, Hingston accepted the offer and joined up in April 1936.

Perhaps the most prominent of these local families was the
Birkins, who owned the largest Nottingham lace company,
the Chesterfield Scarsdale brewery and numerous other business interests. Family members had served with distinction in
the Great War, but a whole new generation of officers emerged
in the 1930s, which did much to shape the history of the regiment in the Second World War. Born on 17 March 1920, Peter
Birkin was the son of Major Harry Birkin, who had commanded
a squadron of the South Notts Hussars in the Great War. After
being educated at Harrow, Peter Birkin was active in the family
lace firm, but was also a very keen rugby player who captained
the Notts Rugby Club. He was soon followed by his cousins:
Philip Gervase (known as Gerry) and Ivor Birkin, who were the
sons of Harry's eldest brother Philip.

Peter Birkin made it his personal mission to recruit the
'right sort' of officer. One such was Charles Laborde, the son of
a colonial administrator in Barbados and Fiji, who later became
a schoolmaster at Harrow. Educated at Harrow, he was a tall,

broad-shouldered man who was captain of rugby before studying economics and geography at Cambridge University from 1934.

> I thought of the Sherwood Foresters, having had some infantry training at school, but then I discovered that the South Notts had quite a Harrow following – the Birkin family of course were all at Harrow. So, one drifted into the South Notts and I became a gunner! Peter Birkin introduced me to Colonel Holden.[4]
>
> Charles Laborde

Another 'rugby' recruit was burly Bill Pringle, the son of a butcher and cattle dealer from Haddington in Scotland. He had decided on a career in farming and was working as tenant farmer at Hardwick Grange near Worksop from 1936.

> I was playing rugby regularly for Nottingham and the captain was a very keen Territorial Army man – Peter Birkin. He was a born leader, strict disciplinarian, fair – and everything he did was done well! They decided to double the Territorial Army and four of us – half the scrum – all joined that night! We were told if we all joined together, we would all get direct commissions. I came home and discussed it with my father, and he said, 'If you can get a commission you go and get it! You'll never need to experience the ranks – and you'll be lucky!' I took his advice![5]
>
> William Pringle

The two batteries soon developed a distinct character, with 425 Battery dominated by the Birkin clan and based on the city area of Nottingham, while 426 Battery had strong links with the Barber family, and many of the men worked in the local collieries at Hucknall.

There was a growing realisation that war with Germany was all but inevitable. The League of Nations, formed after the Great War to try to prevent similar conflicts, had proved toothless. It was incapable of stemming the rise of a resurgent Germany following the election success of Adolf Hitler and the Nazi Party in 1933. Hitler's expansionist policies centred on a 'Greater Germany' were soon obvious. After repudiating the Versailles Peace Treaty of 1919, Hitler expanded the armed forces, introduced conscription and in 1936 remilitarised the Rhineland. In the absence of any effective opposition from France, Britain and the United States, he took another step when, in March 1938, he annexed Austria. Still there was no effective response and, emboldened, he began to press German claims to the Sudetenland area of Czechoslovakia. This time the international tensions reached a new high, and for a while it seemed that war would result. Yet the British Prime Minister, Neville Chamberlain, felt his country was not ready for war and, rightly or wrongly, he brokered an acceptance of the German occupation of the Sudetenland in return for a promise of no further German territorial demands. The result was the much-vaunted – and pilloried – 'scrap of paper' that marked the Munich Agreement of September 1938. War was averted, but for how long? Hitler was incorrigible. In March 1939, he trashed the whole agreement by overrunning the remainder of Czechoslovakia.

In the intervening months British had not been idle, and the army began a rapid growth of its reserve forces. As part of this process, the South Notts Hussars would be expanded to a full regiment, now renamed as 107th Regiment, Royal Horse Artillery (107th RHA), a first-line unit, earmarked for early deployment abroad in support of the 1st Cavalry Division in the event of war. By April 1939, the South Notts Hussars, under the command of Lieutenant Colonel Athole Holden, had reached a total of some 480 personnel, with both batteries now divided into two troops, each boasting four 18-pounder guns. Eventually an entire second-line regiment was formed, the 150th (South Notts Hussars) Field Regiment, Royal Artillery.[6] This reflected the overall enlargement of the Royal Artillery in the last year of peace, with a general doubling in the numbers of field, medium, heavy, anti-aircraft and anti-tank regiments.

Following the Munich Crisis, the obvious urgent requirement for more men to feed the growing regiment saw Peter Birkin build on his recruitment efforts through the Notts Rugby Club, to include the old boys of one of the most prestigious local grammar schools, Nottinghamshire High School. After leaving school, Charles Westlake had gone on to be an articled clerk to a conveyancing legal firm.

> I used to play rugger for one of the teams run by the Old
> Nottinghamians – the Nottingham High School Old Boys. We
> were visited one day by Peter Birkin, who was a prime mover
> in Notts Rugby Club – and also from one of the families who
> provided officers in the South Notts Hussars. He came to talk
> to us on the rugger field. He stressed the need for training in
> one form or another for the army, the dangers which were
> facing Britain at that time and he persuaded quite a group of us
> to join the South Notts Hussars.[7]
>
> Charles Westlake

The urge to control their own destiny was an important motivation for recruitment. Most young men were aware that a system of enforced military service was about to be imposed in readiness for the looming war with Germany. Indeed, in May 1939 a partial system of national conscription was introduced with the Military Training Act, which introduced the call-up of all single men between 20 and 22 years of age to what became known as militiamen. It was intended that they should undergo some six months of military training before being returned to civilian life while continuing training sessions as part of the army reserve. The evident imminence of full conscription thus proved an unintentional boost to voluntary recruitment into the TA. Although it went largely unspoken, there was an awareness that if young men did not sign up as territorials, then they would ultimately be conscripted – and most probably end up in the infantry. Volunteering was the only way to retain an element of choice. The question was, which TA unit should they join? Few men had any idea of what TA units were available to them, so there were many strange reasons why men eventually ended up volunteering for the South Notts Hussars. Some romantic souls, totally ignorant of the change in their status from cavalry to gunners, had visions of galloping into battle. One such was Ray Ellis. Born on 17 March 1920, he was the son of a school teacher in the Arnold suburb of Nottingham. Up until then he had had a varied work career as a junior clerk, a trainee engineer and a furniture salesman.

> I didn't know much about the army. The only regiment I knew about apart from the Guards was the Sherwood Foresters. Soldiers to me were men who wore khaki and fought. I went down one evening to join the Territorial Army as an infantry soldier, and I was going to join the Sherwood Foresters. I got to the Derby Road Drill Hall and there was a sign which was to change my whole life. A simple sign hanging there, a very colourful thing which said, 'South Notts Hussars'. I thought it sounded good! I didn't quite know what a Hussar was: I knew he rode a horse and I knew I couldn't ride, so I wondered if that would be some sort of detriment to me. Strangely enough no-one asked if I could ride a horse – not surprisingly as they were no longer horsed! I joined just on the strength of that sign![8]
>
> Ray Ellis

Many others wanted to 'do their bit' for their country but,

influenced by the experiences of fathers and uncles in the Great War, sought to avoid service in the infantry. The echoes of the carnage and suffering in the trenches on the Western Front were a recurring powerful theme.

> The infantry get too close – I thought let's be in the artillery! They stand off and keep lobbing it in! The infantry was very much footslogging, and to get on a truck and be towing a gun was a far better prospect in my view. I went up with a lot of my friends to join the second regiment of the South Notts Hussars – 150th Regiment. I went up to the Derby Road Drill Hall with my pals, but it was absolutely packed solid with volunteers; the number of people was amazing. I had to fight off the Signals who tried to 'pinch' me and, before I knew it, I'd signed on with Sergeant Major Wigley for the South Notts Hussars – not knowing I'd signed for the 107th not the 150th. Wigley thought, 'I'm not going to lose these!'[9]
>
> Herbert Bonnello

The crowds of new recruits that swarmed down to the Derby Road Drill Hall proved 'easy meat' for the regular permanent staff instructors attached to the South Notts. They were keen to recruit for their own particular unit, rather than swell the ranks of the 'rival' units: the Royal Signal Corps, the Sherwood Foresters, or even the South Notts second-line 150th Regiment, RA, based at the same premises. Albert Parker was one such who found himself duped by Sergeant Majors Edward Wigley and Charles Bennett, who were old hands at this game.

> I didn't go to join the South Notts Hussars. A pal of mine said, 'I'm in the Signal Corps at the drill hall. You want to pop up there – it's lovely!' I walked through the door and a bloke said, 'Can I help you?' I said, 'I want to be a signaller!' He said, 'Just the man – you come with me!' That was it! I was only a lad and

he was an imposing chap. He said, 'Sit down there and I'll send someone to see you!' A bloke came in and said, 'You want to be a signaller?' 'Yes!' 'Right!' 'Just sign there! Have you got your parents' permission?' 'Oh, yes!' 'Sign – that's it!'[10]

Albert Parker

When the dust had settled, Albert Parker found he'd actually joined the 107th RHA.

Each of these potential recruits had to pass a medical examination by a doctor. It was evident to most that this was a mere technicality and the inspection was of an extremely cursory nature.

We had the most rudimentary medical, just the way the comedians describe it: 'Strip off, cough, get on the scale!' They had a look in your mouth and a look at your feet. They used to say, 'Touch him, if he's warm, he's in!' It wasn't quite like that, but they didn't seem to be turning anyone away.[11]

Bob Foulds

All the administration paperwork involved a good deal of hard graft as there were some nine forms for every recruit which all had to be filled in. One new recruit, Bill Hutton, a wealthy farmer's son, found himself at a loose end and volunteered to help in the battery office.

I signed people up – I had this form and I filled it in, 'Do you suffer from coughing, bed-wetting, spitting of the blood? What's your mother's name?' When they were busy, I helped them with the medical. If they couldn't see the board properly, I let them stand a yard nearer, so I think there was a lot of short-sighted people in our regiment – I wasn't the only one![12]

Bill Hutton

As Hutton implies, he himself was as blind as the proverbial bat, and it was a miracle he had passed his own medical. As he had been educated at the prestigious Malvern School, Hutton applied for a commission, but as a lifelong 'joker' who on the surface took little, or nothing, seriously, he failed to impress at his interview. Another recently joined gunner, Ian Sinclair, had also considered a commission, but as a textile sales representative of only limited financial means, he was worried that he couldn't afford to be an officer who, it was considered, required private means to afford their mess bills.

> It was very much a 'county' situation. I got to know the officers of the regiment and it was quite obvious that I was not in their pecuniary situation. I could not possibly afford to be an officer in those days, there was no question of it at all. The 'gentlemen' *were* all 'gentlemen': the Birkins, the Barbers, the Seelys. I was 'here' and they were 'there' financially. That was the only deterrent – I didn't think I couldn't do it![13]
>
> Gunner Ian Sinclair, 425 Battery, 107th RHA

For grammar-school recruits like George Pearson, who had been a relatively early recruit as a gunner back in 1936, this rapid expansion of the South Notts Hussars brought the opportunity of accelerated advancement through the ranks.

> I think one always hoped one might get one's first stripe – and then when it came along one felt very chuffed. A little extra pay, but no real extra responsibility. What it did bring was I grew my first moustache – I thought I was growing up then! Second promotion was up to bombardier and then to lance sergeant. It came about because the regiment had expanded to make two regiments – certain NCOs went to 150th Regiment and that meant promotion opportunities.[14]
>
> Gunner George Pearson, 425 Battery, 107th RHA

For others, like Norman Tebbett, the very same influx of grammar-school types into 425 Battery meant that his own promotion opportunities suddenly evaporated in the face of stiff competition.

> We were generally ordinary working-class fellers. There was a bit of class distinction between the ordinary fellers and the High School people: Ted Whittaker, Geoff Williams, Ian Sinclair, Charles Westlake, John Walker and Ken Tew. They were well educated; some of them were studying to be solicitors and that sort of thing. This was the time when they'd either got to be called up for the militia or they could join the territorials. Of course, most of them were joining the territorials to avoid being called up! We got on well enough, but what I found was that the chances of promotion just went! They seemed to be taking over the regiment! You tried hard – I became a qualified layer – well normally a qualified layer after a while was always given his first stripe. But that wasn't happening! We'd been in a couple of years then, yet you found these new fellers, it didn't seem as if they'd been in five minutes and their promotion was quite rapid. They were taking over all the more senior jobs.[15]

Gunner Norman Tebbett, A Troop, 425 Battery, 107th RHA

In the spring of 1939, the 107th RHA was taking a recognisable shape. The mingled landowners, businessmen, miners, industrial workers, clerks and accountants were a fair reflection of the society from which they emerged: not always easy in each other's company but bound together by the 'greater need'. Some knew next to nothing of the army, of basic military skills, or of the arcane technical skills of gunnery. Others were overly confident that they had mastered their trades. Yet the greatest test lay ahead of them on the battlefields of North Africa, Sicily and North-west Europe. They would collectively learn how little they really knew, slowly master the art of gunnery in a war situation, discover their individual and personal response to danger, and at times explore the limits of human endurance. Many would not survive the war.

3

THE BASICS

> But by the time 1939 came along, I'd put in a lot of work on the Territorial Army and my attitude was, 'Yes, it's got to come! I'm as ready as I ever can be – right let's get on with it!'[1]
>
> Second Lieutenant Bob Hingston, 426 Battery, 107th RHA

IN PEACETIME THE TERRITORIALS WERE looked down on as 'Saturday Night Soldiers' and their units considered as little more than drinking clubs. Yet when war loomed, as it certainly did, the Munich Agreement notwithstanding, their training assumed a far sharper pattern and purpose. They were now preparing themselves for active participation in a terrible war and what they learnt – or failed to learn – could define their future.

Both batteries held their weekday drill nights at the Derby Road Drill Hall. Here they gathered, dressed in their rough khaki uniforms. As with all soldiers, they first had to be taught foot drill: how to march and move as a formed body of men.

> You were taught which was your left leg and which was your right leg – and it's surprising the number of people who didn't know! Once they start to march, they're all over the place. If

you say, 'Left, quick march!' They put their right foot forward
instead of their left.[2]

Gunner Norman Tebbett, A Troop, 425 Battery, 107th RHA

To some this seemed an archaic throwback to Napoleonic
warfare, but the shared experience of drill, the barked orders
of the drill sergeants, the stupid mistakes, the resulting abusive
banter, is one of the eternal foundations of military training.
Drill helped create a sense of teamwork among the recruits, even
if it was only in combatting an external 'enemy', the drill sergeant: teamwork that would serve them well in more serious
challenges. Recruits also did a little rifle drill and some shooting
on the .22 calibre ranges, but their main concentration was their
training on the 18-pounder field gun – given its name to reflect
the weight of the shell it fired. The gun had a heavy box-trail and
iron-rimmed wheels, and its barrel was some seven feet eight
inches long with a calibre of 3.3 inches. During the Great War it
had been a mainstay of the field artillery, one of the new breed
of quick-loading guns which could lay down an effective barrage
with a range of up to 9,000 yards. It was intended that these
guns be replaced with the new 25-pounder gun howitzer, but
these were still only prototypes in 1939. For now, the 18-pound-
ers would still have to be deployed on active service.

A sergeant said, 'This is the Mark IV 18-pounder gun: this is the
trail, this the carriage and this is the breech!' He went round
the whole gun and gave the name for each part of which we
remembered absolutely nothing. I don't think he was an expert
teacher![3]

Gunner Ray Ellis, 425 Battery, 107th RHA

The men were formed into gun sections and began to learn the
rudiments of gun drill, loading dummy rounds time and time
again into the breech. Repetition was imperative, grooving

their actions, allowing them to perform their functions almost without conscious thought; ready for those moments in action when terror could banish all reason.

> We were doing standing gun drill, teaching us to man, aim and fire the gun. There were six in the gun detachment. We fell in and numbered off 1 to 6. The No. 1 was the sergeant in charge of the gun and gun crew; he had to move the trail of the gun round to put it roughly on line. The minor setting of putting the gun on line was done by a traverse on the gun itself. Some No. 1s became extremely good at measuring with their hand the number of degrees that they were moving the gun from the 'zero line' which was the line that all the guns were laid parallel on. The No. 2 opened and closed the breech, on the 18-pounder Mark IV it was a fixed ammunition – the shell and the cartridge case were one fixed unit. The No. 3 was the layer and he sat on the left-hand side of the gun and he elevated the gun by means of a clinometer, a spirit level bubble on the side of the gun; and a dial sight which was 180 degrees either way. He had the most highly skilled job on the gun. No. 4 would load the rounds – he would put the round and No. 2 would close the breech. The Nos. 5 and 6 were ammunition numbers, who would be passing the ammunition to No. 4. It was dummy drill purpose ammunition. We would do this and then change round 'one up', giving the gun detachment a crack of the whip at all the various operations – which was important.[4]
>
> Gunner Bob Foulds, 425 Battery, 107th RHA

After the drill night sessions, many of the men would retire to local hostelries, where friendships were forged that would stand them in good stead.

> On that first night, Fred Lamb and I then went out to a pub at the top of Derby Road called the Sir John Borlase Warren and

had a drink. That was the beginning of our friendship. I did drink a lot. It was the 'in' thing in those days – to be part of the scene you had to have your hair sleeked back with Brylcreem, baggy trousers, smoke with a nonchalant air – and you had to drink and be able to hold your beer![5]

Gunner Ray Ellis, 425 Battery, 107th RHA

There were also weekend sessions with 425 Battery using Ramsdale Park and Jackson's Field, while 426 Battery used the Hucknall Airfield or Annesley Park. Here they would practise dropping into action, using drag ropes to move the heavy guns across often rough and muddy ground.

Sergeant Bennett used to start out about half-past 6 in the morning to rattle the guns out there on their steel 'tyres'. Then we would pick them up and do a bit of gun drill – coming into action. They were all manhandled, there was no gun tower there. Unhitching the gun from the limber, placing the limber beside the gun and pointing the gun left or right, depending on whether you were told, 'Halt, action right!', 'Halt, action left!', 'Halt, action front!' or occasionally, just to confuse the issue, 'Halt, action rear!' Then we'd have sandwiches and Hanson's beer![6]

Gunner John Whitehorn, 425 Battery, 107th RHA

Throughout they would be 'encouraged' by the raucous bellows of their instructors, one of whom earned himself the soubriquet 'Dragropes', such was his enthusiasm for this niche pastime.

I don't think Troop Sergeant Major Greensmith was particularly good with men; I don't think he had very much idea how to handle them. He'd obviously been in the TA quite a number of years and he knew the ins and outs of it quite well, there's no two ways about that, but he'd got very little idea how to impart the knowledge and know-how that he'd got – he just shouted![7]

Gunner David Tickle, 425 Battery, 107th RHA

Those officers and men whose educational attainments indicated a likely ability in mathematics were selected for training as gun position officers and their specialist assistants (known as acks). It would be their responsibility to establish a viable gun position.

When a battery moves into action it doesn't just drive along a road and drop into action anywhere. The ground has got to be suitable. The gun position ack will have put out the flags marking the position for each gun and will also have mentally picked out a track plan so that the guns can come in, sweep off a track, go round a loop, dropping off the guns at each flag point, and then rejoin a track to go to the wagon lines – without leaving tracks going all over the place which would indicate to any enemy aircraft that was a gun position.[8]

Gunner George Pearson, 425 Battery, 107th RHA

Then things all became rather technical.

His job was to help in the 'survey in' of the gun position. That is to get the correct grid reference of the gun position, to use the director, which is rather like a simple theodolite, to lay the guns out on the correct bearing. The guns would pick up an aiming point, some distant spire, chimney or edge of a wood, but would also lay out aiming posts in case fog obscured the original aiming point. Thereafter, to plot the gun position on an artillery board, which is a gridded square. Then any targets that you engage, you also plot in the grid reference of them and you have a metal arm marked out in thousands and hundreds of yards, which swings on a pivot which you put over the gun position. Then there is an arc which measures degrees and you lay the arm out on the 'zero line' that the guns were to be laid on. You set your arc up, the 'zero' in the centre, with the arm on the 'zero', then any reading right or left of the 'zero line' is measured in degrees and can be passed to the guns because they'd been laid out on that same 'zero line'. So, you'd plot all your targets. Any predicted targets, you'd plot in their grid reference on your artillery board and you were able to read off the bearing and the range to those targets.[9]

Gunner George Pearson, 425 Battery, 107th RHA

For anyone familiar with basic trigonometry and the use of logarithms, the actual maths was simple enough. However, some, such as Lieutenant Charles Laborde, suffered a crisis of confidence that even his education at Harrow could not overcome.

My family has a failing for mathematics, we cannot do maths, my father was hopeless at it, I'm hopeless at it! Working out the angles, range and lines of sight, you have an army form to do it on, and I always had to use the army form and the log tables to work these things out. Ivor Birkin was marvellous; he'd do the whole thing in his head and he never got it wrong! I was so envious of him![10]

Lieutenant Charles Laborde, 426 Battery, 107th RHA

The gunnery assistants also had to take note of the effects of the weather on the passage of a shell in flight. The importance of this had been realised through bitter experience during the Great War.

The other thing was to work out from 'meteor' telegrams, provided by the RAF Meteorological Service, the differences that temperature, wind and barometric pressure made to gunnery. If you get a head wind blowing against a shell it reduces its range; if you get a cross-wind the shell can be blown off to the left or right. If you get a freezing-cold temperature when you're firing a shell the cordite doesn't expand as quickly and therefore the shell doesn't get so much punch behind it. All these things had to be corrected for using tables.[11]

Gunner George Pearson, 425 Battery, 107th RHA

Meanwhile the observation post (OP) officers and their acks would go forward to establish an OP post with a direct sight of the intended target.

One of your first jobs would be to draw a panorama of the area of ground which you were supposed to cover by observations. Picking out landmarks and putting them on this sketch – it wasn't supposed to be a work of art but merely a diagram which would identify particular points on the landscape. The idea was that you would make a note when you'd done some firing of what the range and bearing turned out to be for these targets. So that if you could see on your plan that the range and bearing to a barn was so much, if you found a target a bit to the right you could probably more or less guess the correct range and bearing to it.[12]

Gunner Charles Westlake, 425 Battery, 107th RHA

Linked by telephone line to the gun positions command post, the OP job was to identify targets, send down fire orders that indicated the angle of sight and range that the guns needed to open fire on a specific target, then to observe the fall of shot and provide corrections until the shells were hitting the 'bull's eye'.

You always try to bracket a target. If you see a shell which is on line, but is way over the target, you would drop 800 yards. That would drop the round in front of the target. Then you would add 400 yards and hope that dropped your round behind. Then drop 200, then add 100, until you'd got a 100-yard bracket on the target and then go to fire for effect at the 50-yard split.[13]

Gunner George Pearson, 425 Battery, 107th RHA

A further specialisation was that of signaller. For Jack Sykes it was almost inevitable that he would be assigned to signals work as his father, Harry Sykes, was the existing signals sergeant. He spent his drill nights learning the basics of the wireless sets and telephone equipment, whilst at the same time mastering the intricacies of Morse code and the phonetic alphabet.

I was immediately put into the signaller section. We used a No. 1 wireless set transmitting either by Morse code or by speech. We had little telephone field exchanges where you connected all the wires up from the batteries and headquarters. You didn't go a lot into the technical aspects of it, only how to check the circuits, change the valves, and the switchboard was not terribly hard to understand. Morse – I took to it like a duck to water, simply because I was interested in it! I've had trouble learning lots of things, but it came naturally – I can still remember it to this day.[14]

Gunner Jack Sykes, Headquarters, 425 Battery, 107th RHA

THE VARIOUS ELEMENTS of the regiment all came together in typical wet Northumbrian weather at the annual camp at Redesdale in June 1939. However many drill nights they had attended, whatever weekend training they had endured, this would be their first experience of the 'real army'. It was a long overnight journey up from Nottingham and some of the gunners had indulged in a considerable drinking bout before they started. They would come to regret their folly.

We arrived at Redesdale on a cold, damp, misty morning at about 5 o'clock. We detrained and got a lorry that took us up to the camp. There were some bell tents and I thought, 'Oh, thank God, now for a lovely sleep!' The next thing we heard was, 'ON PARADE!' We said, 'Aren't we going to get a sleep?' 'THE BLOODY DAY HASN'T STARTED YET!' And to my horror I realised I had to do a day's work, I had a hangover and I was tired![15]

Gunner Ray Ellis, 425 Battery, 107th RHA

They also sampled just a taste of the culinary delights the army had in store for them in the future.

We were called into the mess hut and there were some pork pies, which looked very good indeed – and bread three-quarters of an inch deep, which was slightly different from the dainty bread and butter I normally took at home. But these pork pies – having cut through them – the outside of the meat was quite a bright green – entirely and absolutely uneatable. We just ate the bread and marge – and went away hungry![16]

Gunner Fred Langford, 425 Battery, 107th RHA

When they eventually got to their lines of tents, the men of the 425 and 426 Batteries, who had separate drill nights at the shared drill hall, had the chance to observe each other closely – often for the first time. There was no doubt that the 'other ranks' of 425 Battery had a more varied composition as they included a fair proportion of former grammar schoolboys and clerical workers in contrast to the predominance of miners within 426 Battery. For some the exposure to working-class culture was an eye-opener. One such was John Walker, a trainee chartered accountant and an old boy of the Nottingham High School.

The first evening, we were practically all from the same school in the same tent. Next to us was a tent of people from the other battery who were practically all miners. I remember saying, 'I am not going to use that particular swear word as long as I'm in the army!' And everybody else said the same thing! I had heard the word, but I'd never heard it used every half-sentence![17]

Gunner John Walker, 425 Battery, 107th RHA

Within 425 Battery there were differences in education and upbringing that could lead to resentment, especially when promotion prospects were materially diminished by the arrival of so many.

The 'cut-glass boys' were the people who came from public school and the High School. The expression came from the likes of Jack Brown, who was a bombardier in those days – an extremely tough Nottinghamian – he had an endless fund of wisecracks and expressions. There wasn't hostility, but there was an 'us and them' situation between the 'cut glass boys' and the remainder. We were fortunate enough to have had a better education than a lot of our contemporaries who had gone to the council schools in Nottingham. I think that in the early days the sergeants gave us a hard time because none of them had any academic qualifications or background. You had to tough it out and stand up for yourself.[18]

Gunner Bob Foulds, 425 Battery, 107th RHA

In turn, it should be appreciated that not everyone in 426 Battery was a hard-bitten miner. Charles Ward was another apprentice accountant – and he too was quite frankly shocked by what he found.

I was lower-middle-class; I'd been to grammar school. I realised when I joined this lot that I'd led a fairly sheltered life! I met some quite extraordinary people from the slums, who'd not been educated well, some had been in prison – some pretty rough types. It was quite an eye opener! They used the 'F-word' literally every other line – it was quite incredible! Of course, to some extent, I must confess that we rather slipped downwards, rather than bringing them up. Our language became worse and worse.[19]

Gunner Charles Ward, 426 Battery, 107th RHA

Accounts clerk Harold Harper also found himself lost and alone in this strange new world.

It rained pretty well for the whole fortnight; I'd never felt so miserable in all my life. The first time I'd left home, roughing it with the food and everything else was just about a disaster as far as I was concerned. Never been used to the boozing habits of the older members, who seemed to think it was wonderful to get away from the wife for a fortnight. They found great fun in coming in and tipping people out of bed at 3 o'clock in the morning! Practical jokes rather than bullying. All I could think of was my girlfriend, who I'd left in Nottingham, and I couldn't get back home fast enough quite frankly. The lack of privacy was really shaking – to come away from a reasonable family background – it was shattering. I was a little bit of a reluctant soldier.[20]

Gunner Harold Harper, 426 Battery, 107th RHA

There was vigorous competition between the two batteries and it soon became evident that they possessed a range of different military virtues. The economic downturn and consequent reduced demand for coal meant that miners were often working on the basis of a shortened three-day week and many would spend their spare time practising their gun drill at the Hucknall Airfield. Bob Hingston found them tolerant of his failings as an inexperienced officer.

I liked the men and I found I had quite a lot to learn about them. I had never really come into contact with this sort of people – miners and other men of that type. It always amazes me really that they did accept this young bloke coming in, not knowing the first thing, and being an officer. Some of them had been in the regiment for some years and knew quite a bit about gunnery, and they had to take orders from me. I should have thought they would have resented me, but I don't think they did. I think it was rather the accepted thing at that time.[21]

Second Lieutenant Bob Hingston, 426 Battery, 107th RHA

The men locked horns in a range of vigorous competitions that placed battery against battery, troop against troop and gun section against gun section. The British Army has always believed in the benefits of competition.

You were vying for points awarded by onlookers who were nothing to do with the regiment. It was a question of getting into action, firing the guns, hitting the target – and there was a Challenge Cup between the two batteries. My pals in 425 Battery used to think they'd got the intelligentsia, so they thought they'd got a head start. But we'd got enough intelligentsia and we'd got these very strong mining lads who could really move things fast. It made you learn a lot quicker – you weren't going to let the other gun be faster at laying than you were, you weren't going to let another gun be any quicker to get into action than you were. If somebody let you down there was hell to pay, even though we were only still playing at war. There was a great rivalry.[22]

Bombardier Herbert Bonnello, C Troop, 426 Battery, 107th RHA

Perhaps sometimes the rivalry got a little out of hand, but it certainly triggered a sense of absolute determination to 'win', as evinced in the attitude of newly promoted Lance Sergeant Ian Sinclair.

> The 426 Battery – you ignored them in my early days. They were a race apart, you only spoke to them to sneer, or be rude! They disliked us probably more than we didn't like them. The rivalry made us what we were – there's no doubt at all about it. If there'd only been one battery, I don't think we would have been anything like the regiment we were. A Troop and B Troop were just the same – they hated each other – as such – with anything to do with the gunnery. Because you were always aiming at being better than the others – that was the thing – always. I enjoyed the rivalry – to me it was always like being on a football field.[23]

Lance Sergeant Ian Sinclair, Headquarters, 425 Battery, 107th RHA

For many of the newer recruits the highlight of the camp was their first live-firing experience with the 18-pounder guns.

> We went up on the moors to actually fire the guns – and this was really something! To hear a gun go off for the first time! I was a gun layer and I'd got my layer's badge. Very proudly I wore an 'L' in a laurel wreath on my arm – this was very coveted amongst young chaps at the time! It was exciting to actually get the fire orders – put the angles on the dial sight and the sight clinometer, to bring the graticule in line with the gun aiming point. Report, 'Ready!' and then, 'Fire!' Then for the first time in your life you pulled back the firing lever and this terrific 'CRACK!' The gun bounces back – the smoke and the smell of cordite – and you've become a gunner![24]

Gunner Ray Ellis, B Troop, 425 Battery, 107th RHA

Yet however much they had learnt and improved, the army always seemed to want a little more – as Ray Ellis found when left behind on guard duty during the regimental excursion to Whitby Bay.

> I was a very smart soldier – at least I thought I was! Marching up and down outside the guard room at Redesdale no guardsman was ever smarter – I was very proud of myself. I noticed Regimental Sergeant Major Porter – a man of some character – coming down the road and he stopped to watch me for a while – and I really put on a good show. Then he walked over, as I thought, to congratulate me on my smartness, and I shall remember his words for ever, 'Boy, do you know what you look like?' I said, 'No, Sir!' He said, 'You look like a bag of shit tied up ugly! SMARTEN YOURSELF UP!' With that he walked away. That was a salutary lesson – he obviously thought this boy needs taking down a peg or two and he did it! Good old Porter! I liked him![25]

Gunner Ray Ellis, B Troop, 425 Battery, 107th RHA

While at Redesdale, the officers of the South Notts Hussars encountered Captain Leonard Gibson, a textile businessman from the Newcastle upon Tyne area. He was serving with the 287 (Elswick) Battery, 72nd Field Royal Artillery, who were based at Blyth Drill Hall but were sharing the same Redesdale summer camp.

> The other regiment was the South Notts Hussars. They were of the same sort of calibre as the officer set-up, but quite a number of them were in the Nottingham coalfields and had served their apprenticeship up here in Northumberland, before going back into their own family coal-owing firms. Pretty posh public school boys – they boasted Etonians and Harrovians. We had the odd Etonian and Harrovian too! In private life we boasted just as they did, solicitors and accountants and that sort of calibre of chap. They were known as being highly efficient and

both of us in turn had won the King's Cup fought for at the shooting camps. We were a pretty efficient amateur army! They had their guest night and most of us went – they were a very wealthy lot of chaps – more so than we were certainly. We had the normal mess games – then there were competitions of 'first over the top of the big mess marquee and down the other side'. They would come to ours and then plots would be hatched. The naughtiest 'boy' in each battery would lay on a raid at 4 or 5 in the morning and get the best trophy they could find in the opposing mess. I seem to remember I might have gone on one or two of them![26]

Captain Leonard Gibson, 287 (Elswick) Battery, 72nd Field RA

THEY GOT BACK FROM REDESDALE just a few weeks before the outbreak of the war. As the political situation darkened, Bob Hingston pondered on what lay ahead of them.

With Munich I can remember being, let's face it, scared stiff – fear for myself – I don't think one ever really envisaged defeat for the country! The relief when Chamberlain came back with his 'piece of paper' was immense – and yet it was tinged very strongly with shame. The thought in the back of my mind was, 'Oh my God, what have we done now?'[27]

Second Lieutenant Bob Hingston, 426 Battery, 107th RHA

4

MOBILISATION

We all had an element of fear – everybody does! If you're going into war, you've a great chance of getting killed or wounded, as have millions more. I was young, I loved cricket, football, rowing – I would sooner have got killed than have my leg shot off so I couldn't pursue my sporting activities.[1]

Gunner Harry Day, A Troop, 425 Battery

THE GERMAN INVASION OF POLAND ON 1 SEPTEMBER 1939 plunged Europe into a state of war. Britain demanded Germany withdraw. When this was ignored, the United Kingdom, France, Australia and New Zealand declared war. The declaration of war on 3 September was almost a relief for many as it ended the uncertainty; the newspapers had been full of 'war talk' for over a year.

The gruff William Pringle was one of those who had had enough.

Everybody was so sick of 'We're going to have a war! No, we're not! Yes, we are! No, we're not!' The strain was getting too much for the people of this country. Thank God it's come – now we can get on with the job and get it cleared up! We wanted rid of Hitler.[2]

Second Lieutenant William Pringle, B Troop, 425 Battery, 107th RHA

A key advance party had already been called up to prepare for the mobilisation, which began in earnest with the call-up of the TA on the afternoon of Friday, 1 September 1939.

> I was in charge of a dental laboratory at Beeston. At 3 o'clock there was the news on the wireless that the TA had been embodied. Off came my white coat and I said, 'That's it, chaps, I'm off!' I came back home, picked up my kit and went up to the drill hall. Everybody was coming in in dribs and drabs.[3]

Lance Sergeant George Pearson, Headquarters, 425 Battery, 107th RHA

Some men betrayed the sensitivity typical of youth in the manner in which they took their leave of their worried parents.

> I remember saying goodbye to my mother, and saying, 'Now, don't expect me back, we shall be away a long time – at least two years!' And she burst into tears. I was merely trying not to raise false hopes on her behalf.[4]

Gunner Dennis Middleton, B Troop, 425 Battery, 107th RHA

One of the best-loved stories of that momentous day concerned Sergeant Major Harry Sykes, who was working as a bus driver. When the call came to report to the Derby Road Drill Hall he certainly responded quickly.

> My dad was driving his bus on the Derby Road route and his mate stopped him and told him, 'We're called up, Harry!' He drove his busload of passengers down to the drill hall – got out and said, 'I've been called up!' And that was it – he just left the bus![5]

Gunner Jack Sykes, A Troop, 425 Battery, 107th RHA

For some of the men who were trapped in 'dead-end jobs,' even the call to participate in a war could seem like a welcome break.

I was on nights at work and I got the telegram and I thought, 'Well that's a relief!' It was a job I was doing to earn money, but I didn't like it! To think we'd be having a break from routine work – night and day and afternoons. I thought, 'Now we're going to be out in the fresh air and breathe some clean air in for a change!'[6]

Gunner Bill Adams, Headquarters, 426 Battery, 107th RHA

But many of the younger men were understandably nervous.

I was at the Boots office and we got a message – nine young lads walked out of an office of about twenty people on that Friday afternoon. I was very down at the mouth. I had seen pictures of the First World War. We had no idea – you always got the impression that *your* regiment wouldn't be involved in that sort of thing! Little did we know! It's perhaps as well we didn't! There was this ridiculous talk that it would be over by Christmas! That was the only thing that kept me going![7]

Gunner Harold Harper, D Troop, 426 Battery, 107th RHA

On arrival at the drill hall, their presence was marked off the nominal roll and they were briefed in a somewhat 'over the top' manner.

We were talked to by a Sergeant Major Burnett who told us we were now in the regular army, no longer territorials. We'd got to smarten ourselves up – and possibly this time tomorrow we might be in trenches in France! Which shook me rigid. But here was a Bombardier Terry Flint, a very tall lad, he broke the tension when he said, 'Sergeant Major, Sir!' 'Yes, Bombardier?' 'Are we proper soldiers now, Sergeant Major?'[8]

Gunner Harry Day, A Troop, 425 Battery, 107th RHA

This thought at least boosted his morale – to think that they were now 'real' soldiers.

While the regimental headquarters remained at the Derby Road Drill Hall, with the officers accommodated close at hand in a small hotel off Derby Road, 425 Battery was billeted in the nearby Hollins factory and the pavilion of the Western Tennis Club, and 426 Battery was quartered in the Radford and Lenton Schools.

The fear of air attack had permeated through society in the inter-war years. There was a horror of the potential of mass bombing and a belief existed that 'the bomber would always get through'. An air raid siren went off on the first night, but it was, fortunately, a false alarm, as it was soon evident that the regiment was by no means prepared.

> On Sunday night I was on fire picket, sleeping downstairs in the drill hall – I had an armband that said, 'Fire picket'. Now that was not well organised! We'd never had any fire drill at all. They told me my particular duty, they told me that if the air raid alarm went, I was to go the third floor to wake the brigadier! Then I was to stand by on that floor till I got further orders. The air raid sirens went. I went upstairs and knocked on this door – and out came this splendid gentleman – he'd got on his pyjamas, but he'd got his hat on with the red band – so I saluted him. I said, 'Fire picket reporting, Sir!' He said, 'Thank you!' He chucked his things on and I stood there near the fire bucket till the all clear. There were wild rumours – they'd bombed Derby – Rolls Royce had been flattened – it was all bunkum of course.[9]
>
> Gunner Ted Whittaker, A Troop, 425 Battery, 107th RHA

Up on the roof above them were the improvised anti-aircraft defences. It was evident that these too had not been thought through.

The one piece of armoury we had was a Lewis gun. I was put on to that with 'Taffy' Stanway stationed on the drill hall roof. We had some ammo, but we weren't called upon to fire the thing. Two sides of the parapet wall and we just rounded it off with sandbags. We couldn't make too heavy a job of it because we were on a boarded roof anyway. I think if we had fired the Lewis gun, we would have descended through it![10]

Gunner Frank Knowles, A Troop, 425 Battery, 107th RHA

For some time, it had been realised that Lieutenant Colonel Athole Holden could not be released from his 'day job' running the Stanton Ironworks Company. He had been retained in command until war was declared in an attempt to ensure that the preparations were not disrupted by a change in command. Now, on 5 September 1939, William Seely, the former commander of 425 Battery, was promoted and took over command of the regiment.

The regiment remained in Nottingham for three weeks learning the basic disciplines of military life. No longer civilians, they all had to absorb, almost from scratch, what it meant to *be* a soldier.

Just learning to be soldiers living together. Accepting the discipline that was necessary in living in billets. Being subject to discipline twenty-four hours a day. Getting people on parade quicker, getting them better dressed, teaching blokes to march that couldn't! Having to exercise authority on things that yesterday didn't matter, when you were still a free man. Being told, 'You must!' or 'You will!' rather than 'Will you?' That was the thing – and some people didn't take kindly to it. Some NCOs didn't find it easy to give orders – they were good at their jobs – but found it very difficult to instil discipline, because they weren't particularly disciplined themselves. I loved it![11]

Lance Sergeant Ian Sinclair, Headquarters, 425 Battery, 107th RHA

Sinclair himself was given the role of physical training sergeant, entrusted with the unenviable task of ensuring that the ravages of sedentary civilian lifestyles were reversed.

As PT sergeant, I was getting blokes out of bed, getting them on parade, going on a cross-country run and doing physical exercises – before they had their breakfasts. I was the most unpopular man in the troop! The physical condition of many of the men was very poor, they'd been taught to be technical soldiers, that's all, not a fighting soldier. It made some of them wish they had never been born! To have to go on a three-hour route march killed them – they were falling out by the wayside. It began to sort out the men from the boys at a very early stage; as to those who really wanted to do it and those who had been doing it just for fun.[12]

Lance Sergeant Ian Sinclair, Headquarters, 425 Battery, 107th RHA

By the time they went overseas, every man needed to be demonstrably physically fit enough to withstand the many and varied rigours of active service. Ray Ellis took part in a route march through Wollaton Park.

We set off with our full kit and boots. At this period, we were not accustomed to wearing army boots – we were used to wearing shoes and it's a big change, you've got to get your feet acclimatised. We had an officer marching smartly in front, but he was not wearing boots – he was wearing a Sam Browne and a pair of light brogues and that was it. We had marched quite a long distance when we passed a parked car in which sat another officer and these two changed so that we now had a fresh young officer wearing shoes. We got back with our feet all bleeding and sore and they told us, 'You have to be toughened up, you never know what might lie in store for you!' We thought, 'Isn't it going to lie in store for you as well? Surely you ought to be doing it!' It rankled![13]

Gunner Ray Ellis, B Troop, 425 Battery, 107th RHA

Ted Whittaker remembered a different kind of frustration in a route march led by the 425 Battery commander, Captain J. K. T. Hanson.

We did an awful lot of route marches which usually ended up at some pub. One of officers, Hanson, he distinguished himself by leading us on a very long route march one morning and we finished up at one of his own pubs – he was a brewer. He went behind the bar and said, 'What are you having?' Everybody rubbed their hands and rushed forward! We thought he was going to buy, but he just went behind the bar to serve! Then there were horrified moans and lots of shouts![14]

Gunner Ted Whittaker, A Troop, 425 Battery, 107th RHA

Warming up to their new lives, they took on a collective identity, with many 'in-jokes' and much singing on the march.

One of our great characters was 'Max' Miller. He used to march at the head of route marches and lead the singing. One of his favourites was a music hall turn called 'Syd Seymour and his Mad Hatters', who had this weird thing, when they came on the stage, he'd shout, 'Are you ready girls?' and they'd shout in very falsetto voices, 'The girls are ready!' Every now and then on the route march 'Max' would shout at the top of his voice, 'Are you ready girls?' and 425 Battery would all reply, 'The girls are ready!' Then they'd break into 'Roll out the Barrel'![15]

Gunner Ted Whittaker, A Troop, 425 Battery, 107th RHA

Slowly, standards of fitness improved.

The outbreak of war brought in its wake the National Service (Armed Forces) Act which, as many had anticipated, imposed conscription on all men between 18 and 41 years of age, unless rendered ineligible by poor health, reserved occupations or an accepted conscientious objection. With the advent of conscription, the necessity for territorials to volunteer for overseas service was removed, a situation subsequently tidied up by the Armed Forces (Conditions of Service) Act which suspended territorial status and rights for the duration of the war. From this point there was only one army; and everyone was eligible for overseas service. The 107th RHA was then designated as one of the three artillery regiments in support of the 1st Cavalry Division – the only cavalry division left in the British Army – which would form up in Yorkshire and Lincolnshire, before being deployed as the garrison force in Palestine.

On 23 September 1939, the unit was packed off to the Rillington area, near Malton in North Yorkshire. Bill Hutton has provided us with an amusing – if slightly apocryphal – anecdote of their unprepossessing departure from Victoria Station in Nottingham.

> We had the band and we marched down from the drill hall down Derby Road. A very fine show it was! I don't know how smart we were, I should think half of us were out of step! We marched to Victoria Station and we all lined up. Lots of people had come to see us off – my parents had come – they were all on the platform. The train came into the station and everyone got on. We put all our kit on the luggage racks, and we all sat down packed tight like sardines. Then we all had to get off the train! Why? Because the officers hadn't got enough room, they wanted two compartments. We all got on to the train again and moved down a bit, so we were more squashed together.

We all got nicely settled, 'Get off the train!' We all got off the train again – and they moved us up again – I think the officers wanted another compartment. My father said, 'God, I hope the Germans are in just as big a muddle as we are!'[16]

Gunner Bill Hutton, B Troop, 425 Battery, 107th RHA

5

GETTING READY

It was accepted, because we thought at the time that this was soldiering and had to be accepted as such. It was absolutely unnecessary at the time, it shouldn't have been like that at all, it was ridiculous. The way we were treated as soldiers in 1939 was appalling. I do feel that our officers had a lot to answer for – they didn't care. It didn't occur to them – there was a big gulf – we were just 'them' – we were not considered.[1]

Gunner Ray Ellis, B Troop, 425 Battery, 107th RHA

THE REGIMENT MOVED TO JOIN the 1st Cavalry Division, with the 425 Battery based at Rillington and 426 Battery nearby at East Barkwith. As part of the 5th Cavalry Brigade (Yorkshire Hussars, Sherwood Rangers Yeomanry and Queen's Own Yorkshire Dragoons) they would be under the command of Brigadier Keith Dunn. One early indication that not everything would be easy was the absence of proper gun tower tractors, which meant they had to manhandle the heavy 18-pounder guns using drag ropes all the way from the station. When they finally got to their billets many of the men were not impressed.

We arrived in the very early hours of the morning and they'd just cleared the pigs out of the pigsty. We had to clean the pigsties up. Personally, I was a little bit lucky as I was in a loft with hay. Quite a lot were sleeping where the pigs had been sleeping. I'd been used to an early-morning wash and shave in a nice warm bathroom. Instead of which I was out in the open, a row of taps had been plumbed in, washing and shaving with a cold north-eastern Yorkshire wind blowing.[2]

Gunner Fred Langford, A Troop, 425 Battery, 107th RHA

Up in the loft they realised that, given the usual cigarette smokers, there was a terrible risk of fire; but nothing was done to minimise the risk.

It was a veritable death trap – if there had been a fire, we'd all have been burnt to death because the only way to get in was up a ladder and through a trap door – and down below was all the hay and straw for the animals. We didn't even have a bucket or water or sand! We lay there smoking and never thought about it![3]

Gunner Ray Ellis, B Troop, 425 Battery, 107th RHA

It soon became apparent that the food rations were going to be of a very low standard. Bob Foulds was based in West Knapton, not far from Rillington, but by the time the food reached them from the battery cooks it was almost always inedible.

The food was really outrageous: it was terrible. It used to come up to us on open lorries. The weather was getting distinctly cold! They used the most inappropriate things: fried bacon and egg – it would come to us in big trays, absolutely congealed to the tray. The tea used to come in hayboxes – which were boxes stuffed with hay with a container of tea inside. Of course, that was stone-cold with a skim on the top! It was most unappetising and sometimes it was quite uneatable the food, even though we were terribly hungry and very young! I think we kept going on large slices of bread and jam![4]

Gunner Bob Foulds, B Troop, 425 Battery, 107th RHA

The officers were aware of the problem, but their inexperience in sorting out the nitty-gritty of army life was evident.

It was bloody awful, but if someone told you to go and improve that food, what would you do, how would you start? You wouldn't know where to start would you? You don't know whether it's bad meat to start with – whether its rotten, or tough – you don't know how to alter any of it![5]

Second Lieutenant William Pringle, B Troop, 425 Battery, 107th RHA

It was the officers' lack of experience that led to their failure to ensure that billets were properly cleaned and supplied with clean blankets. The crowded conditions and dirty bedding led to an outbreak of impetigo, a contagious skin infection resulting in unsightly blisters on the face. This did not improve the morale of the afflicted.

One amusing story of early morning guard duty was recounted by Ronald Miles from his time on 'prowler guard' around their farm billets.

We had been told by the owner of the farm that it was firmly believed that 'ghosts' really roamed the area. So here I was, maybe 100 metres from the farm buildings near to a few trees when I saw this vision of white. 'Who goes there?' I yelled. No answer! Again, I challenged, 'Step forward and be recognised!' I now yelled, even louder. Still no answer so I fired a shot into the air. One minute later the guard commander was at my elbow with another guard. To cover up my embarrassment I said, 'Sergeant, I heard movement – challenged and received no answer!' The three of us moved forward into the darkness and a couple of minutes later we were confronted by two cows with white markings. I cannot recall the exact verbal reaction of my guard commander, but I am sure that it was far from being of the complimentary nature.[6]

Gunner Ronald Miles, B Troop, 425 Battery, 107th RHA

In the absence of any gun towers, there was a concentration on endless gun drill, with even the junior officer required to turn out for training in gun laying under the watchful eye of Sergeant Major Charles Bennett. Men were encouraged to master more than one specialisation, ready for those moments in action when casualties would make it essential that men could cope with whatever was thrown their way.

On 6 November 1939, the 107th RHA moved to the Wragby area in Lincolnshire. To assist with the move, they had been given some old civilian lorries to tow the guns. The journey proved to be not without incident for Ted Coup.

On the move from Rillington to Wragby we used coal lorries adapted with trailing eyes on them. I was to lead one little convoy of four guns, and I was in the front in a pickup truck with this officer. The drivers told me, 'We don't want to go at 10 miles an hour. When old Parsons is not looking just put your foot down, Ted!' We set off from Scampton and we went through Malton. Official orders had been 15 miles an hour and I was knocking up 25mph easily – and the officer said, 'Pull to one side here!' We pulled to one side and watched the convoy go past. When it got to about the third lorry, the gun was missing – it had come off it. We had to stop and turn back – it had gone through a shop window in Malton. I was disgraced then – they caught on I was trying to go fast.[7]

Gunner Ted Coup, A Troop, 425 Battery, 107th RHA

The billets were much improved, and the regiment began to settle into a far more ordered existence. The gun drill was augmented by various training schemes, dropping into gun positions, night convoys and signal exercises. The old Mark IV 18-pounders were taken away to be converted into the new 18/25-pounders. Sadly, the replacements were even older.

> In their place we got a full complement of Mark IIs which had 1917 marked on the breeches. The breeches were clumsier, they had a pole trail, so that you got very little elevation – and thus very little range without actually digging the trail in. Once you had dug it in of course you couldn't move it sideways. They were still steel tyres on wooden wheels – the limbers had pneumatic tyres. They had wooden bungs in the muzzles and 'For Drill Purposes Only' marked clearly in white paint on the trails – they were useless – we couldn't fire them![8]
>
> Sergeant John Whitehorn, A Troop, 425 Battery, 107th RHA

However, with no firing camps scheduled, they were perfectly appropriate for gun drill.

The batteries also began a process of weeding out men who were too unfit, too young, too old, or too incapable to be considered for active service overseas. Some men were returned to civilian life, or despatched back to the second-line unit, the 150 Regiment, RA.

> A lot of the men had lived a very deprived life and quite clearly weren't fit! By this time, we were weeding out: having proper medicals, some of those were invalided out and sent home. Very bad eyesight, cases of suspected tuberculosis on the chest X-rays, some had got very bad feet, which was no good at all, others had some kind of disease that warranted being discharged.[9]
>
> Bombardier Charles Ward, Headquarters, 426 Battery, 107th RHA

To top up the numbers, they had a draft of men called up as part of the first militia who had completed their six-month military training. These proved a welcome addition to the ranks.

> One of the good things the War Department did was include in the draft local people from Nottingham or South Derbyshire. Therefore, they had a lot in common with people in the regiment and there wasn't the resentment that there might have been. There were the odd 'Taffs' and 'Jocks' and 'Brummies', but quite a few locals.[10]
>
> Gunner Frank Knowles, A Troop, 425 Battery, 107th RHA

Many of the territorials were initially dubious of these new arrivals, but they soon came to admire their high standards of fitness, drill and appearance.

> In a way, they were looked down on because they had been conscripted and we had volunteered, but they impressed us. I think we had a grudging admiration for their turnout as they were all quite smart. They'd gone through this six-month intake before being drafted to us. They turned out to be a very valuable bunch when they found their feet and they were an indispensable part of the South Notts.[11]
>
> Gunner Bob Foulds, B Troop, 425 Battery, 107th RHA

One of the militia men was Ted Holmes, who came from Chesterfield. At first he felt equally dubious of the territorials he was now thrust among.

> They were like Fred Karno's Army. The officers had riding boots and britches on – like horsemen. Some of them talked a little bit posh! I liked the Royal Artillery badge with the gun on it! I thought, 'An artillery regiment with an acorn badge – this seems funny – it was odd!'[12]
>
> Gunner Ted Holmes, A Troop, 425 Battery, 107th RHA

Another new arrival was a Tommy Foley, who'd been a professional boxer from Chesterfield.

> He'd beaten a champion pre-war and I think he was contender for lightweight or middleweight championship when war broke out. I'd done a bit of boxing in the Boys Brigade and I came under his wing a bit. We used to train at the Turner's Arms, where there was quite a big club room on the first floor, and the landlord allowed us to use this free of charge. There were about half a dozen, but mainly this Tom Foley used us as sparring partners to keep himself fit.[13]

Gunner Frank Knowles, A Troop, 425 Battery, 107th RHA

A draft of reservists was also sent to the regiment – regular army soldiers who had served their time but were now called up as part of their commitment to the army reserve. If the militia men found the territorials a little strange after just six months' service, these hardened regular soldiers had even more to get used to.

> They weren't used to the fairly relaxed discipline in a yeomanry unit. But most of them fitted in pretty well. They were quite a bit older than we were. They'd got knowledge which we hadn't got; they'd got experiences we hadn't got. Most of them had been abroad, they knew the ropes in India, Egypt and they'd been round the world. A lot of them were fairly unintelligent – a little bit dim – but they knew their particular jobs well. We listened to them, but we very often took what they said with a pinch of salt. You soon realised whether they were 'romancing' or telling you facts.[14]

Gunner Charles Westlake, A Troop, 425 Battery, 107th RHA

The best of them soon buckled down to become excellent soldiers, gaining rapid promotion to sergeant or higher and proving capable of teaching the territorials a great deal about the practicalities of army life. Others were more reprehensible.

> A lot of them were old sweats and old rogues! They'd really come as horse holders for the officers and to give us a bit of age – because we were all very young. They got all the 'cushy' jobs. I think they were better at skiving than us soldiers; we didn't know how to skive when we got into the army, did we? But we soon learnt![15]
>
> Gunner Bill Hutton, B Troop, 425 Battery, 107th RHA

One reservist who soon became a legend in the South Notts Hussars was Gunner Albert Ellis.

> Albert Ellis had been in prison and he was a real pain in the neck! Always in the stores. He could be quite charming; he could also be very belligerent. One day he came in and was making himself a nuisance – he'd been drinking – and he was being very offensive to everybody, throwing his weight about. He fancied himself as a boxer, but he was a smallish man. Albert Swinton just got hold of him and threw him out bodily![16]
>
> Bombardier Charles Ward, Headquarters, 426 Battery, 107th RHA

Another new arrival was a far more treasured recruit. Ted Hayward had trained as a cook at the Westminster Technical Institute and spent ten years working as an elite chef in various hotels. He decided to control his 'destiny' by volunteering before he found himself conscripted to the infantry. It was a life-changing decision.

> It came over the radio that the South Notts Hussars were looking for a sergeant cook – it was then I volunteered. I knew I would be going some time sooner or later, and I thought, 'Well, it's just as well to know what you are going to rather than

trust the lap of the gods, which didn't always turn out to your advantage' – and cooking was my line![17]

Ted Hayward

Hayward was sent to join the South Notts Hussars in Wragby. He had been promised the rank of sergeant cook, but somehow that was lost in the transition and he found himself an ordinary gunner cook. He was appalled by the state of culinary affairs he found on his arrival at 425 Battery.

The food was shocking. A long form was put out and there was a big dixie of stew, which was hard to decipher what it really was! There were some stewed apricots and custard. You had a plate and they seemed to use the same spoon for dishing out the stew as they did the apricots and custard. The taste of it was quite abysmal![18]

Gunner Ted Hayward, Headquarters, 425 Battery, 107th RHA

None of the other cooks had much cooking experience, but Hayward soon came to appreciate the very real difficulties under which they struggled in trying to prepare wholesome meals on inadequate cooking ranges with inappropriate ingredients.

Frozen meat was issued to us for consumption the same day – we would hack it up in bits and hope for the best. It would be pretty hard and inedible. Nobody gave any thought to linking the main element of the meat with any kind of vegetables issued. For instance, I've seen frozen rabbits issued – and the only veg issued were raw beetroots. Now I don't mind who the chef is, I defy any chef to produce a meal from frozen rabbit and raw beetroot! It was always insisted by the medics that tinned pilchards be part of the ration scale – now nobody liked tinned pilchards! It doesn't matter how many pilchards you issued containing vitamins and things which are good for one

– if you don't eat them then they're not a lot of good. Cases and cases of uneaten tinned pilchards were used for making walls around the cookhouse. You were clean to the best of your ability! It wasn't possible, you were dealing with a dirty stove, handling dirty fuel all the time. The complaints were unfair; but not unjust! Unfair because the cooks couldn't do any better; not unjust because they had to eat it![19]

Gunner Ted Hayward, Headquarters, 425 Battery, 107th RHA

Nonetheless many of the men believed that the sheer professionalism Hayward brought to the battery cookhouse meant that food standards gradually began to improve from the point of his arrival.

As all the various elements of the unit got to know each other, men ceased to be defined by their civilian status, or previous origin within the army, and they became all part of the same team.

War was a serious business and gone were the days of the TA when you looked upon it as escapism from your ordinary work. By the time the war had been on about six to eight weeks we were well and truly war orientated. Gradually the cliques were merging together, it was very noticeable. We were aware we were using swear words, we all had to be in the same 'swim' there was a war on and that sort of gave you permission![20]

Gunner Harold Harper, Headquarters, 426 Battery, 107th RHA

Social and cultural differences began to dissolve in the face of shared experiences.

It had been decided that the 1st Cavalry Division were ready to be despatched to garrison Palestine in January 1940. The unit began preparing for the journey out, with most of the men sent home on embarkation leave over the Christmas period. As they faced up to a lengthy separation from their girlfriends, men like Charles Ward had to decide what to do for the best.

> I got engaged that Christmas. I decided not to get married, because I didn't think it was fair! I was just going abroad – I didn't know then I should be abroad for five and a half years I can assure you! But I thought it might be a long time! We were very much in love – and I thought it was a bond.[21]
>
> Bombardier Charles Ward, Headquarters, 426 Battery, 107th RHA

Just before they left there was one last church service attended by a distinguished figure from the past. Honorary Colonel Lancelot Rolleston[22] was a Boer War veteran and pillar of the South Notts Hussar officer 'county' set. He was by then over 90 years old, but he wished to say farewell to his regiment one last time before they went off to war.

> It was a bitterly cold day, one of those frosty mornings with a fog, a really biting day. After the church parade we stood on the school playground and old Rolleston, with no greatcoat, he stood and addressed us. A great old man – and that is where we first heard the words, 'Once a hussar, always a hussar!'[23]
>
> Gunner Ray Ellis, B Troop, 425 Battery, 107th RHA

Then, on 19 January 1940, they marched down to Wragby Railway Station to catch the train to Southampton.

> We were marching along this icy road and it was difficult to keep your feet with all your equipment – rifles, ammunition, field kitbags – we were sliding about trying to march. Somewhere near the church, I heard a woman say, 'God help them, they don't know what they're going to!' No, we didn't![24]
>
> Gunner Ray Ellis, B Troop, 425 Battery, 107th RHA

The South Notts Hussars were on their way to war.

6

PHONEY WAR IN PALESTINE

I walked up the gangplank and I honestly thought I'd never see the shore of England again. I don't know why. I was depressed, very depressed. When we were with one another we never showed signs of depression or anything – we were always laughing and jovial wherever we went. You keep your thoughts to yourself.[1]

Gunner Ernie Hurry, B Troop, 425 Battery, 107th RHA

ON THE WESTERN FRONT NOTHING much was happening in the so-called 'Phoney War' as the British, French and German armies faced each other for eight months in frozen inactivity. As territorials bound for 'sideshow' garrison duties in Palestine, the South Notts Hussars left Wragby with the full pre-war trooping scale of equipment – which meant an enormous quantity of regimental stores packed away into crates and then carefully checked off the official G10/98 War Office list. For the men it made little real difference, but the officers had all their personal kit: civilian clothes, mess dress, sports gear – everything a young officer could need in foreign climes. The packed train took them down to Southampton where they boarded the *Maid of Orleans*. For some of the Midlanders this was the first time they had seen the sea.

Southampton to me only existed on a map. It's not until you
get down there and actually see it that you realise: you see
Southampton docks, all the ships and realise what the sea is
like. I thought it was marvellous. It was still like a big adventure
to me![2]

Gunner Ted Holmes, A Troop, 425 Battery, 107th RHA

But they would not have been human if doubts did not lurk
at the back of their minds: how would they respond in battle?
Would their families be safe left behind ? Would they themselves survive?

The Channel crossing seemed to take for ever, but eventu-
ally they arrived at the port of Cherbourg in Normandy. Ted
Holmes and his chums were astonished to find the French were
French!

Everybody was speaking French, a lot of French sailors with
funny pom-pom hats! They weren't going to let us go out into
Cherbourg, but they said we could go if there was six of you
– and you had to have a NCO in charge. Well 'Taffy' Stanway
was one of the regulars with a badge on his arm because he
was a Lewis gunner. He says, 'We're not having an NCO!
I'll reckon to be the NCO when we go into Cherbourg.' We
sets off and we got to the gate and there's a guard of these
French sailors. When he spotted them, 'Taffy' lines us up and
marched us off. When we got towards them, he's going, 'Left!
Right!' Really regimental – we were all swinging away. These
guards were so amazed they nearly came to attention as we
went past. Anyway, we had a good night, went to a café, had
some egg and chips, dancing with these French lasses. It was
really nice; they sort of put their arms round you and really
hug you! None of us got too much beer or 'owt, – we were just
nice and merry![3]

Gunner Ted Holmes, A Troop, 425 Battery, 107th RHA

Not all of the gunners exercised such self-restraint; used to the 'quaffing ales' of their local pubs, they were undone when they tried more exotic beverages.

> I remember getting absolutely blind drunk because my mate recommended what we should drink. He said, 'We ought to drink red wine and kirsch!' We got in an estaminet and stayed there. I get back to this train and I remember sitting on this metal step and I heaved my bloody heart out – I really did! It tasted worse when it came back, I'll tell you![4]
>
> Gunner Fred Brookes, Headquarters, 425 Battery, 107th RHA

There were many other temptations on offer, but most of the men had little real experience of the 'ways of the world' and had no idea what was going on in various dens of iniquity surrounding the dock area.

> When we got back on to the train, we all got talking and exchanging stories of where we went. One said, 'Did you go in such and such a place?' I said, 'I think we walked in and walked out!' He said, 'Did that girl come up to you making a fuss of you?' I said, 'She did, why?' He said, 'That was a brothel!' 'Ooooh!' I says, 'I've never ever seen one of them before – I always wanted to see what one was like!' 'Aye, she was after taking you upstairs!' 'I missed me chance then!' Of course, they pulled my leg and said, 'You must have been dumb!' I said, 'I must have been!'[5]
>
> Gunner Ernie Hurry, B Troop, 425 Battery, 107th RHA

The train was unheated, and the men were packed in like sardines with all their personal kitbags jammed into the luggage racks above them. The two-day journey seemed a nightmare in the freezing cold. Many of the men went down with a combination of influenza-like symptoms and an extreme sore throat.

Ray Ellis was in a state of collapse by the time they got to Marseilles to board the newly built troopship, the *Devonshire*.

> By this time, I was coughing up blood. Which worried me, but it was nothing really, I'd burst a capillary in my throat. Cough, cough, coughing: I felt really ill. I almost collapsed. They carried me off the train on a stretcher. I lay there shivering on the quayside at Marseilles and eventually I was carried aboard the *Devonshire*. I can remember saying, 'I expected to come back on a stretcher; I didn't expect to go on one!'[6]
>
> Gunner Ray Ellis, B Troop, 425 Battery, 107th RHA

The officers had travelled in much more comfort and they were also trusted to behave on a night out in Marseilles. Whatever their intentions, they showed themselves unworthy of that faith. Among them was Bill Pringle.

> We went round boozers, brothels, restaurants and cafés! Missed the boat! The boat had gone when we got down to the quay. We were told they wouldn't wait – they said that at 6 o'clock they were moving – and they did! They didn't half give us a fright! Mind they were a hell of a lot of officers short! We found a chap and he said that they had only moved so far out and anchored. They agreed to row us out for an enormous sum of money: there were two or three small rowing boats full. They knew who we all were because it was, 'Name, rank and number!' going up the gangplank. It was all part of the game as far as I was concerned! You were going to make the best of it and get on with it. We were all very suitably dressed down the next day![7]
>
> Lieutenant William Pringle, B Troop, 425 Battery, 107th RHA

The men were inexperienced sailors, and many struggled in bad weather at the start of their voyage across the Mediterranean to Haifa in Palestine.

The still ailing Ray Ellis found himself in a hammock on a lower troop deck – sixteen gunners to a very cramped small mess deck.

> The boat was pitching and tossing all over the place and everyone was seasick. Somebody had been to fetch the food and they were coming down the steps – the boat lurched and they fell. All the way down the steps was rice pudding and bully beef all slopping down among the seasick. It was really miserable![8]
>
> Gunner Ray Ellis, B Troop, 425 Battery, 107th RHA

Once the weather improved, they soon settled into the routine of a troopship voyage. The *Devonshire* could carry over a thousand men, so cleanliness and safety precautions were an essential part of their day.

> You had to clean everything up; all the hammocks had to be rolled and stowed. Then you go to your boat stations on the deck, where you would go if there was an emergency, you'd wear life jackets – like being on parade. We'd be there an hour or more and while we were at boat stations the captain would inspect the ship. They were very keen on hygiene. When it was starting to get dusk, no one was allowed on deck because they were afraid of people smoking and giving a light away – and so you were down below. People had to amuse themselves and there wasn't much at all for about eight days.[9]
>
> Gunner Reg McNish, Headquarters, 425 Battery, 107th RHA

The *Devonshire* arrived at Haifa on 29 January 1940.

Their early Palestinian experiences were not auspicious, as an outbreak of meningitis led to the regiment being quarantined for a couple of weeks in a half-completed camp at Sarafand on the coastal plan. Most of the men were accommodated in EP-IP pattern tents.

I remember the very first night! A friend of mine, 'Knobby' Noble, he wanted to go to the toilet – and he picks up Bill's boot and he used his boot! So, when Bill put his boot on next morning, he says, 'My word they have a heavy dew out here don't they' – and emptied his boot! We never stopped laughing – he never knew![10]

Gunner Ernie Hurry, B Troop, 425 Battery, 107th RHA

Their guns and equipment were travelling out in another boat which had been delayed. This left them nothing much to do but foot drill and route marches. The men were soon bored.

We had a period of really low morale, 'Please, Sir, I want a transfer!' 'I'm sorry to hear that, where do you want to go to?' 'I don't mind where, anywhere!' That was the general approach to life. They were all thoroughly fed up. They'd left home quite excited and here we were settled down in this foreign place, which they instinctively disliked, and there was nothing else to do except square-bashing. It was a very nasty period.[11]

Captain Bob Hingston, C Troop, 426 Battery, 107th RHA

In mid February 1940, they moved to a new camp at Gedera in central Palestine (some 8 miles south of Rehovot). After the deep joy of erecting all their tent accommodation, they settled in, but there was still no sign of their guns. One bonus was that by this time the cooks had begun to get a grip of their vocation. Ray Ellis marked this with one of the more amusing stories I have heard in forty years of carrying out oral-history interviews!

The food definitely improved in Palestine. The conditions we ate under were better, we had a better mess tent and we sat at trestle tables. The presentation was better, if a soup or stew type of meal was being served, it was served in a more civilised manner, it wasn't scooped up by some dirty man and dropped

on a cold plate. It was still a bit rough, but much improved.
We used to say, 'We have a fantastic cook in the troop at the
moment, he's a classical scholar!' 'Oh yes!' 'Yes, really, in fact he
has a Latin motto, "Fuck'em; giv'um stew!"'[12]

Gunner Ray Ellis, B Troop, 425 Battery, 107th RHA

Most of the men had little or no realisation of the political
situation in Palestine. The Arab revolt of 1936–9 had just been
quelled, but by 1940 there was an equal and opposite unrest stirring in the Jewish population. Ray Ellis encountered an overt
expression of this.

You could sense a lot of hostility in their looks. One afternoon,
walking along a street in Gedera and passing two Jewish young
ladies, I said, 'Good afternoon!' to them and they spat at my
face! That was rather a shock, because I'd always been brought
up to believe that everyone thought that the British were
marvellous people![13]

Gunner Ray Ellis, B Troop, 425 Battery, 107th RHA

There were legitimate reasons why the British were hated. The
Palestine Police, tasked with maintaining order, were British
recruited and they earned a reputation for brutality second
only to that achieved by the 'Black and Tans' during the 1920s
in Ireland. George Pearson got something of an insight into the
festering hatreds that were created and nurtured on all sides of
the Palestinian conflict.

I was in Jerusalem, sightseeing, and these young Zionists
were coming down the road. The Palestine Police blocked
off the road and wanted them to move further away. I said,
to this sergeant of the Palestine Police, 'What goes on?' He
said, 'We've run a white ribbon across the road, and we've got
loudspeakers. We'll tell them not to cross the line across the

road or they will be charged by the police!' They had these
bloody great long batons, like pick-helves. He said, 'They'll
push all the young women to the front, then they'll push
forwards!' Sure enough, they did! Once they crossed the line
the Palestine Police really waded in and, having come from
England, I thought it was appalling – cracking these rather
luscious German Jewesses on the head with these batons – it
was primitive. I said to this sergeant, 'That's a bit rough isn't it?'
He said, 'Well, you think so, but my mate is going home next
week – he's blind – one of these bitches put a broken glass in
his eyes – so I don't mind!' It gave a different aspect to it! At
first sight to see people bludgeoned it really is shocking, but
then you get the other side and you're not quite so certain.[14]

Lance Sergeant George Pearson, Headquarters, 425 Battery, 107th RHA

Back at Gedera, they managed to play a couple of games of
cricket. They improvised a pitch and Bob Hingston found it a
welcome and amusing diversion.

The locals were accustomed to walking across the village green
whenever they wanted to. The idea of having to stop doing
that for a cricket match never entered their heads. Two women
walked across, being very careful with all these men about to
veil their faces, so they nearly fell over the stumps on the way
through. Donkeys wandered across too. It was a grass wicket –
pretty rough! I don't remember there being any fast bowlers, so
there was no danger – they might have caused havoc! I played,
Joe Comber was our captain, he'd kept wicket for Cambridge,
and he said, 'Bob, you bowl at that end!' I said, 'I can't bowl!'
'You can, you can bowl!' So I proceeded to turn down some
very slow 'tweaky' balls – one of which immediately got a
wicket! 'There you are, Bob, I said you could bowl!!' About the
only time in my life I bowled. I didn't get many runs, double
figures possibly. The officers won, almost entirely owing to Bill

Barber. He came in and hit it all over the place and made a lot of runs.[15]

Captain Bob Hingston, C Troop, 426 Battery, 107th RHA

Charles Ward remembered another game between the officers and NCOs of 426 Battery and the Palestine Police.

Some of the officers had whites, we other ranks – I had a pair of grey flannel trousers and a white shirt I managed to scrounge. I was a spin bowler and on this matting wicket it was very difficult to turn the ball, so the batsman had a big advantage. Never the less, I didn't do too badly, and I got a couple of wickets. They put me in No. 9 and I'd scored eight – got a couple of boundaries – and the last man was in – the other two had lost their wickets. We'd got a chance of playing for a draw, but the idiot at the other end ran halfway down the wicket to a slow bowler, missed it of course – and was stumped. I was furious because I felt absolutely certain we could have held out for a draw![16]

Bombardier Charles Ward, Headquarters, 426 Battery, 107th RHA

Charles Ward *always* took his cricket very seriously and in the postwar year years he would rise to be president of Nottinghamshire County Cricket Club.

On 25 March, there was an Easter Monday boxing competition organised by the 1st Cavalry Division. The South Notts team was led by Lieutenant Harold Clark – and Gunners Harold Thompson and Frank Knowles saw it as a chance to show what they were made of. They had been training with the boxer Tommy Foley and were confident of their abilities, but they were planning how to share their winnings.

One of our officers, a 426 Battery officer named Clark, he'd done a bit of boxing at university and he was our fight manager.

He had set himself up to check that no one was mismatched – that was supposed to be his function! But some of the regiments didn't let them out, they brought them in a 30cwt vehicle with tarpaulins over the back and let them out one at a time. They got more and more like 'Rocky' Marciano. Frightened you to death – they shouted professional! They were marked, they'd had years at it. Tommy Foley, the ex-professional, was quite put out, to put it mildly, he was throwing challenges out left, right and centre. Because we had abided by the rules – Foley could have been included as a member of our team.[17]

Gunner Frank Knowles, A Troop, 425 Battery, 107th RHA

Harold Thompson watched as Knowles took on his opponent in an early bout.

Frank was first and, 'Oooh', he got caught! I looked at him and I said, 'I'm not sharing that lot with you!' Because all his face and eye was cut, blood all over the place. Anyway, it came to my turn and this youth came in with boxing shorts, shoes, gumshields – he'd got everything! I thought, 'Aye, Aye, he's not going to hurt me!' I went straight across and hit him, 'Whhoof!' He sort of shook his head and then he got going. He hit me on top of the head and I thought, 'Aaaah! I'd better go down!' I went down, then I realised he hadn't hit me hard enough! I lasted three rounds, but he hardly laid a glove on me because I was getting out of the road all the time! I hadn't got the 'wind' because we hadn't trained! If I'd have won, I'd got to fight this bloke that Frank had lost to – and I wasn't wearing that![18]

Gunner Harold Thompson, A Troop, 425 Battery, 107th RHA

Even so, Thompson suffered from a perforated eardrum after the fight. Albert Swinton was also in the team, having boxed at school. A fair man, he never abused his considerable strength and boxing abilities. Now what he saw shocked him.

> I was light-heavyweight, and I'd had two bouts before – I won easily. I watched this semi-final and this Scots Grey bloke had taken advantage of one of our blokes, an older bloke – mid thirties – which was old to me. He gave him a rough time, he kept going at our chap, he was inflicting punishment on him that was absolutely unnecessary. I thought to myself, 'Now, if I come up against you, I'm going to give you a hell of a tawsing!' I met him in the final – it was set up for three two-minute rounds. We started off and he landed one on me – right in me breadbasket – and I thought, 'My God, you've got to watch yourself, Swinton, or you're going to get panned out here!' Because it hurt! I back-peddled a bit and sort of got me breath back and then I hit him about three times – and I cut him each time with the force of the blow. He finished up hanging on the ropes with blood pouring from his face and with everybody shouting, 'Finish him! Finish him!' Well I'm afraid I couldn't. I hadn't got that killer instinct! I'd won and that was it finished as far as I'm concerned.[19]

Lance Bombardier Albert Swinton, D Troop, 426 Battery, 107th RHA

There were very few victories for the South Notts Hussars that day.

At the end of March 1940, the regiment moved to Hadera Camp, set on the coast to the north of Haifa. At last the guns arrived and the South Notts recommenced training in earnest. The 425 Battery was given Mark II 18-pounders with rubber tyres, whilst the 426 Battery was equipped with the 4.5-inch howitzers, the other staple of the field artillery from the Great War.

We thought the 4.5-inch howitzers were very good. They were reliable, they fired quite heavy shells. As a howitzer you could pack them close in behind a hill and lob shells over the top. We liked them very much![20]

Captain Bob Hingston, C Troop, 425 Battery, 107th RHA

The resumption of gun drill and command post specialist work was mixed with the usual training schemes: driving in desert conditions, dropping the guns into action and setting up the telephone lines between the OPs and the command posts.

What I remember mostly is the wildflowers which in Palestine at that time of the year are famous. We would drive off the road into a field flaming with colour – lupins about 18 inches high, lilies of the valley – it was really rather sad driving over these and crushing them, putting the guns into action.[21]

Lieutenant Charles Laborde, D Troop, 426 Battery, 107th RHA

On 15 April, their progress was assessed on inspection by General Archibald Wavell, the General Officer Commanding, Palestine.

He walked along the line as generals do and picked up some odd man to speak to. He stopped in front of me and said, 'Do you feel ready to go out and meet the enemy?' To which I replied, 'Yes, Sir!' 'Good man!' he said and walked on. I think that had Hitler known I was ready to go and meet the enemy the Third Reich would have trembled![22]

Gunner Ray Ellis, B Troop, 425 Battery, 107th RHA

As part of the 5th Cavalry Brigade, 107th RHA were still nominally a 'cavalry' unit and the officers were required to learn to ride. This was a problem for some.

When the horses arrived, life changed very considerably for us! We were gunners in a cavalry division and the officer must be able to ride so as to liaise with the cavalry. We had our forty horses with our horse-holders. While a lot of the officers were fairly accomplished horsemen, there were a great number, like myself, who had never ridden. Major Batt instituted an officers' riding school which used to take place at 2.15 in the afternoon, after lunch, when it was very hot. The horses were fairly splendid – high-spirited – and we used to ride round in circles. It must have been a comic sight to watch, because we used to fall off like ninepins. We did in the end persuade 'Teddy' Batt that it was too hot to do it in the middle of the day and we started in the morning at 6.15. It was cool then and pleasant – and not so many other ranks looking on laughing either! It's always fun to see your officers making fools of themselves isn't it? We got to the stage where we could go round the circle without falling off, then we started riding without any stirrups. That was very difficult to start with – when you came to the sharper corners one tended to go straight on while the horse went off to the left, so dismounted very rapidly! We got reasonably proficient at that, but then we started to ride the horse with just a blanket – no saddle at all! I fell off so many times I lost count! Then we did some bareback riding and all sorts of exercises. We had to run alongside the horse holding on to the saddle and then leap into the saddle. The first time I did it, I gave a great leap, as I used to when I jumped for the ball in the line-out at rugger, and I went right over the horse and landed flat on my back on the other side which caused a great deal of mirth! In the end we became very proficient and got up to jumping over a five-bar gate.[23]

Lieutenant Charles Laborde, D Troop, 426 Battery, 107th RHA

The officers' mess was in a large tent and it was still run on peace-time lines, with, at least at first, some insistence on traditional protocols.

We got very 'browned off' with having to wear blue patrols in the evening. Our mess dress was tight blue trousers with a double yellow stripe down the side, a blue jacket with chain mail on the shoulders and it was rather thick blue serge and it was very hot. After a time, a deputation was sent to the colonel to say, 'Please may we not wear this. Please can we wear our dinner jackets?' That was agreed and of course it was much cooler with a white shirt and no waistcoat, just the jacket![24]

Lieutenant Charles Laborde, D Troop, 426 Battery, 107th RHA

Lieutenant Colonel Bill Seely also proved to have a refreshingly tolerant attitude to seniority and place setting around the officers' mess dining tables.

Bill Seely had the tables reorganised and he himself did not have a colonel's seat. He sat anywhere, and he mixed with everybody else. The other senior officers got the idea and it was a very good move on Bill's part; I think it really brought the whole lot together. He believed in the army principle that there should be no rank in the mess. You called the colonel 'Bill' in the mess, but if you met him outside, you called him 'Sir', and saluted him.[25]

Captain Bob Hingston, C Troop, 426 Battery, 107th RHA

The men spent much of their recreational time on the beach. There were strict rules governing the risk of sunburn, which was considered a 'crime'. This was difficult to enforce, as was evident with one victim who should have known better. Harry Day, who had volunteered to act as the orderly to Dr John Finnegan, the regimental medical officer, was one such.

A man was not supposed to work with his shirt off, unless he had been in the desert for some time – desert wise – got his knees brown. There was one particular case: a stupid fool had laid in the sun and went to sleep – that was the medical orderly himself – me! Sunstroke and blistering – I had a temperature of 104 degrees, I treated myself with calamine lotion and Finnegan gave me every possible drug! He couldn't lose his orderly![26]

Medical Orderly Harry Day, Headquarters, 107th RHA

Harry Day was also responsible for advising on the risk of venereal disease. Here there were conflicting sources of advice for the men.

Gonorrhoea was the thing. Lectures were given on the women and brothels. The adjutant, Major Batt, suggested that a man should work off his surplus energy by indulging in sport and as much physical hard work as he could. The doctor, Captain Finnegan, advised that the men should carry and use a condom – and then visit the prophylactic centres afterwards. Everyone used to come; not only other ranks, but officers as well.[27]

Medical Orderly Harry Day, Headquarters, 107th RHA

One wonders which approach was most effective.

In May, the regiment moved to a firing camp deep in the Sinai desert at Asluj. This was a terrible environment, with temperatures recorded of over 95 degrees Fahrenheit in the shade and exacerbated by regular dust storms. Just getting there was a useful training in overcoming desert conditions. Harold Thompson was driving the signals truck and he soon realised that running into soft sand demanded an immediate response if they were not to get bogged in and laboriously have to dig the truck out.

You learned eventually to change gear without using your clutch for quickness. In those vehicles you double de-clutched. Instead of just putting your clutch in and going into gear, you had to put your clutch in, take it out of gear, put your clutch in again and put it into your next gear. Without the clutch you listened to your revs and then put it into gear. It's something you've got to learn how to do. You've got to know exactly when to do it otherwise you get a 'KKKKRRHK'.[28]

Gunner Harold Thompson, A Troop, 425 Battery, 107th RHA

The conditions were also a real practical test for the cooks. The heat and the general desert filth offered an obvious danger of food poisoning. Ted Hayward's skills as a cook had been recognised by promotion to sergeant cook and he realised that in cooking for a mass of men in such circumstances his only realistic option was the somewhat blunt instrument.

The No. 1 Burner used petrol for its fuel. You lit it from the front when you got a terrific gush of petrol come through – threw a bit of lighted paper in and got away as quickly as you could! After a short time, the ring vaporised the petrol, which blew out a line of heat that stretched about six feet. There were little metal stands, to which you could attach dixies. They were very likely to go wrong – the jets got very quickly worn or blocked up.[29]

Sergeant Ted Hayward, Headquarters, 425 Battery, 107th RHA

But what to cook? Speed was of the essence, food could not to be allowed to stand around in these conditions.

It was hot: very, very, very hot! The facilities for storing food was absolutely nil! Everything was kept in the open. No refrigeration whatsoever. It was so bad that if there was any cooked food left from one day, you could not keep it in the camp overnight, because the next day it would be riddled by maggots. We had swill contractors who used to come and take away the swill – and if by 5 o' clock in the evening they had not arrived we had to dig pits and bury the leftover food.[30]

Sergeant Ted Hayward, Headquarters, 425 Battery, 107th RHA

Like so many British Army cooks before him, Hayward soon realised that there was only one real solution.

> Stew – there was no other way. If you're feeding three people, you can get three fillet or sirloin steaks, but when you're feeding that number you had only a small proportion which is fit for roasting or frying. So, therefore, it all has to be stewed – shove it all in the pot and boil it! When you were issued with sausages they arrived in reasonably good condition. But you couldn't keep them because there was no refrigeration, so the only thing you could do was to cook them in boiling water, which didn't make them terribly attractive quite honestly. But it was either that or have rotten sausages. You could keep them cooked for a day or so but they wouldn't keep for a day if they weren't. There is no other item of food that is so liable to contamination than the average sausage – that's under ideal conditions! We served them as soon as we possibly could. The whole regiment could have gone down with diarrhoea or something![31]

Sergeant Ted Hayward, Headquarters, 425 Battery, 107th RHA

Meanwhile, out in the desert the regiment was being put through its paces: every kind of shoot, different types of barrage, the methods of camouflaging positions with nets and desert-coloured scrim. Everything they had learnt in England and Palestine was put to the test in a simulation of 'active service' conditions. One of the inspecting officers monitoring their progress was Brigadier Keith Dunn, who was then the Commander Royal Artillery (CRA) of the 1st Cavalry Division. Dunn was a very 'regular' officer, who was determined that *everything* should be done 'correctly'. The South Notts had encountered him before and were aware of his reputation. Ian Sinclair was acting as temporary troop sergeant major of B Troop when the great man descended on them.

Brigadier Dunn came and gave us the most God awful roasting of all time. For the first time I was afraid of a man – his steely blue eyes! We were sloppy! We didn't know our drill! We were no bloody good! There was nothing really wrong, but there was no way they were going to let you think that you were God's gift! He didn't say that one troop or battery was any better than any other – we were all bloody awful as far as he was concerned! No one ever forgot him, or forgave him for that matter, because we were trying so hard![32]

Lance Sergeant Ian Sinclair, B Troop, 425 Battery, 107th RHA

On one occasion, Brigadier Dunn had a dispute with Captain Colin Barber and ordered him to walk back from a field exercise. Almost every vehicle stopped – knowing full well what had happened – and asked the increasingly red-faced and choleric Colin Barber if he would like a lift.

While at Asluj they were alongside an Australian artillery unit. This was their first contact with the 'Aussies' and they were somewhat bemused. One exchange with newly commissioned Captain Frederick Porter typifies the traditional Australian irreverence and total lack of respect for 'authority'.

One night Captain Fred Porter was taking guard-mounting duty and he dressed in his blue dress uniform. He was walking down towards the parade ground when a group of Australians walked by him. He turned round and said, 'Hey, my man, don't you know when you see an officer!' He said, 'Gor Blimey, we thought you was one of the bloody band!'[33]

Gunner Ernie Hurry, B Troop, 425 Battery, 107th RHA

One tragedy occurred when Gunner Robert Paulson fell ill with appendicitis.

Bob Paulson was a very nice lad, but he was a very obstinate boy and he wouldn't go to the medical officer. Finally, we got the medical officer to see him – by that time the pain had gone off and he was apparently perfectly OK. He said, 'It's nothing! It's a bit of indigestion!' And Doctor Finnegan rather took his word for it. We went out on a night occupation and Paulson was the signaller with me in this OP occupied at night to fire at first light. Bob was in pain that night – it was obvious – and by the following morning he was in agony.[34]

Gunner Bob Foulds, B Troop, 425 Battery, 107th RHA

There are conflicting views as to what happened and who was to blame. Another close friend, Ray Ellis, certainly had a harsher perspective of the unfolding tragedy. He blamed Medical Officer John Finnegan, insisting that he should have realised the seriousness of Poulson's condition.

We'd go out on the range and come back and see poor old Bob there writhing in pain on the floor of this stinking little tent in the desert. He was in absolute agony; sweat was pouring off him. But still the doctor wouldn't do anything about it, until in the end after three days he had to realise that he was seriously ill. He was sent away to Jerusalem, but he had peritonitis – a burst appendix – and he died.[35]

Gunner Ray Ellis, B Troop, 425 Battery, 107th RHA

Bob Paulson[36] died in the Jerusalem Hospital on 16 May 1940. Both Bob Foulds and Ray Ellis were deeply affected, especially when the long journey to the burial ground gave them a small insight into what he had suffered.

Being one of his closest friends I was sent as one of the burial party. We set off across the desert to follow the same track that poor old Bob had made on his last journey. It was an appalling journey. It was so bad the bouncing in the back of this 15cwt that I hit my head on the stanchions that hold the canvas in place – and my nose was pouring with blood. I thought, 'Poor old Bob, coming along a thing like this with a burst appendix!' We saw the sister at the hospital who said that she had never known anyone fight so hard for his life. We buried him in Ramleh Cemetery – and poor old Bob remains there. He shouldn't have died of appendicitis; he should have been sent to hospital straight away. It was an awful shock, because he was so young, you don't expect 19-year-olds to die. A great loss; the first one.[37]

Gunner Ray Ellis, B Troop, 425 Battery, 107th RHA

Ernie Hurry also had a real health scare shortly afterwards. It is evident that he too had doubts as to Finnegan's competence or concern for his patients.

I got this touch of diarrhoea. Oooh, I was ill! I'd got this pain, I couldn't stretch my legs, I couldn't do anything. This chap Paulson had already had peritonitis and I knew he'd died of it – and that was the first thing I thought of, 'I've got peritonitis!' And this damn doctor – 'Aspro' – he won't do anything. So, I went to the doctor next morning, in fact, I was waiting for him to open first thing! Same thing, 'Go back to bed, take an aspirin!' It passed but I was in terrible pain.[38]

Gunner Ernie Hurry, B Troop, 425 Battery, 107th RHA

In the event Hurry made a full recovery. This recovery should cause at least a little sympathy for a medical officer struggling to define exactly what was wrong with men under desert conditions that were foreign to his experience. It was true that some men were malingerers, and in consequence it was all too easy to make mistakes.

On 18 May, the regiment returned to Hadera Camp. This

was meant to be a rest period, but the news soon filtered through of the disastrous events in France as the German Blitzkrieg crashed through the Allied lines and threatened the destruction of the whole British Expeditionary Force (BEF). The second-hand reports of German Stuka dive-bombers and panzers were chastening.

> Seeing how we were armed with the old 18-pounders, the most modern bit of which was the rubber tyres – and then we heard about the Blitzkrieg and the German Air Force! We were out in Palestine and all this was happening in France – the war would be over, and we'd be left out there! I know I began to wonder if I should ever get home again.[39]

Gunner Ted Whittaker, A Troop, 425 Battery, 107th RHA

Day after day the news got worse.

> When we were being pushed right back on to Dunkirk, the news was simply awful – you can imagine being stuck down in a godforsaken part of Palestine, with everything going wrong at home! The one thing that never for one moment entered into our minds was that we should lose the war! Which after all was very much on the cards at that time! Everything was going wrong in Europe. I don't think we thought that England would be invaded – one thought, 'Well the fleet is there! The Germans could never possibly cross the Channel!' It was then that you realised the war was going to last for a long time.[40]

Lieutenant Charles Laborde, D Troop, 426 Battery, 107th RHA

Some of the men felt almost guilty. There was, after all, a very real chance that the British homeland might be invaded – and where were they? Stuck in a sideshow far from the fighting.

There was a lot of discontent: here we were out in Palestine where nothing was happening doing meaningless drill, when we knew that all our people at home – mothers, wives and sweethearts – were at great risk. We thought they were going to be bombed to hell. People were suffering like that in France and at home and you felt rather guilty about it. You felt, 'Why aren't we back there?'[41]

Bombardier Charles Ward, Headquarters, 426 Battery, 107th RHA

7

MERSA MATRUH

We knew we were going into action and we got some chalk and wrote on the side of the train, 'Mussolini, here we come!' How green we were! There was no fear, just exhilaration – at last we were going into action – we were really going to show these Italians what was what![1]

Gunner Ray Ellis, B Troop, 425 Battery, 107th RHA

ON 10 JUNE 1940, ITALY DECLARED WAR on Britain and France. Previously the Italian dictator, Benito Mussolini, had avoided committing himself to either side, aware of the inherent risks of such a course for a country lacking in any real military strength and short of natural resources. At the start of the Great War in August 1914, Italy had deserted the Central Powers and ultimately joined the Allies in June 1915. Following the ascent to power of Benito Mussolini in 1922, the Italians had sought to expand their empire in Africa, first consolidating their grip on Libya and then launching an aggressive war to overrun Ethiopia in 1935–6. Victory led to the amalgamation of Ethiopia with Eritrea and Italian Somaliland to form Italian East Africa. With the outbreak of war in 1939, both sides had again sought Italian backing, but the successful German invasion of France, culminating in the occupation of Paris, seems to have persuaded

Mussolini that the risks of involvement were manageable and that he could pin the Italian colours to the Axis cause. He knew that the main Allied military strength was engaged with the Germans and he saw his chance for easy conquests in Egypt, the Sudan, Kenya and British Somaliland.

The entry of Italy into the war meant a reorganisation of the British forces in Egypt. Given the strength of Mussolini's Africa ambitions, there was an obvious risk of an early Italian thrust across the border from their existing colony of Libya into Egypt, threatening the important naval base of Alexandria, Cairo and the Suez Canal – the crucial link to India, the Far East, Austra-lia and New Zealand. Few things were more important to the continued existence of the British Empire than the Suez Canal. As a result, elements of the 1st Cavalry Division were moved in from Palestine. Despite Brigadier Keith Dunn's strictures during his inspection, the 107th RHA was selected as the artillery com-ponent. The preparations were frenetic.

> Suddenly, we got this seven-days' notice that we were moving. Then things began to happen. First of all, the horses were to go which was very sad. The day before, the colonel organised a so-called 'hunt'. There were no hounds and no 'quarry', but all the officers went out and we had a tremendous gallop about! The horses were off the next day. Then the equipment started to arrive. The poor 104th, the Essex Yeomanry and the Lancashire Yeomanry, the 106th, they were completely denuded of everything. All their guns, their dial sights, their trucks – suddenly we were absolutely smothered with equipment. I must say I didn't envy the quartermaster who had to take it all on and sign for it all! It was a fairly hectic seven days![2]
>
> Lieutenant Charles Laborde, D Troop, 426 Battery, 107th RHA

It was decided that the regiment would be deployed to Mersa Matruh, a small seaside resort some 180 miles west along the coast from Alexandria, while the former garrison moved to face the Italians across the Libyan border.

The South Notts Hussars entrained for Egypt on 23 June 1940. The nervous tension was apparent in a slightly dubious 'spy' scare.

> A man we called 'Palestine Post' was a little Jewish man who followed us around in Palestine. He sold newspapers and had a little stall, which he had permission to set up in our camp. The main paper was called the *Palestine Post* and so he was christened. He went with us, but when he got to the border, somebody saw he was there and there was some talk of him being a spy and he was sent away.[3]
>
> Gunner Ray Ellis, B Troop, 425 Battery, 107th RHA

They broke their journey at the Kantara junction just before they got to the Suez Canal, where they were told to jettison all non-essential stores and equipment to put themselves on a proper war footing. After crossing the canal, they boarded another pair of trains.

> Men used to wait at little wayside stations with trays hanging round their necks carrying pieces of bread and eggs. They used to say, 'Eggs y bread, eggs y bread!' Which in fact were quite tasty and always we used to buy them. These men used to stay on the train to the very last moment to sell as much as they could and then jump from a train doing probably 25 or 30 miles an hour, with bare feet on to the sharp granite chippings at the side of the railway and they were able to do it without spilling their precious eggs and bread![4]
>
> Gunner Ray Ellis, B Troop, 425 Battery, 107th RHA

At Mersa Matruh they were met by the advance party under the second-in-command, Major Edward Batt. They would join the garrison forces consisting of the 22nd Infantry Brigade (2nd Highland Light Infantry, 1st Cheshire Regiment and 1st Welch Regiment) guarding the western approaches to Mersa Matruh, while units of the Egyptian Army units defended the eastern perimeter. The 107th RHA were replacing the 1st Field RA, who were moving forward towards the frontier. Charles Laborde remembered his first somewhat nondescript impressions of Mersa Matruh.

Mersa Matruh had been a seaside resort and had a lot of very attractive villas and what was supposed to have been a nice hotel called 'The Lido' where it was said that the Prince of Wales and Mrs Wallis Simpson had stayed. But it didn't strike me as being very splendid – of course it had been heavily bombed then, all the windows had been blown out and it didn't retain much of its peacetime glory.[5]

Lieutenant Charles Laborde, D Troop, 426 Battery, 107th RHA

Major Batt had warned them of frequent Italian air raids, and within a few hours Ray Ellis had his first experience of being bombed when he was sent with a truck from the B Troop interim gun positions to pick up supplies from the train.

I heard a screaming sound and the next thing there was this vicious explosion and I hurled myself to the ground. It was a stick of bombs falling, but I didn't know at the time. I hadn't heard any aircraft and there had been no air raid warning. There was this devastating flashing, crashing and blast – I was absolutely bewildered. And then it went quiet. Then there was another scream and a soldier came out into the street. He was holding his guts in and all his stomach had been torn open and his entrails were trickling through his fingers. It was an awful sight. He was screaming, then he sank to his knees, his screaming changed to a gurgle and he just sort of dropped almost at my feet. I was appalled. I was terrified, horrified and stupefied. He was the first man I saw die.[6]

Gunner Ray Ellis, B Troop, 425 Battery, 107th RHA

Ray Ellis little realised that high-level Italian air raids would become a part of his daily life for weeks to come. Most of the raids were directed at the railhead and port facilities, but at times bombs were scattered widely across the garrison.

Usually the first warning you got was the first bomb whistle! The aircraft were so high that you couldn't really hear them. They would come over – twelve to fourteen of these aircraft – and drop their bombs across our part of the perimeter. It was quite extraordinary; someone in the mess had always had a bomb land close to them – the bombing was simply terrible. It went on for most of the day, every day! On and on and on! We reckoned we were the most bombed place on the surface of the earth at that time! It was terrible![7]

Lieutenant Charles Laborde, D Troop, 426 Battery, 107th RHA

Initially, they took over the pre-existing gun pits left behind by the 1st Field RA. These looked quite impressive and some of the bigger dugouts offered shelter up to 12 feet deep below ground.

The battery headquarters dugout had an entrance and steps down. In the middle we had the phone and artillery board laid out, then the sleeping quarters were off to the side – not very salubrious. Two signallers, two surveyors where we slept, then there was the battery commander – Major Barber. When you went down it took about 20 minutes before you could get your eyes focused because you'd come out of bright sunshine and all you had down below was paraffin lamps. The walls were corrugated iron, earth and rocks on top – I think if a bomb had ever dropped it would have gone straight through![8]

Gunner Harold Harper, Headquarters, 426 Battery, 107th RHA

There was also a system of slit trenches scattered all over the gun positions, which provided the hope of sanctuary from the effects of blast and scything bomb fragments.

We had slit trenches – about four feet deep, six feet long and about eighteen inches to two feet wide with sandbags on the top. The very first person I ever saw killed in the war was a bandsman. He was in a slit trench only 20 to 30 yards away from the headquarters. The bomb dropped about 20 yards away from him and his slit trench caved in on him. I was one of the people who had to dig him out – that was my first experience of seeing a dead person. I was about 21 years of age.[9]

Gunner Harold Harper, Headquarters, 426 Battery, 107th RHA

Subsequently, the guns were moved into anti-tank positions in the higher ground surrounding Mersa Matruh. The gun sergeants were all allowed a considerable amount of latitude in the design and method of construction of these gun pits and they certainly proved resourceful. The results were a tribute to their ingenuity in acquiring raw materials for the gun pits and attached dugouts. Ray Ellis felt lucky to be in Sergeant Cliff Smedley's gun section.

We first dug the ordinary gun pit. Then we decided to put a roof on the gun pit. This was done with wooden beams and corrugated iron. Whilst this was going on the Royal Engineers were busy building a concrete pillbox for the machine gunners of the Cheshire Regiment. They worked during the day and at about 6 o' clock they packed up and went back to their camp. As soon as they disappeared over the horizon, we started up the concrete mixers again and set to work. First, we built a flash apron in front of the muzzle of the gun so that when we fired, we wouldn't give ourselves away with a big cloud of dust. We built a concrete semicircle for the trail of the gun, so that when you dragged the gun round, it ran in this concrete gully. Then we set to work to build our dugout.[10]

Gunner Ray Ellis, B Troop, 425 Battery, 107th RHA

Although proud of their achievement, with the benefit of his later experience Ellis realised that they had effectively put themselves in a turret with only a 100-degree arc – helpless to an attack from anywhere behind them. The much-vaunted roof would almost have collapsed if hit by a shell or bomb, putting the gun and gun section out of action for good.

Through the summer of 1940, the raids carried out by Italian Caproni and Savoia-Marchetti bombers intensified. There was little warning or aerial defence, as the RAF's biplane Gladiators were not only based too far away, but also lacked the speed and power to have any real chance of successfully intercepting the Italians, and with the Battle of Britain raging, there were many more urgent calls on the services of the modern fighters such as the Spitfire and Hurricane.

One notable victim of the early raids was Major Edward Batt, who was hit by bomb splinters on 18 July 1940.

Major Batt was lying in a shallow trench dugout under a bell tent with Colonel Seely. He was a very tall man – about six foot three – and inadvertently he lifted his leg. A piece of shrapnel took his foot almost off. He was put on a stretcher and I supported the foot. Finnegan told him that artificial limbs meant that he could still partake in his favourite sport of riding. He was evacuated to the underground casualty clearing station in Mersa Matruh and then removed to the 15th Scottish Hospital in Cairo. The amputation proved a success, but some time afterwards a piece of shrapnel was belatedly found in the other foot, which caused gangrene. The foot was amputated but he died.[11]

Medical Orderly Harry Day, Headquarters, 107th RHA

Major Batt had been desperately unlucky, but others had almost miraculous escapes, as John Whitehorn witnessed.

There was a raid came over and from our dugout entrance we saw George Pearson walking across – he made a dash for a slit trench – and disappeared into it. When the raid had gone, we saw that where the slit trench had been there was just a black mark and we said, 'Alas, poor George!' But George got up out of the black circle and walked away – in the wrong direction to start with – but then turned round and went in the direction he was going originally.[12]

Troop Sergeant Major John Whitehorn, A Troop, 425 Battery, 107th RHA

George Pearson had indeed been extraordinarily lucky.

I won't say I was knocked senseless, but I was very badly shaken. When I got up, I found I was on the black rim that just surrounded the bomb hole, but not even touched by a bit of shrapnel – it must have just gone straight over me because I was lying so close. It certainly perforated my eardrums![13]

Sergeant George Pearson, B Troop, 425 Battery, 107th RHA

Given the rain of bombs dropping in the area, there is no doubt that during the early days at Mersa Matruh many of the men became jittery, afflicted by the constant stress.

It did get to you! You were for ever on the alert. Listening all the time to see if you could hear a drone, looking up all the time – especially if you had to go somewhere. You wouldn't say, 'How far is it?' You'd say, 'How many slit trenches is it away?'

Say I had to go from the gun position to headquarters: before I set off, I would be looking all around, then run like the clappers to a slit trench, get down, have another look and so on till I got there. That's how it affected you! People got really scared.[14]

Gunner Harold Thompson, A Troop, 425 Battery, 107th RHA

It was then that the experience of Captain Frederick Porter proved invaluable in stiffening the morale of the territorials. He had been a professional soldier all his adult life and he was a great believer in the power of discipline.

You get far too dependent upon dugouts and trenches when there are air raids about. I was thankful to Captain Porter because when there was an air raid on, we all used to run and jump into a trench. That was absolutely the wrong thing to do because you did more damage to yourself jumping into the trench than anything that would have happened if you'd taken your time in quietly walking. He issued an order that anybody seen running to take cover would be put on a charge.[15]

Bombardier David Tickle, Headquarters, 425 Battery, 107th RHA

It was good advice that was gradually disseminated across the regiment, but it took time for the message to sink in, even when there were slit trenches everywhere, not more than 10–20 yards away from any soldier on the regimental positions.

I was inspecting C Troop on morning parade when the signaller poked his head out of the dugout and said, 'Air raid red!' One or two men swayed a bit – and I heard one of the sergeants say, 'You haven't been given any orders to move yet!' I carried on the inspection, trying to keep as calm a voice as I could, and I said, 'Sergeant, will you let me know if you can hear any enemy aeroplanes?' 'Yes, I can hear one now, Sir!' So, I said, 'Right, well we'd better take cover then!' They broke off – and there

was a shout from one of the NCOs, 'WALK!' And everybody
walked calmly to their slit trenches![16]

Captain Bob Hingston, C Troop, 426 Battery, 107th RHA

Most of the men learnt how to judge the degree of danger and
adjusted their behaviour accordingly.

I've never been a brave man – and I must admit that I took
cover as quick as the next person when an air raid started! But
you became more selective if you could get some indication of
where the bombs were coming. You didn't used to worry if you
knew darn well that they weren't going to land on you! You
could tell by the sound of them whether they were – or not. But
nobody could say that it was a pleasant experience. One treated
them with complete contempt after one had experienced it
because they were quite useless. Thousands of bombs were
dropped on Mersa, and although it was regrettable for the
individuals concerned, there were probably no more than half a
dozen people killed. They were so frightened they flew so high.
One never saw Italian planes coming over, they were like little
dots in the sky and they were more keen to drop their bombs
and go.[17]

Bombardier John Walker, Headquarters, 425 Battery, 107th RHA

In traditional British Army fashion, even as they battled their
own fears, many took a scurrilously humorous view of the efforts
of the six 3-inch guns manned by the Egyptian Army which provided the only anti-aircraft cover.

We used to say that just before a raid they would knock hell
out of the sky. Then whilst the planes were over, they were very
quiet! And as soon as the planes were gone, they knocked hell
out of the sky again.[18]

Sergeant George Pearson, B Troop, 425 Battery, 107th RHA

Humour was regarded as one of the best defences against the debilitating nerves.

> They had a dummy airfield and railhead nearby. The camouflage people used to shift dummies on the latrines each day, they had oil fires which they set off when the Italians came over bombing in the hope that they'd bomb the dummies rather than Matruh. There were a lot of dummy aeroplanes made out of painted mess tables. It was said that they came over and bombed them with wooden practice bombs.[19]
>
> Troop Sergeant Major John Whitehorn, A Troop, 425 Battery, 107th RHA

Never the less, some men did break down under the strain. Many thought that their stress levels were increased by the sheer randomness of the bombing.

> Some of the chaps were very nervous and went rather bomb happy. I hit one bloke in the jaw to quieten him down, because he was raving, shouting, 'We're going to get killed, they're going to kill us!' One or two left us there.[20]
>
> Gunner Bill Adams, Headquarters, 426 Battery, 107th RHA

Ray Ellis recalled a case of an 'old soldier' who used his experience rather less productively than Captain Freddie Porter.

> We had a regular soldier with us who eventually got himself out by tapping his knee with a wet towel and a spoon. Making his knee swell up. We watched him. We all knew he was doing it, we were a bit scornful really. It was a thing you wouldn't have dreamed of doing yourself. But nobody thought of reporting him – he got away with it – he went. A lot of the regular soldiers who came were fine fellows, I'm not denigrating them at all; he was a one off.[21]
>
> Gunner Ray Ellis, B Troop, 425 Battery, 107th RHA

Norman Tebbett took a fatalistic view and managed to conceal his own fears.

> One or two were shook up because a bomb dropped close to them. These people who say they were never scared; I just can't believe them – it can't be true. Yes, you accept it – you're there and there's nothing you can do about it. But I'm blowed if I can accept that anyone who is being bombed is not scared. You know the next one could kill you or badly injure you. You do your job because you're there to do it – and you've got to do it! It's bound to affect you. Of course, you're afraid, but you've got the courage to carry on.[22]
>
> Gunner Norman Tebbett, A Troop, 425 Battery, 107th RHA

In this fashion, most of the men managed to swallow or suppress their fears. The high-level raids would continue for several months, until at last the RAF was reinforced with a fighter capable of reaching the Italian bombers.

> In the autumn, reinforcements were arriving and – *mīrābile dictū* – some Hurricanes! That was the biggest excitement! The Hurricanes got among these bombers and I think they shot down several. The men were standing up and cheering like mad at the sight of these blessed bombers being chased off. They didn't come again![23]
>
> Captain Bob Hingston, C Troop, 426 Battery, 107th RHA

VARIOUS HEALTH PROBLEMS caused more casualties than the bombers flying high above them. One problem soon became apparent – the dugouts swarmed with bedbugs and fleas.

> Some of the wretched men would run out of the dugouts in the middle of the night beating these brutes off them. I discovered

to my great pleasure that they don't like me, they would walk about all over me, but they wouldn't actually bite me! I don't know why! The revolting thing about them is that when they walk on your face and you put up a hand and squash them, they have the most awful stink.[24]

Lieutenant Charles Laborde, D Troop, 426 Battery, 107th RHA

Ian Sinclair would have been deeply envious of Laborde.

The sand fleas used to bite me. Other people used to have them, and they would itch, but I'd be covered in great big weals as big as a half crown after a bad night, which used to stay for several hours before they would go down again. I used to take my bed to bits, give it a good shaking, put DDT powder in it, but I'd lose hours of sleep on account of them.[25]

Sergeant Ian Sinclair, A Troop, 425 Battery, 107th RHA

In the absence of a proper diet of fresh fruit and vegetables, these bites – or any other casual knock and abrasion – would often develop into desert sores.

If you were the type with sensitive skin, like I was, you'd get a little scratch, well that would be infected very soon – and the next thing you knew you had a desert sore. It would finish up like a bomb crater. The skin all round was all sort of tender and red; pussy and sunken in the middle. My legs at times would be completely bandaged.[26]

Lance Bombardier Ken Tew, A Troop, 425 Battery, 107th RHA

As medical orderly, Harry Day was kept busy treating these ugly suppurating sores, which sometimes grew to the size of a small orange, filled with pus.

The treatment was various: some men yielded to one treatment and another man yielded to another. First, we tried Aquaflavine

ointment, then we'd try something else – Eusol, M&B
Sulphonamide powder, hot fomentations or zinc ointment.
They had to be evacuated if they got secondary infections – if
their lymph glands were affected and they had a prolonged
raised temperature.[27]

Medical Orderly Harry Day, Headquarters, 107th RHA

They were also afflicted by a plague of flies that seemed to follow
them around wherever they went. The flies seemed to get everywhere and allowed them no peace.

If you had the slightest cut on the hand, there would be five or
six flies fighting to get at it. The chaps would use old cocoa tin
lids to make a lid for the top of their mugs. When they had had
a drink of their tea, they would put the lid on to try and keep
the flies out of their tea.[28]

Sergeant George Pearson, B Troop, 425 Battery, 107th RHA

Another popular location for the discerning buzzing fly was the
toilets.

Latrines were a trench dug with boxes over the top. On the
top of the boxes was a circular seat and then a lid that would
drop over the seat on which you put a rock to try and keep flies
away.[29]

Sergeant George Pearson, B Troop, 425 Battery, 107th RHA

As the flies meandered between the latrines, the men's rations
and their open sores, there was soon an outbreak of stomach
disorders that could render a man almost helpless.

'Gippy tummy' was a form of bacillary dysentery – not
the amoebic type which was far more serious. A perpetual
diarrhoea. We gave them a starvation treatment – no food!

Plenty of water. If they didn't yield to treatment, then they had to be evacuated because these things were contagious.[30]

Medical Orderly Harry Day, Headquarters, 107th RHA

The men had trouble keeping clean and, given the proximity of the Mersa Matruh lagoon, swimming was a popular pastime. This however left them uniquely exposed to the Italian bombers, as John Whitehorn discovered, much to the amusement of onlookers.

We'd all gone down to the lagoon and were having a bathe down there. It was the only means of washing, because there wasn't much water. A raid came over and we'd been warned that it wasn't a very good idea to be in the water when a bomb was dropped nearby. So, we scuttled out of it and I remembered seeing a slit trench on the other side of the road near a hotel by the lagoon. I dashed out of the water, picked up my steel helmet on the way, went over the road, through the barbed wire, cut a strip out of my backside, landed on the other side – and there wasn't a slit trench there at all! I stood there absolutely naked except for this steel helmet. Everybody else had a jolly good laugh out of it![31]

Troop Sergeant Major John Whitehorn, A Troop, 425 Battery, 107th RHA

Without such Italian interference, the lagoon could be an idyllic setting. John Walker certainly landed on his feet with the extra duties he undertook as the NCO in charge of the battery 'yacht'.

I used to spend quite a bit of my day teaching people to sail in the sea, lagoon and salt lake of Mersa. This was a particularly pleasant way of spending time. It was a *felucca* rigged sailing boat; it had a single main sail and a jib.[32]

Bombardier John Walker, Headquarters, 425 Battery, 107th RHA

The men could buy a selection of goods that originated in the

NAAFI stores back in Mersa Matruh itself, which were then taken round the gun positions by truck. There was little opportunity to drink very much, but the occasional bottles of beer did generate a much-loved comic moment.

> We used to keep beer in the gun barrel to keep it cool. You closed the breech and dropped them down. We had a general officer come to examine the position and by this time we were all black – because we worked naked virtually, just a pair of shorts that's all we wore for months – and he said to someone, 'Is it wise to have native troops so near the front?' The colonel said, 'Bwworrr! These are the South Notts Hussars!' The general was most apologetic! Having said this, he went to the gun and opened the breech and – plonk, plonk, plonk – out came the bottles of beer as they slid down the breech and dropped on the ground. He just looked around, closed the breech silently, nothing was said! He had called us native troops, so he owed us that, didn't he![33]
>
> Gunner Ray Ellis, B Troop, 425 Battery, 107th RHA

The men found humour in almost anything as Ellis discovered.

> Hair was a great problem, because you sweat, and your hair becomes greasy. Then the sand blows, gets into your hair and it matts it. You can't get your comb through it. My brother said, 'I think the best thing we can do is to cut the whole lot off!' We discussed this and thought this was a good idea, so I sat on a petrol tin and George cut off all my hair. Then, when they saw what it looked like, everyone changed their mind and I was the only one with all his hair cut off![34]
>
> Gunner Ray Ellis, B Troop, 425 Battery, 107th RHA

The men near the regimental headquarters sometimes organised small-scale concert parties. This was not a professional show, just men from the regiment playing whatever instruments they could rustle up, comic turns and, of course, men who fancied themselves as impressionists or comedians.

> Sam Hall gave impressions and recited scurrilous songs about officers – and NCOs! He was quite good. He picked on Peter Birkin's stammer, [John] Shakespear's loping walk and his hesitant delivery, pet sayings of officers. He also sang straight songs. Charlie Fisher, a lad from Birmingham – he always sang 'Song of Songs' with a rather high tenor. A chap called C. K. Walker played drums and could drum on anything provided it rattled! 'Max' Miller who had his ukulele did songs and we all joined in! Then we'd all join together to sing all the dirty rugby songs![35]
>
> Gunner Ted Whittaker, Headquarters, 425 Battery, 107th RHA

Occasionally, the underlying stresses that dogged their lives would come to the surface, resulting in disputes and fisticuffs among the men.

> Somebody saying something stupid that somebody would take objection to that probably they wouldn't even have thought about under other circumstances. People would say, 'Say that again, you bastard!' And he'd say it again! That would provoke a fight. You often let them sort it out between themselves, unless it was getting out of hand.[36]
>
> Sergeant Ian Sinclair, A Troop, 425 Battery, 107th RHA

The only chance for real relaxation came when on leave in Cairo. All the men looked forward to this opportunity to get away from it all. They would travel back by rail and immediately indulge in a proper bath to wash away the ingrained grime of the desert.

> What did I do in Cairo? You shouldn't ask questions like that! I stayed in the Continental. The first night on leave I

had a Turkish bath and it was fascinating watching the dust run out of one's pores. You realised how much got in, when you got terribly hot and sweaty and the pores opened – with the sand blowing, it gets into your body. I can just see it running down in yellow streams. Not much to do – except see the sights and booze. You had all your ready money, which you'd saved. I hadn't been able to spend a penny for months, so there was a lot of money – far more money than I'd ever had. Cairo was an interesting place to see. This marvellous club at Gezira, beautiful, wonderful lawns with polo, cricket teams – luxury after the primitiveness of life in the desert! Wonderful![37]

Lieutenant Charles Laborde, D Troop, 426 Battery, 107th RHA

Even the relatively quiet Bob Hingston was ready for a real blow-out when it came to leave in Cairo. Unable to buy much in the desert, most of them the men had plenty of money to spend.

I went with John Shakespear and my God we knocked it back! We used to amble out of the hotel about mid morning, wander round for a bit and about half-past twelve he would say, 'Bob, I think it's time for our morning beer!' Then the session started! We drank a good deal, ate a good lunch and then went and lay down. Woke up with a bit of a hangover, 'Well the only way to deal with a hangover is the hair of the dog that bit you!' And so, it started up again – that was a highly alcoholic leave.[38]

Captain Bob Hingston, C Troop, 426 Battery, 107th RHA

Sadly, one popular young officer, Lieutenant Harry Clark,[39] took it all too far and fell to his death while trying drunkenly to climb from one hotel balcony to another in August 1940.

The men went to different, often less salubrious establishments, but there is little doubt that the same motivations of drink and women motivated most of them.

We went to the Burqa, a whole street of brothels! You go in
an open doorway on the ground floor, a sort of stone hallway
entrance with an open urinal opposite. Upstairs on the first
floor is all the action! By the time you got halfway up the stairs
there was a great queue of men and girls coming out of their
rooms and calling for the Condy's – the old woman went in
with the Condy's fluid for disinfectant purposes. But by golly!
The girls looked rough and the thing was so grim![40]

Gunner Dennis Middleton, B Troop, 425 Battery, 107th RHA

Ray Ellis, as an innocent young virgin, had been shocked the
first time he saw the reality of a cheap brothel. But, like so many
men facing up to the dangers of war, he did not want to die
a virgin. During a second leave he saw a stunningly attractive
Egyptian dancing girl in a rather more upmarket bar. Plucking
up his courage, he struck up a conversation. After a while he
made a clumsy 'move'.

I asked, 'Do you do anything apart from dancing?' She paused
and looked at me and said, 'Are you asking to take me to bed?'
I was flustered and managed to stammer out that it would be a
very nice thing to do – but what would it cost? She laughed and
said, 'Far more than you can afford!' I think it was 500 piastres,
which was about two months' salary for me at the time. Yes,
it was far beyond my pocket, so we just talked and had a
drink. Whilst this was going on, I looked up and saw Frank
Birkenshaw. He saw me and waved. I excused myself and went
over and he said, 'Where did you pick up that dreamboat?' I
said, 'I think dream is the operative word – she's 500 piastres!'
He laughed and went away! I was thoroughly enjoying myself
when I caught sight of Frank again at the door waving to me!
I went over and said, 'What's the matter?' He said, 'Here you
are, the lads have had a whip round – 500 piastres!' That was

the type of comradeship we had – it was fantastic really! I went beaming back to the table![41]

Gunner Ray Ellis, B Troop, 425 Battery, 107th RHA

While the men played away from home, it should not be a surprise that many got unwelcome news from their girlfriends and wives back home. These became known as 'Dear John' letters and often brought the brutal news that a much-loved girlfriend had 'moved on'. Albert Swinton may have been a big, tough bloke, able to deal with punches thrown in the boxing ring, but he was left heartbroken.

Prior to the war I'd been courting a girl – a policeman's daughter – Kathleen. When I was at Mersa Matruh she wrote a horrible letter accusing me of being out of the way. You must remember that we'd just had Dunkirk and all the rest of it – me being out in the Middle East in the sunshine enjoying myself – and couldn't care less about people back home. I wrote and tried to put things right, but she didn't want to know. Next thing I knew, I was told by my parents that she was going out with all and sundry and had gone right off the rails. I thought to myself, 'Well fair enough, perhaps it's just as well I'm out of the way!'[42]

Lance Bombardier Albert Swinton, D Troop, 426 Battery, 107th RHA

He would soon have bigger problems to worry about.

THE ITALIAN FORCES HAD remained static on the Egyptian border since June 1940. However, the Great War had shown the value of giving men a controlled initial battle experience as a partial inoculation against the fears when they were flung into action for the first time. As a result, Sergeant George Pearson was one of several NCOs and officers who were attached for a couple of months to the regulars of 4th Regiment, RHA, who were up at the front facing the Italians in the Fort Capuzzo sector. Pearson soon began to learn some of the practicalities of war, and he was impressed with the slick ease and minimal 'fuss' with which the gunners carried out their tasks.

> If shellfire opened up, don't panic and run like hell, walk and get on with whatever you are doing. If you were travelling by vehicles in the desert, because of the overwhelming air superiority of the Italians, vehicles travelled 400, 500, even 600 yards apart really spread across the desert. You didn't go fast, unless there was any need to, because if you went fast dust blew up and you became easily spotted from the air. Simple things. If there was bombing raid, the vehicles stopped and you dived out – you didn't all run together in a bunch, but you spread out away from the vehicle, found yourself a hole if you could and lay down. If you stopped and you were going to be there for a couple of hours, every man got down to it and dug himself a slit trench – that was automatic. Perhaps in our own unit the sergeants would be going round saying, 'Now get stuck in and dig yourselves a slit trench!' but these fellows had been at it so long that they did these things automatically.[43]

Sergeant George Pearson, (attached) 4th RHA

The 4th RHA were armed with the re-bored 18/25-pounder gun howitzer, an early variant of the 25-pounder proper. Instead of the shell and cartridge being one unit which was loaded in one fluid movement into the breech, the shell and the cartridge were in separate pieces, with a variable cartridge charge size to allow for a higher trajectory of fire.

Pearson also became aware of the impressive figure of Lieutenant Colonel John Campbell, affectionately known as 'Jock'. He developed the tactic of sending out a mixed mobile force to take advantage of the open desert flank to the south of the numerically superior Italians.

> We took a troop of 18/25-pounders, with a couple of light tanks and two lorry loads of infantry as escort. You would go south into the desert and then west behind the enemy lines. An Auster aircraft, or one of your own vehicles, would have 'reccied' ahead of you and endeavoured to find a worthy target. On one of the columns we went on they actually found a concentration of about 400 Italian vehicles. They shadowed them during the day and then, at night, when they put themselves in a laager, we quietly moved up to the ridge about 5,000 yards away, laid out about forty rounds a gun behind the 18/25-pounders and opened up. Up went ammunition vehicles, petrol wagons – the lot – a pyrotechnic picture. Then we hooked up and scuttled off into the night with the intention of getting back to our own lines as quickly as we could. Of course, you never got back in the night, and the next day you would be travelling spread out with probably 500 to 600 yards between vehicles. The Italians would be sending bombers out to find you – they would look for the dust trails and you would get bombed and machine-gunned from the air as you made your way back to your own lines.[44]

Sergeant George Pearson, (attached) 4th RHA

On 13 September, the war took a more serious turn when the Italian commander in Libya, Marshal Rodolfo Graziani, finally gathered his nerve and the Tenth Army began a cautious advance across the border into Egypt. The 7th Armoured Division fell back in front of them, but after advancing some 60 miles to take the town of Sidi Barrani, to general bemusement the Italians stopped their advance. Graziani had never been keen on the invasion and had required continued prodding from Musso-lini before he started moving. The Italian intelligence was poor in the extreme, with estimates that the British forces in Egypt numbered some 200,000 soldiers instead of the reality of, in the first instance, only some 36,000 men. Graziani was concerned at his crippling lack of mechanised transport, with endemic problems across the Tenth Army in inadequate or obsolescent artillery and tanks. Worried by the logistics of the long advance ahead of them, he wanted the reassurance of considerable reinforcements before he would go any further. Instead the Italians began to construct a series of strongly fortified camps at Maktila, Tummar East, Tummar West and Nibeiwa, Bir Rabia and Sofafi.

Despite the Italian pause, their invasion of Egypt triggered additional British defensive precautions at Mersa Matruh, the main set of fortifications barring the way to Cairo. The Egyptians guarding the eastern perimeter were swiftly replaced by the 3rd Coldstream Guards, 1st Durham Light Infantry and 1st Hampshires, accompanied by the 8th Field RA. At first there was an element of overreaction, if not panic, in the Mersa Matruh garrison.

> When the Italians pushed down to Sidi Barrani and everybody thought they were going to come down into Egypt, we dug the guns in as anti-tank guns. The Cheshires, who were machine gunners, were at the back of us. An engineer came round to the gun, he said, 'Now then, can you see the dragon's teeth – the dull ones are wood. So, if they get on to those they'll get through – so watch it!' We were registered on everything from 600 to 1,000 yards and the brigadier came and said, 'They'll be on you in 48 hours; they will outnumber you at 20:1 in men, guns and tanks'. I didn't hold much for my chances on that job – but they never came![45]
>
> Bombardier Herbert Bonnello, Headquarters, 426 Battery, 107th RHA

Gradually it was realised that the Italians were staying put. The question was what to do next?

THE BRITISH COMMANDER IN CHIEF Middle East Command, General Sir Archibald Wavell, directed Lieutenant General Sir Henry Maitland Wilson, his local commander in Egypt, to plan Operation Compass, a large-scale five-day raid by the Western Desert Force (Lieutenant General Richard O'Connor) to try to force the Italians back, but with arrangements in place to exploit any significant successes that might ensue. The main assault forces of the 4th Indian Division would manoeuvre to attack the Nibeiwa and Tummar West and East Camps from behind; the 7th Armoured Division would provide a screen blocking any Italian thrust from Bir Rabia and Sofafi Camps; while the Selby Force (Brigadier Arthur Selby), which was to be drawn from the Mersa Matruh garrison, would attack from the east, thereby pinning down the 1st Libyan Division Sibelle (General Luigi Sibelle), a division formed from Libyan colonial troops, which was holding Maktila Camp, some 10 to 15 miles east of Sidi Barrani. The Selby Force consisted of the 3rd Coldstream Guards, a company of the 1st South Staffordshire Regiment, a platoon of machine gunners from the 1st Royal Northumberland Fusiliers and a Composite Battery, under the command of Major Robert Daniell of 8th Field RA. Daniell's main firepower would be provided by E Troop from 8th Field RA, and the newly created X Troop,[46] equipped with four converted 18/25-pounders and composed of gunners drawn mainly from 426 Battery. X Troop was commanded by Captain Bob Hingston aided and abetted by Troop Sergeant Major John Whitehorn. There was also to be a Dummy Troop under the command of Major Gerry Birkin. This last was a very unorthodox formation.

> He had an OP party from 425 Battery; the gun position officer was Lieutenant Slinn. The gun itself came from the 8th Field Regiment and the sergeant in charge was Sergeant Mallett, who

was known as 'Hammer' and was so addressed by all his gun crew. They were an efficient lot. The gun itself was a 25-pounder, very well worn. We'd been warned that it was liable to be grossly inaccurate and we were also warned not to fire supercharge in case it fell to pieces. It had originally been an 18-pounder Mark V with a split trail.[47]

Troop Sergeant Major John Whitehorn, Dummy Troop, Composite Battery, Selby Force

The other eight dummy 'guns' were nothing more than wood and canvas constructs, with cordite flares used to provide the illusion of a gun flash.

On 7 December, Operation Compass began. The RAF had been pounding the Italian bases and airfields, while the Royal Navy was moving into place along the coast. As the main forces began their approach on Nibeiwa Camp, the Selby Force set off heading west along the coast road towards Maktila Camp. To help disguise what was happening there was an additional deception plan to confuse the Italians as to where the real blow would fall.

We had some Royal Army Ordnance Corps drivers with their 30cwt Morris Commercials, we had drawings made out of three-ply tacked on the side of them to look like a tank. At the back of the vehicle we had some brushwood so it would knock out our tyre marks in the desert. We were going from a point on the map for twenty-four hours at a time, stopping just for a quick meal. Going like the clappers all the time – and then back again. When we stopped, Ivor Birkin came along and said, 'Nobody to brew any tea; we're 7 miles from the enemy lines!' If you had constipation you soon got rid of it![48]

Lance Bombardier Dennis Mayoh, X Troop, Composite Battery, Selby Force

As Selby Force approached Maktila from the south-east, they dropped into action late on 8 December, with E Troop on the left and X Troop on the right. Further round, approaching more directly from the east, was the Dummy Troop.

> Two of us then had to lay a line from the real gun to the OP where Gerry Birkin would be. Just walking with a cable on a bar, reeling it out behind us, about a mile. We passed through a battalion of Coldstream Guards. They were in slit trenches at about 7 o'clock in the morning, buffing up their brasses! I thought, 'Here we are in action and they're cleaning their brasses – I thought you were supposed to dull your brasses not clean them!'[49]

Gunner Dennis Middleton, Dummy Troop, Composite Battery, Selby Force

It was planned that the Royal Navy would support the badly out-numbered Selby Force with a bombardment of Maktila Camp from the Great War veteran superdreadnought *Warspite*, (8 × 15-inch guns) and the monitor, the *Terror*, (2 × 15-inch guns). The guns had an extraordinary range of 33,000 yards, each giant 15-inch shell weighed over 1,900lbs and their destructive force was shudderingly massive. Bob Hingston was in his OP some 4 miles ahead of the X Troop gun positions.

> The *Warspite* – no less. She came up. I'd been anxious to see this, so I'd moved up my OP at the top of the hill. It was really most sensational. I couldn't see much of the actual firing – they must have had flashless cordite on the ship, but then you could suddenly see these terrific burst, hear the 'CRUMP!' and even at the distance we were, the ground shook a bit! Whether they did much damage I don't know, but the effect on the morale of the enemy was absolutely devastating.[50]

Captain Bob Hingston, X Troop, Composite Battery, Selby Force

On the morning of 9 December, the real guns of the Composite Battery opened fire on the Italian camp, while the Dummy

Troop used their thunderflashes and sole real gun to try to magnify the impact.

> We started up! The Italians were utterly lamentable! We were pretty green; but they were appalling soldiers! The first thing I saw four of their guns perched right out in the open, not dug in! Why they'd put them there, when there was quite a bit of cover round about, I simply cannot imagine. They started firing, so I managed to range on to them and gave them a good plastering and that was the end of them – they weren't manned again for the rest of the day.[51]

Captain Bob Hingston, X Troop, Composite Battery, Selby Force

To the south, the main force attacks were successful, as first Nibeiwa and then Tummar West Camps were overrun. The Italian camps were vulnerable to defeat in detail and as their morale started to crumble, they began to fall like dominoes. Meanwhile, elements of the 7th Armoured Division were swooping round to threaten the Italian communications through Sidi Barrani. On the afternoon of 9 December, X Troop was moved round a little further to the west. From this new position Hingston heard the 1st Libyan Division Sibelle begin to withdraw towards Sidi Barrani, covered they hoped by the darkness of night. Hingston and his OP team edged further forward. On the morning of 10 December, he managed to find an OP position that, although in a rather obvious location, offered a decent view of the Italian retreat.

> There were the Italians stretched out along the coast. They'd had a hell of a time, poor devils, bumped into our tanks and generally not got very far away. They were spread out and hopelessly vulnerable. I'd got my signal truck and he started to lay a line, just as the Italians opened up on our OP! The signal truck got away in time and laid the line, but the rest of us were

pinned down pretty badly. They were using very small guns and they weren't frightfully terrifying shells, but it wasn't very nice, and we crawled out.[52]

Captain Bob Hingston, X Troop, Composite Battery, Selby Force

Never a strong man, by the night of 10/11 December Hingston was beginning to suffer from the effects of severe fatigue.

I was bloody cold and there was a cookhouse there manned by the 8th Field Regiment. They had a priceless chap, he had last-war ribbons up and had reached the proud rank of lance bombardier as a reward for years of service. He saw me and he said, 'You look starved, Sir!' I said, 'Well it's been a bit cold out there all day I must admit!' He said, 'Ah, I've got just the thing for you!' He handed me a mug of tea – and it had a hell of a slug of rum in it – it certainly did warm me up nicely![53]

Captain Bob Hingston, X Troop, Composite Battery, Selby Force

On 11 December, he moved forward again with his OP team, ready to support an assault by the 3rd Coldstream Guards and the newly arrived tanks of the 6th Royal Tank Regiment.

I set off again up a sloping hill. There I saw the whole Italian formation spread out down below me in a most ludicrous arrangement all out in the open, a sort of square they'd made with a gun at each corner, almost Napoleonic style. I'd just ranged on to that when the 6th RTR tanks arrived and Colonel Harland said, 'Would you put down a smokescreen to cover my tanks advance?' I think it was completely unnecessary and can't think it did any good at all. I was very annoyed about this because I'd just ranged this beautiful target. So eventually I compromised. We had to get two guns to give them their smokescreen, but the third gun proceeded to pound away at this target and sent all the Eyties under cover. It was a thoroughly disorganised battle and these tanks appeared behind me and came charging line abreast up the hill and over the top. I was sitting out in the open on the ground and as they came over, of course every Italian gun opened up on them. It was quite hectic for a bit. Then there was silence as the tanks disappeared into a dip. A message came from battery headquarters, 'You've fired all the shells you're going to have on that target. What's happening?' I said, 'I don't know. Nothing seems to be happening!' Then I saw a whole lot of Italians appearing out of their holes and stand around. I thought, 'This doesn't seem quite right!' so I landed another shell amongst them. The poor devils – I'm sorry I did because they were only surrendering to our tanks, who shortly afterwards appeared on the scene and took over.[54]

Captain Bob Hingston, X Troop, Composite Battery, Selby Force

Sergeant Ian Sinclair had a good view of the surrender. He was acting as the driver and OP specialist attached to the Dummy Troop.

This Italian general came out with his men holding this white flag. I can remember Birkin saying, 'Good God, they've surrendered!' We couldn't believe it. They were hopeless, shattered – the last thing they had expected, I think, was to be attacked. I don't know what they thought they were there for, quite frankly. They certainly didn't give the appearance that they'd come to fight. They were so dishevelled, so dirty.[55]

Sergeant Ian Sinclair, Dummy Troop, Composite Battery, Selby Force

Gerry Birkin drove forward to take the surrender accompanied by just one officer of the South Staffords and some twenty men.

When we got to the ridge, hundreds of Eyeties and Libyans appeared and threw down their arms. I was a bit frightened, but

I brandished my revolver in the general's face, and he said, 'No ammunition left!' Which was a lie as I found 2,000 rounds on one gun! However, everything seemed peaceful and our twenty men with bayonets controlled the party all right. I took the general's epaulettes and hat – just like Mussolini's – also I got two pistols and an Italian flag. The amount of guns, vehicles, etc., was enormous.[56]

Captain Gerry Birkin, Dummy Troop, Composite Battery, Selby Force

The sheer numbers of Italian prisoners taken posed real problems as they gathered together some 5,000 in a hollow not far from the road. They were cowed, but still had the potential to swamp the guards if something untoward happened. Precautions had to be taken.

Lieutenant Slinn went off to find Birkin and get orders as to what to do with them. They were completely disarmed but I was just left in charge of the whole party with about a platoon of the South Staffords. They were there with fixed bayonets at about 200-yard intervals round this enormous group. Slinn simply gave me the instruction, 'Look after them!' So, we dropped the gun into action about 50 yards away from them, put a round up the spout, made a lot of clanging noises and hoped we were being fairly fearsome and that the Italians wouldn't turn nasty. There were so many of them – it was absolutely ridiculous – we couldn't have done anything if they'd decided to turn on us.[57]

Troop Sergeant Major John Whitehorn, Dummy Troop, Composite Battery, Selby Force

The Italian camp, with all its stores and supplies, lay naked before them – and some of the less-disciplined British soldiers were unable to resist the temptation to explore – and loot.

It was a rather eerie sort of situation being in a deserted enemy camp. I was disturbed by one of the South Staffords who had got very drunk on stuff that had been found in the camp and was persistently trying to get on a stray mule. He was getting on one side and falling off the other – and this went on pretty well through the night.[58]

Troop Sergeant Major John Whitehorn, Dummy Troop, Composite Battery, Selby Force

Their job complete, shortly afterward the Composite Battery returned to Mersa Matruh and disbanded.

A successful action for one side still has dreadful consequences for these who lose the battle. Ray Ellis was unlucky to be left behind with a burial party organised by the Royal Engineers to clear away the corpses that littered the Italian camps.

There were dead all over the place, lying all sorts of grotesque angles everywhere. It is a horrible job. First I thought we'd dig graves, but that was impossible, because it was all rock and there were too many – hundreds and hundreds of them. We hit on the idea of dragging them into any hole we could find and then kicked the rocks and sand in on top of them. After the first day or so, these corpses were beginning to swell and smell. We found some big meat hooks in a cookhouse, so we used those. You stuck it under the shoulder and dragged them. We made no attempt at all to identify anybody, we were treating them like carcasses. We put up a sign with, scratched on it, 'Five Eyties, or six Libyans, or ten Eyties', we didn't even call them Italians. There was no reverence, no service, no prayer, no respect at all, nothing! The main thing was to get them under the ground. I feel ashamed of this, it was wrong – I was wrong – I should have tried to do something, but I didn't know what to do.[59]

Gunner Ray Ellis, Composite Battery, Selby Force

THE SUCCESS OF OPERATION COMPASS had radically

changed the situation in the Western Desert. Lieutenant General Richard O'Connor had achieved a remarkable victory in the 'five-day' raid ordered by Wavell. The Italian system of camps had been overwhelmed or evacuated in unseemly haste. In the first instance, the Western Desert Force had taken some 38,000 prisoner and captured 237 guns and some 73 tanks. What remained of the Tenth Army was in pell-mell retreat back into Libya. In December, the Italian fortress of Bardia was under attack, and would finally fall on 5 January 1941. Still Wavell was not satisfied and ordered an assault on Tobruk, a key port facility, which fell on 21 January. Ultimately, his forces would advance to take Benghazi and finally the remnants of Tenth Army would surrender at Beda Fomm on 7 February. Victory had been achieved. Yet the seeds of defeat were soon sown by the interference of an arch political amateur strategist. On 9 February, Churchill suspended Wavell's offensive and stripped the Western Desert Force to the bone to reinforce British forces for campaigns in Abyssinia and Greece.

For the moment, the pressure was off the Mersa Matruh garrison, now well behind the front line. At this point, some of the most promising South Notts Hussars NCOs and men were being considered for promotion. One such was Herbert Bonnello. After all, he was technically qualified to take a commission from his pre-war schooldays in the Officer Training Corps.

> I was fetched to the office and told I was going to have an interview with a brigadier with a view to being sent down to Officer Cadet Training Unit. They wanted to know what you had been doing in the unit itself. He asked me if I had a private income, not that I think it mattered in wartime as you were not likely to have big mess bills or uniform costs. It was more ability than background once the war had started. You had to be able to show that you could take 'command' and look after

the needs of men. Having joined the South Notts with my pals, I was loath to leave. However, with the fall of France it became quite apparent the war would go on for years; it was more of a case that you have got to go where you can be of better service to the country.[60]

Bombardier Herbert Bonnello, Headquarters, 426 Battery, 107th RHA

At this time there was a widespread suspicion that Lieutenant Colonel Bill Seely and other senior officers wanted to keep as much talent as possible within the regiment for the challenges that lay ahead. Opportunities for a commission were restricted, and Bonnello was refused on the grounds that he had not yet attained sufficiently wide experience on the guns and in technical roles which he would need to have in order to have much chance of success as an artillery officer. From this time onwards, Bonello would seek any opportunities he could to broaden his knowledge – as would many others turned down at this stage. He would eventually be commissioned in October 1941. One who was sent to the Middle East Officer Cadet Training Unit at this time was Troop Sergeant Major John Whitehorn, but this was largely due to personal differences with Major Peter Birkin, whom Whitehorn considered far too aggressive in his manner. Whitehorn was commissioned into the Royal Engineers and would serve with them in the Middle East and Italy.

IN JANUARY 1940, THE 107TH RHA were despatched to the Suez Canal area. Here they had an unusual role for an artillery unit. The canal was in danger of being closed by a mixture of electrical and acoustic mines that were being dropped from German aircraft. The gunners were to be split up into a series of four-man posts all along the canal. These teams had two functions: to shoot down the German aircraft with their Bren light machine guns, which was frankly unlikely; but also to mark the location of any mines that they saw dropped in the canal.

Ted Holmes was attached to Sergeant Staniforth's Bren-gun team when early one morning they got a telephone call warning them that German aircraft were on their way.

> Nowt happened for about half an hour. Then all of a sudden, we saw coming down the canal a big German plane – really low! Sergeant Staniforth lets go at it with the Bren gun. Unfortunately, it had been blowing sand all day and it wouldn't fire automatic and he only got five shots in as it went past. A light appeared, and I says, 'I think tha's got it!' I thought we'd hit it! Next thing, there's a big mine coming down, swinging down on a parachute, about the size of a 50-gallon drum by the look of it – seemingly just above our heads. It landed towards the other side of the canal. We got some bits of stick and we were putting these sticks to point where it had dropped to let the Navy know – when it blew up! It bowled us over, the blast![61]

Gunner Ted Holmes, A Troop, 425 Battery, 107th RHA

On another occasion, Herbert Bonnello and his team managed accurately to locate where a mine had dropped.

> You put two stakes in line from where you were to the mine. 'Jock' Reid was absolutely certain that he heard a splash – so the two markers were put out there. Well, they sent divers, minesweepers, depth charges, a plane with a magnetic hoop and they came to the conclusion he must have been mistaken – there was no mine. Then a naval patrol boat came whizzing down the canal at great speed. It turned round and came up the canal again and 'WWHHUUMP!' up he goes. The theory was that the noise of the engine would set off the acoustic mine, but by the time it went off it was going at such speed that it would

be out of harm's way. That wasn't so! There was nobody killed [in the crew], but one or two ribs had been broken with the blast. The patrol boat drifted down, and we pulled it in at my particular section.[62]

Bombardier Herbert Bonnello, Headquarters, 426 Battery, 107th RHA

Afterwards, Fred Brookes had an explanation for what had happened.

They sent divers down and fetched a mine out. We were most interested – kept well back! They got it up on the side and took it to bits. I take my hat off to people like that! They found out it was a 'ticker' mine: every time a ship went over it, it ticked down one and you could set it from five, six, seven, eight ships to go over before it went up! It was the boat's engines that set it off. Having discovered that we carried on marking the mines and the navy came up in a speedboat and went backwards and forward across where we'd marked it. They relied on the speed of the boat to take them out of trouble when the mine went bang![63]

Battery Quartermaster Sergeant Fred Brookes, Headquarters, 425 Battery, 107th RHA

During this period, Lance Sergeant Bob Foulds and the newly promoted Bombardier Ray Ellis managed to get time to pay a visit to Port Suez. Here they saw a sight that embarrassed them as British soldiers.

We got to Port Suez to see two soldiers walking up the road, dragging a third man by his ankles with his head in the gutter! Absolutely paralytic the three of them! One was so drunk he couldn't walk. I remember saying to Bob Foulds, 'This is disgusting! It's just the type of thing that gets the British Army a bad name abroad!' While we were looking with disgust at these three soldiers, I realised that one was Fred Lamb, and the other was 'Wag' Harris. I said to Bob, 'That's Fred and Wag –

the other must be my brother – the one with his head in the
gutter must be my brother!' It was.[64]

Bombardier Ray Ellis, B Troop, 425 Battery, 107th RHA

The watch on the Suez Canal was a dull task, but the South
Notts Hussars and others had played a small part with other
army units, the RAF and the Royal Navy in nullifying the
German efforts to close the canal. It was later claimed that some
250,000 tons of shipping vital to the British war effort were
released when, as the mine threat diminished, the waterway was
finally reopened.

On 9 March, the regiment moved to Tahag Camp. Here they
were at last equipped with new weapons. Their old 18-pounders
and 4.5-inch howitzers were handed in, never to be seen again,
and they were issued with spanking new 25-pounders. Everyone
was delighted.

We were impressed with the 25-pounder as a weapon. For a
start it was a gun howitzer, in other words the projectile and
the charge were separate, so you had a variable range. You
could either put in the highest charge and elevate the guns to
get the longest range on a flat trajectory, or you could put in
a low charge, cock up the gun and get a much shorter range,
but you could fire over hills. It was very flexible. It was easy to
operate; the sights and the laying was an advance on what we'd
had before with the 18-pounder. It was easy to handle because
it had a gun platform. When the gun was travelling it used to
be hooked up underneath the trail, but when the gun went into
action the platform was dropped and the gun was pulled on the
platform, so that there was no friction from the surface, and you
could spin it round very easily on the platform.[65]

Lance Sergeant Bob Foulds, B Troop, 425 Battery, 107th RHA

By 1941 the 25-pounder was a proven weapon. Previously the

South Notts Hussars had had to make do with Great War vintage weapons. Now they had the real thing.

> It was far more accurate: you could almost drop two shells in the same hole – it was very, very accurate indeed. When the shell landed the fragmentation was very tiny. A big shell may shatter into no more than twenty splinters which could hit or miss – but the 25-pounder fragmented into tiny little pieces, which never got much above knee high as it spread. It was a great killer and – as an artilleryman looking for something that will kill – it was a far more efficient projectile. Picking up the new drill on the 25-pounder was simple – we didn't need a lot of conversion as trained gunners! The No. 1 was in charge, No. 2 operated the breech and rammed the shell home, No. 3 was the layer, No. 4 loaded and No. 5 and No. 6 were the ammunition numbers.[66]

Bombardier Ray Ellis, A Troop, 425 Battery, 107th RHA

By this time Ray Ellis had been posted to Sergeant Staniforth's gun detachment in A Troop to prevent him from being in the same troop as his brother as action loomed. They were also given purpose-built Quad gun towers. This again was a real improvement.

> We'd had lorries before, but the Quads were a curious stubby little vehicle, purpose-built for towing a limber and a gun behind it. It was manoeuvrable – four-wheel drive so that it could get out of difficult situations. It had a flap in the roof, so you could put your head out, could see where you were going and direct the driver. There was room inside for the gun crew, kit and gear. It had the unfortunate impression that it looked like an armoured vehicle because it had flat, slabby, sort of sides. I think it gave people a feeling of security which was totally false – but it wasn't armoured at all. It wasn't terribly easy to get

out of quickly: it was all right for the No. 1 and the driver, but the crew were at the back of it and so if you were being bombed or anything and you had to evacuate in a great hurry it wasn't the easiest vehicle to get out of.[67]

Lance Sergeant Bob Foulds, B Troop, 425 Battery, 107th RHA

They were also issued with limbers, small trailers with two pneumatic tyres which carried the emergency ammunition store for each 25-pounder. They soon mastered the art of being able to drop quickly into action.

First the Quad, then the limber, then there was a hook on the back of the limber on to which you put the gun. When dropping into action, you first unhooked the gun and swung it in the direction which you had been told. Then you unhitched the limber and pushed that on to the left-hand side of the gun looking from the rear. At the back were two doors which opened and inside were trays of ammunition for emergency. Then the Quad would be taken away to wagon lines. The ammunition supply came up in the trucks separately and the ammunition in the limbers was very rarely used.[68]

Bombardier Ray Ellis, A Troop, 425 Battery, 107th RHA

The OP teams and officers were at the same time issued with pickup trucks.

I was put on the wireless of the little 18cwt pickup truck of the battery commander, Major Peter Birkin. A little canvas-covered truck, the wireless set was on one side and a bench on the other. Usually, just one signaller in the back, a driver and the officer. We had to make sure we had spare batteries, make sure it was working, everything was tested.[69]

Gunner Ted Whittaker, Headquarters, 425 Battery, 107th RHA

The South Notts Hussars also received a new second in command, with the arrival of Major Robert Daniell, formerly with the 8th Field RA, who had become known to many of them during his period in command of the Composite Battery during Operation Compass. The idea of territorials did not appeal to Daniell, who was perhaps the epitome of the pre-war regular officer; there was a reciprocal antipathy from the men he was to lead.

> Major Daniell was officious, the caricature of typical 'Colonel Blimp' – a cartoon character in appearance – with a moustache! Never treated anybody with any kind of courtesy at all – he was always 'barking' at them. He never spoke to me, except to 'bark' some order at me! He treated our officers with contempt because, 'All you lot are bloody amateurs!' He would talk to them in a tone of voice that was contemptuous: 'What have you done that for?' I must be fair: he had a great deal of experience and went about his job with a great deal of aplomb and he thought he was efficient. Whether he was efficient or not I don't know, but one thing I do say is his attitude and the way he acted was wrong. He should have appreciated, like Freddie Porter did, that he was coming into a territorial unit, which had a great deal to offer – we were all volunteers with a great deal of goodwill and courage. But you don't get the best out of people like that by treating them as regular soldiers and as semi-illiterate idiots. That's where he made his big mistake. In a territorial unit there is a certain *esprit de corps*.[70]
>
> Battery Quartermaster Sergeant Charles Ward, 426 Battery, 107th RHA

Daniell would never adapt to the men he commanded.

In early 1941, there were plans afoot for an amphibious invasion of the Greek island of Rhodes and the South Notts Hussars were to undergo training for this dangerous task. It involved enormous physical exertions, as the navy had warned they would be restricted to just five vehicles per gun troop.

The powers that be decided that we may not get all our gun-towing vehicles ashore, so that it would be a good idea if you got ten to twelve men with drag ropes and they went on marches pulling along 25-pounders and their ammunition trailers. Manhandling the guns, going off on virtually route marches. The men expressed themselves in typically Nottingham terms on what they thought of the chap who thought up this idea![71]

Sergeant George Pearson, B Troop, 425 Battery, 107th RHA

They also practised disembarking from the landing craft. This proved somewhat problematic as many were, not unnaturally, unwilling to 'get their feet wet'.

They said, 'You will be pleased to know that they expect 80 per cent casualties!' That put the wind up everybody! We got on one boat which took twenty-two men and one vehicle. The pilot took us so far out in the canal and then he'd say, 'Right, we'll come back again to land!' When we came into land we'd say, 'Get closer in – we'll get bloody wet!' 'I can't!' He said, 'This is an invasion. You might be in 9 foot of water! You've got to be prepared for it!'[72]

Gunner Albert Parker, A Troop, 425 Battery, 107th RHA

In the end, they persuaded the sailor to drop them on to the shallow shelf at the edge of the canal – so they ended up paddling ashore with the water only lapping about their ankles.

Our Sergeant Major Jim Hardy said, 'That's no bloody good, don't forget you're going to invade Rhodes – you'll see a lot of water over there! Take it round again and I'll show you how it's done!' He did – he didn't find that shelf – he disappeared! Funny thing – he'd got a tin hat on and it started to float on the water and then disappeared. He was down below – he'd gone!

When they pulled him out, we all said, 'Like that, Sergeant Major?'[73]

Gunner Albert Parker, A Troop, 425 Battery, 107th RHA

8

SIEGE OF TOBRUK

During the first dive-bombing I lay down flat and I would have been glad enough to have got underneath a bit of newspaper! It's just as though they are picking *you* out personally.[1]

Gunner Bill Hutton, Headquarters, 425 Battery, 107th RHA

SUDDENLY EVERYTHING CHANGED. War is not only carrying out your own well-considered plans, but sometimes a rushed, desperate response to the unforeseen actions of the enemy – who have their own strategies. On 3 April 1941, Lieutenant Colonel Bill Seely was called to a conference in Cairo to be briefed on the new enemy in the desert – and told that they were on the move. The Germans, concerned at the fragility of the Italian forces, had sent out the 5th Light Motorised Division to augment the Italians, who had themselves sent across extra motorised and armoured divisions after the collapse of the Tenth Army. Together, they would eventually form the Afrika Korps, a force that would expand into a whole army, while generally retaining the name in the popular vernacular.

They were commanded by Lieutenant General Erwin Rommel, a brilliant and energetic German officer. Born on 15 November 1891, Rommel had a distinguished career as an infantry officer in the Great War, culminating in the award of the *Pour le Mérite* for his leadership in support of the Austrians during the Battle of Caporetto in 1917. He further boosted his reputation in command of the 7th Panzer Division during the Blitzkrieg attack on the BEF in France and Belgium in May 1940. In February 1941, he had been despatched by Hitler to stabilise and then exploit the situation in the Western Desert. Rommel was nominally under the command of General Italo Gariboldi, but Rommel was able to bend Gariboldi to his far more aggressive command style. As the Axis forces began to build up at Sirte, ready for the offensive, the arrival of the Junker Ju 87 Stuka dive-bombers, the Junkers Ju 88 and the Messerschmitt Bf 110 fighters of Fliegerkorps X meant the spectre of Blitzkrieg was approaching for the British in the Middle East.

While the Axis rebuilt their forces in Libya, the British Committee of Imperial Defence, influenced by Prime Minister Winston Churchill, always searching for a 'soft underbelly', had its eyes firmly fixed on the islands and mainland of Greece. In preparing for the invasion of Greece, Wavell had very few forces left to the hold the ground captured in Cyrenaica by the success of Operation Compass. Most of his best generals were also assigned to the Greece operations, leaving the relatively untested Lieutenant General Sir Philip Neame in charge of the Cyrenaica Command, consisting of only the severely under-strength 2nd Armoured Division and the 9th Australian Division. It was realised that, if attacked, they had little chance of holding positions west of El Agheila and plans were in place for a possible withdrawal to Benghazi and then Tobruk. Both the RAF and Royal Navy were similarly distracted, with most of their resources committed to the Greek 'adventure'. Overall, there was no recognition of the increased threat posed by the arrival of German and Italian reinforcements in North Africa. With the gateway to Egypt and the Suez Canal almost unguarded, Rommel saw the chance to strike – and he took it.

When Rommel discovered that the advance British positions at El Agheila were lightly held, he ignored cautionary orders from his German and Italian superiors and on 31 March launched a recce in force that rapidly developed into a full-scale attack. The British crumbled before them; the 2nd Armoured Division fell apart under the pressure of frontal pinning attacks and outflanking manoeuvres, which forced them to withdraw, disrupting their already tenuous logistical supply arrangements. Benghazi fell, and still the Germans surged forward. Rommel seemed to be here, there and everywhere, flying above the battlefield in his Storch light aircraft, landing to drive forward his local commanders and firefighting any tactical and logistical problems as they arose. Neame, in contrast, was helpless: his inadequate forces were outmanoeuvred and fell back in disorder; he himself would be captured on 6 April. The one saving grace was that the 9th Australian Division had managed to escape, falling back almost intact through Derna towards Tobruk. This would be the foundation of the Tobruk garrison in the siege to come.

The consequences were immediate. Hopes of providing effective support for Greece evaporated; now all that mattered was the harsh practicality of moving all available forces up into the Western Desert to stem the onslaught of the Afrika Korps. Among the reinforcements would be the 107th RHA.

At 14.00 on 3 April, Seely telephoned to tell his men that they had to be ready for deployment by dawn on 5 April. This gave them less than two days to prepare. Everyone swung into action: various elements were recalled from training; missing personnel were tracked down; stores were brought right up to war establishment. Albert Swinton found himself rushed off his feet.

> I was quartermaster's assistant, booking stores in and out.
> Each unit has got what they call a G10/98 stores which covers

everything that a regiment needs to perform its duties. That covers a multitude of items, from first field dressings for the soldiers to your guns and ammunition – everything that you want. You're up to your neck in it! Never enough time to do what you're supposed to do! There was stores coming at you from all angles.[2]

Lance Bombardier Albert Swinton, D Troop, 426 Battery, 107th RHA

They moved off on 5 April, stopping overnight at Mena Camp, beneath the Pyramids. Almost nothing can stop British soldiers from letting off steam on such occasions, and many were involved in a boisterous party held in the canteen.

The NAAFI always took a battering on those occasions. You'd walk in over a carpet of beer tins, crushing them as you went. It was drinking and singing really; very much a feeling of live for the day because nobody knew if they were coming back. You had a very short-term outlook. There were a lot of sore heads in the morning![3]

Lance Sergeant Bob Foulds, B Troop, 425 Battery, 107th RHA

Other parties went out to local night clubs. Major Peter Birkin had arranged for the local military police to take a reasonable attitude to men letting off steam before heading off into a situation of extreme peril. Ted Whittaker remembered it well.

My friend Dennis Middleton was a good organiser. We pooled resources and he led a bunch of us, and we had what can only be described as a riotous night out! I can remember Dennis being gently, but firmly, removed from the stage of the cabaret, where he was attempting to accompany one of the belly dancers. Getting home was a bit of a problem – I'm afraid several of us finished up on our hands and knees crawling through a flower bed. Halfway back, I stopped the taxi and was heartily sick on the road. We got back to camp – I don't know how late it was – but Peter Birkin was walking up and down through the camp making sure everybody was safely in. I can remember him telling me that I would be on that truck at first light in the morning even if it killed me. In the morning, I can remember getting into the truck and the major saying to me, 'Have you got a headache?' When I said, 'Yes!', he said, 'Serves you bloody well right!'[4]

Gunner Ted Whittaker, Headquarters, 425 Battery, 107th RHA

For those suffering from a hangover, the seemingly endless coastal road was a severe test – some 410 miles lay ahead of them in the journey from Alexandria to Sollum on the Libyan border. It was not just physical; many were also stressed by the confused nature of their situation – and the fact that no one seemed to know what was happening. It was thought they were going to join the 9th Australian Division, who had been completing their training at Tobruk. Perhaps it was just as well they didn't know what lay ahead.

On and on they drove, with short overnight stops, passing through their deserted former 'home' at Mersa Matruh, until they reached Sidi Barrani on the night of Tuesday, 8 April. As Libya drew closer, they encountered many of the signs of a defeated army in pell-mell retreat.

Troops were coming back at great speed; more and more troops; everything was going east; then we passed rear aerodromes of the RAF where we could see crates being set on fire which we knew contained aircraft engines; then we met convoys of ambulances coming back. It all grew a bit sombre. This trickle developed into a mass exodus of troops – it seemed that everyone in the Army of the Nile was doing their level best to put the greatest distance they could between themselves and the enemy. The only troops moving west were the South Notts Hussars. We didn't like the idea of this at all.[5]

Bombardier Ray Ellis, A Troop, 425 Battery, 107th RHA

Erik Morley expressed his views on the rumoured situation in a robust fashion.

We had some nasty bits of information coming back to us, 'We're going into the retreat!' 'Bloody hell! Well what are we going up there for then if we're going into retreat?' 'Somebody says we're going to take over!' 'Fuck that!' The usual army reaction![6]

Gunner Erik Morley, 425 Battery, 107th RHA

At Sollum, the road ascended a steep hill up on to the main coastal escarpment, a notable feature of that Libyan region.

The Australians had laid mines on the road up the escarpment! When we got there we said, 'We've got to go up there and get through to Tobruk! 'Stupid Pommie bastards!' They'd got to lift the mines that they'd just laid, so we had a pause! My gun tower was tail-end Charlie of the regiment, and my battery commander Peter Birkin, who stuttered a little, came up to me and said, 'N-n-n-now, w-w-when we get on the top, if we get at-at-attacked by tanks, you'll drop your gun and an ammunition trailer off, s-s-send your gun tower on and hold them off as long as you can!' We went on to the top of the escarpment – I was praying that there would be no German tanks anywhere! By the middle of the afternoon, a few tanks appeared on the escarpment side. There I was watching them, they were German tanks, and they kept pace with us, following along and I was shaking in my shoes thinking, 'Oh my God, please, please, don't make me have to drop off!' Luckily, they didn't attack, but I had a distinct looseness of the bowels when I thought of what might have happened.[7]

Sergeant George Pearson, B Troop, 425 Battery, 107th RHA

They were ordered to proceed at the maximum possible convoy speed, so the petrol resupply was done by throwing petrol cans into the back of each truck. Given the fragile nature of British petrol cans this was not a good idea, but they simply could not afford the time to stop and refuel in a conventional manner. The German trap was closing.

We had absolutely awful petrol tins – it was a big bellyache with the troops! They were just normal tin cans, whereas the Germans had these jerry cans. The difference was that all ours leaked out – they were thinner – they were just hopeless, very poorly designed. When you'd taken all these tins of petrol out – half of it was swimming about in the truck! They were jumping up and down in the truck, because the desert isn't all sand, a lot of it is a terrain of rock and stones. Later on, we kept capturing these jerry cans – and half the British Army were using jerry cans![8]

Lance Sergeant Charles Ward, 426 Battery, 107th RHA

As they drew nearer to Tobruk the tension ratcheted up: they could hear the German bombing of the port area and see mysterious lights to the south of them, which presumably marked the path of the encircling panzers.

Ahead of them, Lieutenant Colonel Bill Seely had been establishing contact with Major General Leslie Morshead commanding the 9th Australian Division, who was assigned to take charge of the Tobruk garrison. Morshead was tasked with holding on to the crucial port for eight weeks, until a relief force could be organised and despatched from Egypt. In fact, just by holding the port, the British were putting an effective spoke into

Rommel's wheel. His chaotic style of warfare, seizing fleeting half-opportunities and exploiting gaps, was not suited to the more structured requirements required in attacking a defended perimeter. No matter how hard Rommel drove his commanders and men, no immediate assault was possible. Yet even as he tried to organise his tiring forces for a concerted attack, hour by hour the defences grew marginally stronger: more barbed wire was laid out, the minefields increased in depth, and the Royal Artillery moved into their gun positions, assigned their arcs of fire and registered potential targets.

Morshead and his staff drew up a quick defensive plan, utilising what forces he had available and based on the former Italian perimeter fortifications. For infantry he had the 18th, 20th, 24th and 26th Australian Infantry Brigades, the 18th Indian (Dismounted) Cavalry and the Vickers machine guns of the 1st Royal Northumberland Fusiliers. The perimeter stretched for about 16 miles: from Wadi Sehel, which ran to the sea in the west, the defences went in a rough semicircle some 8 miles from the port itself, to connect with the sea again via Wadi Zeitun in the east. They took over the Italian trenches and concrete posts, and immediately began improving the barbed wire, anti-tank ditch and mine defences. There was much work still to do if Rommel's panzers were to be kept out. Only a few mixed British tanks and crews from the 3rd Armoured Brigade had made it safely into Tobruk, bolstered by elements of the 1st and 4th Royal Tank Regiments. The real underpinning of the defence would be the guns: the 51st Field RA which would cover the western sector of the perimeter; the 1st and 107th Regiments, RHA the centre; while the 104th Regiment, RHA covered the east. Thanks to careful positioning, some forty of the total of seventy-two guns would be able to concentrate on any point where the Axis forces might choose to attack. In addition, there were the 2-pounder anti-tank guns of 3rd Regiment RHA and the 3rd Australian

Anti-Tank Battalion. Protection from German air attacks was provided by the 4th Anti-Aircraft Brigade, RA. A few Hurricanes of 73 Squadron, RAF, provided the only potent aerial deterrent. All in all, around 30,000 men were under Morshead's command. Would it be enough?

Having been briefed on the situation and their role in the artillery plan, Lieutenant Colonel Bill Seely went to meet his regiment at the east entrance of the Tobruk wire fortifications, which they reached by 03.00 on 10 April. The moment the last straggler had been accounted for, the Australian engineers laid one more layer of mines and pulled across the last belts of barbed wire. Tobruk was now besieged. The column pressed on towards their central positions near the Eagle Crossroads, which lay at the junction of the coastal Dena–Sollum road and the El Adem road to the south, leading to the airfield outside the perimeter, and named somewhat prosaically after the buzzard which had been shot and hung up on the crossroads sign. Here utter chaos descended.

> Three artillery regiments got mixed up in the dark. There was confusion everywhere: there were guns that were not ours, there were cap badges that were not ours – everyone was milling about. Had the Luftwaffe come and dropped a few flares they could have wiped out the whole of the artillery power which was to defeat them in a few days' time.[9]
>
> Bombardier Ray Ellis, A Troop, 425 Battery, 107th RHA

The gun troops dropped into anti-tank gun positions as best they could, ready for immediate action. As usual Bill Hutton saw the humorous side.

> They said, 'Dig in!' Well I got out and got a pick and a shovel and it was just like rock. I hit the ground and sparks flew up from the pick. I thought, 'To hell with it!' and I made my bed

and went to bed. I woke up next morning and some cocky chap came along and said, 'We're the last in, Rommel's out there with his panzers!' I said, 'Who's Rommel and what's a panzer?'[10]

Gunner Bill Hutton, Headquarters, 425 Battery, 107th RHA

The overall message was clear: Tobruk had to be held at all costs if the British were to have much chance of retaining their grip on Egypt. The capture of Tobruk would enable Rommel to shorten his supply lines, which stretched all the way back to Benghazi and Tripoli. Without a forward supply base at Tobruk, the Germans had little chance of pressing on successfully beyond the Egyptian border. The South Notts Hussars would be participating in a crucial battle that would decide the outcome of this phase in the North African campaign.

Rommel was desperate to grab Tobruk by *coup de main*, hoping against hope that the defenders could be caught napping. On the morning of 10 April, he rashly sent forward totally inadequate forces under the ad hoc charge of Major General Heinrich von Prittwitz, who had had the misfortune to arrive on the scene in advance of his 15th Panzer Division. The reality was that von Prittwitz was given far too small a force to have any real chance of success. His attack soon collapsed in the face of the heavy fire of the 18-pounders and 4.5-inch howitzers of 51st Field RA, augmented by the Vickers guns of the 1st Royal Northumberland Fusiliers – indeed von Prittwitz himself was killed. The Australian infantry were not yet properly in position, nor were the artillery in their allotted battle stations; but, of course, neither were the German assaulting forces. Rommel's desire for a quick victory was being thwarted. At the time this was not apparent, and the sound of the abortive morning attack by von Prittwitz triggered a good deal of alarm among the South Notts Hussars, exacerbated by a desert storm.

In the morning there was a tremendous dust storm, it was almost impossible to see your hand in front of your face. It was misery. It was really impossible to do anything at the height of a dust storm. We used to wear anti-gas Perspex goggles – they weren't very much use! Wrap a scarf or handkerchief round your mouth and that didn't do anything much either. It used to get everywhere, up your nose, in your hair. You couldn't see to go from one vehicle to the next though it be only 5 or 10 yards away. Then it used to blow itself out. People looked like white-faced clowns; the dust was a very light colour and it settled on to everything. Every part of equipment that had a trace of oil on – it had a thick yellow coating.[11]

Lance Sergeant Bob Foulds, B Troop, 425 Battery, 107th RHA

In such a situation, panic could easily have broken out. Dennis Middleton remembered that his officer certainly got a little overexcited.

We were told we were going to be attacked by German tanks. We were in the wagon lines and the officer in charge was Mr Newman. He said in his 'county' voice, 'When the tanks come, you must rush forward and stick crowbars in the tracks!' This didn't appeal to us a great deal – and I didn't notice anybody looking for crowbars![12]

Lance Bombardier Dennis Middleton, B Troop, 425 Battery, 107th RHA

Middleton's unlikely-sounding story was confirmed by Ernie Hurry.

I was stood there with the signal section wondering what we were doing next, when Lieutenant Newman said to me, 'Hurry, grab a bar or pick shaft to wrench the tracks off the German tanks as they're going by!' I've never heard anything so ridiculous in all my life! We'd heard that much about the

German tanks advancing in Europe. Imagine going up to a German and saying, 'Hey mister, can I knock your tracks off?'[13]

Gunner Ernie Hurry, B Troop, 425 Battery, 107th RHA

In such circumstances, Bill Seely did his rather more pragmatic best to calm his men in the finest tradition of a British officer.

Colonel Bill Seely made a point of walking in front of the guns, pacing up and down carrying a rifle. A gesture – he couldn't have done anything with a rifle. We knew what he was doing. He was saying, 'You're here and I'm in front of you!' No sense of heroics, he wasn't strutting, he might have been walking round his estate in Nottingham with a 12-bore, that was his attitude. He was a slight man, very slight, he didn't give the appearance of some macho tough guy. But something about his demeanour we respected.[14]

Bombardier Ray Ellis, A Troop, 425 Battery, 107th RHA

Shortly afterwards, Seely ordered his regiment to move some 2 to 3 miles to the south, his batteries intermingled with the 1st Regiment RHA, about 5,000 yards from the central section of the outer wire defences. On the east side was 426 Battery, to their right A/E Battery (1st RHA), then 425 Battery, and finally B/O Battery (1st RHA) were on the west side of the central section. Each of the troops sent forward OP parties to take up positions with the Australian infantry, while the signallers busied themselves laying telephone cables all the way from the OPs back to the command posts, winding the telephone wires off reels on the back of signal trucks. These telephone wires were vital to the defence of Tobruk – wireless communications were not reliable and without communications the guns were blind. It was the job of the signallers to keep the lines working when-ever they were cut.

To repair it, all you do is pick up the line in your hand and walk. You've got a telephone over your shoulder and you'd just walk until you find the break – then you'd mend it: bare the two lines, do a suitable knot, then insulation tape.[15]

Bombardier David Tickle, Headquarters, 425 Battery, 107th RHA

On the morning of Good Friday, 11 April 1941, Bob Hingston, by this time commanding D Troop, was manning an OP near the perimeter to the west of El Adem road when he was awoken by the sentry.

I was sleeping just by the telephone on the surface. 'Captain Hingston, Sir, there's something there, I don't see what it is!' He drew my attention, quite correctly in the way he'd been trained, to this lump, a very small lump, right out in the desert. I got my glasses on it and I said, 'No, I don't think it's anything to worry about!' Then suddenly it put its head up – it was a camel![16]

Captain Bob Hingston, D Troop, 426 Battery, 107th RHA

That morning there was a slightly unreal calm as the haze began to dissipate. Some German infantry were sighted and shelled at about 12.00, but the first real attack came at about 15.00 when some fifty German tanks made their unwelcome appearance.

Fairly early on in the afternoon, a number of German tanks appeared on my right, heading very rapidly down towards the perimeter. We got on to them and things really warmed up! Then they stopped and ran across our front and we had a fairly good shoot at them – there were several left behind damaged. I always claimed that I'd hit them, but I think the 1st RHA claimed they had too! They got to the El Adem road and then they withdrew a bit. They were firing light signals; I don't know why! Suddenly they charged down the hill, most impressive, down on either side of the El Adem road going flat out. Our

tanks had arrived, and they pulled them up and a real slugging
match started between the two tank units. Then the trouble set
in – the tanks had cut our telephone line and we could not get
through by radio.[17]

Captain Bob Hingston, D Troop, 426 Battery, 107th RHA

While the Cruiser tanks of the 1st Royal Tank Regiment
harassed the panzers, the signallers desperately worked to repair
any broken phone lines. It had become evident that guns were
by far the best defence against tanks, and the Australian infantry
were dependent on the British guns to protect them. George
Pearson witnessed the application of a long-standing tradition
of the Royal Artillery.

With gunners there are occasions when you can't take cover. If
it was a normal day and you weren't firing, or you were firing on
a relatively unimportant target, and you got shot at by counter-
battery fire, then you would cease firing and take cover. As soon
as it had finished you would go on firing. But when you are in
support of infantry then you don't leave the guns – you must
keep firing in support of your own infantry – you can't just pack
that up because you are being shelled. That was part of Royal
Artillery training.[18]

Sergeant George Pearson, B Troop, 425 Battery, 107th RHA

As the battle intensified, so the gunners warmed to their work.

We were now in our first real wartime situation. Now we were
in action and we were being fired upon – artillery fire. We
hadn't dug in – we were just on the sand. We were just firing,
firing, firing, non-stop for about six hours. We had no idea what
we were firing at – we had no information at all. We had to keep
ramming them up the spout on the line we were on without
any movement sideways, upwards or down; given a range and

a line and just told to keep on firing. One of the guns in the troop seized up because it got so hot. Eventually, we stopped firing in turn to let the guns cool down. You couldn't touch the breech and certainly not the barrel – it was that hot – they say you could have fried eggs on it! We had no water – we couldn't pour water on them. I reckon that my gun alone in that day fired something like 1,200 rounds. We loved it, that's why we'd come, that's what we had expected, or hoped to do, from when we were called up in 1939. Everybody was exhilarated.[19]

Sergeant Ian Sinclair, A Troop, 425 Battery, 107th RHA

Harold Harper saw some of the panzers come over a ridge about 6,000 yards away.

They didn't attack in great strength, probably about fourteen or fifteen tanks altogether. Having got the guns into position and on line, I was in the troop command post responsible for relaying the instructions to the guns, shouting out all the different angles using the megaphone standing 10 to 15 yards behind the guns. The firing was almost incessant. It was rather like going to a cup tie – when you knocked a tank out everybody cheered. I think we managed to knock out about three or four tanks – set them on fire – before they retired.[20]

Lance Bombardier Harold Harper, D Troop, 426 Battery, 107th RHA

In these circumstances, at long range, the guns were mainly firing high-explosive shells, as Ray Ellis explains.

We never did ever have much anti-tank ammunition – a little shell that came to a very sharp point. There was no fuse on the end – it was just a metal projectile designed to penetrate armour. The high explosive (HE) 117 burst on impact. The HE 119 had a slightly delayed fuse on it. At the end of an HE shell there is a little nose cone of brass, like a plunger. As the shell strikes the ground that plunger is pushed in and the shell explodes. When the shell was being carried about, over that plunger it had a 'cap', which screwed on to protect it so that if you dropped the shell, it didn't explode. Before the shell was loaded that cap was removed. But if you wanted a delayed action – as much as you could get – you had the 119 which was delayed a little bit anyway and left the cap on, which we thought might delay it a bit more. A makeshift anti-tank shell. If you could land a 119 on a tank the chances are you'd do a lot of damage: you might go into the turret; you might drop on the engine, set it on fire; you might land on the track and blow a track off.[21]

Bombardier Ray Ellis, A Troop, 425 Battery, 107th RHA

The gunners were soon desperate for more ammunition. Drivers and other spare personnel were pressed into service to keep the ammunition stacked up and ready in the gun pits, and to remove the mounds of empty cartridge cases. Bill Hutton, then acting as a motorcycle despatch rider, was one of those called forward to assist in feeding the guns.

They couldn't get the ammunition to the guns fast enough. Even cooks were carrying ammunition to the guns! You carried a box with two 25-pounder shells in it. Somebody else carried the box of high explosive – that wasn't as heavy as the shells. You had to get them out of the 3-tonner [lorry] and carry it about 100 yards to the nearest gun. They were very awkward things to carry – they banged against you – they were very hard and sharp. There were ropes round the box and your hands got all sore; then you started carrying them on your shoulder and your shoulder got sore. You were being sworn at because you weren't bringing the stuff fast enough. Running around with high explosive in your hand – not a very glamorous job I'll tell you; but it was a job that had got to be done. I hadn't a clue what was going on! I carried ammunition till I dropped. I don't think I've ever been so tired in my life.[22]

Gunner Bill Hutton, Headquarters, 425 Battery, 107th RHA

During these initial tank battles, the battery gun positions began to run short of ammunition as the local supplies held on lorries started to run out. A proper supply system had not yet been established and lorries had to be sent back to a main ammunition dump near the Tobruk port area. This triggered a fondly recalled incident.

The gunners reported they were short of ammunition. Major Peter Birkin put Lieutenant John Newman – the transport officer – who we thought was a bit of a wimp – in our truck and told him to go and get ammunition with lorries. We got to this ammunition dump and there was a sergeant on the gate who refused to let him in and said, 'I must have authority.' To everybody's delight, we were all right close up, Mr Newman replied, 'My authority's coming over that bloody hill in Mark IIIs and IVs – German tanks!' This chap let us in, and we loaded up. When we left this chap in charge was still bemoaning the fact he hadn't got the paperwork – and he didn't know how much we'd taken.[23]

Gunner Ted Whittaker, Headquarters, 425 Battery, 107th RHA

One transient moment during this period attained a near-legendary status due to a gross misunderstanding of what was really happening, deliberate or otherwise, by a press correspondent.

We had a very illiterate, loud-mouthed man as cook; a broad Nottingham accent, ignorant and certainly not a brave man. Our guns were firing over open sights at German tanks who had broken through. This idiot, who I am quite certain didn't realise what was happening, suddenly came out with his serving spoons and shouted, 'Come on, come and get it!' He hadn't been in action before and he hadn't realised what was happening! There was a BBC man there, and he said, 'The morale of the troops there was indescribable. Amidst all this battle I saw a cook waving his spoons, shouting, "Come and get it!" as though nothing was happening!'[24]

Lance Sergeant Charles Ward, 426 Battery, 107th RHA

The shield in front of the 25-pounder was not really to safeguard the gun crew from shrapnel or shells; it was to protect them from the blast coming back from the muzzle of their own gun. But every so often they would 'catch' the blast. It had an effect comparable to being 'boxed' about the ears, resulting in a temporary deafness. After such heavy firing the gunners were left exhausted, with fine sand sticking to the sweat on their faces and bodies, their eyes little more than red slits. Yet there was scant time for rest, as in any overnight lulls they had to continue to dig their guns in as best they could. These gun pits were very different from the 'palaces' constructed at Mersa Matruh.

You dug yourself a gun pit, digging down maybe a foot and a half, couple of feet if you could. Then you put a sandbag wall, two or three sandbags high round the front, so that you had a certain amount of protection for the gun crew and the ammunition which you piled in the gun pit. They were set out, not four guns in a line, but two forward and the wing guns back a little bit, so that if you were attacked by tanks you could always bring two guns to bear even if it was attacking from the flank.[25]

Sergeant George Pearson, B Troop, 425 Battery, 107th RHA

By 13 April, the regiment had managed to establish a series of OPs with the 20th Australian Infantry Brigade (Brigadier John

Murray) in amid the former Italian strongpoints, concrete dugouts and anti-tank ditch that made up the front line. Bombardier Ray Ellis had been sent up as a specialist OP assistant to Captain Charlie Bennett. Under the light of the full moon that night, the forward OPs of both batteries discerned German infantry and vehicles creeping forward and close to their barbed wire – an attack was obviously imminent on the positions held by 2/17th Australian Battalion to the west of the El Adem road.

That Easter Monday morning, 14 April, the assault began through a breach carved through the Australian defences by a combination of German infantry and specialist engineers. Ray Ellis was peering over the top of their OP trench.

> First there was a lot of shellfire landing upon us. Then, looking through the binoculars, I could see these men creeping towards us, running from cover to cover, diving into holes in the ground as they approached. I realised I was really watching German troops advancing towards me in the front line. It was quite a sensation – a game I had played as a boy – it was actually happening![26]
>
> Bombardier Ray Ellis, A Troop, 425 Battery, 107th RHA

At about 05.00, the tanks of the 5th Panzer Regiment began to roll forward through the gap. As the tanks rumbled closer and closer to their position in a dugout at the foot of a former Italian observation pole, Ellis became increasingly aware that this was no longer a 'game'.

> These were the first tanks I'd seen. There was mortar fire, shellfire and Spandau machine-gun fire. You had to stick your head over and look over the top to observe the fire – that was our job – and it wasn't a very pleasant sensation watching this lot come towards you. We weren't panicking – we were terrified – but there's a difference! Bennett gave the orders; I was just

helping him really. We were two men together in a very tight situation and you're passing information to each other, 'Have you seen this, there's one over there!' The signaller would be on the telephone and you're passing the orders. As the tanks advanced so we were reducing the range of the guns, so that our own shells were beginning to fall nearer and nearer. The tanks made short work of the anti-tank ditch and had no problem at all in coming through the barbed-wire defences. Eventually the tanks actually passed through us – some people must have been killed, they were either side a matter of a few yards away. Following the tanks were the German infantry with their bayonets fixed.[27]

Bombardier Ray Ellis, A Troop, 425 Battery, 107th RHA

Charles Bennett was certainly a very cool customer and he carried on communicating his fire orders back to the gun positions even as the tanks overran the OP. David Tickle was the signaller at the other end of the line.

Captain Bennett was at the OP and he'd been overrun. The call came down the telephone line, 'Target me!' We thought, 'Crikey, what's happening?' He kept shouting, 'Target me!' Then it dawned on us what had happened! We realised he had been overrun.[28]

Bombardier David Tickle, Headquarters, 425 Battery, 107th RHA

Major Robert Daniell also claimed the credit for targeting the German infantry as they passed through the gap opened by the tanks in the front-line wire defences. He was determined to isolate the German tanks that had broken through the Australian lines. Tanks cannot 'hold' ground and without infantry support they would ultimately have to fall back.

My role was to try and concentrate the fire of all the guns I possibly could on the gap in the wire that the Germans had cut and through which their tanks were coming. The effect of that was that when they tried to bring their infantry through, they were wiped out. The lorries were blown up and set on fire. At all costs we were to keep out every single infantryman we could.[29]

Major Robert Daniell, Headquarters, 107th RHA

Whatever Daniell might think, some German infantry, accompanied by mortars and artillery pieces, *did* break through. They had managed to establish a strongpoint in the Australian trenches, and it was soon evident that the overall integrity of their front line was in danger. The Australians launched a counter-attack, and in the vicious bayonet fighting that followed, Corporal Jack Edmondson[30] provided an example of inspirational courage and leadership which forced the Germans back into the anti-tank ditch. Sadly, he suffered terrible neck and stomach wounds that would prove fatal. He was awarded a posthumous Victoria Cross. His brigadier, John Murray, left an impression of the intensity of the fighting.

It was something that, unless seen, defies description and is entirely beyond the pen of one puny human. The din was colossal: it rose in an ever-increasing crescendo until one thought one's eardrums would burst. If you can imagine tanks hurling forth their shells; artillery doing likewise; wave after wave of dive-bombers dropping tons of ear-splitting high explosives and the comforting – to my ears anyway – sound of rifle fire; and, above all, a lurid sky suggesting the red blood of brave men, caused by blazing tanks and burning buildings; the huge explosions of burning petrol; to say nothing of the roar of the low-flying aircraft and high revving tanks, you will understand why I fail lamentably to put what is in my heart and mind into words.[31]

Brigadier John Murray, Headquarters, 20th Australian Brigade, 9th Australian Division

On the 426 Battery frontage, Lance Bombardier Albert Swinton was acting as the OP specialist assistant to Captain Colin Barber, when they were ordered to evacuate at once.

They were surrounding us, 'Get out and get out quick!' A lot of sand and tanks milling about. A case of get in the truck and get the hell out of it and hope for the best. I was in the back of the truck; he was in the front. He was a right mad bloke – not mad stupid – but he'd have a go at anything.[32]

Lance Bombardier Albert Swinton, D Troop, 426 Battery, 107th RHA

The German tanks were isolated and found themselves pelted by 25-pounder shells, harassed by 2-pounder anti-tank guns and under attack from the Cruiser tanks of 1st Royal Tank Regiment. The attack lost all cohesion, and by around 07.00 the panzers were in full retreat. Some passed close to where Barber and Swinton had concealed their signals truck after abandoning their OP post. The irrepressible Colin Barber took a series of pot-shots with his revolver at some German infantry clinging to the tanks. As the regimental history ruefully reports, 'Range was only seven yards, but in the best gunner traditions he missed them all!'[33] Not long afterwards, Colin Barber would show a different kind of marksmanship.

Just as it was getting dark, two German staff cars came careering down the El Adem road and horror of horrors there they found us! They must have lost themselves completely. Colin Barber engaged them very correctly, in the best Larkhill fashion, with ranging rounds of gunfire. He did it brilliantly! The two cars were standing together, not very far outside our perimeter defences, when he landed a round of gunfire right on them and they both burst into flames. It was most spectacular because it was dusk and the sight of these flames shooting up – there were a number of Australians around us and they were cheering wildly. One of them rushed up and smote me heavily on the shoulder and said, 'You're the best bloody battery in the British Army!' It was very good for morale![34]

Captain Bob Hingston, D Troop, 426 Battery, 107th RHA

The Germans had suffered severe casualties in the attack, with the 5th Panzer Regiment losing seventeen of the thirty-nine tanks committed, while the anti-tank ditch was later found to be full of dead and dying German soldiers. Rommel had been over-hasty, not giving his men a chance to recuperate after the Cyrenaica campaign. Nor had he allowed his formations time to move forward into position or the newly arrived 15th Panzer Division even to reach the front. In consequence, the breakthrough bridgehead was far too narrow and allowed the garrison to concentrate its artillery to maximum effect. The Royal Artillery had done well enough to establish a solid working relationship with the Australian infantry and the Germans would never get so far again. Rommel could not easily break into Tobruk, but the garrison was trapped, with the Germans in firm control of Fort Capuzzo, Sollum and the Halfaya Pass, which dominated the coastal road from Egypt.

BOTH SIDES HAD THROWN a lot into the opening battles and there was a slight lull in the fighting in the days that followed. Even so, Rommel would persist for a while in scaled-down efforts to break in. On 15 April an attack by the Italian tanks and infantry in the western sector was beaten off, while over the next couple of days more unsuccessful attacks were launched on Ras el Madauur in the south-west corner. After this, even Rommel was forced to accept that the Tobruk fortress was 'established' and that further impromptu assaults had little or no chance of success.

As for the 107th RHA, its 425 and 426 Batteries were still interspersed with the batteries of 1st RHA. These boasted pre-war regular trained and disciplined soldiers, who knew their jobs inside out. At first the South Notts Hussars were almost in awe of their peers.

> We were a yeomanry regiment; we hadn't got discipline instilled into us in the same way as a regular regiment would have. We'd have Rocket Troop or Chestnut Troop one side of us – and when their four guns fired, they fired as one – they went, 'WHHOOF!' Ours went, 'Bang! Bang! Bang! Bang!' They were disciplined to that – we thought, 'Get them off as quickly as you can!'[35]

Battery Quartermaster Sergeant Fred Brookes, 425 Battery, 107th RHA

The presence of the 1st RHA gave them a very handy benchmark for every aspect of gunnery. Soon a desire to emulate became a competition for 'bragging rights'. Charles Westlake expressed it perfectly.

> To begin with we were a bit slower in firing than they were, but we certainly had all the brains – and then some – that they did. Our people knew how to do a job because they would reason *why* it should be done, *how* it should be done; whereas the regular soldier was taught by numbers. Nobody would tell him why it should be done; he was just told how it was done. Their equipment was all shiny – in fact shiny in places where it damn well shouldn't have been shiny because you could see it from miles off. It was 'bull' pure and simple. It would only be a very short time before we got used to the mechanics of firing

and would be able to equal them. We used to reckon that if we couldn't get a round on the ground quicker than the 1st RHA, then we were no ruddy use![36]

Bombardier Charles Westlake, A Troop, 425 Battery, 107th RHA

One wonders if the hard-bitten regulars of 1st RHA were aware of this competition from their junior neighbours?

In the early days of the siege, the gunners had been aware that German Stuka dive-bombers had been carrying out raids on the Tobruk harbour area in an effort to close the port. The Stukas were a potent symbol of the German Blitzkrieg tactics in Europe in 1940. With their distinctive inverted gull wings and screaming Jericho trumpet sirens, they soon made their presence felt over Tobruk. However, the chastening experience of British artillery power during the Easter attacks caused a change in Stuka tactics as they switched their attention to the British guns. The Stukas were vulnerable to modern fighters, but the eleven Hurricanes left behind by the RAF as their contribution to the defence of Tobruk were destroyed within a matter of days. This left the garrison open to Stuka attack.

There was almost no way of hiding the gun positions from the air. Netting and scrim could be used to cover the gun pits, vehicle tracks could be brushed away, but any decent reconnaissance photograph would reveal all: the broad shape of the gun pits could not really be disguised, the buried telephone lines, the command posts, even the paths to the latrines – they all stood out like a sore thumb. Ian Sinclair remembered his impressions of an early Stuka raid on B Troop.

The Stukas come over in formation and then they fan out. Amazement at the noise – they made a dreadful noise. We'd never seen or heard of them before. The noise of them during the dive-bombing – the screams – it was frightening! The shape was frightening – like an eagle coming to pick you up! Then the accuracy with which the wretched people dropped their half-dozen bombs – and they were aiming for YOU as far as you reckoned when they started to come – after your gun pit. You knew when they were coming for you – or whether they were going for somebody else! If they were coming for you, you knew there was only one thing to do – get the hell out of it – in a slit trench if you could and stay there! If you were firing and they came, you stopped firing. There's not much point in us all being dead in a Stuka raid, because the whole raid only lasted 30 seconds in the time you'd normally take to reload your gun. So, there was no point in being brave and sticking to your guns. Under artillery bombardment it was a different matter.[37]

Sergeant Ian Sinclair, A Troop, 425 Battery, 107th RHA

The noise generated by roaring engines and screaming sirens of the diving Stukas was terrifying – far outweighing the actual effects of bombs and machine-gun bullets.

Noise does play a terrific part in fear. I think if you could have a silent battle you wouldn't be anything like so frightened. They usually dropped five bombs; you could actually see the bombs leave the plane. The plane pulls out very close to the ground and you're left with these bombs coming down – you imagine – straight into your slit trench. It is a nerve-racking business: the bombs are dropping; the ground's jumping; and you're being bounced up and down. You had your head well down in the slit trench, crouching, holding your breath and hoping that you would be spared.[38]

Bombardier Ray Ellis, A Troop, 425 Battery, 107th Regiment, RHA

Bob Foulds found that even in such terrifying circumstances there were lessons to be learnt.

You could count the bombs and see them coming at you through the air. We began to learn that if the bombs appeared to be coming straight at you, then they were going to go overhead and hit something behind you. But if they appeared to be coming down in front of you, then they were going to drop on you or very, very close to you, which wasn't a very nice sensation! It's the most naked feeling in the world to see these bombs coming down at you.[39]

Lance Sergeant Bob Foulds, B Troop, 425 Battery, 107th RHA

Ted Holmes was a driver, often working on the water bowser, but he had additional extra duties as an anti-aircraft Bren gunner in a small pit just to the side of the main gun positions.

You could see the planes coming – you could always tell a Stuka because it had got fixed undercarriage and they were like a 'W' to look at! They were really good. They came so low that they nearly scraped the floor by the time they pulled out of the dive. They aimed the Stuka at the target, just let the bomb go at the last minute and machine-gunned you as well. With this fixed undercarriage there used to be a saying that you don't know you've been 'Stukad' till you've got tread marks on your back! This Stuka was coming right towards me and I felt like getting down, but I kept firing and got five shots at it before it went. I'm afraid I didn't hit it![40]

Gunner Ted Holmes, A Troop, 425 Battery, 107th RHA

The Bren was difficult to keep clean in desert conditions and his Bren had jammed for automatic fire, only allowing him to fire single shots. In the circumstances, Holmes did well to get off his five shots.

On 1 May 1941, George Pearson was on the B Troop gun position when the Stukas screamed down yet again. So far, the South Notts Hussars had escaped relatively unscathed, but this time there were casualties.

I dived into a slit trench and another young chap called Phil Collihole[41] dived on top of me. When the bombs had finished exploding and the aircraft were going away, I said, 'Come on, get up, Phil!' He didn't move! I got up and he sort of flopped over on his back. I said, 'Come on, what's the matter, are you hit?' I couldn't see a mark on him, but he was obviously out – and he was in fact dead. A small piece of shrapnel about as big as would cover a thumbnail had gone into the back of his neck and must have severed the spinal column and killed him – just like that.[42]

Sergeant George Pearson, B Troop, 425 Battery, 107th RHA

Three times the Stuka raids attacked their positions. Another casualty was Cliff Smedley,[43] an old school friend of Pearson. This popular NCO had rapidly risen to the rank of battery sergeant major although he was just 21 years old.

Cliff Smedley was a very big chap and when a dive-bombing raid came, he dived into the Boyes anti-tank rifle pit. He and the 500lb bomb had a race for it and the 500lb bomb won. He was not mutilated as such – I think it was blast that killed him more than anything else – because when we picked Cliff up it was rather like picking a fish up, he was all floppy. It must have broken every bone in his body.[44]

Sergeant George Pearson, B Troop, 425 Battery, 107th RHA

Even in these circumstances, there was a black humour evident in their response to tragedy. Herbert Bonnello was still in charge of the pay for 426 Battery and he conceived of an amusing ploy.

Whenever there was an air raid, I used to get this tin box out of our little dugout and put it out in the open. One of the officers one day said, 'What's in the tin box?' I said, 'The pay records and if it gets a direct hit, we're made!' It never did![45]

Bombardier Herbert Bonnello, Headquarters, 426 Battery, 107th RHA

Bill Pringle was confident he knew the best method of reviving the morale of his men.

> Immediately as the last plane was disappearing, man the guns and fire some shots at the German lines: a) it would keep the morale of the men up and b) to let the Germans know that, 'If you shoot at me, I'll shoot you back!'[46]
>
> Captain William Pringle, A Troop, 425 Battery, 107th RHA

The Stuka raids would become a daily backdrop to their lives. Gradually they would learn to cope.

THE GUNS HAD PROVED CRUCIAL to the defence of Tobruk. The concentrated Stuka raids suffered by the 107th RHA were clearly an attempt to knock out the artillery as part of one last attempt by Rommel to take Tobruk, which began on the night of 30 April. This time, he was determined to create a wider breach in the Australian line. The Germans advanced with strong artillery support and their infantry once again managed to establish positions in the Australian front lines in the south-western Ras el Madauur sector, which lay to the right of the 425 Battery. A counter-attack was organised and, as part of the preparations, Ernie Hurry laid out a 'laddered' telephone line forward to the new OP post.

> We laid a laddered cable out to Captain Slinn and, I think, Ted Whittaker in this slit trench out in No Man's Land. We had a steel bar through the drum cable, and we wrapped the bar with plenty of insulating tape. As we walked forward there was a signaller pulling it off. Then every so often the other three signallers would stop and put a ladder from one cable to another, so that should it get shelled there's a way of communication getting through. The job was complete at

about 10 o'clock at night when one of the signallers getting out of the hole tripped over one of the spare drums and clanged it with another. Of course, everything went wild, as Jerry opened up with everything he'd got. He sent these flares up and they machine-gunned us. I lay on my stomach and incendiary bullets were going over my head – I could hear them and see them! Every time the flares went up, I looked for a worm hole I could crawl down! I think it took two or three hours to crawl just over the next hill out of range. I crawled a bit, stopped a bit, crawled a bit, waited a bit – if blood had been brown, I should have bled to death![47]

Gunner Ernie Hurry, B Troop, 425 Battery, 107th RHA

The guns fired, and fired, and fired, and fired. All their records for continuous firing were broken, but still they carried on.

The guns stood up to it very well. The gun barrels became worn, the rifling, which holds the soft copper driving band on the shell, with the heat and the wear of the twisting action of the shell going up the barrel – they wore. As they wore gasses went up past the shell and so it became increasingly inaccurate. There was a very accurate measuring device and when they got beyond a certain tolerance – if possible – the barrel was changed.[48]

Lance Sergeant Bob Foulds, B Troop, 425 Battery, 107th RHA

The unceasing shooting meant that the gun breech and barrels would begin to overheat; in the popular vernacular they became 'white-hot', although this is an exaggeration. In these circumstances, the men soon learnt a crucial safety precaution.

Never to leave guns which are excessively hot loaded with a shell. We did get some premature explosions. If you keep firing, firing and firing as quickly as you can – well the gun gets so hot you definitely cannot touch it. Then if you put a shell up the

breech – and don't fire it almost straight away – the shell can
explode inside the barrel and blow the gun up.[49]

Bombardier Charles Westlake, A Troop, 425 Battery, 107th RHA

After two days, the fighting died down. The Australians had
regained most of the ground, but the Germans had retained
a nasty little salient jutting into the perimeter. However, the
Germans had come to the end of their own tether. During the
attack, Rommel was being closely 'watched' by the august figure
of Lieutenant General Friedrich Paulus, who had been sent out
to North Africa by the German Chief of General Staff, General
Franz Halder, who was deeply concerned by Rommel's failure to
follow orders and his constant demands for precious reinforcements and resources. Halder had in mind the preparations for
imminent attack on the behemoth that was Soviet Russia that
Hitler had ordered to begin in June 1941. Rommel was forced to
accept that another hasty attack on Tobruk would not work, so
began preparation for a more formal and conventional siege. A
ring of defensive posts was established, mirroring the Australian
defences, to ensure the garrison was safely pinned back in its
fortress. The German forward positions on the Egyptian border
were sown with minefields, backed up by strong artillery to seal
off the obvious approach routes that any British relieving force
would have to use to get through to Tobruk.

Meanwhile, Wavell and Admiral Andrew Cunningham,
commanding the Mediterranean Fleet, had their own problems. Churchill's vainglorious Greece campaign had collapsed
in a welter of failure, and tens of thousands of troops had to be
evacuated first from the mainland and then later from Crete. The
Royal Navy was also crucial to the Tobruk garrison. A few old
destroyers, Landing Craft Tanks (LCTs) and a variety of other
miscellaneous small ships made the 'Suicide Run' to Tobruk,
carrying the desperately needed supplies and reinforcements

that sustained the 25,000-strong garrison. Gradually they built up a '60-day reserve' which removed some of the pressure and allowed legitimate confidence that the garrison could hold out.

NOW BEGAN THE SIEGE PROPER and life settled into a routine that would endure for several months. At the gun positions the men now had time to start work, sandbagging around the gun pits, dugouts and command posts. Occasionally they would move battery positions, normally to avoid a 'Stuka run' or to engage a particular target. They also began to improve the OPs located in the front-line area. The original OPs had been built by the Italians as part of their defensive system. They were of simple pole construction type and their proud new proprietors gave them homely names based on their Nottingham homes: such as the Hucknall and Bulwell OPs. Ted Whittaker was sent forward as an assistant to Captain William Pringle at OP 42, just to the left of the El Adem road.

> It was like a crow's nest on top of a 15-foot pole with handholds each side. We'd sandbagged it, we had a seat and a telephone. You could get two of you in at a pinch. At the foot of it was a concrete dugout and a few hundred yards away there was an infantry headquarters – these were Italian fortifications. We were not many yards behind the wire; just in front of the wire was the anti-tank ditch and all round were minefields.[50]

Gunner Ted Whittaker, Headquarters, 425 Battery, 107th RHA

They would climb up the tower before dawn and then stay up there all day.

> You would report you were there and that all was quiet. About midday we sent down a situation report – 'sit-rep' they called it – and then we sent another at night. The usual thing was if you

could see movement on the escarpment a few thousand yards in front. Up to the Italian positions the ground sloped slightly upwards. Then it dropped and there was dead ground that you couldn't see into. Then it rose again steeply to this escarpment, which must have been several hundred feet high, on top of which was the El Adem aerodrome. We could just see the tops of the hangar.[51]

Gunner Ted Whittaker, Headquarters, 425 Battery, 107th RHA

During the evening they would occupy the dugout at the foot of the pole, protected by the Australian infantry. Ray Ellis liked the Australians and found their quaint irreverent attitudes somewhat amusing.

They were friendly, and they had a certain casual way about them which I enjoyed. For instance, the Battery Commander, Major Peter Birkin, had red sandy hair. When he got into the trench, a private soldier would refer to him, 'Hi-yah, Red! How yah doing, Red?' Which I thought was fantastic whereas we would say, 'Good morning, Sir!'[52]

Bombardier Ray Ellis, A Troop, 425 Battery, 107th RHA

However, Harold Harper remembered one amusing incident when their protective screen was breached.

There was a sandstorm raging outside and we were playing cards by the light of a hurricane lamp. Lo and behold, the flap of the tarpaulin came back, and a pair of legs descended. We thought, 'Who the dickens can this be at this time of night?' The next thing was a dixie full of stew – and then this German lad came down – looked to be about 17 or 18. He'd been in the cookhouse and in this sandstorm he'd lost his way, managed to see this chink of light uncovered and thought it was his own crowd and appeared in our dugout. All we did was eat the lad's

stew and then I took him up on top and pointed him back in
the direction of the German lines – told him where to go![53]

Bombardier Harold Harper, D Troop, 426 Battery, 107th RHA

The original poles were augmented as the months passed by a
series of OP scaffolding towers erected by the Royal Engineers.
They were located slightly further back, but their height gave
them a far superior field of vision.

> The scaffolding would be about 6 foot square and stand
> anything between 40 to 60 feet high. It was like a prisoner-
> of-war outlook post. We had to scale up this thing and it was
> absolutely perpendicular! These were put about 1,000 yards
> behind the ridge so that only the top of the towers could see
> over the ridge into the enemy land. Very exposed indeed, you
> got the impression you were there on your own and the rest of
> the world had left you. You felt as though every German in the
> German Army was looking at you.[54]

Bombardier Harold Harper, D Troop, 426 Battery, 107th RHA

The officer and his OP assistant would take it in turns at the
top of the 60-foot-tall scaffolding towers. Albert Swinton soon
found that he had a real problem with vertigo.

> Captain Barber went up and he phoned down and said would
> I take his binoculars up. I said, 'Yes, OK!' Well, I got on this
> ladder thing and I seemed to be going for hours. I looked up
> and, 'Oh dear!' I looked down and nearly fell off. I was scared
> to death I was! I eventually got up to the top and I thought,
> 'Now how do I get in?' There was a double row of sandbags
> with an opening about 18 inches to get through. I got my elbow
> in to lever in – and these sandbags moved and I nearly fell off!
> I was scared to death! I eventually got in and gave Captain
> Barber his binoculars and he says, 'Righto, Bombardier, off you

go!' I says, 'Well, it's all right, Sir, I'll stop up here, you go down and have a break.' Only 'cos I daren't go down! I sat up there for hours and hours and hours![55]

Lance Bombardier Albert Swinton, D Troop, 426 Battery, 107th RHA

Once up the tower, the OP officer and his assistant would have telephone-line communications with the signaller in a dugout at the foot of the tower, who in turn was linked back to the battery positions. Their view was often disrupted by a heat haze or mirages.

By the middle of the morning, as the heat of the day became more intense, you could walk about without compunction. They could see you but in a distorted way. They did the same thing and we would see them walking about but you'd see a man walking upside down 15 feet in the air – distorted visions – you couldn't aim at it, because you didn't know where he was really. Sometimes by a trick of the light, or fate, it would all revert back to normal again in a second – and they had a complete view of the front again, maybe for quarter of an hour – and then it would go again. You'd be looking out and everything would be distorted; then it would all be clear – and everyone dived for cover as the war started again.[56]

Bombardier Ray Ellis, A Troop, 425 Battery, 107th RHA

Early mornings and late afternoon offered the best chance of worthwhile observation.

We could see about half the hangar from the big pole. They built a road that bypassed Tobruk and you could see traffic from the big pole; you'd look through the binoculars – and see maybe a fifty-vehicles convoy moving east, jot the time down and put it in the 'sit-rep'. You'd spot Ju 52s flying backwards and forwards along the ridge – you'd count them for intelligence. If you'd done any shootings you'd put 'Fired on any target so and so; two rounds or whatever!' It was all registered and I did them a brand-new panorama. One target was a leaning telegraph pole; we had a burned-out truck to the west of the road – that was a target; the Italian positions, stone and sandbag sangers, that was a target; an underground well; a deserted village. That was what we could see. Through your binoculars you could see the Italians on this ridge – they'd come out and they'd shake their blankets! One morning Captain Pringle said, 'Do you want to help them shake their blankets!' 'Oh, yes please!' You'd see people running hither and thither. At the time it pleased me, now when I think of it, it was a rotten trick – people just getting up and 25-pounder shells blasting round them.[57]

Gunner Ted Whittaker, Headquarters, 425 Battery, 107th RHA

The OP teams were there to identify targets, give the appropriate fire orders to the gun positions and then correct the fall of shot on to the target. It was a cold-blooded business.

I never thought of it as killing people. That didn't enter into my thinking. You first of all identified the target. If it was a 'GF' target, gunfire, it meant it was a moving target, or one that had got to be engaged very quickly. Say it was some vehicles moving you'd say, 'Troop, GF target!' and everyone ran to the gun even quicker than normal, because the shells had got to be off quickly. You'd then give very fast fire orders. If it was an ordinary target you would just say, 'Troop target!' and that meant there was no great emergency. Then you gave the type of ammunition that was to be fired. If it was HE 119, that meant it was more of a penetration shell; 117 was immediate impact if you wanted to kill troops on the surface; 119 cap on meant that you were firing at something heavy and you wanted a delayed explosion. So you got, 'Troop Target, HE 117!' Then you gave the gun which was going to range,

right-ranging or left-ranging, because only one gun would fire.
Left-ranging meant the gun that was firing was in the middle
of the troop, right-ranging meant the No. 1 gun would fire.
Then you would give your line from the zero line; left or right
of the zero line. If there was any angle of sight you would give
that. Then you'd give the estimated range and then the word,
'Fire!' All that would be passed to the guns. Then all four
guns would move together, but only one would fire. When it
was put on the guns they would say, 'Ready, Fire!' You would
receive from the gun position the words, 'No. 1 shot!' The
shell would come over your head and land and you'd make the
necessary corrections.[58]

Bombardier Ray Ellis, A Troop, 425 Battery, 107th RHA

The fire orders would be received at the troop command post.
Here the gun position officer and his assistant would apply the
necessary mathematical corrections to make sure they could hit
pre-identified targets or new targets. Charles Laborde had great
difficulty with this.

I was the gun position officer passing the orders from the
OPs to the guns. There was a list of all the hostile batteries of
which we had the coordinates. A lot of them must have been
alternative gun positions and so on. Every third or fourth hour
we got another meteorological telegram and we had to set
to and work out the line, range and angle of sight to all these
hostile batteries so that if we were suddenly called upon to
fire on one, all you had to do was look at the list and there was
the line, range and angle of sight all corrected for the weather
conditions. Arithmetic has never been my strong point and we
used to use the army form, specially provided to work it out for
stupid people, we'd go through this and the log tables with the
GPO 'ack'. He would work them out and I would work them

out and if we agreed that was fine – if we didn't then we had to do it all over again.[59]

Lieutenant Charles Laborde, D Troop, 426 Battery, 107th RHA

Laborde was not the only person having problems. Herbert Bonnello had been told to broaden his gunnery experience if he was to have any chance of getting commissioned. He had been acting as gunnery assistant to the battery command post, when he sought permission to join Sergeant William Lake's gun detachment to gain experience in firing a 25-pounder during a night shoot.

I decided it was time I pulled the lever in anger. The spade had been pulled round to fire at a specific target and the first round that I fired the spade shuddered against the ground, I shot off the seat and by the time I landed back on the seat, my spectacles had fallen off! Without my spectacles I'm afraid I can't see a thing. Sergeant Bill Lake was in charge of the gun and I said, 'Bill, my spectacles are off!' Ivor Birkin came racing across, 'What's happened?' I said, 'I can't find my spectacles!' I got out of the seat so the regular layer could get on and eventually with a torch we found my spectacles unharmed. It was then suggested that I was perhaps better off if I went back to the command post office and stuck to my mathematics.[60]

Bombardier Herbert Bonnello, Headquarters, 426 Battery, 107th RHA

Of course, the Germans or Italians would sometimes shoot back, trying to knock out the OP towers which they knew housed their tormentors guiding 25-pounder shells down amidst them.

You could see the guns flash when you were on top of this big pole and you'd say a couple of prayers. Sometimes they'd only fire a few rounds, but sometimes they meant it. If you found they did, you watched the guns flash and as soon as the first shells burst you were over the side. You could just get to the bottom and in the slit trench before the next round fell.[61]

Gunner Ted Whittaker, Headquarters, 425 Battery, 107th RHA

Sometimes the OP officers would accompany Australian night patrols into No Man's Land. Bill Pringle did not enjoy this experience one little bit.

It was hell. I was terrified. It is a funny thing, you notice that each arm of the services is not frightened by being shot at by its own arm. Machine guns and rifles don't worry infantry anything like as much as they worry me! And shells don't worry me anywhere as much as they worried the infantryman! The first thing was to make sure you didn't lose the bloke in front, because he knew his way through the wire – and you didn't! Then you had to make sure you didn't lose your signaller, because you were no bloody good without him! It was a pretty eerie sort of task, I'm not an infantryman at all and I certainly didn't like night patrols, but you had to do it – and that was it. As an officer you had to set an example and not show that you were terrified to death![62]

Captain William Pringle, A Troop, 425 Battery, 107th RHA

The OP teams would be at their post for approximately a week at a time before they were relieved, then went back to the gun positions for 'a rest'.

Beside the original OP posts, the Italians also bequeathed the garrison a plethora of guns of all shapes and sizes – with plentiful supplies of ammunition lying about. The Australians were keen to try to make use of this booty.

They started merely banging away, haphazardly, in the direction of the enemy. The British artillery units showed these Australians how to use the 'bush artillery' effectively. Each gun would be laid on a bearing individually with a prismatic compass. On many of them the sighting equipment had been destroyed by the Italians, so the range was done by a wooden stave which was marked every 6 inches or a foot. That was put in front of the muzzle so that the order for the ranging would be, 'Twenty-eight notches', and the chap would cock his muzzle up until he'd reached the twenty-eighth notch and it would be fired. The Australians did have a rather nasty habit from our point of view. The Italian guns were the split ammunition types where charges were put in behind the rammed shell. If they weren't getting sufficient range from the three or four charge bags that were in the cartridge case they'd cram in an extra bag! 'That'll make the bastard go!' Of course, they blew a few guns to pieces that way. Luckily, they didn't lose any men by it because when they'd done that, they used to fire the gun with a lanyard from a few yards away. But it was not a habit to be recommended. You wouldn't have seen my rear end for dust![63]

Sergeant George Pearson, B Troop, 425 Battery, 107th RHA

Another abandoned battery of Italian guns lay close to the 426 Battery gun positions. These proved an irresistible temptation.

They must have been 150mm: real First World War veterans. They had huge slatted wheels, wooden flaps round the outside of the wheel. Just behind them, they had a movable ramp you had to put into position. They had no dial sights of course, but we used to point them roughly in the right direction of the El Adem aerodrome and then try and fire a shell up on to the escarpment. They were very large shells, much larger than anything we had – they must have weighed over 100lbs. When you'd lined the gun up, you put the ramps behind it in the right position, took hold of the lanyard and retired some distance. You pulled the trigger with this very long lanyard made from signal wire. There was a colossal 'BANG!', off goes the shell and the gun would run straight back, up the ramp at the back and then run forward again. Marvellous sight – it was simply fascinating! You could see the shell going away, then you'd wait for quite a long time and there would be this lovely 'WHHUUMPHH!' in the distance! A great cloud; a huge shell burst! We had no idea of what charge to use! We used to try a little bit more, we put a bigger and bigger charge inside the gun. Eventually, there came the day when we put in one charge too many! The gun flew away! The whole blooming barrel flew off the mounting! We destroyed them all in the end![64]

Lieutenant Charles Laborde, D Troop, 426 Battery, 107th RHA

This was an extremely dangerous pastime, as Albert Swinton could testify. He had been posted to Sergeant William Barker's No. 1 gun detachment in D Troop and was present when one of the Italian guns blew up in similar circumstances.

We wanted a bit more range, so we decided to put a bit more charge in. They fired this gun and we all started running because the gun disintegrated. Old Barker got a lump of the barrel – fortunately for him it hit him flat on – this big lump of cast iron hit him smack on his backside! He was bruised and couldn't sit down for days. That put paid to that nonsense.[65]

Lance Bombardier Albert Swinton, D Troop, 426 Battery, 107th RHA

Perhaps to avoid temptation and more accidents, the Italian ammunition was collected up from all over the Tobruk perimeter and centralised in a large dump. Bill Adams was among those assigned to the task – and he had an extremely narrow escape from disaster. He and the lorry driver had picked up a load and were just approaching the dump.

We were rising up to the top of the escarpment, where we had to run down to this ammunition dump. I saw a glint up in the sky – so I said, 'Stop!' He stopped. It was a shiny silver aeroplane. We waited and waited. That aeroplane dropped one bomb and it dropped right on the ammunition dump! Blew it all up. We stood on the top of that hill looking at it as the ammo went off. After it had died down, we [drove] down, and an MP stopped us, told us to dump it into another dump. We get back and Sergeant Major Beardsall came up and said, 'Thank God you lads are here. I thought you were goners!'[66]

Gunner Bill Adams, Signal Section, Headquarters, 426 Battery, 107th RHA

The siege had settled down. The Germans had passed them by, the battle had moved on. Now they had to exist in a desert for an indeterminate period until they were relieved, or Tobruk fell.

9

A WAY OF LIFE

It was a matter of real economy of priorities really and truly.
Drink first of all. Any water that was left over, that would be
a matter of washing your shirt in it. Maybe, before it got too
thick, you'd have a shave and when it was really no good at all –
that was the time to wash your socks![1]

Sergeant Fred Langford, Headquarters, 425 Battery, 107th RHA

AT TOBRUK THE MEN WERE EFFECTIVELY ON DUTY
twenty-four hours a day, seven days a week, for nine months.
Although it was often relatively quiet, at any moment a shell
could crash down to kill them, so stress levels were high. On the
gun positions there was often nothing to do, just day after day
of sitting in a gun pit with the ever-present risk of sudden death.
In these circumstances, Bill Pringle realised it was important to
try to maintain some basic standards of appearance and hygiene
with the aim of bolstering their self-respect.

I personally was a stickler with my men. I shaved every day
and I insisted that they did. They didn't like it to start with,
but I think they appreciated how much better they felt once
they'd shaved as opposed to being scruffy with a couple of days'
growth and always rubbing their chins. It didn't take them very

long to shave and once we'd got the facts of life established there wasn't any problem.[2]

Captain William Pringle, A Troop, 425 Battery, 107th RHA

In reality, not many officers and NCOs followed this example and standards of appearance varied across the regiment. When nothing ever seemed to change, it was difficult to maintain good morale. Although they had managed to hold the Germans back, it was generally understood that the German forces offered a significantly more dangerous and well-equipped threat than the Italians they had encountered during Operation Compass.

> We went to look at these damaged tanks and there was this great big 75mm gun. The tank gun we were used to was the 2-pounder sticking out in front! In May, we heard about German paratrooper troops taking Crete, and we thought, 'Well, if they can take a great Greek island, what about Tobruk – are they going to drop on us next?' We felt very isolated and very cut off. It was a very different enemy and we began to wonder whether in fact we were going to be able to hold out in Tobruk.[3]

Lance Sergeant Bob Foulds, B Troop, 425 Battery, 107th RHA

Coexisting with these fears of being overrun were rumours flying around the garrison of rescue by a relief force from Egypt. These were based in part on fact: Churchill was naturally keen to break the German grip around Tobruk and put pressure for early action on Wavell. The result was Operation Battleaxe, a premature offensive, undertaken with inadequate resources and preparation. When launched on 15 June 1941 it proved a grim failure, with the armoured forces floundering against the strong German defences. Guns and mines proved as effective there as they had for the British at Tobruk. Terrible tank losses dogged the first day and they only just repulsed strong German counter-attacks, before withdrawing defeated on the third day just in time to avoid entrapment by one of Rommel's trademark wide encircling manoeuvres. It was a disaster that could have been worse. While Rommel's success was recognised by the upgrading of his command to Panzergruppe Afrika, in contrast, the British required someone to take the blame for failure. Within a week Sir Archibald Wavell was replaced by General Claude Auchinleck as the Commander in Chief Middle East. For the men of Tobruk, disillusionment and disenchantment were inevitable as their hopes faded.

> There was supposed to be this great push – and it failed. Now you can imagine, that was a tremendous disappointment and morale went sagging after that. Because we were all buoyed up, you all expected this to be the great relief – and we were all going back to Cairo – and it didn't happen. So that didn't help.[4]
>
> Battery Quartermaster Sergeant Charles Ward, 426 Battery, 107th RHA

Bill Pringle found his methods beginning to flounder in the face of the widespread despondency.

> There was a definite low point when the push that was supposed to get to us didn't. They were uncooperative. You might say, 'Come on, you haven't shaved today!' and he would say, 'So what!' I realised it was no good trying to tell the chap off, because it would only make it worse. I would tell him that life wasn't as bad as that; he was still alive – there were plenty far worse off than him buried in the desert![5]
>
> Captain William Pringle, A Troop, 425 Battery, 107th RHA

In circumstances like this, only comradeship could keep them going amidst the day-to-day discomfort, trials and tedium of life in the desert.

At least Ted Hayward had managed to set up his cookhouse

petrol-burners in a large cave in the escarpment. The cooks only fed the headquarters staff and any of those gunners whose duties allowed them to get back to the cookhouse – usually about eighty men in total, mainly from the nearby 425 Battery. They were fed a monotonous diet of bully beef.

> We were on very simple rations – six days a week corned beef and one day a week tinned M&V – meat and vegetable ration. Never such a thing as menu planning, you went off the cuff – what was there. If we had curry powder, we used to make a curry stew of bully beef with a bowl of rice, not too hot, because most of the chaps wouldn't like it. Then you would mix some of your M&V ration with your bully beef to get a certain amount of vegetables inside a stew. We did meat pies on tin plates: you put your bully beef and vegetables on the plate, put a bit of pastry on the top and push it in the oven. The cave was reasonably cool, and we were able, to a degree, to cut the bully beef so therefore we were able to make bully-beef fritters, which were very popular. Make a flour and water batter, cut a slice of bully beef, drop it in the batter, fry it in a pan on the No. 1 burner for two or three minutes.[6]
>
> Sergeant Ted Hayward, Headquarters, 425 Battery, 107th RHA

The tinned provisions and dry 'dog' biscuits, supposedly nutritious, but utterly tasteless, were distributed by lorry around the gun positions. Bob Hingston was keen to organise gun-pit 'cooking' among his men.

> I said, 'Look here, I'm going to divide these rations to each gun pit, each gun will draw your own rations and you can cook your own food!' The rations were distributed around by these two thoroughly reliable old blighters in charge of the store truck to distribute it. It worked extremely well; they cooked their own food and there were no grumbles about the food at all. Rather

a competition developed as to who could make a real sort of *cordon bleu* dinner for them.[7]

Captain Bob Hingston, D Troop, 426 Battery, 107th RHA

To make up for the lack of fresh vegetables the men were issued with ascorbic acid tablets and very occasionally some real limes. Despite this, the old problem of desert sores caused by an inadequate diet still afflicted many men. A bite, a cut or any kind of abrasion would often develop into a nasty carbuncle.

Charles Ward had been promoted to battery quartermaster sergeant and was given the challenging role of supplying the outlying OP posts with their rations.

In the afternoons, I had to run the gauntlet through the minefields to all the observation posts on the wire. Every day the German artillery used to take pot shots at us – they never hit us; they were miles away We went to each observation post with the rations. We also took up the water in containers – we daren't let the water truck go up there! That would have been terrible if they hit the water truck! One day I was with a driver and we were in between two observation posts and suddenly I looked up and said, 'Christ look!' It was a German fighter coming straight for us! When you're the actual target of this great big plane coming at you, it's the most frightening thing you could ever imagine. All we had time to do was to stop the truck and dive underneath – and then he machine-gunned us. As we came up, I kept saying, 'Are you all right? Are you all right?'[8]

Battery Quartermaster Sergeant Charles Ward, 426 Battery, 107th RHA

If what they had to eat was mundane, then at least there was plenty of it; which was in sharp contrast to the endemic shortage of water. This was after all the desert – almost by definition water was in short supply!

We were allowed half a gallon of water a day and a good portion of that went to the cookhouse. We used to have our water bottle, which holds about a pint and a half, filled every other day. The shortage of water was a bigger enemy than the Germans were in a way. The heat was about 110 degrees in the shade – and no shade! You were really thirsty: your lips used to be cracked and bleeding all the time. We used to dream about putting your head under the tap at home![9]

Gunner Ted Holmes, A Troop, 425 Battery, 107th RHA

Every man had to husband his water and it often demanded enormous personal restraint, especially during the heat of the day. If they snapped, it could all be gone in a few large gulps.

I used to have half a mouthful first thing in the morning, before the sun came up, have a gargle, and then spit it out. That was it until you had your tea. Then, when the sun went down, you drink the rest of it – and think, 'Thank God for that!'[10]

Lance Bombardier Albert Swinton, D Troop, 426 Battery, 107th RHA

The men also had a cigarette ration. Most of the men smoked, but some were heavy smokers used to smoking forty to sixty cigarettes a day. They were soon desperate and eternally on the lookout for extra 'fags'.

I smoked as many as I could get! I've smoked my ration straight off in a day! Your cigarette rations varied. In theory you should get fifty cigarettes a week, but you might have to go three weeks before you get any. At one stage we'd been issued with some Egyptian cigarettes that were ostensibly a present from King Farouk. Most people threw them out, or buried them, because they'd got this 'Turkish' aroma to them – they weren't Virginian tobacco – not what we were normally used to. We thought we were hard done to when we got Craven 'A'

– because we'd started off with Woodbines. Then when [the supply] of British cigarettes dried up – we were looking for those we had slung![11]

Gunner Frank Knowles, Headquarters, 425 Battery, 107th RHA

Harold Harper could have made his fortune.

I didn't smoke at Tobruk. For my fifty cigarettes I used to have a raffle every week. Just bits of toilet paper, anything. The blokes would go mad for cigarettes, everybody would go in for this raffle. I did enormously well with it – but I used to give the money every time to the Red Cross.[12]

Bombardier Harold Harper, D Troop, 426 Battery, 107th RHA

Later in the siege they were also given a rum ration. Albert Swinton remembered the awful pitfalls when he was assigned the responsibility of fetching the rum allotment for the whole of D Troop.

Sergeant Bill Barker said, 'Hey, go across the command post, Bert, there's a rum ration!!' The battery command post was 200 or 300 yards away and I went up there and said, 'I've come for the rum ration!' They said, 'Righto, there it is!', and they gave me a rum jar three parts full of rum. 'That's your ration for the troop'. I set back across the desert and had got halfway back when old Jerry started shelling us something rotten. I thought to myself, 'Do I be British and walk through this lot, or do I hit the deck and break this bottle of rum!' I thought, 'If I lose this rum, I'll get killed anyway!' I was between the devil and the deep blue sea! I eventually got through to the troop – the first rum ration it was![13]

Lance Bombardier Albert Swinton, D Troop, 426 Battery, 107th RHA

Everyone was supposed to drink their rum immediately, but Dennis Middleton and his mates had a better idea.

Geoff Douglas had the bright idea of saving it up for a week and then having a party! So we formed what we called the 'Saturday Club' – this was half a dozen or so of us at battery headquarters. We did this for one or two Saturdays, and then the third Saturday, one of us, I can't remember who it was, overdid this and came out from this dugout absolutely tight, when Peter Birkin was outside. There was the most appalling row! I explained to him, 'I've arranged for the telephone to be properly manned, the guards posted, everything OK!' But he was furious and next morning he had us up and he said, 'If this affair didn't include some of my best NCOs, you'd all be broken, but I can't spare you!' That was the end of the Saturday Club![14]

Lance Sergeant Dennis Middleton, Headquarters, 425 Battery, 107th RHA

Ted Coup was one of those who had 'let himself down'.

We were also issued with limes, which we squeezed to make a passable lime juice. As soon as this corked bottle was full, we mixed the lime and the rum together and we got really drunk. I can remember walking into my dugout – and I hit the cross beam at the entrance with my forehead – that was the last thing I remember! The next morning, we were all on a charge – it finished up with a severe ticking off. From then on you lined up with your mug for your rum ration and there was another man to make sure you drank it![15]

Bombardier Ted Coup, Headquarters, 425 Battery, 107th RHA

Beer was only available occasionally from the canteen truck, replenished when possible from the main NAAFI depot back in Tobruk itself. In the hot, dusty conditions, one can imagine how keen the men were to know when the next shipment of beer would arrive.

" THE BEER SHIPS HERE AGAIN "

They announced, rather rashly, that somebody had paid for a whole consignment of beer. There would be one bottle of beer per man for the whole garrison. And they said when it was coming. The day the ship arrived, in daylight, the Stukas came over as it got into the harbour. All we ever saw was this big plume of smoke. I drew this cartoon with two chaps talking and a big column of smoke in the background just saying, 'Oooh! I see the beer ship's come!'[16]

Gunner Ted Whittaker, Headquarters, 425 Battery, 107th RHA

Whittaker was an excellent amateur cartoonist, whose latest comic offerings[17] were eagerly awaited by many of the men in 425 Battery.

If there was something on the news of something had happened in the day, I'd draw a little cartoon. One of my favourites was Major Birkin appeared in the morning with his solar topee[18] on – the 1st May was the authorised time for putting on your topee. Who the heck would bring a topee up the desert – but he'd got his on! He had a puggaree round it with a South Notts flash on it. In an instant I drew this picture of a topee and a big moustache underneath and simply put 'Prelude to summer' with a little jerboa in the corner saying. 'Does he know one topee doesn't make a summer?' He called me over later, he said, 'Outside, Whittaker!' He just said, 'Watch it!' So, I said, 'Yes, Sir!' and watched it. Eventually I got quite a pack of cartoons and they took them down to show General Morshead,[19] who wrote a little note saying it was good for morale.[20]

Gunner Ted Whittaker, Headquarters, 425 Battery, 107th RHA

The men lived in their gun pits, shallow dugouts, caves, or the former Italian concrete emplacements. One problem, familiar from their months at Mersa Matruh, soon made an unwelcome reappearance.

I just couldn't stand the dugouts. They were so full of fleas. If there was a flea on you and I stood next to you it would jump off you on to me. They love me fleas do. Some people would have fleas crawling over them and it just itched them, but the fleas didn't bite them, or they weren't allergic to them. But if a flea bit me, I used to come up with a great big bump. I used to sleep outside – I was more terrified of fleas than I was of bombs.[21]

Gunner Bill Hutton, Headquarters, 425 Battery, 107th RHA

One liquid that that seemed relatively available was petrol, brought in at great risk by the supply ship convoys from Egypt, and Ernie Hurry remembered a highly dangerous method of dealing with the dugout fleas.

We used to put a lot of petrol on the floor – scattered on the floor – to kill these sand fleas. We were playing cards, when somebody lit a cigarette and threw the match on the floor. All of a sudden, there was a 'BANG!' It didn't set fire – it exploded!

I wasn't the first out through the door, but I was second. When Penny (Penlington) came out he'd got no eyebrows. He looked ever so funny! He said, 'What silly bugger struck a match!'[22]

Gunner Ernie Hurry, B Troop, 425 Battery, 107th RHA

The men also used petrol to try to get rid of pests from their clothes.

Your clothes do get these lice in them and we used to get a half a petrol tin, put petrol in it and soak your overalls, or shirt, in petrol. You'd then put that over a low petrol fire, so that the petrol heated up and that seemed to get rid of these lice. Then you let your shirt dry out and washed it in such water as you could get! It sounds so ridiculous now![23]

Sergeant George Pearson, B Troop, 425 Battery, 107th RHA

Every so often they were plagued by the dreaded sandstorms, which created a veritable hell on earth.

You saw the sandstorm coming along. It just looked like one red mass in the air, blotting out the sun and everything. The sand would hit you so hard that it would even make your skin bleed. We used to dress ourselves up and looked like these cowboys with scarfs over our faces – all you could see was a little bit of two eyes. Of course, your ears all got bunged up and goodness knows what else! The only consolation was that there was never any firing done in a sandstorm.[24]

Bombardier Harold Harper, D Troop, 426 Battery, 107th RHA

People were often filthy. All told, the combination of dust and sand-storms, the prevailing winds and the blistering heat in summer, made for an uncomfortable environment that drained morale.

You couldn't get away from the dust storms – the grime round your eyes, your mouth, your nose. You had a sort of yashmak

covering you tried to fix up. The khamsin, the hot blast of
wind, means you're sweating like fury. The dust, the filth in the
atmosphere sticking to your sweat, you can't move your eyelids,
you try to breathe, you can't blow your nose.[25]

Sergeant Fred Langford, Headquarters, 425 Battery, 107th RHA

Generally, the men looked awful. Some officers, such as Bill
Pringle, may have tried to maintain personal and sartorial standards, but there is plenty of anecdotal and pictorial evidence
that most of the men let themselves go.

I used to wear a pair of shorts, no shirt, no socks, leather army
boots! I once spent three months without a wash, or shave, or
haircut! Apart from dipping my fingers into a bit of water and
just wiping my eyes out. Nothing to clean your teeth with.[26]

Gunner Ted Holmes, A Troop, 425 Battery, 107th RHA

Just to add insult to injury, the nights were often bitterly cold.
The men had to switch from wearing next to nothing to a greatcoat at night.

Where available, the men used the thunderbox trench latrines,
but often they went off alone into the desert to 'do their business'.
Yet they still took care to cover their 'tracks' as best they could.

You usually waited until dark, took a shovel and walked away
until you found an empty area. You did whatever you had to
do – and covered it over again. The men knew that they had to
cover their excreta because of the flies. You lived with the flies
all around your mouth and up your nose. The very thought that
those flies might have been in somebody's excreta made them
really keen, so they did cover over.[27]

Sergeant Ian Sinclair, A Troop, 425 Battery, 107th RHA

Dysentery and various forms of diarrhoea were a very real
danger; after all, these had all but crippled whole British armies

during the Gallipoli and Mesopotamia campaigns of the Great War. Such ailments could reduce men to mere shadows of themselves in a matter of days.

> This was something we learned in the early stages – flies cause dysentery. There was nothing you could do about them. To eat a slice of bread and jam was a nightmare. You'd swat the flies off and in the split second between swatting them off and getting the jam in your mouth, you'd have another couple of flies in your mouth. I had dysentery, but not quite as bad as some poor devils. I recall one very, very strong sergeant major crawling from his dugout on his hands and knees, trying to get to the troop latrine and leaving a trail behind him all the way. He was taken away and we never saw him for about six months, but he recovered.[28]
>
> Bombardier Harold Harper, D Troop, 426 Battery, 107th RHA

The lack of water severely restricted opportunities to wash hands properly, and this poor hygiene further promoted the spread of disease.

> You'd got no means of cleaning yourself. A lot of us had diarrhoea, what we called Gippy tummy. You'd only got to cough sometimes – and it shot out of your backside – like water.[29]
>
> Gunner Ted Holmes, A Troop, 425 Battery, 107th RHA

The problem was that there were just so many men packed into a relatively small area, surrounded by millions of flies buzzing about.

> Everything was black with flies – big black flies. Not surprising when you realise that in a small portion of desert there were thousands of men using shallow latrines! Dead bodies all over the place! Eating and drinking was a great problem – anyone

who has not witnessed it would find it very hard to believe the number of flies that were there. It was such that if you were drinking say a mug of tea, you had to drink it with your right hand holding the mug and your left hand waving continually over the top of the mug, otherwise the whole thing would have been black with flies. And even so you were lucky to be able to drink a mug of tea without at least ten flies drowning themselves in it as you drank.[30]

Bombardier Ray Ellis, A Troop, 425 Battery, 107th RHA

There was also an increasing problem with jaundice, especially during the later stages of the siege, as the poor diet took its toll. One who fell victim was Bill Hutton.

I started to feel ill and every time I ate anything, I just threw it up! I kept being sick and this sort of very bitter, biley, colourless stuff came into my mouth. It was terrible. I had a camp bed and I was lying out in the open. If there was an air raid, I just used to roll off this bed and just lie there – then I hadn't got the strength to get up and get back on to the bed. Finnegan had a tough time because a lot of people were pretending to be ill to get out. He came to see me and didn't reckon there was a deal wrong with me and left me. A couple of days later, 'Max' Miller came and looked at me and I'd gone yellow, like a banana, and my eyes were yellow. So, he went back and fetched the doctor. As soon as he saw me, he had me taken straight down to a hospital place in Tobruk. All I was having up to then was tea, with condensed milk and sugar in it, and bully beef. Well you just spew it up straight away. But with jaundice if you're on the right sort of food, like chicken broth, you don't spew it up. As soon as I got down there and they changed my diet, I didn't feel so terrible.[31]

Gunner Bill Hutton, Headquarters, 425 Battery, 107th RHA

Hutton was eventually evacuated on a destroyer to hospital in Alexandria and would not return for several months. Bob Hingston also began to feel terrible.

The army medical people regarded it seriously and several of the men got slight 'goes' of it and they were promptly evacuated to base. That was apparently the orders. Then the job was getting them back again! I know one of our men, but he was very annoyed because when he was better, he was sent off to some other regiment. I got this jaundice and I didn't know what it was – I wasn't feeling very well. I was lying down in my dugout down at the troop position. When I went to get to pee and then staggering back, I felt my legs collapsing under me and I just managed to get back to fall on to the bed. Ivor, who had seen this, came rushing up furiously worried. Then he sent for a medical orderly, Bombardier Hooper, who took my temperature. 'Yes, I think you should stay in bed, Sir!' I said, 'I can't do that!' 'I think you should, Sir! I'll give you pills.' But he was quite right, whenever I tried to get up I couldn't. So we had to send for Doc Finnegan, who diagnosed the problem straight away. 'You'd better come over the RHQ, Bob, we'll look after you there!' There was Garry Birkin, who was down [with it] at the same time. Now the poor old doctor was faced with a serious a problem! He had formed a sort of small hospital, where he dealt with these mild cases of jaundice among the men; he had not sent them back to base as he should have done, but had kept them up at Tobruk and sent them back to their batteries when they were better. Now he was faced with two officers who were much worse than anything he'd had – and he knew he ought to send us down to base, but he said he couldn't do that to the first two officers who were ill after he'd kept the men up there – because going back to base was a luxury! He was absolutely right of course! He bedded us down in an ambulance, we were lying side by side. We were awfully depressed. Eventually Gerry got very ill and he had to send him down to base – he nearly collapsed on the way down to the ship.[32]

Captain Bob Hingston, D Troop, 426 Battery, 107th RHA

Gerry Birkin was eventually evacuated back to Egypt. Hingston himself recovered and returned to resume command of D Troop.

ENDLESS DAYS AND NIGHTS IN THE DESERT. Warfare has nearly always featured occasional moments of nerve-shredding terror, interspersed with seeming eons of unrelieved tedium. This summed up the Tobruk experience as well as anything. For most of the men the only escape from the battery gun positions was when they were allowed an occasional three-day rest period at a camp in a small bay just to the west of Tobruk port.

You can imagine what the weather was like. This was summer, you didn't need tents – you just had a sleeping bag. You could get a pass for a couple of days and lie on the rocks. Dive into the most gorgeous clear seawater that was possible. It was quite tepid for the top 3 feet, but as you dived further down it got cooler and cooler until it got quite cold. It was just like eating a lovely ice cream in a way, it was delicious.[33]

Lance Sergeant John Walker, A Troop, 425 Battery, 107th RHA

Charles Laborde used to go 'fishing' with hand grenades when he was down there.

We'd all try to 'win' a Mills bomb from the Australians before we were going down. Then you pulled the pin out and tossed this Mills bomb into the water. There was duly a 'WHAM!' underneath, and a great column of water. You waited two or three minutes and then the dead fish started to come up to the surface. We then all popped into the water and picked out the best of the fish – so that we got a change of diet from the bully beef, which was very pleasant as you can imagine![34]

Lieutenant Charles Laborde, D Troop, 426 Battery, 107th RHA

However, the beach rest area was an exception. For most of the time there was nowhere to go; nothing to do. Sat in the gun pits or dugouts, the men had to make their own amusement. Conversation was important, the men chatted, told their stories, described their backgrounds, exchanged the usual manly 'banter' and talked about the war.

Women, usually the number one subject with a soldier! What was happening in the war in the rest of the world. They were always wanting to know what would happen if Hitler won – you always answered that by saying, 'He won't!'[35]

Captain William Pringle, A Troop, 425 Battery, 107th RHA

Letters from home were eagerly awaited. They were dependent on the mailboat surviving a long sea voyage via the Cape of Good Hope, which meant that the exchange of letters could be held up for several weeks.

Mother and father would write that they were all right, that everybody was happy which of course they weren't. Expressing concern and hinting that they knew where I was. I was quite a good letter writer and we had this one green letter per week or month where you were under honour not to write anything military. I wrote to a girl I'd known – she wrote back occasionally! But mostly, I wrote to my parents to let them know that I was all right, because I'd begun to realise that to the folks at home it was all more desperate than it was for us. In Tobruk we never felt in any desperate situation; there was always a tremendous spirit that we were there – we were going to stay there – and *nothing* would shift us![36]

Gunner Ted Whittaker, Headquarters, 425 Battery, 107th RHA

Men were also pleased to receive parcels from home. However, these could also be a disappointment.

I was 21 and I got a parcel that my stepfather had done up. He'd really gone to town on it, put it in sacking and sewn it up. When I got it, the cake was missing, somebody had swiped my birthday cake. Other bits and bobs were in there, but somebody down at the base had pinched me cake. There was me sticking me neck out up the desert and there's people down in Cairo pinching all our stuff.[37]

Lance Bombardier Albert Swinton, D Troop, 426 Battery, 107th RHA

Robert Daniell had a different sort of parcel, one despatched from Cairo by subterfuge, which was clever but somewhat unscrupulous, as it was taking up space on the naval ships running the gauntlet to Tobruk. Not a serious amount of space, but symptomatic of the special treatment and sense of entitlement that could grate on the sensibilities of others forced to follow the rules.

On the four dark nights of the month, they ran the gauntlet from Alexandria bringing letters, ammunition and a few reinforcements. The destroyer only stayed in the harbour for twenty minutes – on one side the wounded were slung aboard, while on the other, boxes of all sorts were sent down a shute into small boats. I was lucky, I had met several of their commanders in Alexandria. They invariably brought with them a sealed 2-gallon tin, filled with welcome whisky, food and clean clothes, carefully packed by my wife and clearly marked 'Nails of all sizes' to delude the wandering Australians. I only lost one to a looter.[38]

Major Robert Daniell, Headquarters, 107th RHA

The men craved news from outside. The signallers would always have their set tuned to the regimental network, but many had managed to get a spare wireless for their own recreation. Music programmes broadcast from Cairo were popular, but more so, perversely, was the sneering drawl of William Joyce, an Irish-American, broadcasting as 'Lord Haw-Haw' on the *Germany Calling* propaganda programme. Joyce often included details omitted from the British official BBC reports, which were understandably economical with any information revealed.

We'd listen to the wireless at night and pass the news round to the troops. For instance, the BBC announced one night, 'A Midlands town has been heavily bombed, some casualties.' We switched to 'Lord Haw Haw' and he said, 'Good evening South Notts Hussars, as you've heard Nottingham has been obliterated tonight.' Often, he was more informative than the BBC! Once he said, 'Good evening South Notts Hussars! Have you said good morning to the Luftwaffe?'[39]

Gunner Ted Whittaker, Headquarters, 425 Battery, 107th RHA

The intent was to demoralise, but the obvious lies and propaganda also provoked derision or amusement.

We used to listen to 'Lord Haw Haw', we used to have a good laugh about him! In one particular case he was on about a big battle taking place out in the Mediterranean. His aircraft had sunk our ships and shot down our planes – and he played a record, 'How deep is the ocean; how high is the sky!' He used to call us the 'Rats of Tobruk'. He would say, 'Good morning, "Rats of Tobruk". Have you said, "Good Morning" to your air force? Oh, I beg your pardon, don't worry, ours will be over to visit you soon!' We used to think it was very humorous! We didn't believe him – I can honestly say that when things got really tough, I can put my hand on heart and say that we never, ever thought we would lose.[40]

Bombardier Dennis Mayoh, D Troop, 426 Battery, 107th RHA

There was one form of pernicious propaganda that sometimes hit home with soldiers far from home.

The only effect I can ever remember of German propaganda getting through to certain members of the battery was the lady[41] who originally sang 'Lili Marlene'. She used to call us the 'self-contained prisoners of Tobruk' and this seductive voice would say, 'Of course, while you are here and slaving away, your girlfriends and your wives are enjoying life back in England.' Occasionally you would get a bloke who would say, 'I haven't heard from my wife for six months!' And it would get through to him that way.[42]

Bombardier Harold Harper, D Troop, 426 Battery, 107th RHA

For a few, religion offered some solace and Padre H. Parry was keen to hold church services. Parry was a short, chubby figure who looked rather like a country parson. He was popular with the men as he was blessed with a friendly nature and always 'on the move' visiting the gun positions. Many may not have appreciated his religion, but they enjoyed his company. He also had a reputation of never flinching from the grim realities of war, by supervising the burial of bodies – and bits of bodies. They knew he would also write letters to the bereaved families back home.

Padre Parry came to me and he asked if he could have a church session. I said, 'No, not under any circumstances can you have a collection of men in the evening which could be dive-bombed and lose casualties. But what you can do is walk about until you can find a large cave. If you can find that you can certainly hold any religious functions that you wish! He found a bier – where they used to keep the corn. A large bier dug by hand, and when the corn was ripe, they filled this with corn, and they put a large stone at the top so that nobody else could know where it was. He found one in Tobruk and we held Sunday services and Communion. He was extremely well liked and admired enormously. Because he was always first in any place where action was taking place and men were dying.[43]

Major Robert Daniell, Headquarters, 107th RHA

The padre himself did not reciprocate Daniell's high regard, and many officers very much appreciated Parry's irreverent – *sotto voce* – habit of calling this august figure 'Gunner Daniell'.

Reading was a popular pastime with many of the men, but the problem was a shortage of books. Ray Ellis came up with a pragmatic solution that also filled up some of his spare time.

I borrowed a 15cwt truck and went all around the regiment scrounging books. In the end I got quite a collection and I made a 'library' in my dugout on the gun position. I'd got 200 or 300 books and made shelves in the dugout and put them up. I used to have library periods during the day when men could come and change their library books. I went to a lot of trouble documenting the books, got men's names and filled in the library system and they'd come and change their books.[44]

Bombardier Ray Ellis, A Troop, 425 Battery, 107th RHA

Cards was a great method of whiling away the hours. Of course, many played the old favourite gambling games, betting for cigarettes and such, but there was a refined school of thought that favoured the more aesthetic skills of contract bridge.

Sergeant Pat Bland taught us bridge; his family were county bridge players. Bridge proved to be a magnificent mental therapy. We would play for hours, learning the 'alphabet' of bridge. Pat was a very strong-minded young man, 'Now, you are here to learn!' We learnt! And he would tell us off horribly if we made silly mistakes! It drilled it in![45]

Lance Sergeant John Walker, A Troop, 425 Battery, 107th RHA

Others sought to try to keep up their physical fitness by sparring with the pre-war boxer Tommy Foley.

He used to take one after the other of us on and lightly touch us for a round at a time to keep himself fit. As many as twelve or fifteen people would put up their fists against him for one round – and he would never stop. You had to try and hit him, but he never really hit you. The only way you could ever get Tommy down was to tickle him, he used to laugh like mad; he couldn't stand being tickled![46]

Lance Sergeant John Walker, A Troop, 425 Battery, 107th RHA

In recording the interviews, one of my favourite sections was always the more esoteric pastimes that the men evolved to alleviate the boredom.

Bill Barker, he organised himself a garden. Sounds a bit stupid I know! He was a very keen gardener in civvy life. He'd go round the desert, got little bits of scrub and planted them into this little patch. Any spare water, with tea leaves, he'd go and water his garden! He was a great fisherman too and he'd sit there for hours with a bit of stick casting – as though he was fishing. Everybody said he was puddled – he wasn't – but it makes you think![47]

Lance Bombardier Albert Swinton, D Troop, 426 Battery, 107th RHA

Ray Ellis and his pals were particularly daft. At times I could hardly believe what he was telling me!

> We sometimes played cowboys and Indians from the films we'd grown up with – schoolboy games around the gun pits! Once we were doing this and I was an Indian with a stick, which was supposed to be a tomahawk. This is ridiculous – this is men in action! Jim Hardy, the sergeant major, was a cowboy. He came charging up and, in the excitement of the thing, he forgot, drew his revolver and fired and nearly put a bullet through me! That sobered us down a bit![48]
>
> Bombardier Ray Ellis, A Troop, 425 Battery, 107th RHA

They also formed a lodge which they named the 'Noble Antediluvian and Most Noble Order of Jerboas' after the local desert rats. Like the real-life Masons, their activities ranged from amusingly eccentric to downright strange.

> We would all sit round and 'The Lodge is now in session!' When in session we were not allowed to laugh, you had to keep your face straight. You had to sing the Lodge anthem. It was a song from the Boer War and the words went like this, '*The Boers have got my Dad they have, My soldier Daddy*'. We changed it to:
>
> *The whores have got my Dad they have*
> *My soldier Daddy*
> *I don't like to see my Mummy sigh*
> *I don't like to see my Mummy cry*
> *I'm going across the ocean on a big ship*
> *I'm going to fight the whores I am*
> *And bring my Daddy safely home!*
>
> You had to sing this without laughing! It was so bloody ridiculous. A lot of hairy-arsed gunners sitting round in a circle

singing these stupid little childish songs! If you laughed, you had to pay a forfeit, and these were pretty terrible! You might have to piss in your boot or take out your penis and allow one member of the team to lash it three times with a bootlace! Horrific things! While this was taking place everybody could laugh, but when the punishment had taken place, Jim Hardy, who was usually in charge, would say, 'Calling the Lodge to order!' and you'd have to somehow take any smile off your face. Of course, you couldn't![49]

Bombardier Ray Ellis, A Troop, 425 Battery, 107th RHA

But for me the most surrealistic of all the pastimes was that revealed by Charles Ward. I almost choked trying to suppress the laughter that would have ruined the tape recording.

In front of the gun position there was a knocked out Italian tank. One day, we went forward to it and we levered off the turret – and there was 200 or 300 ball bearings. We confiscated these and set up a marbles league! In the charge cases there was a cardboard cup about 2 inches in diameter and about 1½ inches deep. We used to set these out into the desert and scrape a board along so that all the sand was level like a miniature golf course. We'd flick these ball bearings into these various cups. One day the colonel came along – and there was all his troop on their hands and knees flicking these ball bearings about! He said, 'Most intriguing! What's happening?' We told him and he said, 'Oh! Can I have a go?' And there was the colonel on his hands and knees playing marbles with us![50]

Lance Bombardier Albert Swinton, D Troop, 426 Battery, 107th RHA

Try as they might, the combination of boredom, fear and tension caused men to get tetchy with each other. Transgressions that might have been tolerated. or not even noticed in better circumstances, could become flashpoints to serious rows or even fights.

We were getting bloody fed up of standing around doing nothing! 'Taffy' Stanway and I were arguing about gun-laying or something like that! He turned round and said, 'Right, I'll knock your bloody block off!!' I said, 'All right! You just try it! The best thing to do is get the gloves and we'll have a box!' We did! There was Sammy Hall, 'Spraggy' Cooper, Sergeant Inger – we were all there! No refereeing, just kept going! I gave him a good hiding – you see with me being small and him a bit taller than me, he thought he could take the rattle out of us! But I showed him that a little man can beat a big man – and fetch him down! I knocked him out! It came and went![51]

Gunner George Loyley, A Troop, 425 Battery, 107th RHA

The men gradually got over the disappointment of the failure of Operation Battleaxe, but as the interminable months wore on, and summer turned to autumn, their morale began to fade again.

By the time it got to October, and there were no signs at all of another attempt to relieve us, gradually the accumulative effect of all the bombing and shelling tended to get you down. Although I can't remember anybody becoming what we called 'bomb happy', there were signs of a certain amount of tenseness. I felt twitchy, my nerves a bit on edge. The tendency was to run for a slit trench rather than walk there. I think there were certain people 'worked their ticket' to get back. One or two of them simulated certain illnesses that were difficult to detect and got evacuated: stomach disorders, bowel complaints, fever – that sort of thing. It was never proved, so we never bothered about it. It didn't affect us.[52]

Battery Quartermaster Sergeant Charles Ward, Headquarters, 426 Battery, 107th RHA

It was not unnatural for many of the better-educated, or OTC-trained men to start to wonder whether they could be doing more for their country than sitting in the desert for months on end. However, the continued apparent unwillingness of Lieutenant Colonel Bill Seely to sanction his better NCOs going forward for a commission was a serious frustration.

> If ever there was any resentment, it was because we reckoned we ought to have been sent to be officers, because of the way that we had done our work – and knowing that they must be needing them. Several of us felt that we had been passed over because we had spent all that time in Mersa Matruh and Tobruk and nobody knew anything at all about us. We found out that we were being kept in the regiment because of the feeling by the colonel and the officers that they didn't want to lose anybody – wanted it kept as a family. They kept sending 'nil' reports in for people for Officer Cadet Training Units. We kept hearing of other people going, but nobody from South Notts ever went! Eventually they were detailed at RHQ that they would send somebody: 'This regiment of yours, that is supposed to be so bloody wonderful, how is it that you have no officer material?' Well of course we had, we'd got lots and lots of officer material – and Bill Seely didn't want to lose us![53]
>
> Sergeant Ian Sinclair, A Troop, 425 Battery, 107th RHA

This rather changed the focus of the senior officers in the regiment, and at last they began to encourage the 'right sort' of people to apply for commissions.

> Really the three of us, Bob Foulds, Dennis Middleton and myself, we were very reluctant to leave the unit. But we were promptly told by our battery commander, Major Peter Birkin, that officers were in short supply and artillery officers were even shorter in supply. He thought we were sufficiently equipped

to pass the course and it was our duty to go and get on with it. We were taken to be interviewed by the brigadier and General Morshead, the Australian commander of the Tobruk garrison – who approved us. They had your history – our powers of leadership such as they were and your gunnery knowledge such as it was had already been assessed by your unit – it was more or less a formality that the general would support the application going forward.[54]

Sergeant George Pearson, B Troop, 425 Battery, 107th RHA

They would eventually leave to attend the course at the Middle East Officers' Cadet Training Unit at Kasir el Nir Barracks and Royal Artillery Base Depot at Almaza in January 1942. Ian Sinclair was upset not to be chosen in this tranche, but he would follow later. Other NCOs selected at this time were Troop Sergeant Major Claude Earnshaw and Bombardier Herbert Bonnello. There proved to be a problem with Earnshaw, who had a strong Nottinghamshire accent. Before going off, he had been deeply concerned that he might not 'fit in' to the officers' mess.

I was sitting talking to him and he was worried about this, 'I don't think I ought to go there, Sir! I don't think I'm up to it!' I said, 'Damn it all, Earnshaw, you can do the job as a second lieutenant on your head – you know it all!' 'Ah, but I don't talk like an officer!' I said – and I believed it! – 'I don't think that matters now – I quite agree it would have a few years back, but now I don't think that will matter at all!' He said, 'I hope you're right, Sir!' He went with Bonnello, but after a bit he was returned to unit (RTU). When the end of the course came, they were asked for comments and an Australian said, 'Aye, yes I've got a comment, you RTU'd the best man on the course, Mr

Earnshaw!' It upset him rather badly, I think. That was a thing I was very angry about! He would have been a good officer.[55]

Captain Bob Hingston, D Troop, 426 Battery, 107th RHA

IT WASN'T JUST BOREDOM. Although there were long periods of tedium, people still died. Ray Ellis spent much time thinking about death and survival. How one man could be 'selected' for a random death, while others are unscathed not feet away.

You looked for all sorts of omens – I can remember looking for omens in the sky – shapes of clouds which would suggest good things. Your mind was involved in this sort of thing. But I never thought of being killed – it was always the other man who was going to die! You had this feeling that, yes, you would survive. Really at the back of your mind you realised you were kidding yourself.[56]

Bombardier Ray Ellis, A Troop, 425 Battery, 107th RHA

Not everyone could cope, and Ellis was adamant that one NCO in his troop had 'earned his ticket' by pretending to be going mad. Their attitude to cowardice was very mixed: they had all felt apprehension, they knew they would feel it again, but they never the less had contempt for those who gave way to their fears.

We all lost our nerve sometimes. Even if he didn't run, he wished he could! We understood. There was a lot of bravado, but we all knew that we were pretending, we all knew that each other were frightened. If a man broke for a few moments, you sort of forgot it – you didn't notice it because you knew he'd been all right till then – and he'd be all right again. Anyone who was really cowardly, he was out. We had no pity for people who couldn't sustain their courage.[57]

Bombardier Ray Ellis, A Troop, 425 Battery, 107th RHA

Some men could cope with bombing, but hated shellfire; others were the reverse. George Pearson remembered one bad case.

I had one gunner in my sub-section he'd only got to hear the drone of an aeroplane and he would get fidgety. If it became obvious that you were going to be bombed, he would just rush madly around. We just used to knock his feet from under him and a couple of us would lie on him. It was just a sheer panic that it set off in him. You might say, 'Oh he's not a very good chap to have in a gun crew!' But when we were being fired on by shellfire it didn't bother him a bit! He was a loader and he happily went on loading – not a bit bothered! To me it was far more dangerous to be engaged by the enemy artillery because once they've got your range, they can drop shells on you all day, whereas an aeroplane comes, it drops its load of bombs and it's got to go off and load up again.[58]

Sergeant George Pearson, B Troop, 425 Battery, 107th RHA

In the end morale is a very complicated business. Different men respond in different fashions to different threats, different situations. Some were capable of great heroism in short bursts, but found their courage worn down by the length of the siege. Some became ill and found that to be the final straw. It was difficult to be brave if you had dysentery or jaundice. Boredom undermined their convictions: the endless routine, the same dugout, same people, same food and same 'bloody Germans' tormenting them. It almost seemed that if only the siege would end, then everything would be all right again.

10

BREAKOUT FROM TOBRUK

Suddenly, in the still of the morning, the wail of the bagpipes as the piper started up. There was about half a minute, a minute, no more than that, and then everything opened up and of course you couldn't hear anything more. They started to go forward. As soon as the guns started to fire, the clouds of smoke and dust – it was just like a thick fog – you couldn't see anything at all![1]

Lieutenant Charles Laborde, D Troop, 426 Battery, 107th RHA

WHETHER THEY APPRECIATED IT OR NOT, from the moment Tobruk was besieged planning was under way for the garrison's relief. But the campaign in the Western Desert was not waged in isolation to the rest of the war. On 22 June 1941, Hitler had ordered the invasion of the USSR. At a stroke, North Africa became a secondary front. The great questions would now be asked – and answered – on the Eastern Front. But, sideshow or not, the defence of Egypt was still a priority to the British Empire. The new Middle East Commander in Chief, General Sir Claude Auchinleck, was charged with hurling back Rommel. Like Wavell before him, Auchinleck judged that the forces at his command were far too weak and inexperienced to allow for any chances of an immediate successful attack. This was particularly the case as Rommel's 5th Light Division had been upgraded to become the 21st Panzer Division, while in addition the 15th Panzer Division had arrived in North Africa. Together they were the Deutsches Afrika Korps. Auchinleck therefore demanded not only more reinforcements, but also the time to train them under desert conditions. This would be a recurring theme of his period of command. After a vigorous row with Churchill, in which Auchinleck stood his ground, it was decided that the relieving offensive would now start in early November.

By August 1941, only one German and three Italian divisions were around Tobruk; the rest had moved up to the Egyptian border. Every so often one side or the other would launch a minor attack, seeking to improve their tactical position, but little was achieved. One big change for the South Notts Hussars came in August when they were 'separated' from the 1st RHA, who moved to take on the central southern section, while the 107th RHA were assigned the east sector on the left of the perimeter.

In the later months there was an emphasis on moving guns forward to carry out harassing fire. The 51st Field RA had been re-equipped and their old 4.5-inch howitzers had been used to form a makeshift third troop in 425 Battery. This was placed under the command of Sergeant Ian Sinclair and granted the nickname of 'Glamour Troop' in an amusing recognition of his dashing good looks.

> I was sent up with our 'Glamour Troop' to a forward position. We had four spare guns: 4.5-inch gun howitzers we took only skeleton gun crews – three or four men per gun. We went up, well forward, within 1,000 metres of the wire, and took up position with these guns and fired regularly – for no good reason! We were only in touch with the command post and we were told to fire on a certain line because they thought there was a target there. We'd get an order: 'Righto, fire five rounds

of gunfire at five minutes past ten on this line!' but nobody was observing for us. We fired about ten rounds per gun per day. There was no urgency about it – it was a nuisance value. The whole idea was to make the enemy think that we had a damn sight more guns than we had.[2]

Sergeant Ian Sinclair, A Troop, 425 Battery, 107th RHA

On 17 October, a memorable, but horrific, incident occurred at the 40-foot scaffolding tower where Bob Hingston, now recovered from jaundice, was engaged in his usual OP duties.

I went up to the OP and we had a squadron of King's Dragoon Guards – armoured cars that had been swept into the fortress. An officer called out to me, 'Can I come up there? Whenever I appear on top of the ridge in front of us, I get shelled off it.' I said, 'Yes, come along up – a bit of company would be very nice.' Lieutenant Weaver turned out to be a very nice chap. An ardent politician – he was a Conservative – he was talking about his political career in a rather more pleasant way than most politicians talk. He was telling comic stories about it, which were really very funny. We were having quite a good time when, for some reason or other, the Germans decided they didn't like us up there and a battery opened up on us. That gunner, I hand it to him, he knew his job. He landed a shell short of us and then another over us. I remember remarking in a rather tight voice, with a rather dry mouth, 'Damn, they've bracketed us!' Then he landed two shells right at the base of the tower. Weaver looked at me and said, 'Should we get down?' I said, 'I don't think so, I think it's very unlikely he'd ever hit us up here and these things can stand an awful lot of battering around. They might see you getting down and then promptly land one on the ground just as you get there!' I'm sorry I made that decision. Hardly had I done so, than they got a direct hit

on this arm that was sticking out holding a [camouflage] net.
There was a roar, it wasn't a bang, it was more of a roar in my
ear. And something hit my right leg like a stone. The silly things
one does – I remember shouting out to the world at large,
'That's buggered me!' Then I looked to Weaver[3] and there he
was sitting beside me with the top of his head blown off! I was
splattered with blood and everything.[4]

Captain Bob Hingston, D Troop, 426 Battery, 107th RHA

Hingston had been badly wounded in the thigh of his right leg.
One of his men climbed up with a first field dressing to stem
the bleeding. Luckily, the Germans had stopped firing. Weaver's
corpse was covered over with a waterproof. Hingston was in no
great pain but his leg was useless and there was a real problem in
working out how to get him down, until some practical Australian infantrymen took a hand.

Two Australians came up the ladder with a roll of telephone
wire. They said, 'Could you manage to climb down the ladder,
if we tie this round and we can hold you a bit?' Well, my old
mountaineering ability – I knew how to tie a knot round
me that wouldn't slip! They paid out the 'rope' and I sort of
hopped down a step at a time holding on with both hands –
and got down to the bottom. The next person to arrive was
Battery Captain Freddie Porter – he was looking after his
equipment! 'Ah, Bob, I'm sorry to hear this, awful bad luck!
Can I have your revolver and your binoculars' – he knew I had
an issue revolver and binoculars! A thoroughly efficient bloke![5]

Captain Bob Hingston, D Troop, 426 Battery, 107th RHA

There were multiple witnesses to what happened to Hingston,
but in view of contradictions that appear between the testimony
of Major Robert Daniell and other witnesses in various key incidents in our overall story, it is perhaps appropriate also to give

Daniell's account of this incident to illustrate why I have tended to be wary of using his version of events. With personal experience accounts we must take into consideration likelihood and corroboration in deciding what probably took place. It is by no means a precise business working out exactly what happened eighty years ago.

> One day Captain Hingston was up in the tower and a young cavalry officer, who got stranded in Tobruk and was bored to tears, asked me if he could go and spend the day up in this tower and see what he could see. I said, 'Certainly!' It happened that the Italians opened fire on the tower and for the first time they hit the arm that was holding the camouflage net, snapped it off, and it took the head off the cavalry officer. He was left lying next to Hingston, on the platform at the top, which was not very big. I got a telephone message to tell me that this had happened. I got on the phone to Hingston and told him to come down off the tower. He said he couldn't move because he was so shocked with the body of this man next to him – he wasn't touched. I said, 'I'll come and get you down!' I went there and climbed up to the top of the tower, I kicked the decapitated corpse off the top, Hingston was sick – and then I said, 'You've got to come down!' He said, 'I can't move!' I said, 'Don't be an idiot! You slide over my back, put your arms round my neck and I'll bring you down' – which I did![6]

Major Robert Daniell, Headquarters, 107th RHA

I would merely point out that Hingston *was* badly wounded. He was taken to the Australian regimental aid post then back to the Tobruk Hospital. He remembered the voyage aboard HMS *Kandahar* to Alexandria.

> In the evening it was deadly quiet. We were all carried out, fifty or so I should think, and laid on a sort of raft, tied alongside

some very aged paddle steamer. We lay there for a bit. It was rather nerve-racking lying there quite helpless. At intervals you would see gun flashes from around the perimeter and hope, 'Oh my God, I hope that's not coming this way!' One's ear was cocked for bombers! Nothing happened. A voice said, 'Won't be long, we're just going to start the engine!' The most appalling crashes and bangs occurred, and a frightfully noisy engine started up in this ghastly old tub! We were manoeuvred out, I glanced to my left and there was a destroyer. The whole thing was beautifully organised, there were lashings of men heaving up the stretchers. There were two burly matelots on the deck of the destroyer and as each stretcher was pushed up towards them, they seized it and passed it on to a chain of men who carted it off. Incredibly quickly we were moved up into the destroyer, HMS *Kandahar*. On the other side of the ship they'd heaved off all the ammunition and supplies they'd brought up; then they were out again. The orders were they were not to stay in Tobruk longer than absolutely necessary because it was bombed so much![7]

Captain Bob Hingston, D Troop, 426 Battery, 107th RHA

His leg proved to be badly injured, requiring several operations to reconnect the nerves. Ultimately, his medical category was downgraded and his active service was over.

BY OCTOBER, the Tobruk garrison had radically changed. Australian senior commanders and politicians were insistent that the Australian formations should be concentrated and deployed as a single force. Churchill grudgingly acquiesced to this, and consequently the 9th Australian Division began to be withdrawn in stages from Tobruk by sea. They were replaced by the 70th Division, commanded by Major General Robert

Scobie, who also took over from Morshead in overall charge of the garrison. Among the new units to arrive were the 1st Polish Carpathian Brigade in August 1941; the 16th Brigade and elements of the 32rd Army Tank Brigade in September; and finally the 14th and 23rd Brigades in October. By 25 October over 47,000 men had been evacuated, replaced by some 34,000 men, which represented another sterling effort by the Royal Navy. The replacements had the advantage of being fresher, not ground down as their predecessors had been by six months in the Tobruk trenches. The Tobruk artillery was also reinforced by the arrival of the 144th Field RA and the 149th Anti-Tank RA. Only the 107th RHA, accompanied by the 1st RHA, the 104th RHA, the 1st Royal Northumberland Fusiliers and the 2/15th Australian Infantry Battalion (left behind when they ran out of moonless nights suitable to evacuate them) would serve through the whole of the siege of Tobruk.

One might have thought that, of all these reinforcements, the Polish soldiers would cause most linguistic incomprehension, but one delightful – possibly apocryphal – story has a different perspective. Jack Sykes was out carrying out his signalling duties when he got quite a shock.

> We were repairing this wire and these blokes came over the cliff and I could hear them talking and I thought, 'Christ!' I couldn't understand them hardly and I thought they were bloody Germans! It frightened the life out of me! It turned out they were Durham Light Infantry – you know how they talk, 'Wye aye, lad!' and all that![8]
>
> Sergeant Jack Sykes, Headquarters, 426 Battery, 107th RHA

He had indeed encountered some of the 1st Durham Light Infantry, part of the newly arrived 23rd Brigade.

Auchinleck was acutely aware that Churchill still required the relief of Tobruk as a matter of urgency. After the arrival of more reinforcements and some months of preparation, on 18 November he felt able to commit his newly formed Eighth Army (General Alan Cunningham) to the offensive. Ironically, he would thereby beat the Germans to the punch and thwart the Afrika Korps offensive against Tobruk, planned by Rommel for a week later. Cunningham's forces consisted of XXX Corps (7th Armoured Division, 1st South African Division) and XIII Corps (New Zealand Division, 4th Indian Division and 1st Army Tank Brigade).

Auchinleck's overall intention with Operation Crusader was to drive the Axis forces away from the Suez Canal, and thereby remove the threat to Egypt. He envisioned two distinct phases: first, destroying the Axis forces in eastern Cyrenaica, and second, pushing forward and occupying Tripolitania. On 18 November, the XIII Corps were to launch an attack at Sidi Omar, looking to push north behind the German defensive lines; while the XXX Corps would push right round Rommel's southern flank, to seek out and destroy the German armoured units in the Gabr Saleh sector. They would then move forward in conjunction with a breakout from the Tobruk garrison to capture the Sidi Rezegh and Ed Duda Ridges which lay to the south-east of Tobruk. The South Notts Hussars' role was to cover the attack launched by the 70th Division against the 25th Infantry Division (Bologna), pushing out to the south-east from the perimeter towards the El Duda Ridge some 11 miles away. Here it was hoped they would rendezvous with the tanks of XXX Corps.

Intensive briefings were conducted for the Tobruk garrison officers with the aid of a detailed sand-table model. The plans were then disseminated in accordance with the expressed intention of Major General Robert Scobie that everyone should be told the outline of the plan and the specifics of their personal role within the greater scheme of things. Ted Whittaker found himself playing a part in this 'trickle down' of information.

I learnt a great deal because Major Birkin spent a lot of time telling me what he hoped for from the battery. His great aim was that ideally everybody could do everybody else's job and you'd be a team. He explained this in great detail to me and he expected me to go round and chat to the men on the gun positions and tell them what we were going to do, putting them in the picture.[9]

Lance Bombardier Ted Whittaker, Headquarters, 425 Battery, 107th RHA

In brief, 425 Battery was to support the advance of 32nd Armoured Brigade and the 2nd Black Watch as they burst out of the fortress to take by surprise the strongpoint 'Tiger'. Meanwhile the 426 Battery was to fire its first barrage from outside the fortress perimeter minefields and would then support the attack by the 1st Bedfordshire and Hertfordshire Regiment and 1st Royal Tank Regiment on the 'Jack' strongpoint.

Covered by darkness at night, the gunners dug new gun positions, dumping copious forward ammunition supplies before camouflaging the results of their hard work. They also prepared the telephone cable signals trucks which would accompany the OP team in their Bren Carrier as they advanced to 'Tiger'. The idea was to get a telephone line forward as quickly as possible to supplement the less than reliable wireless communications.

We had to prepare Bombardier Keaton's vehicle, which was this soft-skinned 15cwt, which was fortified with sandbags. It was piled with sandbags inside, all round, leaving a small space in the centre on which we mounted a windlass for a reel of cable. The truck was going to go forward with the tanks, immediately behind the Black Watch, reeling out the cable behind it. Stan Keaton was given this enviable task! Peter Birkin would be in his Bren Carrier with Ted Whittaker manning the radio.[10]

Lance Sergeant Dennis Middleton, Headquarters, 425 Battery, 107th RHA

After a period of uncertainty as to the actual start date, the news arrived on 20 November that the moment had come. At 04.00 on 21 November 1941 there would be a diversionary attack towards El Adem, but the real attack would commence at 06.00. The officers and their specialist assistants set about preparing the detailed fire programmes for their guns.

> A predicted barrage is where you draw on the map where you want the barrage to fall. If it moves forward 100 yards every three minutes, you draw each line of the barrage on the map. Each gun sergeant then gets a gun programme that says every three minutes he's got to add 100 yards and go right or left so many degrees. Of course, they had to be accurate because your infantry were moving up to within 200 yards of the line shells. If you dropped shells on your own infantry, you weren't very popular.[11]
>
> Sergeant George Pearson, Headquarters, 425 Battery, 107th RHA

Ray Ellis had been promoted and had taken over Sergeant Ian Sinclair's gun in A Troop. When the programme was ready, the results were handed out to the gun sergeants.

> You were given a programme which gave the line, range, angle of sight and the times that they were to be fired. This was printed on a piece of paper which was given to the No. 1 of the gun. When the 'Zero Hour' arrived, you fired the first salvo and then you followed the programme, according to the times as they were laid down for you.[12]
>
> Lance Sergeant Ray Ellis, A Troop, 425 Battery, 107th RHA

First, they would fire on 'Butch' for eight minutes, which would cover the advance of 16th Brigade and cover the left flank of the main advance; they would switch to fire for ten minutes on the heavily mined 'Jill' Ridge; then the main barrage would fall on the two main 'Tiger' and 'Jack' strongpoints, before switching to a counter-battery role against the German batteries. Bob Foulds remembered the frenetic pace of the firing.

> We fired something like 600 rounds a gun before breakfast. That was our all-time record! We were all pretty shattered. The gun barrels were glowing red, I don't think I've ever seen them so hot. As you put the charge in and closed the breech – the gun went off – there was no question of pulling the trigger.[13]

Lance Sergeant Bob Foulds, B Troop, 425 Battery, 107th RHA

At one point David Tickle, who had helped work out the gun programme, was panicking when he thought they had got the calculations all wrong.

> They had a hue and cry from the gun positions, 'We're running out of ammunition!' I said, 'Don't be bloody silly! You can't!' I thought, 'Crikey! What have I done?' I quickly did some critical calculations through the gun programme. I thought, 'Well, the rapid rate of fire of 25-pounders was about seven a minute!' And I'd based all my calculations on that – which was the right thing to do. But the gunners thought otherwise. 'What rate are you firing at?' They didn't know – they were just putting them up – they were that enthusiastic! I calculated that they must have been firing at about ten or twelve a minute. The guns were red hot – you could have fried an egg on them. We should not have been firing that fast![14]

Bombardier David Tickle, Headquarters. 425 Battery, 107th RHA

The Black Watch had been hard at work on fitness training to minimise the time it would take to get to 'Tiger'. The mobile OP team of 425 Battery were ready and waiting to follow them.

We brewed up. Peter said, 'Now, you all know what you're going to do?', poured a rather large rum ration into all our drinks – and off we went![15]

Lance Bombardier Ted Whittaker, Headquarters, 425 Battery, 107th RHA

Frank Penlington was given the unenviable task of driving Bombardier Stan Keaton's 15cwt signals truck as it accompanied Peter Birkin's Bren Carrier. He was not happy.

We should have had a tracked vehicle! Nobody said to me, 'You're going to go with the infantry, the Black Watch, in the first wave!' Dawn hadn't broken. I was in the front on the start line. The sergeant major of the Black Watch says, 'Where's your mugs, lads?' I thought we were having tea! All the lads had got their mugs and he filled it up with rum! I sipped mine just to wet my lips, 'Anyone want this?' A soldier says, I'll have it!' I gave it to him – he had the lot – so he had two – half a pint! There was something on the bagpipes and we went forwards. Stan was in charge; we just went forward. There were three signallers in the back, reeling out the line. Going at 4 miles an hour if that – very slow! All hell blew loose! Nothing but shell bursts – black plumes! Bullets coming towards me! As we laid it out, they blew it up – it was a waste of time. Five of us risking our lives for nothing.[16]

Gunner Frank Penlington, Headquarters, 425 Battery, 107th RHA

The OP Bren Carrier passed through the gap in the barbed-wire defences, then over the tank trap which had already been filled in. Now they were in No Man's Land. Birkin was in the back of the Bren Carrier, with Ted Whittaker and the driver in front. Peter Birkin was due to rendezvous with Lieutenant Colonel George Rusk commanding the 2nd Black Watch to assess their progress and further artillery requirements.

There was the most incredible noise, I have never in my life, before or since, heard anything like it. For some minutes it was impossible. There was our barrage, people firing back, tanks, trucks. In the middle of all this, a Black Watch piper, standing there, we couldn't hear a thing, but he was stood there with these pipes! Shortly after that we met Colonel Rusk and, again, I was absolutely flabbergasted. There stands this colonel, stood there with his greatcoat, steel helmet and a proper ash walking stick with a knob on top! 'Morning, Peter!' We set off, constantly checking that we were on the right line. The tanks ran on to a minefield, so that was the tanks gone! This was horrifying because we were going to follow them. German machine guns sounded just like a piece of calico tearing, they seemed to fire ten times as fast as ours! Occasional bits of stuff hitting the sides of the Bren Carrier.[17]

Lance Bombardier Ted Whittaker, Headquarters, 425 Battery. 107th RHA

During the advance, a shell had hit the Black Watch signals truck and put it out of action. Whittaker switched to the back of the Bren Carrier and took up station on the wireless, sending messages on behalf of the 2nd Black Watch. The Scots had strayed left of their intended line of advance and had inadvertently taken 'Jack' as well as 'Tiger'.

The colonel came and said, 'Tell them I've lost 60 per cent of my chaps and I want reinforcements as soon as possible.' We had a code book and reserves were [known as] 'pigeons'. And the message said something like, 'Sixty per cent casualties, need urgent pigeons!' Within an incredibly short space of time, this regiment, who had been held in reserve, came over the hill. Colonel Rusk said, 'How the bloody hell did they get here?' I said, 'Brigade are listening to us!' Of course, it made all the difference, because it kept him up to strength.[18]

Lance Bombardier Ted Whittaker, Headquarters, 425 Battery, 107th RHA

Behind them careened the sandbagged signals lorry.

> Occasionally Stan Keaton in his truck would catch up with us, shouting and waving to us, and reeling the [telephone] line out in the middle of all this lot! The line was getting broken as fast as they laid it! There was still the odd tank and Bren Carriers going backwards and forwards, the occasional trucks picking up the wounded. We'd had to alter the barrage of course: it had all run late and we'd said, 'Fire Phase II again!' They'd asked us for extra fire on various points. These were the sort of messages I was passing. Mostly it was fixed targets – I didn't have to give any ranges or anything. Everybody was on the ball; you didn't have to go through all the rigmarole. Eventually, we arrived at this so-called strongpoint. The most miserable little selection of holes and things you've ever seen – that was 'Tiger'! I got a message just after we got there. A voice told me it was Brigade HQ and said, 'Report your position!' I very proudly said, '"Tiger", repeat, "Tiger"!'[19]

Lance Bombardier Ted Whittaker, Headquarters, 425 Battery, 107th RHA

'Tiger' had fallen at 10.15. The OP teams were by no means out of danger, as they then came under fire from the deadly multi-purpose German 88mm guns.

> These were firing at close range and after the first few shots, everyone's expression was, 'Christ almighty, what's that?' There were two bangs: the second one you heard was the gun going off. The shell was so fast, I think it was almost supersonic. You'd hear an enormous 'BANG' as the shell burst close to you, then then next 'Bang' was safe. As someone said. 'If you hear the second "Bang" you're still alive!'[20]

Lance Bombardier Ted Whittaker, Headquarters, 425 Battery, 107th RHA

Gunner Ernie Hurry was out with Bruce Meakin in another

signals 'monkey truck' when he encountered one of the other great dangers of desert warfare – mines.

> We were working our way round on the outside of the perimeter, and we ran into a minefield. Somebody happened to look down over the front, he was standing up looking over my head. We'd actually run on to this minefield! He shouted, 'Pull up!' Which I did! It was good job somebody spotted them, they were these long 'coffin' mines. You could see them! Some of the sand had moved away and they were long boxes under just about quarter of an inch of sand covering them. You could see the shape of them. We were practically halfway through it! We had to be very, very careful as to how we got out of the vehicle, because they were alongside us. They were that close! We worked our way to the front – and we thought it was too dangerous to drive off. We pushed it and manhandled the steering wheel, bit by bit, till we pushed it off.[21]

Gunner Ernie Hurry, B Troop, 425 Battery, 107th RHA

Initially, 426 Battery had a slightly quieter time as the attack by the 1st Beds and Herts was rendered somewhat redundant when the Black Watch captured the position. It soon became apparent that the 'Tugan' strongpoint which lay between them and El Duda was still strongly held and resistance began to stiffen. By the time 'Tugan' fell at 15.37 it was obvious that the 70th Division did not have the strength left to force a passage through to the El Duda Ridge.

Meanwhile, the Eighth Army push towards El Duda had stalled. The strength of the German defensive positions, together with the British failure to combine armour, infantry and artillery into one single well-directed punch, led to a sequence of isolated attacks and painful losses in the face of determined resistance, culminating in a series of counter-attacks on 21 November by the 15th and 21st Panzer Divisions on the key Sidi Rezegh Ridge.

This fighting would rage for three days. It was soon evident that the German Mark III and IV panzers still had a clear edge in firepower over the General Stuart (Honey) and Crusader Cruiser tanks – especially when backed up by the deadly batteries of 50mm Pak 38 and 88mm guns. This failure to capture El Duda Ridge left the Tobruk garrison force, including the 426 Battery, in an exposed 'corridor' strung out from Tobruk towards El Duda.

> We'd got Germans on three sides and got hammered something rotten; we were being shelled and all sorts – it was a right dodgy place – shells flying all over the place. The padre came round – and he was a big fat man – Parry. He'd got a little tiny tin hat on the top of his head and he was walking about in among all this lot saying, 'Have faith, my boys!' We used to say to him, 'Why don't you 'eff off, you silly old sod!' Anybody with any sense would have been down under the ground, but he was walking about among it, 'Have faith my boys!' You've got to admire the man – because he was a hell of a target![22]
>
> Lance Bombardier Albert Swinton, D Troop, 426 Battery, 107th RHA

Swinton was also not deaf to the religious message Padre Parry was peddling.

> You can talk to who you like but there's no atheist on the battlefield, I can say that in all sincerity. I've known blokes say, 'No, I've got no time for religion.' You put them in a battle and they're all there praying, mate. There are no atheists on a battlefield![23]
>
> Lance Bombardier Albert Swinton, D Troop, 426 Battery, 107th RHA

Exposed as they were, the battery moved position and in the course of this move Harold Harper made a memorable mistake.

We had to move out very, very quickly in the late afternoon. We were under full observation from the enemy, that was why we were getting well and truly hammered. We had a fair number of casualties. We moved to this position about 500 to 600 yards to the right-rear. It wasn't until we reached there that I found that I'd left the director stand behind. My officer, Captain Garry Birkin, was not pleased, although he and I were the very best of friends! He said, 'You'll go and get it as soon as it's dusk!' Dusk arrived about two hours later and I walked across this No Man's Land. I'd just got there when the Germans suddenly let fly – somebody must have spotted me walking across. I got these all to myself and I dived for the very first trench I could find. That first trench was the troop latrine and I finished up ankle-deep in it! Nobody wanted to speak to me for two or three days after that![24]

Lance Sergeant Harold Harper, D Troop, 426 Battery, 107th RHA

Shell holes sprouted up all around the gun positions – yet there were minimal casualties. As the guns were in constant demand to support the operations of the infantry and tanks, this was one of those situations where the gunners had no option but to grit their teeth – and carry on firing.

There was no backing down and getting under cover because you're being shelled. Come what may you've got a programme and you've got to do it – them blokes in front are relying on you. Relying on you to put this barrage in front of them so that they can keep up at the back of it. Or if they're attacking a post and they want covering fire – you've got to do it![25]

Lance Bombardier Albert Swinton, D Troop, 426 Battery, 107th RHA

As the situation deteriorated, both batteries were often firing as fast as physically possible. Once again, man and machine were being pushed to the very limit.

The Germans put in a heavy attack and the OP, who thought he was going to be overrun, just gave the quite unconventional order, 'And fire like bloody hell!' The wireless set went dead and 'we went to town' – we got rid of the whole 240 rounds behind the gun. We were engaged by counter-battery fire – some rotten German was firing back at us – most unsporting. The excitement of firing was a distraction: your guns were making a noise, your neighbour's gun is banging off as well, so the noise you are making distracts from the explosion of shells on your position. The normal rate for a 25-pounder is three rounds a minute, intense is five rounds a minute, but I clocked my gun firing off between twelve and thirteen rounds a minute firing at an 'area' target. My gun was just beginning to glow red round the jacket, the thicker part that goes round the barrel. That was very dangerous.[26]

Sergeant George Pearson, B Troop, 425 Battery, 107th RHA

Then came a sudden earthshattering calamity.

We had the order, 'Stop!' which simply means stop whatever you're doing, because you're going to change on to another target. By that time the guns were tremendously hot – almost glowing – very, very hot. We called to the command post, 'Guns loaded; guns hot!' But before we had chance to do anything else my gun, No. 4, and No. 2 – the shells both exploded. My gun was still elevated: we'd taken the cartridge out, but the round was rammed up the bore. No. 2 had depressed the gun slightly. My round went off in the barrel – the breech was open fortunately – blowing it front and back and bulging the barrel. The front half of the shell went out of the front and the rear part of the shell went off in my gun and it hit some ammunition at the back – that added to the confusion with an explosion at the back of the pit as well. My crew were OK. Unfortunately, on the No. 2 gun, the round went off and there were casualties – a young soldier was killed, and Lance Sergeant 'Ginger' Barker was wounded. A great character, a heavily tattooed man, he was evacuated, the hospital ship was sunk – and we lost him.[27]

Lance Sergeant Bob Foulds, B Troop, 425 Battery, 107th RHA

Meanwhile disaster also stalked the OP party, led by Captain Ted London operating from a Bren Carrier, as they moved out to a captured position ready to bring support fire down should the Germans launch a counter-attack.

We had got stuck so we were out of our vehicle and in the dugout in contact with the troop, bringing fire down on infantry and trucks who were regrouping and coming back at us. We were in a bit of a mess and we were shot up. We were resting at lunchtime in this low dugout: Sergeant Tew who was doing signaller, Ted London, a South African and myself. A German shell came into the dugout and went straight through the South African. He was dead – there was no doubt at all about that; shrapnel took Ted's right arm off, Ken Tew had back injuries – I was completely untouched! The dugout was in a bit of a mess so we got out and I radioed to the troop that we could no longer do anything. Ted laid out and covered up with a blanket, I put a field dressing on his arm, you could see the bone. He was totally conscious but in a shocked state. He knew he was badly wounded. Eventually, ambulances came.[28]

Sergeant Ian Sinclair, A Troop, 425 Battery, 107th RHA

Sinclair had been very lucky.

When Rommel weakened his frontier forces to counter-attack the 7th Armoured Division at Sidi Rezegh, the XIII Corps attack slowly began to gain traction. The 4th Indian Division captured Sidi Omar, while the 2nd New Zealand Division (Major General Bernard Freyberg) had managed to cut off the

Bardia fortress. For the next few days, the battle was incredibly complex, with rapid tactical ebbs and flows. Even the official historian despairs, describing the situation as: 'The forces of both sides were sandwiched like layers of a Neapolitan ice.'[29] The Eighth Army seemed to be teetering on the brink of defeat and Auchinleck had to intervene to prevent the shaken Cunningham from giving up on the offensive and withdrawing back to the Egyptian frontier. Auchinleck reasoned that Rommel must also be suffering extensive casualties in the severe fighting and that his supply situation must be dire, especially with the revitalised Tobruk garrison lurking behind his lines – Auchinleck resolved to bring up his reserves and keep up the pressure.

On 24 November, Rommel, confident that he had already overwhelmed the British armoured strength, launched an impetuous thrust by the Afrika Korps panzer divisions down the Trigh el Abd track, intending to raid into Egypt and cut the logistical supply routes to XIII Corps. This dramatic move, 'The Dash for the Wire', was probably overly bold, as it not only ignored the advance of the 2nd New Zealand Division, but also allowed recovery time for the battered remnants of the 7th Armoured Division south of Sidi Rezegh. Little was achieved by Rommel's brief 'invasion' of Egypt, although perhaps it did accelerate the dismissal of the hapless Cunningham, who was replaced by Lieutenant General Neil Ritchie.

Rommel failed to find the British forward supply bases and, frustrated, swung across towards Bardia before falling back to counter-attack at Sidi Rezegh, which had by then been taken by the continued advance of the 2nd New Zealand Division on the night of 26 November. The New Zealanders sent out a battalion to try to meet up with the 70th Division, which duly managed to reach El Duda on the morning of 27 November.

We woke up one morning to see a line of trucks which said, 'Eighth Army'. They were coming in and it was the New Zealanders. Somebody said to the leading officer or NCO, 'Thank goodness you've come and Tobruk's relieved!' They said, 'Relieved nothing! We've been chased in by the Germans!'[30]

Lance Sergeant Bob Foulds, B Troop, 425 Battery, 107th RHA

The truth of this was illustrated when Rommel's counter-attack once more severed the links between El Duda and Sidi Rezegh. There was considerable retrospective amusement at this turn of events, and the veterans would always claim that they had relieved the Eighth Army who were stranded in the desert. Still the fighting continued to rage on, with both sides suffering severe losses. However, Rommel could not replace his exhausted troops, while Auchinleck could move forward the 4th Indian Division, the 2nd South African Division and the very first elements of the 1st Armoured Division, which was in the process of landing in Egypt. Rommel was caught in a battle of attrition he could not win.

On 4 December, Rommel's attack on El Duda was repulsed by the 14th Brigade of 70th Division. By this time Rommel's supply situation was fast becoming impossible. He abandoned the eastern perimeter of Tobruk and turned to face the advancing XIII Corps, but on 5 December he was forced to retreat to secure his supply lines. Once again the Axis forces were hustled out of Cyrenaica, retreating all the way back to defensive lines anchored at Gazala. On 15 December the Eighth Army began a frontal attack, with the usual outflanking southern thrust. Rommel had no option but to fall all the way back to El Agheila, right back to where he started in February 1941. The siege of Tobruk was over; Operation Crusader had succeeded, but it had been a close-run thing. Auchinleck deserved enormous credit for his steadfast reliance on traditional military values, maintaining his focus in the face of dramatic, but ultimately pointless, armoured manoeuvring by Rommel. He concentrated on applying his superior strength forces to a churning battle of attrition until his enemy was broken, then harvested the rewards of victory. Operation Crusader gave the British their first victory against a major force of the German Army in the Second World War. It deserves to be remembered.

After the fighting died down, the men of 107th RHA were left mentally and physically exhausted. This was not just the impact of a fortnight's hard fighting, but the accumulated effects of an eight-month siege.

> There were no great celebrations or parties, we were too tired and weary for that! There was a great feeling of relief that it was over, because until that moment we didn't know that Tobruk was going to be relieved – we didn't know that we were going to win any battle. All the time we were in Tobruk there was always a constant fear that we would be overcome and taken. Until I saw that columns of New Zealanders coming in – you heaved a sigh – at least that threat after all those months had been lifted.[31]
>
> Lance Sergeant Ray Ellis, A Troop, 425 Battery, 107th RHA

They moved westwards behind the general advance of the Eighth Army, but only as far as Timimi. Here they ran out of petrol as the British supply line became overstretched. The South Notts Hussars were left behind in a bare patch of desert. With their vehicles and guns handed over to other artillery units, the 107th RHA had ceased for the moment to be a fighting regiment. The men decided to celebrate with an impromptu party. There were many versions as to how they came by the necessary drink to make it 'go with a swing', but I think Albert Swinton catches the 'spirit' of what happened.

Ivor Birkin, he would say, 'There's a truck, there's two blokes, off you go, find something to drink! Never mind about where you get it! Go and find, it, buy it, pinch it, do what you like but get back here with something to drink!' On this occasion they came back with some horrible purple-looking Italian wine in 44-gallon drums! The sort of wallop where the first mouthful tasted of potash or something – but after a couple of mugs it tasted all right. That was where Ivor Birkin made his first mistake – he put me in charge of it! We messed about with this drink and we decided it would be better warm with some sugar in it! We had a hell of a party![32]

Lance Bombardier Albert Swinton, D Troop, 426 Battery, 107th RHA

A huge bonfire was built, and three sheep were 'purchased' from an Arab shepherd for half a pound of tea.

The cooks cooked up this sheep and then we settled into this Chianti. We were all well and truly plastered! The troop sergeant major was sat astride this barrel of chianti, ladling it out in mugs. We only had two non-drinkers in the troop, and they had a stretcher. As fast as people folded over and passed out – they put them on this stretcher and carried them back to their vehicle. It was a paralytic night![33]

Sergeant George Pearson, B Troop, 425 Battery, 107th RHA

The fireside singsong and the instrumental musicianship deteriorated in proportion to the amount of chianti drunk.

We had a bloke who played the piano accordion – he played all night and gradually his playing got wilder and wilder as he got drunker and drunker until eventually it came home in a great 'WRRRRRHHH!' last chord and he collapsed![34]

Lance Sergeant Bob Foulds, B Troop, 425 Battery, 107th RHA

Albert Parker was one of those who fell *hors de combat*. There were no stretcher-bearers for him.

> I got gloriously drunk and I went outside. I don't know whether you've had a lot of wine to drink, but if you get out in the fresh air it tends to make you keel over! Jack Billington said to the others, 'Parker's outside. I think he's dead – I kicked him twice and he never moved!' Next morning when I got up all my ribs were bruised. I felt rough, really rough![35]
>
> Bombardier Albert Parker, A Troop, 425 Battery, 107th RHA

Ray Ellis had only recently been promoted and he seems to have tried to calm things down. It was a doomed effort.

> It occurred to me what was happening, so I went and got Sergeant Frank Burkinshaw and said, 'Frank, stop drinking, everyone's going to get paralytic – we'd better stay sober!' It was no use telling everyone to stay sober – the men were not in the mood to be told to stop drinking![36]
>
> Lance Sergeant Ray Ellis, A Troop, 425 Battery, 107th RHA

From his relatively sober viewpoint Ellis had a good perspective of what happened as the evening wore on.

> It was amazing because every man went through the same changes as they got drunk. They were happy for a start. Everyone was laughing and happy – it relieved all the tensions – we were out of Tobruk. Backslapping, weak jokes were laughed at – all the normal things of men getting drunk. Gradually it changed and they stopped laughing and became maudlin. It was mothers, sweethearts and wives – tears rolling down! Then eventually they just collapsed unconscious – dropped down on to the ground. Frank and I went round all the gun towers collecting blankets and covering them, because it was bitterly cold, and they could have died of exposure.[37]
>
> Lance Sergeant Ray Ellis, A Troop, 425 Battery, 107th RHA

As is so often the case, come the dawn, the men would regret their heroic inebriation. On 30 December 1941, the South Notts Hussars were recalled to Cairo.

> Next morning, we had the news that we were being withdrawn and going back to the Cairo for rest, re-equipment and leave. We travelled in the Quad gun towers with blinding thick heads over a bumpy desert – we paid dearly for our night before – believe me![38]
>
> Sergeant George Pearson, B Troop, 425 Battery, 107th RHA

It was estimated that during the siege the regiment had fired some 70,000 shells. They had certainly played a vital role in the defence of Tobruk. The cost was painful: some nineteen men dead and thirty-seven wounded. But most had survived.

Surely, they had endured the worst the war could throw at them. They were desert veterans.

11

BATTLE OF KNIGHTSBRIDGE,
27 MAY 1942

I was tired, physically tired; tired of battles, fighting, deserts and killing – sick of the whole thing. I was only 22, but as far as warfare went, I was an old man.[1]

Sergeant Ray Ellis, A Troop, 425 Battery, 107th RHA

BY THE END OF OPERATION CRUSADER, the Eighth Army had driven the Axis forces all the way back to El Agheila. Yet even as they celebrated success in North Africa, the global war situation would have severe consequences for Auchinleck. The declaration of war on Japan following its assault on the United States at Pearl Harbor on 7 December 1941 deflected most of the reinforcements originally intended for North Africa to Singapore and the new Far East theatre of war. At the same time the overall naval and air situation in the Mediterranean continued to deteriorate. This meant little to the South Notts Hussars, however, who were more interested in enjoying their well-earned rest period. They came back to Tahag Camp, not far from Cairo, and it seemed that life began again. They lived in reasonably comfortable tents, they had fresh meat, vegetables and as much water as they could drink. During the siege many of them had lost weight and this was their chance to build themselves up again. Most had a week of leave in Cairo, where they could work off their frustrations, drink alcohol to excess or simply relax, depending on their inclinations. Meanwhile, Ray Ellis had been promoted to sergeant and he relished the new freedom to enter the sacred inner sanctum that was the sergeants' mess.

> There was a bar with plenty of beer and whisky. We used to go up every night at about 7 o'clock, a whole gang of us, to 'write letters'! No one ever wrote a word of course – we would start drinking and drink steadily through until about two or three in the morning. When you got there, you ordered a crate of beer and you put it at the side of you. You didn't go buying rounds like you do in the pub; everybody had a crate and you drank your own. Talking and drinking, laughing and joking. The officers used to come in – they always stood at the door for a second – and someone would say, 'Ah! Hello Sir, do come in!' One night we were there at about 1 o'clock in the morning when Peter Birkin fell off his chair into the sand! We picked him up, carried him to his tent and put him to bed. About twenty minutes later he crawled in under the tent and said, 'Whhosh had the audacsshitty to put me to bed?'[2]
>
> Sergeant Ray Ellis, A Troop, 425 Battery, 107th RHA

By this time, the South Notts Hussars had been abroad for two years, and the more optimistic were beginning to hope against hope that they might be sent back to the UK.

> We went abroad thinking that we'd probably be abroad for six months. Then a year passed, and we thought, 'Well we must be getting towards the end of our time now.' Then two years had gone and, 'Well, surely now we must be getting near.' It seemed a long way from home; England was farther away than

the moon! We were always thinking about coming home. It's a sort of hope that soldiers have, 'I've heard a rumour!' or 'Next month we're going home, there's a ship already packed in the harbour to take us!'[3]

Sergeant Ray Ellis, A Troop, 425 Battery, 107th RHA

Such thoughts should probably have been disabused when, on 20 January 1942, the 107th RHA were issued with a brand new set of 25-pounders and Quad gun towers. However, after a ceremonial parade and inspection on 28 January, they were thoroughly distracted again by a belated Christmas party, organised and paid for by Lieutenant Colonel Bill Seely with contributions from the 'Ladies' Committee' back in Nottingham. Once again it proved to be a wild affair!

We took over the NAAFI and all the drinks were free – I must say that was a fatal mistake in those days! Turkey, mince pies, plum puddings! It was all lads together and it was a riot! Peter Birkin led everybody who could still stand in all the old filthy rugby songs. It was a party and a half, and I don't think half of us ever got back to our tents that night, it was lay down and sleep wherever. Anyone who was sober ought to have been court martialled. Can't remember the next day or two![4]

Bombardier Ted Whittaker, Headquarters, 425 Battery, 107th RHA

On 21 February they moved to Sid Bishr Camp, near Alexandria, where they joined the 22nd Armoured Brigade commanded by Brigadier William Carr. The brigade consisted of the 2nd Royal Gloucestershire Hussars (2nd RGH), the 3rd County of London Yeomanry (3rd CLY), the 4th County of London Yeomanry (4th CLY), the 107th RHA and the 50th Reconnaissance Regiment. Training was gradually stepped up as the South Notts Hussars eased their way back into a warlike shape. On 24 March, they moved on to Bene Yusef Camp near Cairo. Here the training process was complicated by the decision to create a new battery based on the regiment.

The 520 Battery was to be commanded by Major Gerry Birkin, who was considered by his men as one of the best officers in the Royal Artillery. Courageous and competent, he was possessed with a direct air of command that did not require shouting and he was never seen to 'look down on' the men he commanded. Over two hundred reinforcements arrived to help form the battery, together with some seven new officers. One of them proved to be a familiar face: Second Lieutenant Herbert Bonnello, a former NCO who had returned from his period training at the Middle East Officer Cadet Training Unit and now was destined to be the command post officer with 520 Battery. Others, such as Lieutenants Charles Rickard, Alan Smith and David Elliott, will become prominent players in our story. Lieutenant Colonel Bill Seely was aware that they might be going into action soon, and he was keen that the newcomers should be spread throughout the regiment. He arranged that B Troop should be transferred from 425 Battery and D Troop from 426 Battery to create the new 520 Battery. The end result was 425 Battery (Major Peter Birkin), composed of A and E Troops; 426 Battery (Major William Barber) with C and F Troops; and 520 Battery (Major Gerry Birkin) with B and D Troops. Although several officers and NCOs had been 'juggled' around, it was the case that, with two 'veteran' troops, 520 Battery had ended up as the most experienced battery of them all. The South Notts Hussars also had attached to them the 2-pounder guns of 287 Battery, 102 Anti-Tank Regiment (Northumberland Hussars) RA, commanded by Major D. J. Cowan, and an anti-tank company of the Northumberland Fusiliers.

In readiness for their new mobile role with the 22nd Armoured Brigade, the battery commanders and OP officers were issued with Marmon-Herrington armoured cars which had their turrets removed to enable them to act as OP vehicles. They were equipped with No. 11 wireless sets to communicate direct back to their own battery, with an additional No. 9 crystal set to allow them to liaise with the tank units for which they supplied artillery support. Bobby Feakins, newly posted as Major Gerry Birkin's driver, had his doubts about the Marmon-Herrington.

> It was solid steel, made in South Africa, with a Ford V8 engine which was a pig to get at! With that weight behind it, it wasn't the easiest of vehicles to manoeuvre, because your vision wasn't all that good. I was in the driving seat, front right, next to me on my left was Gerry Birkin; directly behind me was a wireless operator and behind Gerry there would be two wireless operators. One [linked] into the regiment, the other into brigade and one direct back to our own battery.[5]
>
> Bombardier Bobby Feakins, Headquarters, 520 Battery, 107th RHA

Frank Knowles also had little faith in the new Marmon-Herrington.

> Whilst it was so-called armoured, it wouldn't resist a normal .303 bullet. One of the lad's rifles went off accidentally and it went through one wall of the armoured car and through a heavy-duty battery the other side![6]
>
> Lance Bombardier Frank Knowles, Headquarters, 425 Battery, 107th RHA

In late April, the South Notts Hussars moved up to rejoin the rest of 22nd Armoured Brigade at Fort Capuzzo near the Libyan border. They now embarked upon an intensive programme of 'box' training which was radically different from anything they had attempted before. Each battery was allotted to a specific tank regiment: thus 425 Battery to 3rd CLY, 426 Battery to 4th CLY and 520 Battery to 2nd RGH. These yeomanry 'cavalry' regiments had recently had one squadron re-equipped with the Grant tanks, which boasted the more powerful 75mm guns, but were still for the most part reliant on the badly outclassed Crusaders with their ineffective 2-pounders.

> All our plans were geared to attack. We were training not as a complete regiment, but more as three separate batteries, concentrating on being an armoured box. You might have been called on to do anti-tank, to support tanks, to support infantry, to shell certain distant targets. The main thing was manoeuvrability – and this is one thing we'd not had a great deal of training in – we'd been static for so long. We were excellent at gun drill, at firing, even the new gun teams, but we were still not accustomed to packing up and getting out quickly. The trucks always withdrew, and so you were left. If things weren't going quite well and you'd got to withdraw, it's a different thing to get your trucks up, to get the guns on tow again and off! They wanted to concentrate on doing an orderly withdrawal – the circumstances made that impossible as I found out later! The idea was that all trucks should go down to the starting line of withdrawal and turn round and come back. I used to argue that by the time the last truck had got down to the starting line they would be captured. The best thing was everybody turn right round, scarper like hell and reorganise.[7]

Second Lieutenant Herbert Bonnello, Headquarters, 520 Battery, 107th RHA

As the 107th RHA moved forward into the desert, they gradually got used to moving as part of a 'brigade box'. The combination of so many vehicles moving in tandem in the desert was a dramatic sight.

> The 'soft' vehicles were in the middle. The guns were on the outside, with the armoured units coming up in the rear in their own box formation. These huge dispositions moved about the desert very much like ships at sea – like a flotilla of naval vessels

sailing. It was rather like that in effect, because as the vehicles moved along through the sand, they left a trail of dust behind them just as ships leave the wake in the water![8]

Sergeant Ray Ellis, A Troop, 425 Battery, 107th RHA

One element of the new training that caused some degree of consternation among the gunners was the strange idea that the guns were to act as decoys, placed as they were on the edge of the 'box'.

The idea was that the guns should be placed in a vulnerable situation to attract the German tanks – tempting the tanks to attack us. When the German tanks came out, our armoured units would come in and destroy them. It was a stupid theory. The amount of time it would have taken for German tanks to come on to our position and wipe us out didn't allow enough time for our tanks to come from wherever they were in hiding to protect us. The time limits were too fine. We didn't like it at all; we were all well aware that the 25-pounder was not an anti-tank gun. It was not manoeuvrable enough – it would only traverse a certain distance with the traverse wheel and if you wanted to move the gun you had to move the whole bloody gun round by moving the trail; it was too high, with a shield that gave you no protection except from blast.[9]

Sergeant Ray Ellis, A Troop, 425 Battery, 107th RHA

Most of all they feared that the 25-pounders would be isolated at the mercy of the German tanks.

The crew of each Quad, armoured car, lorry and pickup truck would now be responsible for its own cooking arrangements. Lance Sergeant Harold Harper had been appointed as OP assistant to Captain Ivor Birkin, who was by then commanding D Troop. Harper, his driver and their two signallers decided that this time they would make sure that they had a little more variety in their diet in the desert.

> We all clubbed together, including the officer, and we went
> to various shops and the NAAFI in Cairo and stocked up to
> capacity with tinned fruit, custard powder, milk powder, bottles
> of whisky, tins of beer, bags of sugar, all the luxuries. We took
> it in turns to do the cooking. Rations were issued at night, by
> a 3-ton vehicle coming round to each individual vehicle to give
> them their rations.[10]

Lance Sergeant Harold Harper, D Troop, 520 Battery, 107th RHA

New arrivals like David Elliott benefited from the accumulated
experience of these desert veterans. The son of a farmer from
Bramley in Surrey, he had already served in the ranks with the
141st Field Ambulance, Royal Army Medical Corps, during the
Dunkirk campaign in 1940. Now he was facing very different
challenges in the desert.

> The 25-pounder cordite came in metal boxes which were very
> useful for your own personal belongings. People soon adapted
> the vehicles they travelled in – bolted the boxes on the side –
> and in them your batman would store tinned food, or cigarettes
> or anything else you'd managed to acquire in extra rations to
> improve your living conditions. They were quite important
> things to have – your own kit box.[11]

Second Lieutenant David Elliott, Headquarters, 520 Battery, 107th RHA

They may have been a little perturbed by the 'box' tactics, but
the South Notts Hussars were confident in their skills and drills.
As their training was completed in mid May, some of the OP
officers were issued with light Honey tanks to render them less
conspicuous when moving forward with the tank regiments.
The attached 287 Battery, 102 Anti-Tank RA were also issued
with the splendid new 6-pounder anti-tank gun, although this
was left so late that their gunners had little chance to familiarise
themselves with its use in action before the 'balloon went up'.

The main features of desert warfare had by this time become established. Logistics were of prime importance: without copious quantities of fuel, the divisions could not move, the aircraft could not fly. Vast quantities of munitions, replacement vehicles, spare parts, food and water were required at the right point at the right time – or disaster could ensue. Ultimately, almost everything had to be sent out from the home countries – thousands of miles away. Both sides had overextended supply lines, which were under constant threat. The harsh desert environment was rough on the soldiers, but it was also tough on machines bouncing across a stony terrain.

Plagued by the logistical consequences of their recent advance, the British had paused while they attempted to improve their supply links. They also suffered from the consequences of a further deterioration in the situation in the Mediterranean. The British base at Malta was effectively 'masked' by heavy German air attacks launched from Sicily which improved the Axis supply route, thereby allowing a plethora of reinforcements to reach North Africa. While intelligence reports available to Auchinleck led him to believe that his opponents numbered only some 35,000, in fact Rommel had more than 50,000 German and 30,000 Italian troops under his command by January 1942. The timely arrival of a convoy had brought strong reinforcements and copious supplies of fuel. The 'Desert Fox' was by no means finished. Indeed, from February 1942 his command was upgraded to the Panzerarmee Afrika.

Rommel lunched a sharp counter-attack on 21 January, which on 3 February recaptured first Benghazi and then Timimi. The situation only stabilised on 4 February, with the establishment of a new British line based on the coastal town of Gazala just 30 miles west of Tobruk, stretching inland for 15 miles from Gazala, with a further detached strongpoint at Bir Hacheim, some 50 miles from the sea. The defences were patterned on a series of 'brigade boxes', dug in behind strong minefields with further deep minefields linking the boxes together. A further two rearward defensive boxes were prepared: one defending the town of Acroma; the other, the Knightsbridge Box, so named after the 'Knightsbridge' sign marking the junction of the desert track leading from Acroma to Bir Hacheim and the Trig Capuzzo road. The XIII Corps (Lieutenant General William Gott), supported by the 1st Armoured Brigade, was responsible for holding the line, with the 1st South African Division deployed on the coast, the 50th Northumbrian Division to the south and the 1st Free French Brigade Group holding Bir Hacheim. The XXX Corps (Lieutenant General Charles Norrie) had the 1st Armoured Division (Major General Herbert Lumsden) near the Knightsbridge Box, with the 7th Armoured Division (Major General Frank Messervy) further south. Behind them the Tobruk fortress was garrisoned by the 2nd South African Division, while the 5th Indian Division was held in army reserve.

As part of the 1st Armoured Division, the 22nd Armoured Brigade was moving forward to take up its allotted battle positions in the featureless area of stony desert around Knightsbridge.

> On route we were training, dropping into action on imaginary targets. On May 26th, I remember Ivor Birkin turning to me and saying, 'I do not know what else we can do to make this troop more efficient.' By that time, we'd reached the situation where we could be driving along and suddenly get the order – and within 35 seconds we would have a round up the spout and in the air.[12]

> Lance Sergeant Harold Harper, D Troop, 520 Battery, 107th RHA

The 425 and 426 Batteries were located close to the Knightsbridge junction, while the 520 Battery and the 2nd RGH were some distance to the south-west, closer to the Bir el Harmat minefield. They were desert veterans, fresh from nine months facing everything the Germans could throw at them at Tobruk. What could go wrong? What indeed.

BOTH THE AXIS FORCES and the British were preparing to launch major offensives in May 1942. The Axis forces deployed some 90,000 men, 560 tanks and 542 aircraft, while the British had 110,000 men, 843 tanks and 604 aircraft. Auchinleck was planning a thrust for Benghazi on 15 May, but his continuing logistical problems eventually forced a postponement until 1 June 1942. As a result, Rommel was able to strike first. His plans were simple but devastating: the attack, codenamed Operation Venice, began at 14.00 on 26 May 1942. The Italian X and XXI Corps launched head-on attacks on the XIII Corps defensive boxes, attempting to convince the British commanders that this was the main attack. As soon as darkness fell, the Italian Ariete Armoured Division pinned the Free French in their Bir Hacheim Box at the south of the Gazala Line, while the 15th and 21st Panzer Divisions swirled round to the south to strike hard to the north – *behind* the British lines, in an attempt to destroy the 7th and 1st Armoured Divisions. This in turn would cut off the retreat of the infantry of XIII Corps, who could then be defeated in detail by attacks on their boxes from both front and rear. The 90th Light Division would swing even further round to the south, heading for El Adem, and sever the British supply lines from Tobruk. Meanwhile, the Italian XX Motorised Corps (Ariete, Littorio and Trieste Divisions) would open up a wide gap in the British minefields south of Bir el Harmat, aiming to pinch out the Sidi Muftah Box (occupied by the 150th Brigade, 50th Northumbrian Division) and thereby open a short and direct supply route to the manoeuvring armoured divisions.

That evening, the South Notts Hussars had no idea of the

seriousness of the threat facing them and were far more focused on their next move. After all, they were surely safe – as they were miles behind the lines.

> It was just like any other night. We had got into the near vicinity of a minefield and we said, 'Right, we'll dig in here!' We certainly dug a slit trench; the guns did not dig in. They were pointing westwards over the minefield and all the supporting trucks were in line dispersed at the back of them. I can remember we kicked a football about that night. As I was getting ready to get down in the old sleeping bag, I noticed there was a tremendous amount of activity by flares on the other side of the minefield. No one realised the import of these flares.[13]
>
> Second Lieutenant Herbert Bonnello, Headquarters, 520 Battery, 107th RHA

Nonetheless, Lieutenant Colonel Bill Seely felt the 520 Battery was a little isolated and he planned to move them closer to the other batteries on 27 May.

> Colonel Seely came round, and I heard him telling everybody, 'We're having a very early move in the morning, so nobody need dig in!' Well that suited me – I wasn't very fond of digging, I was very pleased about that![14]
>
> Gunner Bill Hutton, B Troop, 520 Battery, 107th RHA

They would have been safer with slit trenches, but all was quiet; all was calm.

> Sergeant Major Earnshaw, the battery sergeant major, and myself went across to one of the B Troop positions and sat in the back of a 15cwt truck where, under the direction of Sergeant Bland, who was an excellent bridge player, we were taught the elements of contract bridge by the help of a hurricane lamp.

When we left just after midnight and wound our way across the
moonlit desert you could have heard a pin drop.[15]

Lance Sergeant Harold Harper, D Troop, 520 Battery, 107th RHA

Sergeant Patrick Bland[16] would be dead within hours, killed by
a German shell.

While the South Notts Hussars slept, the Germans over-
whelmed the defences of the 7th and 3rd Indian Motorised
Brigade. The 90th Light Division, swinging round even further
to the south, was able to overrun the advanced headquarters of
Major General Frank Messervy commanding the 7th Armoured
Division. However, not everything went Rommel's way. The 1st
Free French Brigade holding the Bir Hacheim Box stood firm.
In fact, the French would hold out until 10 June in a remarkable
display of sustained heroism. Never the less, on the morning of
27 May, the massed tanks of the 15th and 21st Panzer Divisions
were able to swing north to attack the 1st Armoured Division in
the Knightsbridge Box area.

The men of the South Notts Hussars were still in complete
ignorance of the peril they were in. As they sat in the desert the
Germans grew ever closer.

We had just about finished breakfast when we saw this dust
cloud on the horizon. Paid no attention whatsoever, assumed
it was some of our troops on manoeuvres. We were attached to
the Royal Gloucestershire Hussars. The guns were just parked
with their vehicles, we had laagered for the night, expecting to
move next morning. Then along came the battery commander,
Major Gerry Birkin, and he said, 'I think they're Germans!' He
gave instructions for the D Troop OP to follow him.[17]

Lance Sergeant Harold Harper, D Troop, 520 Battery, 107th RHA

Bombardier Bobby Feakins was driving the Marmon-Herrington
commanded by Major Gerry Birkin that morning.

I dived straight in, started the engine and away. Gerry Birkin said words to the effect of: 'There is a possibility we may come into action; I know you'll do your best!' I pulled up when he told me to stop. He said, 'Turn the car round!' I knew something was going to happen – we were facing back the way we came. He got his glasses out, he was up in the turret – he'd sighted a lot of dust and we were getting firing lines – so many thousand yards from the battery to the dust. I would verify just to check we were in unison. He was up through the turret and he said, 'Bombardier, would you just check this?' He came down, I went up and a shell landed a bit behind us. He said, 'Whoops!' Then I said, 'Oh Sir! Quick!' I thought I'd seen a vehicle moving in direct line towards us rather than dust. I came down and sat in my seat and he went up. I had a map on my lap facing the front of the vehicle, he was up through the turret, looking out of the back of the turret facing the Germans. The next round came straight inside the armoured car. I didn't realise it had hit us and I turned and there were the two radio operators without heads – absolutely nothing from the shoulders. I had blood and muck all over me. Gerry[18] slumped into my arms and he was actually dead at that point, hit right in the abdomen. I was wounded in the legs. On the inter-battery radio, I said, 'We've been hit! We've been hit!'[19]

Bombardier Bobby Feakins, Headquarters, 520 Battery, 107th RHA

The beheaded radio operators were Gunner Walter White[20] and Gunner William Lloyd.[21] A third signaller, Gunner J. H. Wright, had survived unscathed, but Bobby Feakins had been left in a dreadful state.

I was bleeding profusely from shrapnel fragments all around my legs, so I decided to make it back to the battery to get out of a sitting duck position. I said to the chap, I didn't even look round, 'Hang on!' I slammed it into gear to try and get out of a sitting duck position and get back to the battery. I tried to put my foot on the accelerator because I was losing the strength in my legs and I hit a slit trench. It just went, 'Whuumph!' Straight in – and I can assure you it was a very nasty smack – everything came forward and the seat hit me in the back – that caused the back injury. I turned round, and there was nobody there! I wondered what had happened. I crawled out as best I could, pulling myself out and I was hanging on the back of the vehicle when Sergeant Harper came racing across to us. I suppose I was in a bit of shock – headless bodies – the inside of my armoured car was just nothing but blood and flesh, bits of body all over the place.[22]

Bombardier Bobby Feakins, Headquarters, 520 Battery, 107th RHA

Unfortunately, Gunner J. H. Wright had already jumped out of the back of the armoured car and sought shelter in the selfsame slit trench. He leg was broken, and he was left trapped under the front wheels of the armoured car.

Harold Harper and Gerry Birkin's brother, Ivor Birkin, were close by in their own Marmon-Herrington.

We had only gone about 600 or 700 yards, when we heard a gabbling on the battery commander's radio which immediately told us something was wrong. Captain Ivor Birkin jumped out and dashed across, 50 to 60 yards.[23]

Lance Sergeant Harold Harper, D Troop, 520 Battery, 107th RHA

Harper tried to follow in his armoured car, while at the same time attempting to get in touch with the battery. Then a further calamity struck.

Out of a cloud of sand came a Royal Gloucester Hussars Grant tank. We hit it head on and we literally bounced back 5 or 6 yards. I was standing in the turret and I was crushed; the impact broke my ribs down the right-hand side. The next thing we saw our engine was on fire. We dashed across and told Captain Birkin what had happened. There we were, stranded.[24]

Lance Sergeant Harold Harper, D Troop, 520 Battery, 107th RHA

A dreadful scene met their eyes.

I've never seen anything like it in my life. Major Gerry Birkin[25] lay flat on the floor, obviously dead. I went to the back and opened up the two doors at the back of the armoured car. Apparently, the armour-piercing shell had gone clear through the middle of the battery commander as he was standing up and then chopped off the heads of the two radio operators. All you could see was these two lads, their hands still holding their mouthpieces, although their heads had rolled on to the floor – a bit of a gory sight. My biggest problem was to persuade Captain Ivor Birkin to leave his brother – he was in a very distressed state. I said, 'Come along, you must come back!' He said, 'No, you get back, I'll see what I can do.'[26]

Lance Sergeant Harold Harper, D Troop, 520 Battery, 107th RHA

Harper managed to get the hapless Wright from under the front wheels of the armoured car. By then, Ivor Birkin had also been wounded in the ankle by fire from the fast-approaching German tanks. In the chaos, neither of the OP teams had managed to get any coherent wireless message back to 520 Battery. Their supporting tanks of the 2nd Gloucestershire Hussars were also surprised.

Only four tanks got away from the first 'stand', and they only moved when the enemy were within 600 yards. Fire of every kind was intense, and the dust and smoke of high explosive made it immensely difficult to follow what was happening. Tanks were burning on every side, and the thick black pall of smoke caused by the fires added to the confusion. No orders could be given, and it was impossible to see signals, so every crew fought its own battle. Armour-piercing shells slammed against the front plate, knocking equipment and showers of paint to the floor inside.[27]

Captain Stuart Pitman, F Squadron, 2nd Royal Gloucestershire Hussars, 22nd Armoured Brigade

Trooper Victor Bridle was in one of the Grants commanded by Lieutenant Edmond Ades. They were hit early in the battle.

We had four direct hits in less than a minute. The first shattered a track and I felt it go, almost instantaneously. Another came in through the final drives, wounding the 75mm gunner and must have just missed me; the third came clean in through the side door, just missing the high-explosive box and killing Buxton, the loader, and Corporal Chamberlain. It must have been a powerful shot, for it was a very neat hole and wasn't even burred. The fourth shot must have gone straight into the engine, for almost immediately the flames roared through on both sides of the turret and Mr Ades shouted to bail out. I asked Solovitch if Buxton[28] was dead, though I saw him drop myself, and he said he was definitely killed, so I told him to get out, and he crossed over me and straight into the turret and out the far side. I went out last and took a quick glance at Johnnie Chamberlain.[29] There was no doubt whatsoever, he was definitely killed. I went out the side door, and Mr Ades was waiting there. He was very confident, and said, 'Don't worry, lad, we'll get out of this yet!'[30]

Trooper Victor Bridle, F Squadron, 2nd Royal Gloucestershire Hussars, 22nd Armoured Brigade

Their luck ran out a little later.

Mr Ades suggested that those who could, and wanted to, should make a run for it, at least to try and hide in a dugout until the boys came in again; to try to get right away would have been suicide, as it was proved. The German tanks were about 400 or 500 yards in front of us and already passed on the flanks. But never the less, he went, telling us to run at intervals, so as not to bunch together. Corporal Pavitt was just running off, and I was going to follow, although my leg was very stiff through a small wound which had tightened the muscles, but I didn't run, for Mr Ades[31] hadn't gone 40 yards before he was hit by a belt of explosive bullets. Corporal Pavitt went up to him and turned him over, but it was useless. During this time there was a constant flow of machine-gun bullets, and we had to be extremely careful. By this time the Germans were up to us, and one of their tank officers told us to put our hands up and walk towards their rear. Just then our own 25-pounders opened up and we had to contend with them, and believe me, they were shooting well![32]

Trooper Victor Bridle, F Squadron, 2nd Royal Gloucestershire Hussars, 22nd Armoured Brigade

In all this chaos, survival was the only preoccupation for Harold Harper and Bobby Feakins as they found themselves in the middle of this full-scale tank battle with the other squadrons of 22nd Armoured Brigade joining the fight. In a state of near desperation, Harper picked up Ivor Birkin and carried him bodily in a kind of fireman's lift the 30 yards to join the other OP team survivors clinging to the back of a stray Crusader tank from the County of London Yeomanry.

The tank commander had no idea we were there and kept firing. We had to keep dodging as best we could when the turret and barrel kept swinging round. I don't know quite how we managed it; how we didn't get thrown off is a miracle.

We slithered around and hoped for the best, hung on to what you could. I remember the gun firing within about 6 inches of my ear! One of our fellows fell off and we thought he'd been crushed to death. Most of us received wounds of some description from the German shelling, although at the time we weren't aware of their extent – there was too much happening. Later, I found I'd got some shrapnel in my left knee.[33]

Lance Sergeant Harold Harper, D Troop, 520 Battery, 107th RHA

Unsurprisingly, it was the injured Bobby Feakins that had fallen off the back of the bouncing tank.

Ivor Birkin's driver was hanging on to me like grim death with the fear of God in us! We hadn't gone very far when he was hit right across the bottom! When you get hit like that on the cheeks of your arse the immediate thing is to grab them. Of course, in doing this he let me go – and I fell off the tank! The tank continued on its way, and I was left out in the open, miles from anywhere in No Man's Land. Where tanks turn, their tracks throw up a 'ridge' and I was hiding behind the tank tracks! Nonsensical of course but to me it was a haven. The pain had started to come in, I don't think I was paralysed, but I just couldn't use them. I had a great gaping hole in my right leg and my left leg and knee was full of shrapnel. I must have still been in shock, but I was compos mentis. I knew what was going on around me and my one issue was to keep safe.[34]

Bombardier Bobby Feakins, Headquarters, 520 Battery, 107th RHA

Badly wounded and left all alone in the hostile desert, Feakins' survival prospects did not seem very good at all.

After a while another tank came by, saw me out in the open and came over. He said, 'What the hell are you doing here?' I said, 'Having an afternoon cup of tea, you silly bugger!' He said, 'Well, I'm sorry old chap, I'm going into action now, but on my way back I'll come and pick you up!' Away he went. An hour and a half to two hours. Hell on earth, watching the shells drop all around me, but none too close! Just wondering about the things you've done and the things you'd like to do! I hadn't given up – I think my mind was too full. An element of fear because you didn't know what was going to happen. But he did come back – and I felt heaven had opened up! One of the crew got out, lifted me on and made me safe and they drove me back.[35]

Bombardier Bobby Feakins, Headquarters, 520 Battery, 107th RHA

He was dropped off at a first aid post where he was examined somewhat cursorily by the doctor.

The doctor examined my wounds, dressed them, gave me some painkillers. I know I felt an awful lot better when he had finished. They stuck a luggage label on my tunic, on which the doctor had written, and when I looked it said, 'Amputation right femur'. That put a shock wave through me – to think that I was going to lose my right leg! My mind was running over what I would do whenever I got home with one leg. I really loved dancing and I couldn't imagine doing a quickstep with one leg. A million other things were going through my mind.[36]

Bombardier Bobby Feakins, Headquarters, 520 Battery, 107th RHA

He was then taken by a 3-ton lorry to the 42nd General Hospital inside the Tobruk lines.

We were lined up in a corridor on stretchers on the floor. Then the queue for the 'surgery' – a great big hall. You were plonked on this trestle table – and that was the operating table. There were no nurses at all, one doctor and one RAMC person helping him. The screen would go round the patient, the doctor would operate and every now and again you'd hear a 'Clonk!' in a bucket where some physical part of the body had been sawn off – and you could hear the actual sawing. Knowing full well what the first aid post doctor had written on my label, I was beginning to get very uptight. When he eventually got to me and put the screen round me, he said, 'Well, you're the last, I've been operating now for twenty-four hours! I'm dog-tired and I couldn't do any more!' I said to the doctor, 'As I'm your last, I wonder if you could spare a little time to see if you can save my leg, obviously I would be very, very grateful!' He said, 'All right young man, I will see what I can do!' The anaesthetist, a padre, who was about to put the hood over my nose with the ether drops which they used in those barbaric days, said, 'Now go to sleep, think of your wife!' I said, 'I'm not married.' 'Well think of your fiancée.' 'I'm not engaged padre!' 'Think of your girlfriend!' 'I haven't got a girlfriend!' His last remark was, 'Think of somebody's bloody wife!' Which rather shook me coming from a padre! I woke up in bed, I sat bolt upright, dived with my hands down the bed to see if I'd got two legs. I was very grateful to find that I did! I went straight back to sleep again.[37]

Bombardier Bobby Feakins, Headquarters, 520 Battery, 107th RHA

Feakins' luck held and he was safely evacuated to Egypt. His leg and back injuries eventually responded to treatment, but the mental effects of his traumatic experiences would linger.

I couldn't sleep. Nightmares of Germans raiding and me running away – being chased by Germans with bayonets. I just couldn't sleep. I'd be thinking of the carnage in my armoured car: the memory of the headless bodies in my armoured car, the loss of Gerry Birkin. It was to stay with me for a very long time – each night they gave me a sleeping draught to put me to sleep.[38]

Bombardier Bobby Feakins, Headquarters, 520 Battery, 107th RHA

MEANWHILE HARPER'S NIGHTMARE journey on the back of the tank had come to an end when the tank commander dropped off his shaken – and stirred – 'passengers' at the CLY wagon lines before returning to the fray. One of the trucks took them to the advanced field dressing station about 2 miles down a track. However, they were not there long before the German panzers arrived.

> I was in the bag! They just walked in, a German sergeant walked in and took my pistol, had a look at my wallet with my money in – he gave me the money back because he said they'd got plenty of it already printed for when they went into Cairo![39]

Lance Sergeant Harold Harper, D Troop, 520 Battery, 107th RHA

Harper had excelled at German while at school and it now came in useful as he was able to chat to his captors to try to find out what was happening. The dressing station carried on functioning with both German and British wounded being brought in for treatment. For the next few days the battle ebbed and flowed around them, but eventually Harper saw an opportunity to escape, when the Germans seemed to have been pushed back. This was despite his rib injuries and damaged knee.

> A Welsh anti-tank sergeant and I decided to make a break for it. My theory was that if we went due south-east we would be edging out into the desert where there was less likelihood of anybody being around because nearly all the fighting was in the coastal zone. All I had was a pair of shorts, full stop! We waited until after dusk. We passed one tank full of Germans, so I started speaking in German, just to make sure that if we were spotted they would think that we were part of them. At first light we laid up. We found one or two derelict British vehicles, put our hands under the radiator and swilled our mouths out with the radiator water. We had the sense not to appear in the

daytime when the sun was belting down, we just got under a vehicle. We never slept to any great extent, kept awake all the time, because you daren't sleep. Then unfortunately the next night, when we were walking, this laddie trod on a land mine and that was the end of him. I'd made quite a big friend out this lad – he came from Cardiff. It made me a little bit wary, looking for any sand that had been ruffled up. I was left on my own. Eventually, I had to drink my own urine, you started by swilling your mouth out with it and hoping for the best. We'd got used in the desert to reading the stars, so I knew which direction I was going in pretty well, and I could tell from the firing where the battle was – where it was and the right way to approach. My only fear was when I got near to our lines – I walked in with my hands up and started shouting as much in English as I possibly could. I was in a bit of a bedraggled state when I got to the Guards Brigade Headquarters.[40]

Lance Sergeant Harold Harper, D Troop, 520 Battery, 107th RHA

At last, on 6 June, Harper got back to the British lines. In his debriefing he was able to give some useful intelligence from his observations behind the German lines. From there he was evacuated back to hospital in the Nile Delta. For the moment his war was over.

BACK AT THE ISOLATED 520 BATTERY most were still blissfully unaware of anything untoward. On the ground, B Troop were facing south towards the action, while D Troop were facing west. Ernie Hurry had just had a NAAFI canteen truck delivery and he set off in his signals pickup truck to distribute it round the battery.

I had to give it out to the men. Cigarettes, all sort of tins of fruit, anything. I'd left my vehicle and walked across to another

one. They hadn't been dispersed, they were still in column
of route, one behind another. All of a sudden, I heard the
'Schmozzle' the other side of the hill. Gunfire, machine-gun
fire. I said to a chap, 'Somebody's having it pretty rough over
the other side!' I didn't know how far or how near it was,
because sound travels in the desert. We were sat there talking –
and then I saw this German tank come over the hill![41]

Gunner Ernie Hurry, B Troop, 520 Battery, 107th RHA

Bill Hutton was caught with his pants down; both literally and
figuratively.

I'd made myself a permanent lavatory seat out of a petrol
tin – all cut with a pear-shaped hole. I took that and a spade,
dug myself a little hole, put this seat on top of it and I sat on
it reading some magazine. I was sitting there and in the sand
round me there were bits of stuff flying up all round me. 'What
the bloody hell's that?' I couldn't hear any bangs or whistles,
I thought, 'Some bugger's shooting at me!' I could see a tank
way back on the horizon – I presumed it was one of ours
practising, trying his gun out, and not seen me. I smartly pulled
my trousers up! All of a sudden, one of the new officers came
rushing up and said, 'We want every spare man to help dig the
guns in!'[42]

Gunner Bill Hutton, B Troop, 520 Battery, 107th RHA

In the confusion Ernie Hurry ran back to his truck and tried to
get it out of the guns' line of fire.

More tanks appeared over the hill – I should say six or seven.
I zigzagged down and took position at the back of the guns,
waiting there to see what was going to happen. They were
turning the guns round, taking up positions. The guns opened
up – firing down the column of vehicles. The Germans were

very close then – let's face it they were close on the back of our
vehicles when they came over the hill – about half a mile.[43]

Gunner Ernie Hurry, B Troop, 520 Battery, 107th RHA

It all happened so suddenly; the men had no warning of what
was going on.

We were more flabbergasted than panicked. D Troop were
able to go; they were on the other side of all this line of vehicles
that shielded them, and they managed to get their gun towers,
limber up and push off. B Troop had to turn round and face
south, firing virtually over open sights. You could see these tanks
coming up in a sort of feathered 'V-Shape' formation. They
were smallish dots in the distance. The guns started firing and
it was pretty plain that things were not going the right way. The
tanks kept coming closer and closer. The poor chaps on the guns
were having a rough time – knocked quite a few tanks out – the
problem was they were getting hit as well. All you could do was
stand and watch. Both Battery Captain Bennett and myself just
stood and watched. I said, 'Look, I'm going down there to help
those lads on the guns!' He said, 'No you don't, you stop here.
There's nothing you can do; there's nothing I can do!'[44]

Lance Sergeant David Tickle, Headquarters, 520 Battery, 107th RHA

It was an impossible situation and in truth the resistance did
not last long. Herbert Bonello had a good view of a heroic deed
performed by Sergeant Fred Taylor in the final stages.

It was an amazing thing – he did an open sight action all on
his own because most of his chaps had been killed. He hit this
tank, it seemed to me to be so close – 50 yards – and it was just
like a knife going through butter. The turret came straight off
and bounced at the back. The driver went on and hit a limber –
I think everyone else in the tank had been killed.[45]

Second Lieutenant Herbert Bonnello, Headquarters, 520 Battery, 107th RHA

This was described in the regimental history as 'his Parthian shot'.[46] Later on, Bill Hutton heard the 'real' story of what had happened from Fred Taylor himself.

> MacNamara was Taylor's gun layer and this tank was coming straight for the gun. MacNamara looked through his telescopic sight and the thing was so near that he didn't see anything, just a grey mass. Fred Taylor was telling him to fire, and he turned round to Fred, off his gun seat, and said, 'I can't see a fucking thing!' Taylor said, 'Pull the bloody trigger, man!' He pulled the trigger – just as the tank was going to climb over the gun. It blew the turret right off and killed everybody in the tank and it carried on and climbed over the gun.[47]
>
> Gunner Bill Hutton, B Troop, 520 Battery, 107th RHA

Moments later, their position was completely overrun. Bonnello found himself trapped in a slit trench under fire from the German tanks. For the rest of his life he would ponder whether they might have escaped if they had been given different orders.

> There were two distinctly different orders: one said 'Action!' and one said 'Scarper!' Too late for me – I should have gone – gone like lightning. Clearly the attack was coming from the south and it was too late to go back towards Cairo, you had got to go towards the coastline – north. We should have gone much sooner. When do you scarper? When do you go into action? That was the biggest worry; that's the nightmare.[48]
>
> Second Lieutenant Herbert Bonnello, Headquarters, 520 Battery, 107th RHA

Bonnello was trapped, but Charles Bennett managed to organise the destruction of damaged lorries and then controlled the evacuation of all those vehicles still able to move.

Captain Bennett, he stood up in his vehicle with a blue flag, which meant everybody was to withdraw. I went back on the gun position and picked up three or four signallers – Bruce Meakin was one of them – I'd got them on the running boards as well. I was fired at and chased by one of the German tanks, I could see the machine-gun bullets spurting in the ground in front of me. I put speed on and kept going![49]

Gunner Ernie Hurry, B Troop, 520 Battery, 107th RHA

Major Daniell appears to have arrived at the end of the resistance, just as the last few vehicles were making their escape.

Beside me, out of the corner of my eye, I saw Padre Parry hauling a couple of wounded into the back of his truck. I shouted to him, 'GO! GO!' Just in time he disappeared, six wounded in the truck and four bullets in Padre Parry. Exhorting his driver to go faster, yet faster, they eventually reached safety.[50]

Major Robert Daniell, Headquarters, 107th RHA

Despite his wounds, Padre Parry survived, treated by Harry Day back at the regimental aid post.

Padre Parry had machine-gun bullets through the window screen of the vehicle he was travelling in which had entered his chest and he was brought in in a truck. He was highly shocked, and we had to give him morphia, tetanus injections, put shell dressings round it. He was evacuated.[51]

Medical Orderly Harry Day, Headquarters, 107th RHA

After the last vehicles had left, Robert Daniell then claims to have 'played dead' and driven off once the German tanks had moved away. Herbert Bonnello had no such luck; he found himself in a hopeless predicament.

If tank crew see enemy in a slit trench, they can crush you – that was a big worry. I saw this big tank coming and it just missed us. Eventually the position was completely overrun and the tank people captured us – I'd got a revolver and I didn't fancy my chance – I've got to admit it was left in the slit trench![52]

Second Lieutenant Herbert Bonnello, Headquarters, 520 Battery, 107th RHA

He was taken off by a truck to be a prisoner of war in Italy and Germany for four long years.

Meanwhile, Bill Hutton was still alone in his slit trench.

I could hear this squeaking, creaking noise that tanks make. I bobbed my head up and I soon put it down quick again – they'd got dirty big black crosses! Three German tanks all within damn nigh spitting distance. Our guns are shooting at these tanks – and they're shooting at our guns. All bloody hell was let loose. There's a hell of a difference from being in action with one of your pals, so that you can make silly jokes about it, but being on your own it's a different cup of tea altogether. I sat in there and I thought, 'If I was Errol Flynn and I'd got some sticky bombs, I'd got a perfect chance to put all those tanks out of action! Well, thank God, I haven't got any sticky bombs!'[53]

Gunner Bill Hutton, B Troop, 520 Battery, 107th RHA

Not unreasonably, Hutton surrendered when he saw the fighting was over. The prisoners from 520 Battery were gathered into a large column with Italian armoured cars at the front and back. The guards were lax and on the first night several were able to escape, including Lieutenant Charles Rickard. Next day, Bill Hutton and a friend managed to slip off, after hiding themselves under a derelict vehicle. After many more adventures in the desert they eventually made their way back to the unit. This marked the end of Hutton's service with the South

Notts Hussars as not long afterwards his appalling eyesight was diagnosed, and he was posted to the Field Security Section at General Headquarters back in Egypt.

WHILE THIS FIGHTING RAGED, some 15 miles away the 425 and 426 Batteries were still located near the Knightsbridge cross-roads. Sergeant John Walker had been promoted to command a gun in Captain Bill Pringle's E Troop, and as an experienced desert veteran he felt sure that something bad was happening.

> We felt the ground shaking, which we knew by experience was either artillery or dive-bombers. You could feel the vibration the same as one would with a minor earth tremor. We immediately went to our guns and we could then see smoke on the horizon.[54]
>
> Sergeant John Walker, E Troop, 425 Battery, 107th RHA

Then came the alarm and the most tremendous 'flap' as 425 Battery moved off following the tanks of the 3rd CLY. After a series of seemingly random moves, they fell back to take up positions facing south and adjoining the Knightsbridge Box (held by the 201st Guards Brigade), with, alongside them, the escaped D Troop from 520 Battery. Soon, through the distortions and mirages that plagued visibility, they could just make out the German panzers getting closer and closer.

> 'Willie' Pringle, our captain, a Scotsman, walked along and said, 'Under no circumstances must you fire until you're given an order.' The heat haze slowly dissolved itself into physical things. On the horizon you saw a vehicle which looked like a shadow and the heat haze made it jump up and down – and it slowly became a vehicle or tank. We simply looked at this in silence. We all lay down; we didn't sit on our guns because

they were too far away for us to shoot at them. Sergeant Major George Attewell walked round and asked if we were all right. We just lay there until they started to shoot at us![55]

Sergeant John Walker, E Troop, 425 Battery, 107th RHA

The men stayed under cover, as Bill Pringle planned to hold their fire until the panzers were at the closest possible range.

The German tanks wouldn't face concentrated 25-pounder fire when they got within close range. You had to be sure to get more accuracy. I prefer high explosive – it's more 'universal'. Armour-piercing (AP) is no good over distances because it must have a flat trajectory. If you don't hit the tank with AP it is a complete waste, but if an HE shell lands quite close to a tank it is pretty noisy inside with the bits of shell hitting: it might damage some of the trolley wheels that the tracks run on; it might even burst a track; it could kill the interior occupants![56]

Captain William Pringle, E Troop, 425 Battery, 107th RHA

Both the troop commanders of 425 Battery followed the same policy, but the disadvantage of holding fire to a few thousand yards was that gunners would be within range of the tanks' secondary armament – machine guns. Nearby, Ted Holmes, who was acting as a loader on one of the A Troop guns, found the hold-up extremely frustrating – and dangerous.

They were machine-gunning along the front of our guns, hitting the wheels and gun shields, everywhere, with bullets pinging off. These tanks came a bit closer. We'd got a round up the spout ready. We'd been told to load, but not fire until they came in close – we hadn't got to fire until we could see the whites of their eyes! Daft! We had to just sit there. I remember this Irish gun layer said, 'I wish they'd let us fire, I've got two in me sights!'[57]

Gunner Ted Holmes, A Troop, 425 Battery, 107th RHA

Under heavy fire it was inevitable there would be casualties.

We were under a hail of machine-gun bullets and we lost fairly quickly the layer on the next gun to me and one of my team got a bullet through his leg. Lying there being shot at by machine guns. George Attewell stood at the side of me and I said, 'For God's sake, George, get down – you'll get hit!' He didn't say a word, he just carried on staying there. There were bullets streaming into my limber. It didn't blow anything up, but they were hitting it just a yard to the left of where I was. I thought, 'Well, you're a better man then me, George, and yet why shouldn't I be like that?' That was exactly the feeling – he did inspire you! Then we were told to 'Take post!'[58]

Sergeant John Walker, E Troop, 425 Battery, 107th RHA

At last, the guns blazed out. Once they started firing, at this close range, it was the gun sergeants that controlled the guns.

I would pick the target and then help lift the trail round to get it on to the one I wanted. We were all scared to hell, but we were not scared in the least once we started firing. We were firing-cap on HE – the shell had its percussion cap left on which just gave it a fractional delayed action – it hit and exploded fractionally later – the idea being that it would blow up inside the tank rather than outside. The first one that we hit – the whole tank went red – my layer, Frank Bush, threw his hat in the air. 'Willie' Pringle said in his Scotch accent, 'Never mind that, get another one!'[59]

Sergeant John Walker, E Troop, 425 Battery, 107th RHA

But the German tanks were also scoring hits as they closed the range.

> If you hit him it's OK – but meantime he's firing at you with his gun and machine-gunning you at the same time, twisting and turning, zigzagging towards you. We got one or two shots off – when this one hit us. I believe it was an 88mm from a tank – there was such a lot of velocity with them that the first you knew about them was when it had hit you! It dropped just underneath the gun shield as far as I know. I was on the left-hand side of the gun, where you load up with your right hand, crouched down, my head right under the gun layer's seat with this 25-pounder round ready to load up again. It was just like someone gave me a big bang on the shoulder. My arm went all dead, it was just like a bit of old rope, just hanging all sort of any road. You could see the bones through me flesh. I reeled away.[60]
>
> Gunner Ted Holmes, A Troop, 425 Battery, 107th RHA

Holmes staggered back to the regimental aid post. He had wounds all down the left-hand side of his body. Here he encountered Harold Thompson, who had also been wounded.

> I got wounded by a shrapnel airburst there – on the forehead. There was blood streaming down my face. They took me down to the doctors – and that's where I met Ted Holmes after he'd been wounded. You couldn't stick a pin into anywhere that hadn't got shrapnel in it! He was absolutely splattered with shrapnel. Not really serious wounds, but combined they were! The doctor just come and looked, cleaned me up and said, 'You'll be all right and go back!' Which I did! Ted Holmes was evacuated back to base.[61]
>
> Gunner Harold Thompson, A Troop, 425 Battery, 107th RHA

Despite the casualties the battery held firm and the tanks were forced to retire when they got to about 3,000 yards from the gun pits. It had been a magnificent demonstration of the power of guns. But it had been a close-run thing.

That day, Lance Sergeant Ted Whittaker and Gunner David Worley were part of Major Peter Birkin's OP team, when Birkin went forward to liaise closely with Lieutenant Colonel Anthony Grafftey-Smith of the 3rd CLY. It was their task to provide the artillery support required by the squadrons of Grant and Crusader tanks.

> This Colonel was operating his tanks just like a fleet of ships at sea. It was more than a bit exciting, because you could see through the binoculars these big grey monsters with umpteen times more range – German tanks. Our tanks were engaging them, they'd fire and gradually drop back. The General Grants had gone in within an hour or two because they picked them out. We were bringing fire down – coordinating it. Wherever the colonel went we stuck close to him. It was absolute chaos! A scrap – then fall back – because our tanks were no match for these Germans – they were outgunned.[62]
>
> Lance Sergeant Ted Whittaker, Headquarters, 425 Battery, 107th RHA

At one point Birkin's OP team found themselves right in the middle of a tank battle, with shells and bullets whizzing around them. Then, suddenly, disaster loomed as their Marmon-Herrington lurched wildly to one side as a tyre was burst.

> David Worley said something gentle like, 'What the fucking hell's happened to us?' We hopped out – and we'd got a puncture – front wheel. Major Birkin said, 'Change the bloody wheel!' The tanks were at fairly long range, but by this time they'd come over the hill and there was quite a bunch of them. Machine-gun bullets were landing round us, one or two did hit the car with a bit of a rattle; if they'd been closer, they'd go

through it! You can imagine! We couldn't get the spare wheel off – I don't know whether it was because we were terrified or if the nuts were tight. Talk about fingers and thumbs! We finally got the spare wheel off. Then jacking up an armoured car – it's heavy – we were frantic! We got this ruddy wheel off. We put two wheel bolts on, and Dave said to me, 'What do you reckon?' I said, 'In the bloody car!' We hopped in, the major said, 'OK?' and off we went.[63]

Lance Sergeant Ted Whittaker, Headquarters, 425 Battery, 107th RHA

To the amusement of all, later investigation revealed that in his desperate haste, David Worley had managed to cross-thread both nuts![64]

The 426 Battery then moved forward to support the 4th CLY in a series of fighting withdrawals, with each squadron of tanks falling back in turn covered by the 25-pounders. The whole of the South Notts Hussars then formed part of an outer defensive ring being supplied by 22nd Armoured Brigade to the Knightsbridge Box, which was garrisoned 'inside the wire' by the 201st Guards Brigade and 2nd RHA. The worst was yet to come.

12

THE LAST ROUND, 6 JUNE 1942

> To be honest, all you're looking at are the few tanks that are
> coming near your gun. All you're thinking about is knocking
> out any tanks that look dangerous to you – not saving the
> British Empire![1]
>
> Sergeant Ray Ellis, A Troop, 425 Battery, 107th RHA

THE BATTLE OF KNIGHTSBRIDGE RAGED ON. It was a
complex business and, to be fair, few oral history accounts give
us any real guidance as to what was actually happening. There
is substantial confusion evident in both the order and timing of
events. To crudely summarise, Rommel's plan had been stymied
in several respects. Bir Hacheim had still not fallen, while the
sweep round to the north had made good initial progress but
had then been stemmed by the determined resistance of the 1st
Armoured Division. By this time Rommel had lost something
like a third of his tanks. The German panzer units were taken
by surprise by both the hitting power of the Grant 75mm guns
and the challenge posed by the Crusaders taking up protected
hull-down positions – with only their turret peaking above a
sand dune – to compensate for their inadequate 2-pounder
guns. To make matters worse, the assault to drive a direct supply
line past the Sidi Muftah Box and through the minefields had

not succeeded. Rommel ordered his panzers to fall back into Sidi Muftah Depression (known as the Cauldron) between the Knightsbridge Box and the Sidi Muftah Box facing east, using the British minefield to defend his rear.

Rommel's tanks were beginning to be immobilised through lack of petrol, and they were also short of ammunition, food and water. They could not carry on like this. In desperation, Rommel ordered them to turn their backs on the enemies to the east and to push west. He was determined to smash a viable supply route past the 150th Brigade Box by attacking it from both sides at once. His gamble worked: the garrison was crushed by a combination of overwhelming forces and mass Stuka attacks. The box was finally overrun on the afternoon of 1 June. The direct supply route was freed up and by this one bold stroke everything had changed: Rommel's armoured divisions were now resupplied and concentrated in a central position, thrusting right into the heart of the Eighth Army defensive lines.

This transformation in the tactical situation was not appreciated by the British High Command. Wary of losing the initiative, Auchinleck favoured either a direct assault to the west by XIII Corps, or a wide sweeping counter-attack round Rommel's southern flank. Given the reality of the situation, both these schemes were problematic, but Ritchie's alternative plan to launch a direct assault on the German forces in the Cauldron on 5 June represented the greatest risk, as it would be an attack on Rommel's strongest point.

The trouble was that the High Command would not accept the local reports of the strength of the German forces gathered in the Cauldron. Typical was the fate of the warning sent by Ted Whittaker, who was on OP duty when he tried to tell an intelligence officer at headquarters what was really happening. It was all to no avail.

We could see the big minefield and we were shooting at vehicles which were coming through from west to east. Instantly we reported this because the only known path at that time was further towards Bir Hacheim where it was fairly narrow. We reported this: back came someone from brigade on our frequency who said, 'Regards your sit-rep. Suggest you mean east to west, enemy retreating.' We were incensed at this and Birkin got on the mike himself and said, 'Troop movements: west to east, through minefield.' Blow me they came back again and said, 'Other reports definitely indicate east to west, enemy retreating.' This was one of the fatal mistakes. They'd opened a huge gap through the minefield and were pouring supplies through.[2]

Lance Sergeant Ted Whittaker, Headquarters, 425 Battery, 107th RHA

As a result, plans were made for Operation Aberdeen to be carried out on the night of 4/5 June. After a heavy artillery barrage, the 10th Infantry Brigade (5th Indian Division) and the 22nd Armoured Brigade were to thrust westwards directly into the Cauldron, breaking through the minefields and anti-tank gun defences to take Aslagh Ridge and push on to the Cauldron, ready for the 32nd Army Tank Brigade to attack from the north, looking to capture the Sidra Ridge that overlooked the Cauldron. Finally, the 7th Armoured Division, in conjunction with the 9th Indian Brigade, was to destroy whatever German forces remained in the Cauldron itself. The 1st Armoured Division would 'hold the ring' to prevent Rommel breaking out to the north or north-east, before moving in at the 'kill' to exploit the expected success.

On 5 June 1942, the 107th RHA was attached to the 10th Indian Brigade, to take part in the heavy preliminary barrage planned to commence at 03.30. Ray Ellis was only 22, but war had made him a man old before his time. Another battle, another barrage, the prospect of more deaths.

The worst part of a battle is before the battle: that is when you have the fear. My gun crew were new, and this was their first experience of warfare. I felt sorry for them because they were all obviously frightened. They were also homesick. It was only a matter of months since they'd been at home in England with their wives and sweethearts. I felt sorry for these men who were homesick, frightened and cold. I knew what it would be like when the barrage started: the first 'FLASH' and 'CRASH'. All the noise and the screaming of shells. Then you knew the enemy would reply and back into the old carnage. I wished that no gun would ever fire again. I was war-weary. Then you got the, 'Take Post!' You get on the gun – just tensing yourself. Everything is very still and quiet, then the shout through the megaphone, 'Zero, minus five, four, three, two, one, FIRE!' A screaming 'CRASH' as every gun along the front opens up and the battle is started. There is no longer then time to think about being wounded, or killed, or lonely, or tired – you're involved, the gun is firing and leaping about and you're firing the programme.[3]

Sergeant Ray Ellis, A Troop, 425 Battery, 107th RHA

After firing a barrage of some 135 rounds per gun they were to move forward with the 10th Indian Brigade and secure the high ground of Aslagh Ridge, which it was hoped would then give a good observation over the whole of Rommel's 'defeated' forces in the Cauldron area. They little knew that they were advancing to disaster.

After the barrage was fired, it was, 'Cease Firing!' We closed down, clamped the gun, hooked it on to the limber, the gun towers came up and we moved into the advance as the whole front moved forwards. It was just before dawn when we came up to this crest and everything opened up around us. He was waiting for us – he must have had it all ranged and ready – because the very first shells landed right among us. It was appalling. The sky ahead became a sea of flames as all their guns opened up. It was carnage, but we just kept going – because what the hell else could you do?[4]

Sergeant Ray Ellis, A Troop, 425 Battery, 107th RHA

As they reached the ridge the scale of the ambush was evident: the Germans had fallen back slightly and the barrage had been wasted on empty desert. Now it was time for the German retaliation.

In the distance there was this big arc of little tongues of fire. I realised to my horror that this was practically the whole of the Afrika Korps waiting for us. Soon after the first flashes, everything fell on us! The fire was absolutely murder. We were on this down slope and they were sitting at the edge of this shallow bowl. Absolute chaos, that really was the beginning of the end.[5]

Lance Sergeant Ted Whittaker, Headquarters, 425 Battery, 107th RHA

The Grant, Stuart and Crusader tanks of the 22nd Armoured Brigade were exposed to this terrible barrage of fire. Bill Pringle was moving forward in his Honey tank while on advanced OP duty with 3rd CLY when they encountered a German 88mm battery in a wadi. Pringle is a fascinating character whose gruff nature did not endear him to everyone, but he certainly had common sense.

The colonel spun round and waved his flag, 'Yoicks, tally ho to it, tally ho, tally ho!' A bit childish – we were there to win a war as far as I was concerned. When I eventually got him on the radio, because he wouldn't answer to start with, he told me that he knew where he was going, what he intended to do and that it was my job to do as I was told! We went straight at them. The barrels were facing that way. The first gun was on him in seconds and 'BWHUUFF' he'd gone and the whole lot came to a screaming halt. There was total chaos everywhere. The tank I was in had a burst petrol tank, so they'd tied 100 gallons in 5-gallon tins tied on the back with string! I tried to bring some gunfire down on the positions, but there was that much smoke and dust around you couldn't see it! I thought, 'Well, there's only one place for Pringle and that's out of here!' The British government spent a lot of time training me – I was an expensive asset! I said to the driver, 'Turn round and get on back!' 'I can't!' I said, 'Why not?' 'Can't get it into gear – the clutch has gone!' I said, 'Stop your engine and start it!' 'I've tried that, Sir, it doesn't work!' I told him to 'Rev it up, full revs, put the gear in a reverse position, then let me get my feet in it, and I'll see if I can push it in with my legs!' The Honey gear lever went down into the entrails of the tank. The first time it didn't go in. There was a right old battle going on outside of the tank, but I was more interested in getting this bloody engine started. There was no getting out on foot because you'd have been shot to bits. I said, 'Keep the revs on whatever you do and if we go – don't you stop!' I straightened my legs; the tank gave one hell of a 'bunny jump' and kept going backwards. We reversed 7 miles! I told the chap, 'Don't you stop, I'll murder you if you stop!'[6]

Captain William Pringle, E Troop, 425 Battery, 107th RHA

That day the 22nd Armoured Brigade would lose some sixty of its 156 tanks. The attack from the north by the 32nd Tank Brigade had met a similar fate, running into a minefield then being hit hard by 21st Panzer Division, losing some fifty of its seventy tanks. There would be no help from that quarter. The 9th and 10th Indian Brigades and their supporting gunners – including the 107th RHA – were left in a terrible situation facing most of the 15th Panzer Division and Ariete Armoured Division in the

Cauldron area without any proper armoured support. Brigadier Bernard Fletcher was left seething at the situation in which his men found themselves.

Our left flank had evidently not been guarded. Its protection was such an obvious necessity that it never occurred to me personally to ask what that protection was. I assumed that my brigade and 10th Brigade would not be asked to advance 5 to 8 miles into the enemy positions without adequate steps having been taken to protect the southern flank. There appears to have been a complete misunderstanding between the 22nd Armoured Brigade and 9th Brigade as to the capabilities and tasks of the two brigades. The 22nd Armoured Brigade appears to have thought that a battalion could establish itself in a box in the desert in a matter of half an hour; while 9th Brigade thought that the 22nd Armoured Brigade, with its 100 tanks, had been given the task of destroying the enemy tanks in this area in which it was to establish itself. In point of fact, the Armoured Brigade appears to have made no attempt to go to the assistance of the 2nd West Yorkshires when they were attacked by forty tanks and seventeen armoured cars; and when the position held by the 2nd Highland Light Infantry was attacked by forty tanks, the 22nd Armoured Brigade began a slow withdrawal. Later, it reported itself faced by ninety tanks. The opportunity of destroying the two small concentrations of enemy tanks had passed. I consider that infantry who have to operate with tanks should be trained with them. There would not then be this wide divergence of opinion as to the tasks and capabilities of the two parts of a force engaged in any one operation. In the desert, infantry require forty-eight hours in which to establish a box which can stand by itself against an enemy tank attack. In addition, they must be allowed to lay mines. Lack of mutual understanding and of common doctrines extended beyond the failure of tanks and infantry to understand each other.[7]

Brigadier Bernard Fletcher, Headquarters, 9th Indian Brigade, 5th Indian Division

To make matters worse, on the night of the 5/6 June, what few tanks that remained were withdrawn to the north-east towards the Knightsbridge Box. In their absence the Germans, covered by darkness, began to creep forward. The situation certainly irritated Bill Pringle.

We couldn't see our tanks anywhere, until that night we saw them behind us trailing away up to the north, which was the last place they should have gone. The British High Command said that all the German tanks were up north and the ones that were opposite us were wooden ones! Well I nearly exploded because we'd been in the desert three years, we'd seen every German tank that ever came into the bloody desert and if we didn't flipping well know, then I didn't know who the devil did! I went and saw Peter Birkin and played hell and said, 'If we don't get out of here tonight, we've had it!' He agreed with me and we both went to the colonel. He said he'd put it to the Divisional Command. I said, 'We've got to have more ammunition – and a lot of it!' He said, 'Don't worry, Bill, don't worry, there's plenty of ammunition on the way!' I said, 'Well, I hope it gets here before daylight!' He said, 'Why?' I said, 'The German tanks are round behind, and they'll shoot it up!' 'How do you know?' 'I can hear them!' You can't move tanks around without making a horrible squawking of tracks and God knows what! I was annoyed, probably wrongly, with his lack of ability to convince higher command that they'd got it wrong. There's different ways of putting things, but I'm afraid I should have sworn at them – it's one of the ways to make people listen to you! Take a bit more notice! I went back to E Troop and got some sleep – I didn't think there was any more I could do![8]

Captain William Pringle, E Troop, 425 Battery, 107th RHA

Robert Daniell seems to have argued with the 22nd Armoured Brigade commander, Brigadier William Carr, pressing for a retirement from this potentially suicidal position. It was his belief that they should pull back towards the Knightsbridge escarpment, masked by a mass of smoke shells, hoping to dissuade the German tanks from following too closely into an artificial cloud. He was met with short shrift and the vehemence of Carr's response would inform Daniell's conduct throughout the battle that followed.

He said, 'Bob, you are to stand and fight in the position where you are now, you are not to move! Do you understand me? You are not to move at all!' I told him that if I obeyed, I would lose every single man I had. He replied, 'You are a Horse Artillery officer, you have been properly brought up and you know that in battle you will obey orders – or take the consequences.'[9]

Major Robert Daniell, Headquarters, 107th RHA

David Elliott was designated to accompany an ammunition supply column as it returned to the regimental wagon lines of the night of 5/6 June. It was obvious that the German steel ring was closing about them.

I was quite frightened – I think you wanted to be doing something, I had nothing to do at all. I remember the sun going down, a very, very bright red. Seeing a German armoured piercing shell coming towards us, at the end of its trajectory – like a cricket ball! It was just bouncing and turning over. I thought, 'Well, these people are a bit too close to me to be comfortable!' I was quite glad when evening came and we collected up six 3-tonners and a small Maurice pickup, which Jack Attewell drove, and he made me sit in the cab of one of the 3-tonners at the back. It was routine to him! The track was well marked and off we set. We found there was fighting going on closer than we thought, by the look of the flashes. The moon hadn't come up, it was terribly dark. At one stage we all had to stop rather suddenly. I walked forward to find out what was happening, and Jack got out of his vehicle and he was pointing to the front – there was a light moving where he wasn't expecting anybody to be. We kept quiet. Then there was more firing in front, and he decided to turn a different way. Around the middle of the night there was a bang and the head of the column stopped again. Again, I went forward and this time it was because a lorry had driven into a slit trench. That caused a lot of kerfuffle – we had a chain to pull it out. It was getting lighter – the moon was coming up – and Jack suggested I walk in front. We weren't travelling fast, there was not even dipped lights. I think it was a decision that saved some of our lives because within half an hour I'd tripped over barbed wire 8 or 9 inches high and he knew immediately it was the wire of a minefield. We turned down the wire a little bit and came across the German skull and crossbones, a yellow triangle that they hung on the wire, 'Achtung Minen!' We knew there were gaps through if we could find them, so we drove along the wire until we came to quite a well-worn gap. We turned through that, travelling east, and when we got to the other side of the minefield, we started following tracks. We met vehicles, but there was bombing going on behind us, the flickering of the fighting down to the south and we were nonplussed as to what was happening. We got back to the wagon lines and went to sleep.[10]

Second Lieutenant David Elliott, Headquarters, 520 Battery, 107th RHA

FEW OF THE SOUTH NOTTS HUSSARS slept much that night. The remnants of D Troop, 520 Battery were on the left, with 425 Battery in the middle, both facing south, while 426 Battery was on the right with C Troop facing west and F Troop looking north-west. They were in a saucer-like depression, with a raised 'rim' running all around them, allowing the Germans to approach and threaten their flanks with impunity until they crossed the rim – about 1,200 yards from the guns. Also trapped close by in the Cauldron were the 4/10th Baluch Regiment, the 2/4th Gurkha Rifles, the 3/9th Jat Regiment and the 4th, 28th and 157th Field RA – the divisional artillery of 5th Indian Division. But we must concentrate on the South Notts Hussars. The men knew that their position was untenable. They would not have been human if they were not afraid.

> Then you knew that was it! I felt shattered. How does a young man feel when he thinks his life's going to finish there and then? You'd made a picture in your mind of the German: he was a big figure about 9 feet tall, strong and swarthy – invincible.[11]
>
> Bombardier Albert Parker, Headquarters, 425 Battery, 107th RHA

Ray Ellis found very little to reassure him when he chatted to a couple of his officers as they did the rounds of the positions. There was no point in sugar-coating this situation.

> I was standing by the gun when two figures approached, Captain Slinn and Lieutenant Geoffrey Timms. They stopped for a chat and I asked, 'What's the situation, Sir?' Captain Slinn said, 'We're being left to fight a rearguard, Sergeant. We're going to stop and its one of these fight to the last man and last round jobs! It's going to be a bloody awful day – a real hell of a job this one! I think there will be very few of us left alive at the end of this day.'[12]
>
> Sergeant Ray Ellis, A Troop, 425 Battery, 107th RHA

Graham Slinn would be proved right.

Just before dawn, another supply column from regimental wagon lines reached the regiment. With them was Charles Ward, with a lieutenant of the Northumberland Hussars who was nominally in charge.

> We got there more or less at first light and it was quite obvious that the Germans had practically surrounded them. This lieutenant said, 'Quartermaster, I'm going to take the petrol and ammunition in. It's up to you to take back all the other soft vehicles with the food and everything!' I rounded the others up and told them, and suddenly he came dashing up and said, 'I'm taking the lot through!' I think really, he was after a medal, I can't think of any other reason, because what he did was stupid! As we went in, we were actually machine-gunned. I'd got a driver who'd just come out from England – he was not very good and certainly not very brave. As we were machine-gunned, he almost went to pieces, and said, 'What do I do? What do I do?' I said, 'Drive on, and put your "so and so" foot down!' He did and we got in just as the Germans closed the ring. The first thing I saw was all the petrol trucks we brought in going up in flames.[13]

Battery Quartermaster Sergeant Charles Ward, 426 Battery, 107th RHA

As the light improved, Ted Whittaker had looked eagerly for the return of the British tanks as they had been promised. He was to be sorely disappointed.

> During the night they told us not to be alarmed: the British tanks were going out to refuel and rearm. On 6 June we stood to from before first light. As it got light, we looked up the ridge and yes – there were the tanks in position – you could just see the tops of them – silhouetted. As it got just a bit lighter then we knew we were for it – they were German tanks hull-down.[14]

Lance Sergeant Ted Whittaker, Headquarters, 425 Battery, 107th RHA

Just after dawn some Stukas flew across the battlefield and in response the purple German recognition smoke signals went up – they were all around the South Notts Hussars.

The first attack was launched at 08.30 with a mass tank attack pushing in from the south-west and aimed squarely at 425 Battery.

> The colonel's armoured car was seen travelling at high speed in our direction. The car turned parallel to the guns and the colonel almost hanging out of the vehicle was yelling, 'Tank alert! Independent gunfire! Zero elevation!' That meant each gun for itself. I said a prayer or two as I scrambled on to the seat. I swung my scope to front vision and saw four or five tanks moving towards us at about 800 yards. I slapped my backside which indicated to John Walker that I was on target, he yelled 'AP up the spout'. As soon as I heard the breech slam to, I heard John yell, 'Fire!' I fired. I watched as the blue light at the rear of the shell moved to the second tank in line. A bulls-eye! Smoke and flame shot out of the turret of the tank. I moved my scope on to the next moving target and achieved the same result. The tanks were now closing in and stopped at about 500 yards. Simultaneously they did a 90 degree turn and moved to my left. I saw one tank turn its turret back on to me and then a flash! The tank shell hit the left side of my gun shield and ripped a huge chunk of flesh from my left thigh. John pulled me from the seat and yelled for Frank Bush to take over. As John moved me to the rear of the gun, I felt something hit me in the throat. I knew no more.[15]

Gunner Ronald Miles, E Troop, 425 Battery, 107th RHA

In a close-range action like this, all that mattered were the gun sections; almost everybody else was irrelevant. Bill Pringle chose to go forward and stand with his gunners.

You were saying to the chaps as they fired a shot, 'For Christ's sake go easy – we won't have any left!' I was quite happy we could cope with the situation – we could have done if we'd had enough ammunition. We wanted lorry loads of the damn stuff![16]

Captain William Pringle, E Troop, 425 Battery, 107th RHA

In various estimates the panzers got as close as 500 to 700 yards before falling back.

They wheeled off and went back. Once they were out of effective range, we stopped firing, because we were concerned with ammunition. I doubt if we had more than twenty rounds per gun of armour-piercing, which is not many! I always tried to keep a few in reserve, so that if something did get through and was looking really dangerous, at least I'd got an armour-piercing as a reserve. Then you cleared all the shell cases from the back of the gun, made sure the ammunition is to hand, generally tidy up the position to make it as efficient as possible. See if you can find a few more stones to pile up in front of the gun, or scrape a bit more depth to the slit trench you are in.[17]

Sergeant Ray Ellis, A Troop, 425 Battery, 107th RHA

At 09.30, Bill Seely sent a wireless message to Brigadier Carr, again requesting permission to retire. Carr was intransigent, informing Seely that a relief force, the 32nd Army Tank Brigade under the command of Brigadier Arthur Willison, was already on its way to rescue them. It proved a vain boast, as Willison's tanks could make no headway against the heavy German fire.

Rebuffed in their first attempt, the Germans began to adopt a slightly more patient, cautious approach, with German infantry moving up in support around the 'saucer' rim. They also moved up their artillery and began to drop airburst shells across the 107th RHA gun positions. Dennis Mayoh left a vivid memory of what the fighting was like as the layer with Sergeant Faulkner's gun section.

> If the tank was going sideways from right to left, or left to right, we had to hit him in the tracks. If the tank was coming for you, as it moved up and down, we had to try and aim for the belly. If not the belly, then the top of the gun, which should have knocked his turret off – but it didn't! That was how we were trained to hit them. Although I say it myself, we were good! Sergeant Faulkner was at the trail giving orders, and at the same time looking for any danger to the left, or to the right. I was laying the gun. On the telescope you've got a cross and you would wait for the tank to come across there and as he got there you would say, 'On! On! On! Fire!' You would fire just as the tank's nose reached the cross, allowing for the distance.[18]

Bombardier Dennis Mayoh, D Troop, 520 Battery, 107th RHA

Jack Sykes was in charge of the signals for Major William Barber commanding 426 Battery. As is sometimes the case with wartime memories originating in times of great stress, he was somewhat forthright in his assessment of Barber.

> I was with Barber in a converted armoured car as a mobile command post. There was a driver. Two wirelesses: one, which Walter Dobson was on, was through to our guns; and I was through to the brigade. Barber was a bit of a dodderer – I got the impression that he didn't seem to know too well what he was really up to. He was adequate rather than exceptional. I passed back orders to Barber, who passed them on to the guns for them to do whatever was necessary – to take up positions, fire to support infantry, or tanks – or whatever. The only thing I could see was through a bit of a slit in the side – and I could see

shells exploding, movements, that kind of thing. I stayed there all the time.[19]

Sergeant Jack Sykes, Headquarters, 426 Battery, 107th RHA

Even with the limited visibility through the slit, he could see that the German tanks were getting nearer.

I was sitting there passing messages when – all of a sudden – there was a bloody great bang! It filled with cordite and smoke. I remember Walter shouting, 'Jack! Jack!' I was pretty well half-unconscious because the shell had hit underneath my seat and I got the blast of it in my back. I got shrapnel in my back, some in my knee and all my arms were scratched and bruised – all swollen. I wasn't feeling very happy with myself! I remember he dragged me out and put me at the bottom of the slit trench. After that I took no further part in it.[20]

Sergeant Jack Sykes, Headquarters, 426 Battery, 107th RHA

Battery Quartermaster Sergeant Charles Ward soon realised that he was serving very little purpose as the shells dropped all around the command post.

The guns were in front of the battery headquarters and really there was nothing for me to do. I made a half-hearted attempt to distribute rations, but every few yards you were shot at! Major Barber said, 'Just go and put your truck somewhere, where they can go and get them!' Which I did! A few people went. What it says in the regimental history, that I went round distributing rations as though nothing was happening, was rubbish! Quite frankly, I didn't! With shells dropping all around and chaos, to go around the guns with the rations, with the Germans taking pot-shots at a few hundred yards, would have been suicidal – to put it bluntly – and serve no purpose.[21]

Battery Quartermaster Sergeant Charles Ward, Headquarters, 426 Battery, 107th RHA

Ward encountered Bill Seely, who was walking around the position with Major Cowan of the Northumbrian Hussars.

> I thought, 'Dammit, I'm going to report direct to Colonel Seely!' I went up to him, saluted. Seely was very nice; the [officer] of the Northumberland Hussars looked at me as though I was a piece of cheese! I told him I'd been to look for ammunition and there's none available! 'Oh, thank you very much! All right!' He was quiet, totally relaxed. Amazing really.[22]

Battery Quartermaster Sergeant Charles Ward, Headquarters, 426 Battery, 107th RHA

Ted Whittaker, as a specialist OP assistant, also found himself redundant as the battle raged all around them.

> Peter Birkin said, 'You'd better make yourself useful where you can!' What use is a forward observation expert when the enemy is on your position – it's like the proverbial spare at the wedding. I've never felt so helpless. I had a word with my mates, told them what Colonel Seely had said: 'We've only got to hang on twelve hours!' And the reply to that was, 'A fat lot of effing use that's going to be!'[23]

Lance Sergeant Ted Whittaker, Headquarters, 425 Battery, 107th RHA

A good soldier, Whittaker resolved to make himself useful. One obvious mission was to help in gathering and caring for the wounded. In the first couple of hours of the action casualties had been surprisingly light, but now they were mounting fast as the airburst shells sent metal shards scything across the gun positions.

> Going from one trench to another with field dressings. This was horrifying! One of the first people I saw was Birkin's batman, in a slit trench with a big hole in the top of his steel helmet.

Previously, it had been very exciting, and I was almost enjoying it, but I began to realise that these were my friends, people I knew. I'd got back to where our armoured car had been dug in and there were half a dozen drivers who'd taken refuge in this big hole we'd dug. They began to shell us, right over us – this airburst – and I dropped into a slit trench and I sat there for ages, petrified. All of a sudden there was one burst really close, some terrible noises came from this hole. I jumped up and these poor chaps – there were one or two still alive, but it was terrible – terrible! Miraculously nothing where I was just a couple of yards away.[24]

Lance Sergeant Ted Whittaker, Headquarters, 425 Battery, 107th RHA

Bombardier Albert Parker was also driving round in his pickup truck collecting casualties and taking them to regimental aid position. He had a dreadful experience he could never forget.

People were scattered all over the place. I picked up one bloke and he was like a rag doll – no arms, no legs and smoking – on fire – it frightened me to death. Terrible.[25]

Bombardier Albert Parker, Headquarters, 425 Battery, 107th RHA

Frank Knowles was one of the men treated by Parker.

I received leg wounds in two places – the thigh and the back of the lower right leg. It was from shrapnel or rock splinters – we were on hard ground. On reflection I think it might have been an 88mm, because we didn't hear it coming and 88s were faster than sound – you got them before you hear the whistle. It numbed the leg and I fell over. I was lying beside the pickup. Albert Parker rolled me into a slit trench and applied a field dressing.[26]

Lance Bombardier Frank Knowles, Headquarters, 425 Battery, 107th RHA

1. Officers of the South Notts Hussars at the start of the war. Tallest at the middle back is Lieutenant Graham Slinn, first on left front row is Captain John Shakespear, second on left Major Peter Birkin, middle, Lieutenant Colonel William Seely.

2. Ted Holmes taken on leave in Cairo, 1940. One of my favourite informants – a lovely man who would become a gravedigger in civilian life working at Hasland Church.

3. Frank Knowles on leave in Cairo, 1940.

4. Braving muddy conditions in the tented camp at Gedera in Palestine, 1940.

5. Officers on a sea bathing parade in Palestine, 1940. From left to right:
a cheeky Peter Birkin, Ivor Birkin and an unidentified officer.

6. Bill Hutton – a cheery character, he got a position as a despatch rider. Here he is with his pride-and-joy motorcycle in Palestine, 1940.

7. Ray Ellis sat on the trail of an 18-pounder Mark II in Palestine, 1940.

8. A lovely photograph of Ted Whittaker taken in 1939 to mark his first appearance in uniform having volunteered to join the South Notts Hussars. He little knew of what he was letting himself in for.

9. Harry Day was taken prisoner at the Battle of Knightsbridge but escaped in Italy and was sheltered by friendly Italians. This photo was taken in 1945.

10. Fred Langford had worked for Ericson Telephone Ltd in Beeston before the war. He gravitated towards the signals and rose to be a signal sergeant by 1941.

11. Jack Sykes followed the footsteps of his father, Sergeant Harry Sykes, into the regiment and ended up as a signal sergeant. Here he is in 1942.

12. Group photograph of pals taken in Palestine, 1940. From the left Bill Hutton, Ray Ellis, Cliff Lilbourne, Bob Paulson and Ian Sinclair. Poor Bob Paulson would be the first man in the regiment to die, stricken down with appendicitis he died on 16 May 1940.

13. Ronald Miles was not one of the men that I interviewed as he had emigrated in the post-war years to Australia. His son, Paul Miles, heard of the book and sent his late father's memoirs and this photo.

14. Bombardier Albert Swinton in action in the boxing final on the divisional sports day in Palestine, 1940.

15. Gunner Mills cutting Ivor Birkin's hair in Palestine, 1940.

16. Practice firing with an 18-pounder at Mersa Matruh, Egypt, 1940.

17. Gunner Ronald Monteith with signalling equipment in
the desert at Asluj Firing Camp, Palestine, 1940.

18. View of the long straight road into Mersa Matruh, Egypt, 1940. The South Notts Hussars would be part of the defence of Cairo and Alexandria from the threatening Italian Tenth Army.

19. Ted Whittaker standing on top of a pyramid whilst on leave in Egypt.

20. Quad 25-pounder gun tower as issued to the regiment at Kabrit Camp in Egypt, 1941.

21. Bob Hingston using theodolite with Geof Neale standing by during calibration of new 25-pounder guns at Kabrit in 1941.

22. Command post dugout of D Troop, 426 Battery at Tobruk, Libya, 1941. Conditions were harsh, with men living in shallow holes in the ground. It was too hot during the day and frequently cold at night.

23. Sergeant Bob Foulds with D Gun, B Troop, 425 Bty at Tobruk, Libya, 1941. When I interviewed Bob he still looked in his mid-fifties – in fact he looked younger than me!

24. The regimental water bowser with Ted Holmes on the right in Tobruk, Libya, 1941. Bowsers and cookhouse trucks, indeed transport of any kind, were invaluable and the South Notts Hussars soon became adept at winning 'extra' vehicles.

25. Sergeant Ian Sinclair's gun team with him in centre, on the left Tommy Foley and on the right Ray Ellis. Picture taken in Tobruk in 1941. A tough and determined group of men.

26. One of the most important roles of the 5.5" medium gun was to 'take out' the German batteries that threatened slaughter to the advancing infantry if they were not knocked out before the Battle of Alamein, 1942.

27. Boarding the landing ships was a complex puzzle prior to the invasion of Sicily in July 1943. Space was at a premium and a high degree of skill was needed from the Quad gun tower drivers.

28. A group photograph of the South Notts Hussars with one of the mighty 5.5" guns in Sicily in 1943. These changed the nature of the war for the gunners. No longer in the front line, now they could wreak destruction of the Germans from miles behind the line – no longer at 'close range'.

29. Signallers of 425 Battery in 1944.

30. Dug in command post of 425 Battery in 1944.

31. From 1943, the regiments armed with the 5.5" medium guns were banded together to form an Army Group Royal Artillery or AGRAs to maximise their destructive power. Here is a typically strong concentration amassed to cover the Rhine crossing in March 1945.

32. The campaign could be fast moving in north-west Europe. Captain Bob Foulds has his 425 Battery command post set up in a 3-ton lorry ready for the next advance.

The medical facilities were inadequate for this kind of situation. The newly arrived Doctor McFarland (replacing Doctor Finnegan), and his orderly Harry Day set up a regimental aid post in a slight depression in and around a 3-ton covered lorry equipped with just four stretchers. The ground was soon covered with the wounded. Harry Day was rushed off his feet.

> Many of them were very badly wounded. They had to have morphia. We just had to lay them on the ground, we had no more stretchers. We splinted all that we could. We used all the wire splinting and had to use temporary splints of rolled-up paper magazines on fractures to arms and legs – caused by shell splinters. Some head wounds.[27]
>
> Medical Orderly Harry Day, Headquarters, 107th RHA

Day recalled one particularly terrifying close escape.

> One of the wounded had a compound fracture of the humerus. The doctor was replacing the splint and I was supporting the humerus with the man's head resting on my thigh as I was kneeling on the floor of the truck. An 88mm armour-piercing shell came straight through the truck and hit him under the throat, taking the man's head completely off. His remains were spattered on the canvas of the truck. I rolled over with the near-miss and my shorts were covered with his blood. At first, I thought I had been wounded myself, thought my cricketing and sporting activities had finished. Putting my hands down my shorts I found I was still in one piece.[28]
>
> Medical Orderly Harry Day, Headquarters, 107th RHA

As the long day wore on, the wounded continued to pour in. They simply couldn't cope.

> I had great difficulty in restraining men – who were suffering from shock and in a comatose condition – from walking away

from the comparative shelter of the shallow basin around the truck and walking towards the enemy guns. One had to be very careful, they were very badly wounded, and they had to be slowly shepherded back. They didn't know where they were going, they wanted to go away.[29]

Medical Orderly Harry Day, Headquarters, 107th RHA

The airbursts seem to have caused the most casualties. One exploded above the headquarters of 425 Battery close to Frank Knowles.

Looking out the rear of my truck, I saw a shell airburst fell Captain Slinn and Lieutenant Timms. They had severe head wounds. That was within 12 feet of the rear of my vehicle and I got out to see if I could do anything, but Peter Birkin told me to get back in and leave it to the medical officer and his orderly.[30]

Lance Bombardier Frank Knowles, Headquarters, 425 Battery, 107th RHA

Harry Day was called to the scene by a runner. By this time, movement in the open was fraught with extreme danger.

We had seen airbursts from the German tanks – and one such had mortally wounded Captain Slinn and Lieutenant Timms. The doctor went across and a few minutes later the runner came back again and asked me to go across with another medical pannier. The runner went – and I saw him within a few yards blown to bits. I put the medical pannier on my back, and I ran zigzag across to 425 Headquarters. The doctor had received an injury in the knee. Captain Slinn and Lieutenant Timms were both taken by stretcher back to the RAP. I put my arm around the doctor to assist him back and he told me to walk in front. At first, I couldn't understand this order, but obviously one of us had to be left alive! Had a shell burst when we were both together, it would have killed us both and nobody of any consequence would have been left to look after the wounded. Eventually we arrived back at the RAP. Captain Slinn and Lieutenant Timms' wounds were – I can't elaborate – they were beyond talking about. They were beyond the possibility of medical treatment. The actual decision about giving these men a lethal dose of morphine by hypodermic syringe rested entirely with the doctor – who was completely justified. They would never have been normal human beings again; I saw that it was a relief for them.[31]

Medical Orderly Harry Day, Headquarters, 107th RHA

By the end there were over seventy badly wounded men at the regimental aid post.

The morphia had gone. We weren't as a RAP equipped to deal with that amount of wounded. The situation was a thing that happened once in a lifetime. Some were dying, some we couldn't do anything about. People bleeding got tourniquets put on as best we can. But what they wanted immediately was surgical treatment and hospitalisation. They must have that. There was nothing else we could do – we were a RAP.[32]

Medical Orderly Harry Day, Headquarters, 107th RHA

Charles Ward visited the RAP and tried to bring some comfort to some of his wounded friends.

I like to think it wasn't deliberate, but the Germans seemed to be pinpointing this place more than anywhere else. Claude Earnshaw, who'd got a shot, I think through his knee, he was such an enthusiastic soldier and he was cursing because he couldn't take any further part in the battle. He refused to go down in the dugout and sat on the top. He said, 'Come on, come and talk to me!' We sat chatting away for half an hour with all these shells – you could feel the blast sometimes, it

actually lifted you! I saw Sergeant Bill Lake[33] coming in badly
wounded, he'd been hit all down his side. He was moaning,
'Don't touch me, don't touch me!' He died of course. It was
a terrible business; they were bringing them in by the dozen.
How Harry Day coped with it I don't know![34]

Battery Quartermaster Sergeant Charles Ward, Headquarters, 426
Battery, 107th RHA

Some men showed amazing sang-froid as the shells rained
down and the tanks rumbled forward. One incident was almost
bizarre.

During the last hour or more, I was in the same slit trench with
this chap Sergeant Buckley, he was the battery clerk, and we
were pinned down completely. He was an amazing bloke, he
got out a piece of paper, drew on it and said, 'C'mon, let's have
a game of Battleships!' There we were in this slit trench playing
battleships with all this hell let loose.[35]

Battery Quartermaster Sergeant Charles Ward, Headquarters, 426
Battery, 107th RHA

Understandably, some men could not cope with the danger, the
noise, the loss of their friends. Perhaps it is more amazing that
most found the courage and determination to carry on their
duties to the end.

One officer broke down and lost his nerve, he was laid in a slit
trench behind my gun, screaming, 'Keep them back! Please
keep them back!' He gave us no help at all! At the time we
judged him very harshly, but now who am I to judge? Willie
Pringle was on the gun position all this time. He wasn't hiding
in a hole or anything. Peter Birkin was very evident, he'd got
a little Honey tank; he came round to my gun late in the
afternoon. He said, 'We're not finished yet are we, Sergeant!'
I said, 'No, Sir, we're not!' Jim Hardy was with him and as

they drove off the position they were hit. A shell went straight through, killed the driver, went between Peter Birkin's legs and cut poor old Jim Hardy in two and killed him.[36]

Sergeant Ray Ellis, A Troop, 425 Battery, 107th RHA

Bill Seely aroused nothing but admiration from his men. Throughout the battle he moved round the gun positions in his Honey tank, accompanied by his adjutant Captain Henry Peal, a wireless operator, and his driver Gunner Chadbourn. He regularly checked with his troop and battery commanders and visited the men in their gun pits. He survived for nearly the whole battle but ran out of luck in the most terrible fashion, when a shell scored a direct hit, causing the Honey to burst into flames. Chadbourne escaped, but heroically dived back in to try to rescue the others. Bill Seely[37] and his wireless operator were clearly beyond either reach or help, but Chadbourne managed to drag out the adjutant – all in vain, however, for Henry Peal[38] died next day from a combination of his wounds and terrible burns.

In these closing stages the guns were almost completely surrounded, and the tanks had edged forward to open fire with their machine-gun secondary armaments. Major Robert Daniell was touring the gun positions attempting to form scratch gun detachments from any spare personnel he could find. Although his intention was admirable, his abrasive manner raised some hackles.

When the tanks knew that they completely encircled us and there was very little resistance left from our lads, they came quite close, like a bloody dog looking at its prey. A bloke called 'Tiny' Williams (he was about 6 foot 2) he'd been hit with a bit of shrapnel in his shoulder. I was going to find the situation – some blokes had been killed – and see if they wanted any help [on the gun]. I was actually walking towards it when Major

Daniell says, 'GET ON THAT GUN!' He was in a slit trench!
I said, 'Why don't you get on the bloody gun?' To me he was
just a bloke shouting out of a hole – I didn't know who he was.
He says, 'I am Major Daniell!' I said, 'I don't care a bugger who
you are! If you want a gunner, why don't you go on the gun?'
I walked forward to the gun and started to pick up the ammo
and put it up the breech! I bent down to pick up the next shell
and the next thing I knew my face was covered in blood. They'd
fired at us – I must have had a splinter – it nicked near the left
eye.[39]

Bombardier Albert Parker, Headquarters, 425 Battery, 107th RHA

Ted Whittaker recalled a similar incident.

I heard Major Daniell shouting, 'Are there some gunners? I've
got a 25-pounder here – somebody man it!' I thought, 'Well,
I can't sit here!' I jumped up and said, 'Here, Sir!' And there
were two other fellows. He said, 'There's a few rounds in there,
you might as well fire them!' Then off he drove. There was this
German tank a few hundred yards away. I guessed the range.
There were three rounds in the limber, no armour-piercing. We
loaded this HE and fired, and it went over the top of this Mark
IV tank. The turret turned and, 'BRRRRUUUMPPHH!'
To my horror, I was the only one standing. The machine-gun
bullets had gone straight through the gun shield. He fired one
burst and left us.[40]

Lance Sergeant Ted Whittaker, Headquarters, 425 Battery, 107th RHA

Both the other men on that makeshift gun crew were wounded.

Daniell was still determined never to surrender under any
circumstances. The remarks of Brigadier Carr the previous night
had aroused and exacerbated his natural pride in his status as a
regular officer of the Royal Horse Artillery.

Never mind. We were told to stand and fight to the last man
and the last round and that's what we did! I was directly given
the order and I had no idea of surrender at all. My natural
inclination had been to move the whole bloody lot half a
day earlier and get them out of trouble. I never would order
anybody to surrender and no Horse Artillery gunner officer has
ever surrendered.[41]

Major Robert Daniell, Headquarters, 107th RHA

However, the next action that Daniell took earned him the
lasting enmity of nearly all the survivors of the Knightsbridge
battle. As he expressed his intentions it appeared a reasonable
course of action.

I knew that the guns behind me had no ammunition. I knew
that Barber's battery had got ammunition if I could get guns
to it. If I could get the four guns together I could face four
ways. I could therefore stop any tank from running over them.
You must remember I'd seen the German tank run right over
the British gun. I found these two guns and shouted to them
to follow me, I was in my 8cwt truck and I started to drive off
towards Barber's position. I never saw them again.[42]

Major Robert Daniell, Headquarters, 107th RHA

John Walker was the No. 1 of one of the two E Troop guns
ordered to pull out of the line. His views of the orders he was
given are obvious.

Our second in command, Major Daniell, drove on the position
in a staff car, and he told us to pull our guns out and form 'a
hollow British square'. He immediately pushed off – he didn't
stay there to organise it. I was able to pull my gun out, my
driver came up with the vehicle, I hitched in and we started
to climb into the vehicle, when a shell came right through my

driver and the front of the vehicle. The vehicle was wrecked, and my driver was killed – and we decided that was enough. There was nothing we could do. The German tank was about 15 yards away, no more! Other guns on the same site had already surrendered and they were just driving through us.[43]

Sergeant John Walker, E Troop, 425 Battery, 107th RHA

Ted Whittaker had the best – and worst – perspective of the terrible consequences of Daniell's headstrong action.

There was ammunition exploding, gun limbers and ammunition trucks blowing up. Flames, smoke, horrible stink of gunpowder. I went up to E Troop, I thought if this was it, I might as well be with my mates. Major Daniell drove up and shouted, 'Form British square – go and form up on 426 Battery!' They were over to our right. What he meant was to get back to back and fight it out! I rushed up when I heard this – the gunners had got Quads which were still in action and they hooked the guns on. I went to get on the limber of the first gun in the troop. There were two or three chaps sitting on the limber. The nearest one, Harrison, was a Derby County footballer. They told me to 'Eff off'. The truck was moving, and I grabbed hold of the door and put one foot in the footrest – so I was hanging on the side of the door. We went a few yards and there was the most horrible 'WHHUUMMMPH'. I glanced round – couldn't quite see what had happened – there was some awful moans at the back. 'WHHUUMMMPH'. The most enormous crash brought us to a standstill. As I jumped off, I looked back and it was a terrible sight. The first shell had hit these blokes – this poor Harrison[44] was practically in half. I dropped off the door and threw myself flat. The driver, Stevenson, he'd got half out of the door and the next armour-piercing shell came straight through the driving cab and there was poor Stevenson[45] left hanging over the door. I dropped in a slit trench. Three shots: 'Bang, Bang, Bang!' I was absolutely horrified at what had happened to these people I had been talking to only a moment before. I felt I could have sat down and cried.[46]

Lance Sergeant Ted Whittaker, Headquarters, 425 Battery, 107th RHA

Both these guns had been from Bill Pringle's E Troop and it is fair to say that he was livid at Daniell's intervention.

The first thing I knew was a gun was going across my rear heading north. It was nonsensical – it broke up what was a very tenable position. I reckon that if we'd had enough ammunition, we could have seen that job out till dark – and then gone! I shall always be convinced of that! They never got where they were supposed to get to – they couldn't have got to where they were supposed to go – straight into the tanks – they were shot to bits 20 or 30 yards out of the gun positions. I told the other guns to stay where they were; I wasn't going to have them shot up.[47]

Captain William Pringle, E Troop, 425 Battery, 107th RHA

Pringle is clearly exaggerating – there was no chance of holding on as they had no more ammunition – but he did recognise the futility of Daniell's 'gesture'. To make matters worse, Daniell was perceived not to have stayed to share the fate of the men he commanded – and in this case sent to their deaths. He simply drove off to the 426 Battery position.

One of the German tanks blew a wheel off my truck. I got out and walked across to where one of the subalterns, Chadburn, was sitting behind a gun in his Honey tank. Behind him were blazing lorries and the place was covered with smoke. It was 5 o'clock and I knew I had an hour of light to get through before it would be dark. Machine-gun fire was very heavy all round. I rolled into the smoke, but I found I couldn't breathe in it. So, I rolled back again, and I was on my way walking across the ground, the machine-gun fire was coming up like hail. I wasn't touched! I walked as far as Chadburn's gun and I saw a German tank about 120 yards away. He was in his tank and I shouted at him to jump down and help me with the gun – and a wounded gunner appeared from somewhere. He and I swung the gun round, loaded it and I pulled the trigger and blew the tank sky high – I couldn't miss it.[48]

Major Robert Daniell, Headquarters, 107th RHA

His story has no external corroboration but is typical of the narrative promulgated by Daniell: he is the instigator; the man of action, and the rest of the officers are simply not up to his standards as a regular.

Bill Pringle, as one might expect, had a far more pragmatic attitude. The situation was hopeless so he would 'spike' his guns to deny them to the enemy and then surrender to save as many as possible of his men.

The tanks were nearly on top of me, they were so close behind me. There was no more left to fire – we left the last two rounds to blow the guns up. You put one down one end and one up the other and pull the trigger.[49]

Captain William Pringle, E Troop, 425 Battery, 107th RHA

Pringle also witnessed the death of Captain Alan Chadburn, which shows him in a different light to that portrayed in Daniell's account.

Alan Chadburn[50] stood on top of tank and waved his .38 pistol. Waving and shouting, I don't know what he was shouting – I couldn't hear. For somebody to do that he must have been partially mentally deranged. You're committing suicide aren't

you? And what was the point? You couldn't win the battle. All
of a sudden, he was machine-gunned down.[51]

Captain William Pringle, E Troop, 425 Battery, 107th RHA

With the German tanks actually moving across the gun positions, for those gunners still left alive surrender was the only
realistic proposition.

Three tanks appeared round the escarpment. Dr McFarland
said, 'Harry, we're saved – it's the Gloucester Hussars!' I said,
'Well Sir, the Gloucester Hussars don't have white crosses on
them.' He said. 'Oh my God, we're going in the bag! Will you
please get my personal kit from the 15cwt truck!' – which was
about 200 yards away. I had my Red Cross brassard on my
left arm, the tanks were on my right – so I walked backwards
showing my Red Cross brassard and pointing to it. I walked
slowly![52]

Medical Orderly Harry Day, Headquarters, 107th RHA

Fred Longford remembered the sudden silence after the terrible
din that had afflicted them all day.

When things became completely silent, you could hardly hear
yourself speak because of the silence. The Jerries came out
and told us to gather together in a little group. The standard
remark was: 'Hard luck, Englander, for you the war is over!' In
a guttural tone of course! The thing that hurt my ego was they
wanted the acorn cap badge. I took my cap badge off – that's
how I lost my cap badge. One chap was shot – just like that –
because he virtually told the Jerry demanding it to get stuffed.
I'm afraid I'm no hero to that extent![53]

Sergeant Fred Langford, Headquarters, 425 Battery, 107th RHA

By this time the wounded Frank Knowles had regained some
use of his leg and he sought some means of escape.

I could hobble about a bit. There were some vehicles of ours nearby and three of us made a 'dash', as far as one could! Dave Worley, the driver, a chap named Geoff Douglas, who had a wound in the arm – the three of us hobbled and Geoff Douglas supported me as we made track for a pickup parked fairly near. We reached it and tried to start it, but the engine had been machine-gunned, there was no compression and we couldn't start it! While we were still trying to start it a burst of machine-gun fire came over our heads as much as to say, 'Dismount!' We did and hobbled off into captivity.[54]

Lance Bombardier Frank Knowles, Headquarters, 425 Battery, 107th RHA

Ted Whittaker knew he was going to be a prisoner of war and he tried to make sure he had as much useful kit as he could amass in the short time left to him.

Right in front of me was my armoured car. I looked at my big pack; I thought, 'No – a bit too heavy.' I got my small pack with my shaving kit, collected my water bottle and greatcoat. I had a look in the car and there was a great big hole through the left-hand side and an armour-piercing shot had gone straight through Sergeant Major Jim Hardy. By this time German tanks were with us. I saw a bunch of people and I thought, 'Well I'll go and join them!' I hadn't gone far when there was a big 'Clank! Clank! Clank!' right at the side of me and a German tank stopped. A German officer, a pleasant young man, with his cap on and earphones, he leaned out and said, 'Where are you going?' I looked at him and made the classic remark, 'With you!' 'Hop up!' I climbed up and he said, 'For you the war is over!' He said, 'What's Cairo like?' With a bit of bravado, I said, 'You won't see Cairo!' He shrugged and laughed at me![55]

Lance Sergeant Ted Whittaker, Headquarters, 425 Battery, 107th RHA

Ray Ellis, whose story was recounted in our Preface (pp.ix–xiv) was generally acknowledged to have fired the last shot of the battle. He was left utterly exhausted, physically battered and emotionally traumatised. As he surrendered, he suddenly had a flicker of fellow feeling for his captor. A realisation that they were both human beings, with far more in common than what separated them.

> A German Mark IV tank rolled up and there was a German with his head poking out the top. He just beckoned me up on to the tank. I jumped up and I could see he was a sergeant. We looked at one another, we'd been fighting each other all day – and we both shrugged our shoulders and looked up to heaven, 'What a bloody silly thing it was!' It was a matter of two enemies who had no enmity.[56]
>
> Sergeant Ray Ellis, A Troop, 425 Battery, 107th RHA

For them the war *was* over.

THE SOUTH NOTTS HUSSARS WERE gathered together by their German captors and then marched to a concentration point for all the British POWs captured in the Knightsbridge area. Charles Ward was, in a way, relieved that it was all over.

> The first thing was, 'How lucky I am to still be alive after this "lot" when there's so many you could see had been wounded and killed. Not that you were very happy about being captured. But the basic human nature of survival – you had to accept it![57]
>
> Battery Quartermaster Sergeant Charles Ward, Headquarters, 426 Battery, 107th RHA

There was, however, one more tragic incident when Captain Colin Barber was callously murdered by one of his captors.

A British officer was wearing his binoculars round his neck on the normal leather strap. A German officer went up to him and obviously asked for the glasses – you could tell by his gesticulations. The officer refused – he was not used to being a prisoner – whereupon the German officer drew his revolver and shot him in the chest – just as coolly as that. The officer fell to the ground and was kicking out his life on the sand and this German bent down and calmly took the glasses off – and swaggered away.[58]

Sergeant Ray Ellis, A Troop, 425 Battery, 107th RHA

Then one final tragic episode showed that you were never truly safe in a war. Several of the prisoners of war remember their column being attacked by British aircraft on 7 June.

Next morning, these aircraft with a shark's head, fighters, came down and machine-gunned. It was an amazing reaction from the lads – they all shouted and cheered, 'Go on, give 'em hell!' Even though they were firing at us. What the fighters were trying to do amazed me! Because they must have known what we were! Whether they were trying to hit the Germans to give us a chance to escape – that's the only thing I can think of![59]

Battery Quartermaster Sergeant Charles Ward, Headquarters, 426 Battery, 107th RHA

The wounded Frank Knowles remembered the aircraft striking as they were passing along a narrow path through a minefield – so they could hardly scatter.

We were marched through a minefield on a well-worn track. And we were bombed by our own planes – Hurricanes. The bloke who was supporting me, Fred Charles,[60] was killed. He was acting like a crutch – that's how near he was to me! Prior to that we'd shared some cigarettes that I'd found – he was probably buried with his share still in his pocket![61]

Lance Bombardier Frank Knowles, Headquarters, 425 Battery, 107th RHA

Ray Ellis was scathing as he considered the pilot's actions.

We all waved madly to him – he must have been a man of very scant intelligence – he should have realised we were prisoners. But he didn't! He came diving down, with all his machine guns blazing – he cut a swathe through the press of bodies. Some of the men attempted to scatter and as they did the German guards opened fire on them. I saw one or two men fall – they didn't get far. We saw the bomb leave the plane and he got a bullseye – right in the middle. Stan Keaton and I were standing on this press of bodies which saved our lives. The other bodies took the brunt of the explosion. Some men were blown to pieces, others were horribly wounded and screaming – it was absolute carnage.[62]

Sergeant Ray Ellis, A Troop, 425 Battery, 107th RHA

Most of them would be POWs for three years.

ONE MAN DID ESCAPE THE LAST STAND. Robert Daniell, whatever people might think of him, was clearly a man of his word. He had promised himself he would not surrender, and he did not.

I walked back to my vehicle, which I saw about 40 yards away. By this time, it was half-past five. There were Germans collecting wounded and picking up dead – here, there and everywhere. The driver said, 'I've just changed the wheel!' I said, 'Well, thank God for that! You've got one minute to make your mind up! Do you see those six German tanks that are approaching in line towards this position? – I'm going to drive straight for them, they will be taken by surprise and unable to swing round their turrets to open up with their machine guns!' He said, 'Major, you are asking to be killed. I'm sorry, but I'm going to leave you!' He went to the back of the truck, took out his bundle and I saw him walk off to join two or three Germans to surrender. I jumped in my truck and did what I said! I drove straight for the tanks. Five of them were unable to get their turrets round. One did and blew off my canopy at the back of the 8cwt truck. I swung hard left – right round them.[63]

Major Robert Daniell, Headquarters, 107th RHA

As ever, his story of how he escaped is in some senses unbelievable, but it is undeniable that he did get away. He would never be forgiven by the men he left behind. The regimental history[64] estimated that over the ten days of fighting during the Battle of Knightsbridge some seventy-six South Notts Hussars were killed, with a further sixteen dying from their wounds or as POWs. Many of the rest of the 500-man total strength were now prisoners. For all intents and purposes, the South Notts Hussars had ceased to exist.

13

REBUILDING

The battery was formed out of a lot of ragtags: cooks, office clerks, quartermaster stores blokes, quite a few had prison service for desertion! The number of Nottingham people was probably about 10 per cent. All sorts of people were being flung together to try and make this battery with a bunch of new officers.[1]

Lance Sergeant Harold Harper, B Troop, 107 Battery, 7th Medium RA

THE ADMINISTRATIVE REAR ECHELONS of the regiment had no idea what was happening to their friends in the Cauldron on 6 June 1942. Communications had gone dead and they could not get any firm news. Within hours, reports started to trickle through, but even as they began to piece the picture together, many could still barely believe the scale of the disaster that had befallen them.

The officer went forward to see what was happening and then, about mid morning, he came back to us and he said, 'The regiment's gone!' It didn't mean anything to us – because we just thought they'd moved. What he meant was they'd been overrun. You felt shattered. It didn't really sink in until next morning when they had us on parade. He said, '425 Battery,

'shun!' I suddenly realised we were all that was left – I counted
the blokes – only twenty-two![2]

Gunner Reg McNish, Headquarters, 425 Battery, 107th RHA

They were desperately in need of leadership, something positive
to jolt them out of their lethargy. Someone had to get a grip.

We were sitting round in the B Echelon area, concerned at what
the future was going to hold for us. It was pretty obvious that
we were in a low state of morale; basically, because we didn't
know what was happening. Battery Sergeant Major Charles
Beardall saw this fairly quickly. He just came walking smartly
into the echelon area, issuing some pretty sharp orders about
gathering up and getting a move on! And really that is all we
wanted: somebody to tell us to get on with it! Which we did![3]

Lance Sergeant David Tickle, Headquarters, 520 Battery, 107th RHA

One of the first survivors to arrive back at the rear echelon was
Major Robert Daniell.

This vehicle came driving very fast with Bob Daniell driving
it. He was covered in sand, his eyes were red-rimmed, he was
wearing a neckerchief round his collar. He climbed out of the
vehicle and said, 'The regiment has had it!' We all clambered
round him saying, 'What do you mean?' He said, 'They'd been
overrun by the panzers and it was all over!'[4]

Second Lieutenant David Elliott, Headquarters, 520 Battery, 107th RHA

Daniell did not stay long; in view of his dismissive attitude to
the sacrifices of the men under his command, perhaps it was just
as well. As an experienced regular officer, he was whisked away
to command the 4th Field RA. His temporary replacement was
the memorably named Captain William Williamson of the
Northumberland Fusiliers.

Gradually, over the next few days, the survivors would

coalesce as the rear echelon formations fell back in stages towards Buq Buq. One of the luckiest men in the regiment was Albert Swinton, who had earlier on been sent on an 'urgent mission' back to Cairo.

> I was detailed off with a couple of trucks and two or three NCOs to go to Kasr el Nil Barracks in Cairo to pick up 1,200 bottles of English beer which had been supplied by two breweries – Watney Combe & Reid and Whitbread – gave each man who had been in Tobruk from start to finish two bottles per man. There was no desperate rush, so it took me about three days, then a few days swanning about Cairo, then we eventually set off back up the desert.[5]

Lance Bombardier Albert Swinton, D Troop, 426 Battery, 107th RHA

When he got back, he was told to stay well out of the way, and he would ultimately fall back with the other retreating Eighth Army units. As each man rejoined the unit, he was given three bottles from Swinton's beer supplies. Nevertheless, the mood was melancholy.

> We were absolutely shattered. It was obvious that the morale had gone. Who suggested it I don't know, but we got people together and we had a singsong: sang all the old First World War songs, plus a few from this war. Towards the end this gunner, a Welsh miner, he had a beautiful voice and he sang the Welsh national anthem in that desert night evening – it stuck in my mind.[6]

Second Lieutenant David Elliott, Headquarters, 520 Battery, 107th RHA

BEHIND THEM THE WAR RAGED on without them. Rommel's risky plan had worked, and on the night of 13 June his troops were able to pinch out the Knightsbridge Box. The Gazala Line was comprehensively breached, and a pell-mell retreat ensued as on 14 June the 50th (Northumbrian) Division and the 1st South African fell back. There was hope of another stand at Tobruk, which by 18 June was once more cut off and besieged. However, the fortress defences had fallen into disrepair, and this time Rommel concentrated his artillery, panzers and infantry into a strong focused assault. On 20 June, the 15th and 21 Panzer Divisions broke through, and in a matter of hours had overrun the whole of Tobruk. Next day some 33,000 British, South African and Indian troops were taken prisoner. Huge quantities of vital stores, munitions and fuels, had fallen into German hands. Tobruk: the symbol of resistance to the Nazis in 1941 had fallen.

Rommel was the man of the moment and his achievements were recognised by Hitler with an immediate promotion to field marshal. Never one to rest on his laurels, Rommel was determined to hammer home his advantage, and his forces pressed forward right up to the Egyptian frontier. This was as far as he was meant to go: the Italian High Command, who were still his nominal superiors, wanted to consolidate the success and wait for the completion of the planned capture of Malta before any further advance into the Nile Delta. Their logic was sound: with Malta removed from the equation, the Mediterranean would be effectively an Axis lake and their logistical situation secure. But Rommel also had his justifications for boldness: a successful Italian intelligence operation had secured the American codes which allowed the Axis commanders to read the reports of the American military attaché in Cairo. These revealed the seriousness of British tank losses – it was reported that of 742 tanks they had only 133 left. Rommel was determined to seize his chance and make a grab for the ultimate prize – the Suez Canal. On 21 June he issued a stirring order of the day to his men.

Soldiers of the Panzerarmee Afrika! Now for the complete destruction of the enemy. We will not rest until we have shattered the last remnants of the British Eighth Army. During the days to come, I shall call on you for one more great effort to bring us to this final goal.[7]

Field Marshal Erwin Rommel, Headquarters, Panzerarmee Afrika

Hitler was dubious as to the reality of the Italian commitment to the capture of Malta, suspecting it might become yet another serious strain on German resources. In these circumstances, he decided to back Rommel: the invasion of Malta was postponed, and the invasion of Egypt was sanctioned.

On, on, surged Rommel's armoured columns, driving across the border and deep into Egypt. On 25 June, faced with a desperate situation, Auchinleck intervened to replace Ritchie and take personal command of the Eighth Army. He brought an admirable sense of purpose with his ingrained ability to focus on what mattered and being unafraid of decisive action to avoid the spectre of defeat. Recognising that the demoralised Eighth Army could not hold the isolated Mersa Matruh positions, on 26 June Auchinleck ordered a resumption of the retreat, but there was a marked change in tone. The Eighth Army would avoid static positions and keep mobile, not allowing units to be pinned down and destroyed, while it carried out a fighting retreat a further 150 miles to a defensive line anchored on El Alamein. Auchinleck was fully aware that every mile Rommel advanced added greater strain to the Axis supply lines, and he therefore attempted to ensure that all British supply depots and logistical facilities were destroyed before they were abandoned. Every mile Rommel advanced also brought them within closer range of the strongly reinforced Desert Air Force and a mile further from his own Luftwaffe bases. As the RAF fighter squadrons secured an effective air superiority, they opened the gate to massed squadrons of medium bombers that flayed the Germans on the ground. Axis forces amassing for an attack were vulnerable to devastating bombing, with their supply chains being further disrupted.

The new Eighth Army defensive line stretched 40 miles from El Alamein on the coast down to the almost impassable Qauttara Depression, made up of areas of soft sand and salt marshes. There were some defence works dating back to 1941, but much work needed to be done – and this was immediately put under way. Although still 160 miles from Cairo, it was just 70 miles from the crucial Royal Navy base at Alexandria. Despite being determined to make a stand, Auchinleck also ordered the preparation of more defences further back in the Nile Delta – just in case things went wrong. His underlying intention was to keep the Eighth Army as an 'army in being'.

Recognising the tactical inadequacies revealed in the recent fighting, Auchinleck began the centralisation of control of the previously dispersed artillery, to allow for a tactically significant concentration of firepower, while his armoured forces were also to be reorganised. These measures would take time to bear fruit. All in all, Auchinleck demonstrated an impressive grip on the situation. Not so his subordinate generals, many of whom lapsed into a state of despair, which mirrored the understandable panic among the Egyptian populace on the streets of Cairo. He challenged his men to take a more positive attitude.

> The enemy is stretching to his limits and thinks we are a broken army. He hopes to take Egypt by bluff. Show him where he gets off.[8]
>
> General Claude Auchinleck, Headquarters, Eighth Army

His men were exhausted and many of his units had suffered severe casualties during running battles with the Axis armour. But the Eighth Army was still extant; still capable of fighting as an organised command. It had not been defeated in detail. There *was* still hope: it was backed by the concentrated strength of the Desert Air Force; it was close to huge supply dumps, and strong reinforcements were on their way. Auchinleck just needed time.

Rommel had his own problems as he approached El Alamein, but he was nonetheless determined to deny the British any time to recover. He would drive his men forward – despite his difficulties he was confident. On 30 June 1942, the First Battle of Alamein began. The Qauttara Depression ruled out Rommel's favourite southern outflanking manoeuvre – this time he would have to break through the British line. The British resistance was much stiffer than Rommel expected, and it was soon apparent that the Italian and German divisions were approaching exhaustion, tottering as they were at the end of a very long supply line and with little air support. Rommel sought victory through dramatic strokes and swift manoeuvrist warfare; what Auchinleck intended to give them was grim resistance and a war of grinding attrition. Rommel certainly noticed the power of the better-concentrated British artillery fire.

> Furious artillery fire again struck into our ranks. British shells came streaming in from three directions, north, east and south; anti-aircraft tracer streaked through our force. Under this tremendous weight of fire, our attack came to a standstill. Hastily we scattered our vehicles and took cover, as shell after shell crashed into the area we were holding.[9]
>
> Field Marshal Erwin Rommel, Headquarters, Panzerarmee Afrika

On 2 July, the Germans launched an attack on Ruweisat Ridge. Again, the British artillery blazed out in unison, augmented by the 6-pounder anti-tank guns which the British had now successfully added to the tactical mix. The Desert Air Force (Air Vice Marshal Sir Arthur Coningham) played a vital role in supporting the ground forces. Soon panzer hulks littered the battlefield as the Germans could make no progress, and on 4 July Rommel had no option but to call off the attack: the advance on the Nile would be postponed indefinitely. For the rest of the month, Auchinleck launched a series of counter-attacks, but he too lacked the strength to break through. Both sides awaited the next move: who would be ready to strike first?

Where did the South Notts Hussars fit into this bigger picture? Initially, they were irrelevant, as they only had one 25-pounder to their name – and that was *hors de combat* with a round firmly jammed in the barrel. The first plan was for them all to move back to the main Royal Artillery Base Depot, Almaza in Cairo. Here they would be reformed as 107 Battery, RHA[10] for attachment to their sister regiment, the 104 (Essex Yeomanry) RHA, to replace the Essex battery destroyed in the recent fighting. The regimental headquarters staff were to stay at Almaza, where it was intended they would act as a nucleus on which the regiment could be reformed at some point in the future.

By the time they got to Almaza, they had gathered up some nine officers, of which only Captain Charles Laborde was an 'original', with another sixteen NCOs and roughly 150 men. Reinforcements began to flood in to top up their numbers, but they proved a strange mixture. Among the arrivals was Reg Cutter, a Geordie from East Boldon, a fitter driver who had served with the 74th Field RA and who had been evacuated from Dunkirk back in 1940.

> I joined the South Notts Hussars. Never heard of them. You didn't know what to expect. You were just saying to yourself, 'Oh hell, I've got to start making pals and that again' – a different mob! I mean I'm an artillery man – I'm not a hussar. That's the way you feel; that's the way you were educated. When you're in a regiment that's your home, that's your mam, your

dad – that's YOUR regiment. I didn't want to be a hussar. But you do what you're told. I was a bit dubious at first. I thought, 'Well, I'm here now, there's nowhere else to go so you've just got to make the best of it!'[11]

Gunner Reg Cutter, 107 Battery, RHA

Ernie Hurry encountered some of the rougher elements that had been posted in to join to the South Notts Hussars.

We had to have a load of reinforcements and we had a load of people come from out of these detention camps. Believe you me there were some 'right ones', some hard cases, oh dear. To be with them in action – you couldn't have had any better blokes, but you couldn't trust them; they'd pick the laces out of your shoes. I palled up with one and he was a nice guy, Maclean from Scotland. I found him a very nice chap. I said to him, 'Mac, how come you are with this lot in prison?' 'Well, I was engaged, and I got a letter while I was out here in Cairo, that my girlfriend had got married. When I got this letter, I went mad. I went into this cabaret and the band was upstairs. I went up there and went mad – I threw some of the band over the balcony. I got sent down for two to three months in this prison!'[12]

Gunner Ernie Hurry, 107 Battery, RHA

Shortly after their arrival in Almaza, Major Albert Lewis-Jones was appointed to command 107 Battery. He was a strong character, indeed many thought him positively abrasive, perhaps even slightly uncouth in his manner. Yet he had a tough job on his hands to weld the disparate elements of his new battery together to form an effective team.

Soon it was evident that the plans had changed radically. Now the two troops (A and B) of 107 Battery would be posted to form part of the 7th Medium Regiment, RA. This regular regiment had earned a splendid record fighting in the Western Desert in 1940, before being committed to the campaigns in Greece and Crete in 1941. They were successfully evacuated and returned to fight in the Western Desert between 1941 and 1942. The 107 Battery was to replace the 25/26 Battery, which had been destroyed in the fall of 150th Brigade Box at Gazala in June 1942. The South Notts Hussars would now fight side by side with the 27/28 Battery, which was equipped with 4.5-inch howitzers. In contrast, 107 Battery was the beneficiary of the first overseas deployment of the brand new 5.5-inch medium guns capable of firing a 100lb shell some 16,000 yards. Hitherto the Eighth Army had been reliant on medium artillery that dated back to the Great War – and the 5.5-inch marked a great step forward. The men rejoiced in the idea that their shells would certainly pack a very healthy 'wallop', with four times the explosive power of the 25-pounder.

As they struggled to form the new 5.5-inch gun sections, they found themselves desperately short of gunners, most of whom were dead or prisoners. Tradesmen of all sorts, including specialist assistants, fitters, signallers and storemen, were pressed into service, given little option but to retrain as gunners. One such was Harold Harper, who was made a gun sergeant and set to mastering all aspects of 5.5-inch gun drill. In theory, it differed little from the 25-pounder.

> The No. 1 was the sergeant: he theoretically did nothing, except to oversee what was happening on his gun. The No. 2: he closed the barrel of the gun from the right-hand side of the gun. The No. 3 was the layer: he sat in the seat and laid the gun, responsible for putting the gun in the right direction with the dial sight. Nos. 4 and 5 were the chappies responsible for sliding the shell into the barrel of the gun and ramming the shell. Nos. 6, 7 and 8 were ammunition numbers responsible for preparing the ammunition and passing the shells on to the tray.[13]
>
> Lance Sergeant Harold Harper, B Troop, 107 Battery, 7th Medium RA

In practice, the sheer size of the guns and their shells was intimidating. Some, like Gunner Ted Holmes, who had officially recovered from the wounds he suffered on 27 May, found that his weakened wounded arm simply could not cope with the repetitive strain of lifting 100lb shells. In consequence, he had to be taken off the guns. Even the fit and well found it hard going.

> We'd been used to handling 25-pounder shells – and found ourselves handling a 100lb shell. It seemed a very laborious exercise. We were told that of all the hand-loaded guns this was the heaviest. Manoeuvring the gun into position was very difficult – we had very little instruction. We had the comfort of knowing that this gun fired probably 4–5,000 yards farther, so we'd be a bit farther away from the enemy – I suppose that was the only consolation we got! Every time we saw a 25-pounder we were almost reduced to tears![14]
>
> Lance Sergeant Harold Harper, B Troop, 107 Battery, 7th Medium RA

Despite the difficulties, Harper rose to the challenge and soon came to enjoy his new role.

They also had to get used to their new purpose-built, four-wheel-drive (six-wheel) diesel-engine AEC Matador gun towers. These created a good impression: well made, manoeuvrable and mechanically reliable, with a powerful engine that was intended to allow them to tow the 5.5-inch gun at 30mph. They soon learnt that if they – illicitly – took the speed control governor device off, then they could easily achieve 50mph when necessary. They also had a high cab which gave a good field of vision for the driver. There were two seats in the back which could each hold five gunners. In addition, they performed the function of a limber, for they could carry an additional load of about 3 tons which equated to sixty shells, spare wheels, digging tools and rations. They had a winch and hooks at both the front and the back – all told, a flexible tower. Experience showed that it was advisable to cut down the cab, so that they threw less of a shadow in desert conditions and allowed the gunners to get out quickly in the event of an air raid.

One new arrival in the troop who would have great problems with gun drill was Gunner Ken Giles. Before the war, the bespectacled Giles was an optician and was a keen amateur musician who had attained near-professional standards playing the concert piano. Having toyed with conscientious objection, his reluctance to get involved in the war had been eroded by his experiences as a volunteer fire watcher. He was called up in June 1941 and, given his obvious intelligence, was trained in survey work at the School of Artillery at Larkhill. Here his ability to memorise and play any piece of music on the canteen pianos made him a popular figure. He was then sent out to the RABD at Almaza, where, despite his protests, he was reclassified as a gunner and attached to the 107 Battery. Throughout his life he would demonstrate a mastery of intellectual pursuits, but it is fair to say that he was not a natural gunner.

These medium guns were huge monsters! The barrel was terrifically long, and the trail behind the firing end was able to be split open and it took two or three men to lift it. Things like spades were dug in so that when the gun was ready for action it was so spreadeagled that it looked like a capital 'Y' upside down. I was put on the guns – on Sergeant Tickle's gun. I had never in my life had anything to do with guns – so I was completely at sea. I was not exactly a tremendous physical specimen and I've always been underweight! On that first day, I had to take charge of the rammer. This is a pole about 6–8 feet long with a kind of mop on the end. I was to throw the rammer, rather as one would throw the javelin, to pass it to one of the other numbers to ram the shell home. My aim was terrific – terrifically bad! The rammer hit Sergeant Tickle full in the face. There was a tremendous gasp of horror. I shivered and practically shrank into the ground, but to his eternal credit, Sergeant Tickle never turned a hair, his face just expressed surprise and his eyes streamed with tears – and he said, 'I think you'd better change numbers, Gunner Giles!' It was soon realised that I would be quite useless on a gun![15]

Gunner Ken Giles, A Troop, 107 Battery, 7th Medium RA

He was immediately transferred for training as specialist gun position officer's assistant. Whatever his manifest failings as a gunner, Ken Giles soon settled down with his new comrades.

We were a pretty friendly lot. Nobody ever seemed to pull rank on you. Nobody seemed to say, 'I'm the sergeant major, do this, do that – and look out if you don't!' Nobody seemed to be like that. Obviously, you had to obey orders from anybody who was senior to you, but they were given not in a sharp tone of voice, 'Get on with this, Ken!' 'Do that, George!' 'See this is all right!' That kind of thing – and the job was done. We would say, 'OK, Sarge!' Officers it was, 'Sir!' It was the friendly, easy-going manner which produced results far more than any martinet type of command. I settled down quite well and I believe all the new intake did. We did seem to amalgamate and mix well with all the veteran survivors of Knightsbridge and with those that had come in.[16]

Gunner Ken Giles, A Troop, 107 Battery, 7th Medium RA

It is one of the strange marks of this period that many of the ordinary gunners were oblivious to the domineering nature of the role played by Major Lewis-Jones, who was by no means 'friendly and easy-going'. It was largely the officers and senior NCOs that felt the lash of his tongue as he strove to get the unit licked into shape.

DRIVEN ON BY MAJOR LEWIS-JONES, they spent days learning the rudiments of gun drill. There was a sense of urgency as Lewis-Jones had been informed that within a month they would be moving up into the line. After a couple of weeks, they calibrated all of the eighteen 5.5-inch guns that had been sent out to the Middle East. The idea was to establish how each gun performed as against the standard, so that the gunners could allow for the built-in deviations present in each individual gun and thus attain the desired accuracy. Newly arrived Eric Dobson was taken with the imposing sight of the guns firing for the first time.

> The eighteen guns were calibrated on Almaza ranges, making an impressive sight as these giants stood wheel to wheel, with every now and then one of them spitting flame and emitting a most fearsome noise. At the time one felt it was unfair on inexperienced gunners to have to calibrate all the guns that were in the country; actually, it was most useful, for Major Lewis-Jones was able to select a 'matched set' of eight.[17]

Second Lieutenant Eric Dobson, B Troop, 107 Battery, 7th Medium RA

The calibrated performance of the guns was astounding to men used to the 25-pounders. The 5.5-inch guns proved to be quite extraordinarily accurate, capable of dropping shells almost in the same holes, time after time.

However, except for this calibration they never had another chance to fire their new guns 'live'. The pressing need for the heavier guns at the front meant that their time was almost up. After only a month, they left Almaza and moved up to join the rest of 7th Medium RA at El Alamein, arriving on 15 July 1942. The South Notts Hussars were back in action!

14

BATTLE OF EL ALAMEIN

There were guns in front of us, guns at the side of us, guns at the back of us! When they opened up, it was a tremendous salvo – you've never heard anything like it! Guns all around you – and these flashes! All we heard was one shell came back – it came right over – it landed well behind us![1]

Gunner Ernie Hurry, A Troop, 107 Battery, 7th Medium RA

THE TIMES THEY WERE A-CHANGING for the Eighth Army as well as the South Notts Hussars. Following his success at the First Battle of Alamein, General Claude Auchinleck believed that the long-term advantage now lay with the Allies and he commenced the planning process for the next offensive, intending to utilise the stream of reinforcements that were at last beginning to reach the Western Desert. The forces sent out earlier in 1942 had been eroded in the Gazala fighting, but there was a healthy contingent of divisions arriving from across the Empire, as Australia, India, New Zealand and South Africa all answered the call. The units they sent would prove to be valuable additions to the Eighth Army once they had acclimatised to desert warfare. However, Winston Churchill, ignorant of military practicalities, sought an immediate attack and seethed at Auchinleck's more cautious approach. In fact, Auchinleck had been by no means passive and had launched a series of relatively minor military operations in July. They were intended to keep Rommel off-balance, but floundered on the strong Axis defences. The Eighth Army was capable of resolute defence, but the underlying problems with poor doctrine, inter-arm cooperation and training were soon exposed when they moved on to the offensive. In response to these problems, Auchinleck was determined to improve cooperation between his infantry and armoured units, rejigging his divisions to increase the infantry component of armoured divisions, while attaching armoured brigades to infantry divisions. He also instigated a series of measures to improve all-arms training and liaison. Auchinleck considered that until mid September 1942 at the earliest, the Axis positions were too strong to be successfully assaulted. He began planning for an attack in the coastal sector, with extensive deception measures to keep Rommel's eyes fixed on his more open southern flank. Until then the Eighth Army would stand on the defensive, with a continuation of the programme of precautionary defensive preparations back in the Nile Delta.

Auchinleck's honesty in reporting the situation as it *was*, rather than through rose-tinted spectacles, proved fatal in dealing with Churchill, who needed to be reassured – and obeyed. It is also undeniable that Auchinleck failed to motivate his subordinate generals. Many kicked against the required organisational changes, while few grasped why they should simultaneously prepare for both defence and attack. In mid August, Churchill struck: ever the consummate politician, he overwhelmed the objections of his long-suffering Chief of Imperial General Staff, General Sir Alan Brooke, who eventually suggested a replacement commander for the Eighth Army: General Sir Bernard Montgomery.

Bernard Montgomery was born in London on 17 November 1887. He attended the Royal Military College, Sandhurst and was commissioned into the Royal Warwickshire Regiment in 1908. When the Great War began, he was badly wounded in 1914, but would return to the Western Front as a staff officer, rising to become chief of staff with the 47th Division by November 1918. After attending Staff College, his career continued to prosper as he rose to command the 8th Division in Palestine. In 1939 he returned to England and was given command of the 3rd Division, with which he was considered to have done well during the BEF advance into Belgium and subsequent retreat to Dunkirk in May 1940. Montgomery was beginning to attract favourable attention as a competent professional soldier, but his trenchant criticisms of the higher command of the BEF had also created some antipathy. In July 1940, Montgomery was promoted to be the acting lieutenant general commanding V Corps, which was charged with defending Hampshire and Dorset in the event of a German invasion. His relationship with the Commander in Chief, Southern Command – one Claude Auchinleck – soon degenerated. In April 1941, Montgomery moved to command XII Corps in Kent. Here he attracted both admiration and scorn for his obsession with improving the physical fitness of his men. He was also harsh with any officer he considered might 'fold' under the pressure of action and unceremoniously removed such men from command posts. He then took over the South-Eastern Command, where he further refined his ideas of careful training before committing men to action.

In view of his history of mutual antipathy with Montgomery, Auchinleck would also be peremptorily removed from his 'other' role as Middle East Commander in Chief, to be replaced by General Sir Harold Alexander. Auchinleck rejected the proffered alternative of being transferred to the newly created Persia–Iraq Command and on 15 August he disappeared from the North African stage. He may have been dismissed in some ignominy, but Auchinleck's role in stabilising the situation of the Eighth Army should not be forgotten.

Whatever the merits of the departure of Auchinleck, Montgomery instituted a further shake-up across the Eighth Army, building on the sound foundation laid by Auchinleck. He immediately stamped down hard on any idea of preparing for possible failure by suspending further work on the defensive preparations in the Nile Delta. To Montgomery, morale was a crucial element of success, and although his stance was essentially a posture – and the existing defensive arrangements remained in place in the Delta – his strictures somehow did the trick in boosting everyone's spirits.

> What is the use of digging trenches in the Delta? It is quite useless; if we lose this position we lose Egypt; all the fighting troops now in the Delta must come here at once, and will. *Here*, we will stand and fight; there will be no further withdrawal. I have ordered that all plans and instructions dealing with further withdrawal are to be burnt, and at once. We will stand and fight *here*. If we can't stay here alive, then let us stay here dead.[2]
>
> Lieutenant General Bernard Montgomery, Headquarters, Eighth Army

He softened the message by pointing to the imminent arrival of strong reinforcements. Montgomery insisted that he would not attack until he was completely ready; ironic indeed given the dismissal of Auchinleck for delaying going on to the offensive. However, it is evident that Montgomery was a more 'modern' general than Auchinleck, in that he prioritised morale and recognised that 'image' was all-important.

> Morale is the big thing in war. We must raise the morale of our soldiery to the highest pitch; they must be made enthusiastic, and must enter the battle with their tails high in the air and with the will to win.[3]
>
> Lieutenant General Bernard Montgomery, Headquarters, Eighth Army

He embarked on a programme of personal visits all around Eighth Army, discussing the plans, first, of course, with generals and staff, but then trying actively to engage the interest and support of as many as possible of his junior officers and the lower ranks. Montgomery was a strange man, very self-confident, prickly in the extreme; yet, somehow, he was blessed with the ability to give his men the impression that they were being taken into his confidence.

Montgomery engaged in a thorough clear-out of senior commanders to get the men he wanted; some of his cull was thoroughly justified by previous inadequate performance, some of it was unfair. Fortunately, most of the replacements proved competent. He also continued the reform of the armoured formations, creating a *corps de chasse* for future decisive operations, made up of the 1st Armoured Division, the 10th Armoured Division and the motorised 2nd New Zealand Division. At last American Sherman tanks were being delivered and, while they had their faults, they still represented a qualitative improvement on previous armour as, with their 75mm guns, they could engage the German panzers on equal terms. There was also the welcome addition of around 100 Crusader IIIs with the 6-pounder gun. Finally, at last, the Eighth Army was getting self-propelled guns: some ninety 105mm Priests and eighty 25-pounder Bishops. Together these would offer mobile artillery support to the armoured divisions.

BACK ON THE GROUND at El Alamein the men of the 107 Battery were meeting their new comrades of 7th Medium Regiment and the 27/28 Battery. They also received a welcome draft of new officers to the battery, who had served as NCOs with the South Notts Hussars before being sent to the OCTU and commissioned. Among them were Bob Foulds, Ian Sinclair and

Charles Westlake. At first, they were nonplussed by what they found: everything seemed to have changed – and not for the better.

> Morale wasn't high. As we understood it, the battery had been made up from the military prisons of Cairo. They were wonderful rogues if they were on your side! But they weren't too good if you were agin 'em! If they were short of anything they would go and pinch it from someone else! They got a very scratch crew together. They hadn't developed what we might call a corporate spirit at that time because they'd come from so many different areas. There were quite a number of original South Notts, but there were more people from all over the place.[4]

Second Lieutenant Charles Westlake, A Troop, 107 Battery, 7th Medium RA

Bob Foulds found it difficult to settle down; indeed, he felt more than a little unwelcome in the officers' mess. This was not the South Notts Hussars he remembered so fondly.

> At first, I found it a bit unhappy and depressing in that environment. We had the feeling that we were 'outnumbered' as the 'old' South Notts Hussars element there and we weren't very welcomed by the people who had recently arrived. I think their tone was taken from Major Lewis-Jones, who was the battery commander: he was an excellent soldier, no question about that, extremely knowledgeable and he knew his gunnery. His drive was unshakeable. He was very competent, and he got that battery to be a fighting unit by sheer force of personality. Having said that, he wasn't a particularly pleasant man. He was a bully to junior officers. We all expected to be driven hard, that's what we were there for, but there was unnecessary harshness.[5]

Second Lieutenant Bob Foulds, B Troop, 107 Battery, 7th Medium RA

The 7th Medium RA was commanded by Lieutenant Colonel Horace Elton, who had a considerable reputation as a disciplinarian.

> 'Toc' Elton was a bit of an abrasive individual! He was very much a 'regular' soldier, he didn't like TA soldiers, he objected to us wearing our acorn and oak leaf cap badge. He thought we ought to be wearing our Royal Artillery gun badge. He had three of us up before him – wanting to know what the hell we were doing wearing this 'awful badge'! Jack Attewell spoke up and said, 'Well, I was commissioned into the South Nottinghamshire Hussars and I'm entitled to wear it!' We never wore anything else and defied anybody to take it off us. It was very important to us; we were primarily South Notts Hussars and after that we were gunners – we got the best of both worlds I reckon![6]
>
> Second Lieutenant Charles Westlake, A Troop, 107 Battery, 7th Medium RA

Having made his point of view clear, Elton had the good sense to let it lie. However, Elton was a lot more than just a hidebound regular; he was also brilliant gunner. He was operating at the very cutting edge of a variety of new methods to maximise the results that could be achieved by the medium guns under his command. The South Notts Hussars would benefit from their association with this brilliant officer.

MANY OF THE MORE RECENT 'HUSSARS' had been understandably nervous as they approached the front line at El Alamein for the first time.

> I saw one shell burst – and I suddenly thought, 'This is war! This is it!' I was a bit nervous. I didn't want to be killed out

here and buried in the sand. I felt the first 'turnings over' in my stomach. But it soon passed. I never mentioned it and who knows if the other 'rookies' had the same feelings – I wouldn't be at all surprised.[7]

Gunner Ken Giles, A Troop, 107 Battery, 7th Medium RA

They were assigned to gun positions only some 200 yards from the sea, some 1,000 yards ahead of the 27/28 Battery whose 4.5-inch howitzers had a lighter shell but slightly longer range. They were to support the 9th Australian Division, part of the XXX Corps which was holding the coastal sector, while the XIII Corps was in the line to the south stretching down to the Qauttara Depression.

Immediately on arrival, the 107 Battery became aware of one drawback to their new guns. As they toiled to dig the vast gun pits required in the soft sand, many of the gunners swore that for every spadesful they threw out, two spadesful of sand came tumbling back in.

There was some trepidation about digging gun pits for these monsters, for no one knew the size required. A number of South African bulldozers came to offer their help and, though they saved a lot of back-aching work, they were really something of an embarrassment. Their scoopings made it even more difficult to shape these auditorium-like gun pits. And so it was that when the guns were due to move on the following afternoon not a single one of the pits was really ready. However, the guns had to be brought in – they arrived one by one, as ordered, and there were Herculean struggles to get them into their holes before nightfall. Some detachments succeeded, others did not, but all guns were in action line and on line by midnight when the first target came over the telephones. The eight guns belched in unison and the first 5.5 shells flew towards the Afrika Korps – the first, in fact, against the enemy anywhere.[8]

Second Lieutenant Eric Dobson, B Troop, 107 Battery, 7th Medium RA

Albert Swinton had been promoted to sergeant and he was given command of the No. 1 gun of B Troop. He had a proud boast as the literal right of the line.

I was right on the beach – the right-hand gun of the whole lot at Alamein. We were still learning, and we were being compared with the 7th Medium who were a very efficient regular mob – which was most unfair. I think we got a bit of an inferiority complex. So, we had to really pull finger until eventually we were as good and probably better than them.[9]

Sergeant Albert Swinton, B Troop, 107 Battery, 7th Medium RA

All the officers were soon made painfully aware that the battery had by no means reached the level of efficiency demanded by Major Lewis-Jones.

Lewis-Jones thought we weren't as quick getting a round on the ground as the 4.5-inch battery – and he wouldn't have that! Which is fair enough! He instigated a rule that every day one gun would be pulled out of action and everybody, including sergeant majors and officers, would be trained on that gun! We thought it was pretty tough – it was very hot! I think in retrospect it was very good. Very sensible.[10]

Lieutenant David Elliott, Headquarters, 107 Battery, 7th Medium RA

With competition with the 27/28 Battery as the spur, they were driven hard by Lewis-Jones. Not only in gun drill, but also in taking the guns out of their gun pits and practising dropping them into action; always with the intent of reducing to the minimum the time between an 'alarm' given while driving along to getting the 'first round' in the air. Meanwhile the signallers and specialists were put through their paces to ensure that they were right up to standard and to eliminate any weak links identified in the 'chain'.

During this period the battery had two main forward observation posts. David Elliott remembered a stint at the 'Orange' coastal OP on the forward slope of a coastal hill.

> You couldn't see much at all – everything was shimmering. I don't think I fired at all. When you wanted to do a piddle, you piddled into a tin and chucked it right upon the sand. You weren't allowed to get out to do anything; the fear was it would be targeted by artillery fire. You were in there with an assistant, you had a telephone line back. You reported back to the gun position if you saw the Germans out in the sea and any air activity. It was boring! It was very hot under that tin roof and I heard pebbles scuffling and I thought, 'Oh, dear, what's happening?' I looked out behind me to be surprised to see an Australian infantryman, with a tin hat on the back of his head, his rifle slung over his bare shoulder, and nothing on except shorts and boots. He came up and I was signalling to him to keep down off the skyline – he was completely oblivious that he might be giving away our OP positions. He said in a broad drawl, 'Hey cobber, what are you doing hiding in that hole?' He just stood there and talked to us! 'Anything you want, would you like some butter or sausages?' He went off back and an hour or so later he came back with some tinned stuff for us – back over the skyline again! It did not attract any fire! To me it made a farce of the fact we crawled out there at night.[11]

Lieutenant David Elliott, Headquarters, 107 Battery, 7th Medium RA

The other OP, known, not without reason, as 'Nuts', was a mobile armoured car position a little further inland. It was in a slight hollow in the middle of an otherwise flat plain, some 500 yards in front of the minefield and the safety of the Australian lines. By this time Charles Laborde had been promoted and was in command of B Troop.

> One had to stand up in the OP and one was terribly exposed, because the land was very flat. You covered your head with netting and peered at the enemy. It was very hot. We had one terrible day there; the Germans must have had an OP higher than usual, and they could see the truck. He started to fire at us – we decided that discretion was the better part of valour. We hopped out of the armoured car, into a very small slit trench which had a sheet of corrugated iron over it and a few sandbags. The shelling went on, and on, and on, and in the end, I said to my 'ack', 'I think if we stay here much longer one of these shells is actually going to hit the top of this thing!' They were all round us you see! 'I think we'll hop into the truck and we'll move it!' We must have moved out of sight, because the shelling then stopped.[12]

Captain Charles Laborde, B Troop, 107 Battery, 7th Medium RA

It was not only the German mortar and shellfire that made their lives a misery at 'Nuts'. There was also a plethora of an old desert friend – the flies.

> Flies by the million, grown fat from the numerous bodies unburied out in No Man's Land, filled the armoured car and made observation and eating equally impossible. After a time, crews found the perfect fly-catcher and conditions improved slightly. The idea was to set up beer bottles all round, each with half an inch of beer in the bottom; the bottles became jammed tight with the hideous bodies within two hours.[13]

Lieutenant Eric Dobson, B Troop, 107 Battery 7th Medium RA

The OPs were not only identifying good targets of opportunity, such as distant vehicles or visible infantry, but were also registering the guns on to all potential significant points in the area.

As the 5.5-inch guns were mainly intended for a counter-battery role, they received lists of all the identified German gun batteries in their area. These were collated from the reports of RAF reconnaissance aircraft and the hard graft of an attached battery of the 4th Survey Regiment, who used flash spotting and sound ranging to locate the German guns.

> I was in the command post working out the counter-battery lists, which came through from – presumably – divisional headquarters, giving the coordinates of enemy gun positions, the enemy batteries, which would have been found out through flash spotting or sound ranging. There were sometimes upwards of 200 of these batteries. They all had code numbers such as 'XC' 'CY' 'DJ' – that sort of thing. When we were required to fire on an enemy battery we would get an order from our battery command post through to our troop, 'Target Counter Battery XY!' Instead of having to work out the coordinates, to save time they would have already been worked out, so that I had them down on a list and I didn't have to refer to the artillery board, or anything else. So one was able to pass the fire orders immediately to the guns who would then engage the target. Of course, if we fired too much from one gun position the enemy would have done precisely the same thing – and we ourselves would have been shelled.[14]

Gunner Ken Giles, A Troop, 107 Battery, 7th Medium RA

As the guns were now further apart than had been the case with the 25-pounders, firing orders were transmitted from the command post by a simple tannoy system.

When it was realised that some of the potential counter-battery targets were out of range from the main gun positions, Bob Foulds was ordered to prepare some forward gun positions for B Troop. Given the size of the gun pits this promised to be no mean task.

The word got round that we were going to attack, so we made a start on digging some forward gun positions to put our range well forward from where it was at that time – perhaps 1,000 yards in front of the normal gun positions. I was given the job of digging with the help of some South African bulldozer people – at night – a gun position so that we could camouflage it by day and go on and finish it. We went out with these lads as soon as it had got dark. We had staked out where these guns were to be. We made a start. We dug all night, the bulldozers going and then when a bulldozer had finished a pit, because it made a big scooped mess, our people had to square it up and sandbag round. Just before daylight we packed this job up and came back and fell into our beds! The next thing I knew, Lewis-Jones was on my tail because these gun pits were not deep enough – although they were so vast – like circus amphitheatres – but they hadn't gone down deep enough. Now, it was very hard to tell in the dark! Anyway it didn't suit 'His Lordship' at all – so back we were out the next night to finish off these pits by hand.[15]

Second Lieutenant Bob Foulds, B Troop, 107 Battery, 7th Medium RA

All through July and August, the South Notts Hussars strove to match the regulars of 27/28 Battery. In the absence of much counter-battery response from the Germans they were able to achieve significant improvements, despite the continued flow of criticism and brickbats received from Major Lewis-Jones.

MEANWHILE THE 'DESERT FOX' WAS STIRRING. Although plagued by a crippling shortage of fuel and the general logistical difficulties of being at the end of very overstretched supply lines, Rommel was once again looking to go on the offensive. Indeed, given the intransigent attitude Hitler demonstrated on the Eastern Front – where he would countermand orders, push for unsustainable attacks, and dismiss officers he deemed insufficiently aggressive – retreat was not really an option. Having received reinforcements in the shape of the German 164 Leichte Division, the Fallschirmjäger Brigade 'Ramcke' and the Italian Divisione Paracadutisti 'Folgore', Rommel decided to attempt a further attack on the night of 30 August. He planned to swing an assault force south, around the British left flank, before taking the Alam Halfa Ridge running parallel to the coast to the rear of the Eighth Army. Unfortunately for Rommel, Montgomery was warned in good time of an imminent attack by the ULTRA intelligence system, which allowed the British to break the German secret codes. The British could predict the Axis thrust to the south and the maligned Auchinleck had already done much valuable work to secure the defence of the Alam Halfa Ridge. Montgomery intended to let the Germans make progress towards the ridge, with the 7th Armoured Division giving ground, before the 5th Indian Division and the 2nd New Zealand Division would strike from the north, driving into the left flank of the German advance.

On 30 August 1942 the Battle of Alam Halfa began. Right from the start the Germans had problems. The clearance of the minefields caused huge delays as they tried to force their way forward, the German and Italian armoured formations were bombed from the air, hit by the new 6-pounder anti-tank guns, blasted by the artillery and then attacked by the Allied tanks. On 1 September, the 107 Battery was ordered south to support the advance of the 2nd New Zealand Division. Over the next few days they would fire an enormous number of rounds attached to the command of the 64th Medium Regiment, RA. It would prove a torrid experience.

We were suddenly told to up sticks and go down to the south, into the real desert area. There was absolutely no cover; it was all gravel and sand. We took up a gun position back from a ridge, near destroyed 88mm guns. We had a static OP right on the edge of this escarpment. The other troop had a mobile OP in the armoured car. We sat looking over this quite extraordinary view. The escarpment was several hundred feet high and then there was this plain running out below it. It was a stupendous sight, it was simply swarming with German motor transport, infantry, a few tanks – we had a wonderful day's shooting, giving these Germans down below the most fearful stick, setting fire to the vehicles and no doubt doing a great deal of damage.[16]

Captain Charles Laborde, B Troop, 107 Battery, 7th Medium RA

The Germans certainly noticed their contribution to the battle and took immediate retaliatory action. Shells began to crash down on the gun positions – and then came the scream of the Stukas, seemingly lining up for their attack on B Troop by using the nearby line of destroyed 88mm guns as a landmark.

Methodically they plastered the gun positions, not wasting a single bomb. Three men only, amazingly, were touched: Lance Bombardier Brown received serious wounds, and Sergeant Hewson and Lance Bombardier Clark had to receive treatment. One gun tower was destroyed and a range dial damaged. It was really fantastic that so many bombs should have been concentrated in so small a space and yet so little damage done.[17]

Lieutenant Eric Dobson, B Troop, 107 Battery 7th Medium RA

They had been lucky. But next day the Stukas were back – twelve of them this time.

The second time the Stukas came over, I had come back from the OP and was on the gun position. They destroyed one of the Matador gun towers and they killed a number of the men. I think we were all pretty badly shaken; the bombing was fairly hairy, and we only had slit trenches. No Stuka raid in which you are in the target area is any fun at all – and that is the truth of it![18]

Captain Charles Laborde, B Troop, 107 Battery, 7th Medium RA

This time they took a hell of a battering.

There were near misses on all guns, three craters round the command post, and a direct hit on a loaded Matador that was delivering ammunition to Sergeant Swinton's gun. Two members of his detachment were killed, Gunners Brownlow[19] and Becks,[20] and three more wounded, Gunners Truss, Wilkinson and Cartledge. The whole troop showed the utmost gallantry in trying to drag clear the killed and wounded, and the Matador driver, Hoggart, made heroic attempts to put out the fire that was licking at the shells and cartridges. The fire quickly spread, and the work of rescue continued with 5.5-inch shells whistling through the air in all directions, and some exploding.[21]

Lieutenant Eric Dobson, B Troop, 107 Battery 7th Medium RA

Ian Sinclair was one of those first rescuers to get to the scene.

A driver named Becks, I can see him now, ever so little fellow he was, he had his whole stomach ripped out. He was cut almost in half. I can remember him being alive, with his stomach out. Wrapping him in a blanket and thinking, 'Oh, my God!' He never lost consciousness, until the ambulance came. The ambulance men wouldn't take him, because they knew he was going to die, 'Oh no, he can't live, leave him!' Just left him in the blanket – he did die very soon. They were right – it was their business – he *was* going to die. I wish he'd have died straight away, because I can remember the look on his face.[22]

Second Lieutenant Ian Sinclair, B Troop, 107 Battery, 7th Medium RA

As the operations wound down, the battery returned to their coastal gun positions.

The British resistance had proved far too strong, and from 2 September Rommel began to pull back his assault divisions, recognising that his attempt to take Alam Halfa Ridge had failed.

Montgomery did not follow up immediately. When it came to the crunch, he was a cautious general and preferred to build up his strength, complete his reorganisation and strike only when the time was right. Of course, Churchill wanted an attack at once, well before the landings planned for the British First Army (Lieutenant General Kenneth Anderson) under Operation Torch in Algeria and Morocco in early November 1942; but Montgomery, supported by the Commander in Chief Middle East, General Harold Alexander, followed Auchinleck's well-trodden path in demanding more time. Meanwhile, the revitalised Desert Air Force would continue to harass the Axis forces. Exploratory, small-scale counter-attacks served only to confirm that the German and Italian units arrayed in front of them were still more than capable of a resolute and effective defence. Whenever the great offensive was launched it would not be easy.

THE ROLE OF ARTILLERY WAS RADICALLY CHANGING by this stage of the North African campaign. The lessons of the Great War had been belatedly relearnt: artillery fire was most effective in battle when it was concentrated. This message was truly rammed home when, in September 1942, Brigadier Sidney

Kirkman was posted out as Commander Royal Artillery in the Eighth Army. Kirkman was an impressive figure who had hammered out an effective method of securing the quickest and heaviest concentration of fire on a target by all artillery within range. His basic thesis[23] was that tactical command of units in an operational situation should be at the highest level possible – i.e. preferably at corps headquarters – but that actual fire observation and control of the guns should be decentralised to the forward observation officer – the man on the spot on the battlefield. Kirkham had already tested out his theories during large-scale exercises in England and it was apparent that the forward observation officer had the best opportunity of accurately judging a situation and deciding on the appropriate response – whether it be fire from just a troop of guns, or a corps artillery defensive barrage to fend off a full-scale German attack. If the command of artillery was too decentralised, then local commanders could interfere to prevent rapid concentrations of fire across higher formation boundaries. Up until then in the North African campaign, artillery strength had been dissipated with command exercised at brigade level, or even lower in the widespread use of ad hoc 'Jock Columns'. With the deployment of just a troop, battery, or at most a regiment of artillery, then the guns were still useful, but perforce lacked the collective concentration of fire radically to alter any given tactical situation. By the summer of 1942, the policy of deploying the guns in 'penny-packets' – present everywhere but nowhere in strength – had finally been overturned. From now on the guns would be collected together to achieve significant objectives. Effective cooperation was prioritised between the artillery, infantry and armoured formations, with the view of producing an artillery plan which meshed perfectly with the needs of the overall operational plan. The process of concentrating resources was assisted by the timely arrival of the new 6-pounder anti-tank gun, which proved an excellent weapon, capable of taking on the German panzers, and thereby allowing the 25-pounder units to be removed from an anti-tank role and enfolded back into the overall artillery plan.

There were also technical advances to achieve that concentrated effect based on the work back in the UK of another gunner officer, Brigadier Jack Parham. He had managed to simplify the whole process of focusing the fire of hundreds of guns on a single target at the behest of a forward observation officer. Parham had recognised the essential truth, demonstrated throughout the Great War, that artillery is not a precision weapon and that fire could only be directed at the area containing the target – not an exact point. This demanded a large number of guns, copious amounts of ammunition and a simple, rapid and effective means of wireless communication between the forward observation officers and the gun batteries. The latter was attained by the definition of targets according to their importance and hence the scale of artillery response required: regimental targets requiring twenty-four guns, divisional targets requiring seventy-two guns and corps targets which could entail the deployment of hundreds of guns.

More lessons taken from the Great War were reflected in the meticulous care with which the gunners drew up complex artillery fire plans, with carefully calibrated guns, accurately surveyed maps and the use of up-to-date meteorological corrections to allow for the effects of air pressure and weather on a shell in flight. Bombardments would be synchronised by the BBC time signal so that the opening shells would all burst on their targets together for maximum effect. German batteries that had been identified would be 'neutralised' by a torrent of shells at Zero Hour – although the international ban on the use of poisonous gas (in place since 1928) had made this far more difficult than back in late 1918. The old 'creeping barrage' tactic would also be employed to create a 'wall' of shells moving forward in front of the attacking infantry, while standing barrages protected captured positions from counter-attacks. This mix of old and new methods would be deployed to devastating effect in the barrages fired during the Battle of El Alamein.

Meticulous preparations began, with Montgomery seeking to take advantage of the period of full moon in late October. With no easily accessible open flank, established German defensive positions on a narrow frontage, and with 5-mile-deep minefields in front of them, his plans for Operation Lightfoot envisioned two separate attacks. Lieutenant General Sir Oliver Leese's XXX Corps (9th Australian, 51st Highland Division, 2nd New Zealand Division and 1st South African Division), supported by the 23rd Armoured Brigade, were to make the main attack in the north, cutting paths through the minefields and breaking through to create viable bridgeheads. These would be the jumping-off points for exploitation – before first light – by Lieutenant General Herbert Lumsden's X Corps (1st and 10th Armoured Divisions) which was to cut the German supply routes and thereby trigger an engagement with the German armoured formations. Meanwhile, Lieutenant General Brian Horrocks' XIII Corps (7th Armoured Division), 44th Division and Free French Brigade was to launch an attack aimed at pinning German armour in the southern sector. Deception measures would be enacted to convince the Germans that the main thrust would be in the south, complete with dummy tanks, fake supply dumps and wireless 'dummy' signals indicating non-existent unit deployments. Later, Montgomery modified his tactics by introducing the idea of a series of 'crumbling' operations after the bridgehead had been made, striking hard at the Italian infantry, to try to provoke German armoured retaliation. This attritional intent was informed by the knowledge that Montgomery had gained a clear numerical supremacy in men, tanks and aircraft. Ironically, given Montgomery's subsequent habit of criticising Great War generals, the planning process drew on much of the assimilated knowledge of that conflict.

BACK IN THEIR COASTAL GUN POSITIONS the South Notts Hussars resumed their daily routine. As the day of the offensive approached, the observations taken from the OP had more and more urgent relevance. Bob Foulds was sent ahead to act as a relief observation officer at Point 32 on a forward ridge.

We had an OP on the side of Point 32. Some distance from what I would call the most dangerous area, but it was an OP that you had to occupy before first light, and you couldn't move out till after dark. It was quite a deep pit cut in the side of the hill and we faced south-west. It gave a very good view over the German lines, but visibility was always a problem, because as soon as the desert got hot you used to get this mirage effect, unless there was a clear, fine day with no sand blowing around. We used to have an officer and two signallers who could relieve each other and look after meals. A panorama was left in the OP with all the recorded targets identified, a list of all the other targets for night firing. Looking with the naked eye you'd see something on the broad horizon and then you'd try and identify what it was with binoculars. When I saw troops or vehicles moving near to a recorded target, I did one or two shoots, put one or two rounds of gunfire down. It was hard to keep your concentration up all day. You were reporting any enemy activity: if there was excessive shelling on the OPs on Point 32, we always reported that and tried to give a bearing on the guns that appeared to be firing. The command post made use of all this data and if it was considered valuable enough, they'd pass that back to Survey Regiment for counter-battery use by the corps as a whole.[24]

Second Lieutenant Bob Foulds, B Troop, 107 Battery, 7th Medium RA

Colonel 'Toc' Elton was beginning to have an impact with his advanced ideas of gunnery. One new method linked with his name was the development of the 'Stonk', which demonstrated his adherence to the same principles as Brigadier Jack Parham in securing the fastest effective concentration of massed fire.

The word 'stonk' being given it meant a concentration of all available guns, whoever they belonged to, on to a target that needed every available gun. The word 'stonk' went down everywhere and the map reference where the 'stonk' was to take place. You knew where you were on the map, you got a line using a compass bearing on the map reference you'd been given, you point the gun at it: one round, load, 'Fire!' An airburst for everybody else to get a line on it. Everybody else set up their zero lines on this round in the air – and you all get into action.[25]

Second Lieutenant Ian Sinclair, B Troop, 107 Battery, 7th Medium RA

Such a concentration of fire coming from massed batteries meant that the target was almost certain to be destroyed.

The 'stonk' was splendid idea. It was simply worked out on a 1,000 metre square, one of the map grid squares. You got the map reference of the grid square and the word 'stonk!'. Then every gun involved in it – any number of 25-pounders and all the medium guns – fired into a certain area of that square. It was the most marvellous way of breaking up a German attack and it was done with tremendous success. It was devastating in the desert.[26]

Captain Charles Laborde, B Troop, 107 Battery, 7th Medium RA

Also, work was done on the 'rolling ball of fire' – a 'stonk' that moved forward on a certain axis. As might be imagined, these experiments with new methods didn't always turn out as expected.

> We were doing experimental airburst ranging. If you got a lot of infantry and you could crack a shell about 50–60 yards over their heads, then the spray of the shrapnel would cause greater effect than a shell just hitting the ground. You had to put a fresh fuse cap and set the fuse on a timescale. You calculated this timescale from special tables which were issued. In the dark, with the help of a torch, you had to set this fuse, and unfortunately my gunner responsible for setting the fuse put it on 20 seconds instead of 30 seconds! The result being that the thing would have cracked over our own troops if we had fired it. I happened to spot it at the last second and reported that the wrong fuse had been set. But it was already up the barrel. We had to take the gun out of the pit and fire it out to sea! The Germans would wonder what the dickens was going off![27]
>
> Sergeant Harold Harper, B Troop, 107 Battery, 7th Medium RA

On another occasion, the accuracy of fire exceeded all expectations amid an informal competition to hit a threatening German OP scaffolding tower, which had appeared a fair distance behind their front lines.

> 'Toc' Elton bet a bottle of Scotch that nobody could knock this tower out. I was fortunate enough to be up at the OP when somebody came up to do the shoot – I was extremely sceptical, because an OP tower is incredibly difficult to hit, especially at that range.[28]
>
> Second Lieutenant Bob Foulds, B Troop, 107 Battery, 7th Medium RA

His doubts were shared by Albert Swinton, whose gun was

assigned to the task. His story also reflects an amusing inflation in the imagined size of the bet.

> I was told that the bet was six bottles of whisky. I was chosen as the gun to do it! When they said to me, 'We're going to knock an OP down!' I said, 'Don't talk such a load of tripe – we never do it! They fired at us for nine months in Tobruk and never hit an OP – so why should we do it now?'[29]

Sergeant Albert Swinton, B Troop, 107 Battery, 7th Medium RA

Bob Foulds watched the shoot unfold at a range of over 12,000 yards.

> Observation was good that day, it was clear, which was unusual, because usually there is some sand and haze and things used to disappear into the mirage. We could see the fall of shot. In about three or four rounds, this thing disappeared – to our amazement. They'd put a ranging round so close to this tower that they only made the smallest corrections and then they hit it![30]

Second Lieutenant Bob Foulds, B Troop, 107 Battery, 7th Medium RA

Charles Laborde was also watching.

> Whether we hit a supporting wire, or whether we actually hit the OP itself it's difficult to say! When the shell hit the ground, it made a tremendous cloud of smoke and dust. But the fact is that it fell down, to a great deal of joy and surprise![31]

Captain Charles Laborde, B Troop, 107 Battery, 7th Medium RA

Albert Swinton had triumphed, but as he rather ruefully remarked, he never got a sniff of the fabled whisky bottles.

> I shall never forget it. We had got the Survey Regiment there, sound ranging, visual ranging and all sorts of things. I think it was about the fifth round we hit it – and we gave it five

rounds of gunfire just for good luck. It came down all right. My goodness it came down. Our colonel won six bottles of whisky – I never even got a smell.[32]

Sergeant Albert Swinton, B Troop, 107 Battery, 7th Medium RA

BY OCTOBER, PREPARATIONS FOR THE BATTLE had begun in earnest. More forward gun positions were laboriously dug and some 500 rounds per gun moved up and buried. All the guns had by now fired over 2,000 rounds, so they were carefully recalibrated to allow compensatory adjustments to ensure that they remained accurate. On 20 October, 107 Battery moved forward into their new gun positions situated just north of the main coast road, with B Troop next to the sea and A Troop beside them. The wagon lines and rear echelons moved up to occupy the old gun pits.

First definite news of coming operations reached the battery officers in the mess dugout on the night of 22nd October. Colonel Elton walked in after giving five minutes' warning of his coming; usually the colonel's visits concerned an unfortunate event of that day, but everyone sensed that this was something different and the party was in a jovial mood by the time he arrived, jovial perhaps because a few bottles of a strange brew called 'Vin Marco' had just come up from Alexandria. Colonel Elton explained that the new commander in chief had directed that every man in the line should understand in general the full objectives and aims of the Battle of Alamein, and he gave the detailed plan: 7th Medium Regiment, under orders of XXX Corps Royal Artillery, commanded by Brigadier Mead Dennis, the former South Notts adjutant, was to support all the attacking moves in the northern sector, first with a monster counter-battery programme and later with infantry-supporting shoots. Colonel Elton, unquestionably the finest ever passer-on of verbal orders, left the whole mess keyed up to a high pitch of excitement over coming events; he left behind, too, something more practical – the whole counter-battery programme for the attack.[33]

Lieutenant Eric Dobson, Headquarters, 107 Battery, 7th Medium RA

This triggered the massive amount of hard work necessary if they were to have any chance of being ready in time for the scheduled start of the artillery bombardment at 21.40 on 23 October. The infantry attack would go in some twenty minutes later at 22.00.

I helped in doing the calculations for B Troop along with Eric Dobson. We were given the reference points of this barrage taken from the map – we used to have to work out the line and range for every single step, so that we could convert into fire orders for the guns. On top of all of that you had to apply – come the day – the meteorological element. How much the wind was going to turn the shells, how much the atmosphere was going to hold them back or let them go further forward. Harold Harper, who was an extremely good mathematician, went over the whole of our calculation on his own before sending it back to the battery. There were no calculators, no means of doing it other than manually. It was very important these calculations were checked and rechecked.[34]

Second Lieutenant Bob Foulds, B Troop, 107 Battery, 7th Medium RA

The South Notts Hussars were once again ready for battle.

WHEN THE GUNS ROARED OUT the effect was incredible. Although it could not really be compared in scale to the stupendous barrages of the Great War, it was still an awe-inspiring sight and a true cacophony.

It was the biggest artillery bombardment in which we'd ever taken part – principally from the very, very, very considerable number of guns that took part in it. When it opened up there were guns in front of you, behind you, beside you – all over the place. Guns that you'd never realised were there until they actually fired. The gun flashes were all around you![35]

Second Lieutenant Charles Westlake, A Troop, 107 Battery, 7th Medium RA

The more thoughtful men could not help wondering what it must be like for the Germans on the receiving end of this deluge of shells. But after what had happened to their friends in the Cauldron, few of them really cared.

The staggering noise when all the guns opened together. One was absolutely shattered by the noise – it was tremendous! The whole heavens lit up with 'Monty's moonlight', the searchlights put up to brighten up the moon. Every now and then when we were firing there would be the most tremendous explosion in the German lines when one of the shells had hit an ammunition dump. A tremendous flash. The men were supposed to fire four rounds a minute, but were actually firing something like six rounds a minute. The guns got violently hot and were leaping about in the gun pits, because the oil in the buffer recuperator had got so thin with the heat. You could see the gun barrels glowing, they were so hot.[36]

Captain Charles Laborde, B Troop, 107 Battery, 7th Medium RA

There were serious mechanical problems, almost inevitable with this rate of continuous firing.

I heard a tremendous bang and looked out – no shell had landed. The No. 4 gun had just fired. I couldn't make out what this was. Then it fired again and there was another tremendous 'BANG!' The shell was prematuring just outside the bore, scattering bits of shell far and wide. We had to stop it from firing and the artificer came up and did all his tests. He said, 'It's a very dirty barrel!' He cleaned it out a bit and said, 'All right, try another one!' No one was very keen to pull the lanyard, so it was obviously the officer's business to fire it. I went in, gave it a tug and off it went – it was OK.[37]

Second Lieutenant Bob Foulds, B Troop, 107 Battery, 7th Medium RA

On a personal level, Harold Harper had one member of his gun section who was afflicted badly by nerves.

After we'd fired about ten to twelve rounds I thought, 'Blimey, it's beginning to get hard work!' I noticed one bloke was missing! He was the biggest bloke in the crew, and he was hiding in a slit trench behind the gun! That sort of thing become contagious – so I had to do something drastic to get things back on an equilibrium. I had to go and drag him out in the middle of the barrage, get him by the scruff of the neck and threaten to shoot him if didn't get back on the job! It sounds terrible now, but you were a different sort of animal in those days.[38]

Sergeant Harold Harper, B Troop, 107 Battery, 7th Medium RA

The gunner returned to his post, but Harper considered that he never really recovered his spirit. Indeed, shortly afterwards a pretext was found for him to be evacuated back to base.

By dawn the medium guns had switched their fire to the German strongpoints reported to be holding up the advance. It was unfortunate for the Germans that at this decisive moment in the North African campaign Rommel was away on sick leave, while to make matters worse, his replacement, General Georg Stumme, died of a heart attack while under an air attack. Rommel was swiftly recalled, but for two days the Germans lacked any strong leadership at the higher levels of command.

In the XXX Corps sector, things went reasonably well, with the 9th Australian Division, 51st Highland Division and 2nd New Zealand Division all making some progress, but in places failing to take key objectives in time to allow the planned pre-dawn early advance of the armour. This left the situation very much in the balance.

Ken Giles would see at first hand the evidence of the initial successes.

> The following morning at dawn, I was standing by one of the gun pits and saw thousands upon thousands of German prisoners marching through the wadi below us. They were about eight to ten abreast and the column seemed to extend for miles. They looked absolutely worn out: they were dirty, dejected, mostly very young – 18, 19, 20. They walked with their heads down. They all looked very dazed – and I think they would have been with a bombardment such as we put over! It would have a devastating effect – they would be disorientated and worried what was to happen to them. On the *qui vive*, glancing right and left, 'Are we all right? Are we going to be mown down?' Whilst they were passing, I recall somebody running out into the line of prisoners, commandeering this watch and rushing back with it – I thought that was a pretty rotten thing to do![39]

Gunner Ken Giles, A Troop, 107 Battery, 7th Medium RA

The barrage was relentless, and the men had no chance to properly rest. It was soon all hands to the pump as badges of rank were forgotten in the collective effort to keep the guns firing.

> The length of time you went without any sleep. It was days on end you were in action – firing or taking charge of the gun positions. The troop leader would go round the gun pits doing anything he could to assist whatever it was. If it was

humping ammunition; you humped ammunition! If the No. 1 wanted some help you would give it to him! Most of the time it was a matter of making sure that your presence was known – that they knew you were there – having a word with them as you went round from one gun pit to the next. I think most of us went thirty-six to forty-eight hours without any sleep whatsoever. You seem to get into a sort of zombie-like routine where you just keep going – you know what your job is – and you just get on with it! You do get heavy-headed, your eyes ache like the devil. All you want to do is go to sleep for a couple of days – you just can't! We realised were just going to drop dead on our feet, and we had to organise it so that you snatch a little bit of sleep whenever you could, while somebody took over.[40]

Second Lieutenant Charles Westlake, A Troop, 107 Battery, 7th Medium RA

Ernie Hurry was one who tried his best to 'pitch in', although he did not cover himself in glory during his brief foray as a 'gunner'.

I was in the gun position taking turns, helping on the ammunition and everything. I never touched the dial sight, but I was doing everything else. To fire these guns, you had to put a cartridge in the breech. Then you pulled a lanyard! I'd helped them with loading, then you stand back to fire it – and nothing happened! They said 'Right, fire again!' Pulled it again! Nothing happened! 'Try again!' Nothing happened! We wait a few seconds, then we opened the breech. When they opened the breech, I hadn't put a cartridge in! So they told me to, 'Piss off!'[41]

Gunner Ernie Hurry, A Troop, 107 Battery, 7th Medium RA

On one night, B Troop was required to carry out harassing fire every three minutes throughout the whole night. Harold Harper saw this as a chance to give some of his gun section a well-earned rest.

It was to keep the Germans awake really – and not quite knowing what was going to happen. I said to my detachment – you've not had a sleep for about four nights, go and get yourself away from the gun, get yourself down and my lance sergeant and myself can manage this between us – one round every three minutes was chickenfeed. We had no sooner started this when we got a report that another gun that was going to fire spasmodically with us was out of action. The message I got from the Gun Position Officer Lieutenant Foulds, was 'You'll have to double up!' I told him my situation and next thing was the GPO came on the gun and the three of us managed to fire these rounds between us – he had previously been a gun sergeant in Tobruk.[42]

Sergeant Harold Harper, B Troop, 107 Battery, 7th Medium RA

In the end it was not obvious which gave up first: his gun section or the gun itself. Harper maintained it was the gun.

When we looked up the barrel there was no rifling left in the barrel at all, all smooth all the way up! We found out afterwards that my shells were dropping about 1,000 yards short – there's no doubt about it that we probably dropped rounds in our own infantry. My gun got taken out of action and I was told to report to the REME workshops to have a fresh barrel put in.[43]

Sergeant Harold Harper, B Troop, 107 Battery, 7th Medium RA

The absence of a single shell falling on their gun positions throughout the battle was a testament to the efficacy of the early deluge of counter-battery fire they had inflicted on the German artillery.

However, not everything was going according to plan. On the night of 23 October, the efforts of the Royal Engineers to cut two wide lanes through the minefields to allow the passage of the 1st and 10th Armoured Divisions had fallen well behind an unfeasibly tight timetable and in consequence, the attacks of the advance tank units were thrown back. By the time dawn broke there was a 'traffic jam' of masses of static tanks, guns and vehicles stretched out in the two 'corridors' reaching back from the German lines. During the day a defensive screen had to be established around the small bridgeheads. On the night of 24 October, the tanks attempted to break out, but were thrown back again by a ring of German tanks and anti-tank guns gathered around the minefield exits. The Germans also began to counter-attack, which was still more threatening in a weak tactical situation, although there was some hope given by the sterling performance in battle of the new Sherman tanks and their powerful 75mm guns.

Meanwhile, the 107 Battery observation officers had been pressing forwards, looking for a new vantage point to set up an OP. On the morning of 24 October, Charles Laborde had gone forward for B Troop.

> I found myself in a 15cwt with my wireless, my ack and a driver, and off into the enemy's territory. There was a narrow path which had been opened up through the minefields by the engineers. It was rather like a county road in this country: running between the wire on either side with the white lines of tapes marking the road to run on. Just the tracks made by the vehicles where all the surface scrub had been worn away. On either side were these poor fellows who had been killed in the assault lying about in the wire and on the minefields. We went up as far as we could go – we found a convenient trench as an OP, where we set up with the Australian infantry roundabout. There we had a fair amount of firing, with the Germans trying to reorganise. Infantry moving about, occasional tanks, the odd vehicle. We could fire at things beyond the 25-pounders. I think you could say it was a fairly hectic day![44]

Captain Charles Laborde, B Troop, 107 Battery, 7th Medium RA

While occupying this OP, Laborde found himself gifted with the once-in-a-lifetime opportunity to trigger a 'stonk'. It was one he seized with alacrity.

> I could see these German tanks, vehicles and everything clustering in front, all lining up to put in a big assault. That was duly reported back to the gun position and went back to brigade headquarters – and further back. Suddenly there was this most colossal outburst of firing into this area where the Germans were forming up! The whole desert erupted! I think it was ten rounds of gunfire, every gun fired – that's an awful lot of shells on the ground. It became a vast cloud of dust! That was it! It simply disintegrated and finished off any large-scale counter-attack they were going to have. Never developed at all![45]
>
> Captain Charles Laborde, B Troop, 107 Battery, 7th Medium RA

THE BATTLE HAD MOVED into the stage Montgomery had referred to as 'crumbling'. He sought to draw in German counter-attacks and engage them in a battle of attrition, confident that he had the whip hand given the massed power of the Eighth Army arsenal of guns, backed up by the increasing dominance of the Desert Air Force. On 25 October, Rommel's subordinates ordered a series of armoured counter-attacks and their panzer losses started to escalate. They had fallen into Montgomery's less than subtle trap. Rommel's return that evening did not change the approach, as even more counter-attacks were launched to no avail. Rommel's strength was draining away and his excessively long supply lines meant he was fast running out of fuel.

Montgomery had his own problems. The 'crumbling' process by its nature was slow and had not achieved any significant progress. On 26 October, Montgomery and his staff reassessed the situation. They had started the offensive with 1,060 tanks and had suffered 306 losses, while the Eighth Army had also suffered some 6,140 casualties killed, wounded and missing. There were even increasing concerns over artillery ammunition if the battle lasted too much longer. Montgomery decided to modify his overall plans. He planned a new major thrust to be known as Operation Supercharge, to be carried out by the substantially reinforced 2nd New Zealand Division, the 10th Armoured Division and the 9th Armoured Brigade. The necessary reorganisation would be undertaken between 26 and 28 October and was to be covered by a series of niggling offensive operations to be launched by the 9th Australian Division. This triggered much vicious fighting at a considerable sacrifice of Australian lives.

As the line edged forward, the OP teams found it difficult to find good concealed positions not exposed to excessive retaliatory fire. Captain Alan Smith had established an OP on the forward slope of a ridge, but he had already been forced out by heavy shelling. When Laborde went up to take over as forward observation officer there, he found the situation nightmarish. Although the OP offered a good vantage point looking through a slit facing towards the British lines – i.e. the wrong way – it had an open entrance facing the Germans. Laborde and his signaller did their best to sandbag up the hole and create a viable OP position. He also took the precaution of getting his signaller to lay a complex ladder of telephone lines back to the wireless set in the truck hidden behind the ridge – just in case the shelling resumed.

> We waited for the dawn. None of us knew that it was actually a German flash spotting point, the position of which they knew to the last metre! With the dawn came the first of the shells – and they rained shells on this OP at a fairly steady interval for hours. We did a little bit of firing at targets we could see, but by

about 9 o'clock we no longer had any communications with the truck – all my beautiful ladder had been broken. [46]

Captain Charles Laborde, B Troop, 107 Battery, 7th Medium RA

Without communications back to the guns, they were enduring hell for no purpose.

It was absolutely dreadful – one thought, 'Any minute a shell is going come on the top and that will be it – thank you very much!' It was a terrifying experience! Then they started to fire a very big gun at us, the shells making a hole about 6 to 8 feet across, 5 feet deep! Eventually we heard this shell arriving, then there was the most tremendous thump, it landed the other side of our little sandbag wall. Whatever God was looking after us that day I don't know, but the shell didn't go off! It sent up a column of earth and muck, high up into the sky, and it descended all over us! The sides of the dugout fell in and I was completely buried – it didn't do me much good. I edged my way backwards to discover my 'ack' was three-quarters buried too. We wriggled ourselves out of that! I thought, 'Well what do we do now?' It was about 10 o'clock in the morning, three-quarters buried, no communication, the space in the dugout was about 2½ feet between the roof and what had fallen in. We were pretty badly shaken you can imagine! All you can say for that very fortunate escape was that they must have reckoned they had 'fixed us' because they didn't fire at us after that – the shelling stopped. [47]

Captain Charles Laborde, B Troop, 107 Battery, 7th Medium RA

His horrendous day was by no means over. With great difficulty, Laborde managed to get a viewpoint open, but the Germans must have noticed some movements, as they opened up again – this time with a Spandau.

I put my head down very quickly! For some hours, this wretched gun was firing bursts at odd intervals. It was fairly accurate, and sprayed the whole top of the OP, the sandbags disintegrated, and all the sand fell down on top of us. They had completely neutralised us, we couldn't get out and in the OP we could do nothing! It was quite well on into the afternoon, occasional shelling, when an Aussie crawled up a trench which must have led to the OP and he called out, 'Is there anybody there?' I said, 'Yes! I can't come out because of this Spandau!' 'Ah, we've fixed that bugger!' I said to my 'ack', 'Let's get out!' We thought we'd better go together. We both crouched in this very shallow little hole in the front, then I said, 'Right! Off we go!' We leapt out on to the top and ran like hell back to the truck. We only got halfway when we heard the shell arriving. We flattened ourselves on the ground and there was a tremendous thump and bits fell about. We ran back, they fired about half a dozen other shells, seeing if they could get us![48]

Captain Charles Laborde, B Troop, 107 Battery, 7th Medium RA

This terrible experience had a very real effect on Charles Laborde.

I was very shaken. I'd had hours of this, it was demoralising. I was glad to be away – great relief that I had actually survived. I went back to my little dugout, a covered slit trench. I fell asleep and I slept like a log through the barrage going on through the night – which was all going on about 60 yards away. Never heard a thing, I was absolutely finished. This was the worst day I had in the whole war. In the morning I was fine – the resilience of youth![49]

Captain Charles Laborde, B Troop, 107 Battery, 7th Medium RA

With the same confidence of youth, he thought he had got over it, but he would suffer nightmares of being trapped in that OP for decades. Not long afterwards, Laborde left the South Notts

Hussars, when he was detached as a signal instructor for the Artillery Wing of Royal Corps of Signals School, Maadi, Cairo.

THE MAIN OPERATION SUPERCHARGE ATTACK commenced at 01.00 on 2 November. The focus was further south than the existing main operations, as it was intended to strike at the junction of the German and Italian forces. With Churchill again starting to stir impatiently back in London, it was important that something concrete was achieved soon, or Montgomery might well have followed Auchinleck into the wilderness. It was primarily carried out by the 50th Northumbrian Division, which had been attached to the 2nd New Zealand Division. They would attack behind a powerful creeping barrage, supported by the Valentine tanks of the 23rd Armoured Brigade. Their objective was the Sidi Abd El-Rahman track which ran from the coast road, south towards the Qattara Depression. Once this had been achieved, the 9th Armoured Brigade was to push on and exploit the advance.

The fighting was hard, but the British armour, supported closely by the massed guns, the self-propelled guns and the deadly interventions of the Desert Air Force, was beginning to hold sway. German counter-attacks only frittered away yet more of their precious panzer strength. The British advance was eventually stopped, but at such cost that Rommel was warned that he was almost out of panzers, desperately short of fuel and running low on ammunition. He realised the game was up and ordered a withdrawal to defensive positions at El Fuka. His message back to Germany must have made for pleasant reading to the British High Command when decoded by ULTRA.

An orderly withdrawal of the six Italian and two German non-motorised divisions and brigades is impossible for lack of MT.

A large part of these formations will probably fall into the hands of the enemy who is fully motorised. Even the mobile troops are so closely involved in the battle that only elements will be able to disengage from the enemy. The stocks of ammunition which are still available are at the front but no more than nominal stocks are at our disposal in rear. The shortage of fuel will not allow of a withdrawal to any great distance. There is only one road available and the Army, as it passes along it, will almost certainly be attacked day and night by the enemy air force. In these circumstances, we must therefore expect the gradual destruction of the Army in spite of the heroic resistance and exceptionally high morale of the troops.[50]

Field Marshal Erwin Rommel, Headquarters, Panzerarmee Afrika

Hitler issued orders to stand and fight, but although Rommel made one last effort, he knew it was useless.

It was evident that Operation Supercharge had succeeded. It had triggered a more effective version of the 'crumbling' attritional fighting intended under Operation Lightfoot, but as it was conducted on a far narrower front, the power of the British guns and Desert Air Force could be concentrated to overwhelm the German resistance. The only question was whether Montgomery could go on to gain a decisive victory.

On 3 November the British began another series of attacks – not all of which were successful. The fighting was still hard; it was rarely anything else in the Western Desert against determined German and Italian opposition. Left with little real choice, Rommel prioritised the retreat of his Afrika Korps, leaving most of his Italian units to their fate. The soldiers of the Ariete, Littorio and Trieste Divisions fought on as best they could to hold up the British advance, but most of their tanks were destroyed, their artillery silenced, and the infantry surrounded and forced to surrender.

On 5 November 107 Battery was ordered to advance some 10,000 yards to take up new positions amid what had been the German lines. In freezing cold and pouring rain they dug new gun pits. Many celebrated at the signs of the slaughter and damage their guns had wreaked. Others found it more disturbing.

> We passed an out-of-action German gun. One or two members of the dead German gun crew were lying on the sand, a greatcoat over them, a stick or rifle dug in the ground where their heads rested, with a German helmet over the top. That made a very great impact upon me. It was so unnerving; you could feel an atmosphere around such abandoned guns.[51]

> Gunner Ken Giles, A Troop, 107 Battery, 7th Medium RA

The South Notts Hussars had taken a grim revenge for the Battle of Knightsbridge.

15

ADVANCE TO VICTORY IN NORTH AFRICA

It was commonly said that the gunner would never be an infantryman: first because the infantryman had to walk, and we always rode; secondly because he was sent in in attacks against small arms fire which we didn't normally experience. On the other hand, the infantryman said he would never be a gunner because we were always being bombed and shelled – far more than they were. It's every man to his job![1]

Second Lieutenant Charles Westlake, A Troop, 107 Battery, 7th Medium RA

THE EIGHTH ARMY SUCCESS WAS CELEBRATED wildly by the British back home – perhaps more out of relief than anything else. This, despite the disappointment that most of the retreating Axis forces had managed to escape. However, a pernicious combination of a lack of deployable reserves, over-crowded roads, the heavy rain and a general sense of exhaustion that settled over the men of the Eighth Army overwhelmed Montgomery's intentions of pressing home the Allied advantage. Never the less, he and his men had a achieved a significant victory and it marked the beginning of the end in North Africa.

The Axis forces suffered some 20,000 killed and wounded, with a further 30,000 men taken into captivity. The Eighth Army had some 13,500 casualties. When considered on the world stage, the Battle of El Alamein was little more than a skirmish, compared to the titanic clashes waged by millions of men in the Russo-German war on the Eastern Front. Yet, for the British Empire, it was a vital campaign that it simply could not afford to lose. Defeat and the loss of the Suez Canal link to the east would have brought dire consequences, not only in the Mediterranean and Middle East but across the globe.

The character of the operations would change for the South Notts Hussars during the next phase of the desert war. Except for their forward observation teams, the bulk of the men were often remote from the face-to-face battle, unless they had a visit from the dreaded Stukas. In a war of movement, the medium guns would move up, fire a barrage, and then move on to the next stopping point. They would rarely have time to dig gun pits, usually dropping into action on the open ground.

After a couple of days, the South Notts Hussars moved on to El Fuka airfield. Here they engaged in some basic maintenance and calibration of their guns, several of which had new barrels fitted. They also practised dropping into action as quickly as possible: in what promised to be a war of movement, every second could make the difference between life and death.

> The purpose of 'crash action' was to get from guns on the move to an aimed round 'on the ground' in the shortest possible time. An OP travelling in front of the guns would see a target and bring the guns into action using his map reference to get a 'round on the ground' and then correcting from there.[2]
>
> Second Lieutenant Bob Foulds, B Troop, 107 Battery, 7th Medium RA

On 22 November they began a 'forced march' to support the 51st Highland Division, who had run into the German 'stop line' established at El Agheila. This proved a long trek, passing through all the old desert war staging posts. Mersa Matruh, Sidi Barrani, Sollum, Tobruk and Gazala. On their way they passed close to the Cauldron battlefield by the Knightsbridge Box.

> Battery Sergeant Major Beardall paid a visit to the scene of the South Notts great stand. He found Major Barber's armoured car with its wireless aerial still in its bracket. Three guns of Captain Chadburn's troop were still in their pits, all spiked, and there were many burnt-out vehicles. He picked up a notebook belonging to Bombardier Bowden, a 25-pounder rammer from C Troop's position and a telephone. The whole area was as it had been left, though a foot-deep layer of fine sand covered everything.[3]

Lieutenant Eric Dobson, Headquarters, 107 Battery, 7th Medium RA

Still the advance went on as, without a fight, the port of Benghazi fell on 20 November.

When 107th RHA reached El Agheilla, they joined with other medium regiments in providing a massive support barrage ready for the assault of the 51st Highland Division. However, Rommel was aware of the competing priorities of the Eastern Front and the requirement to counter the Allied Operation Torch launched on 8 November in Algeria. In these circumstances he would receive nothing like the reinforcements and supplies needed to replenish his army. Fearful of the outflanking manoeuvre by the 2nd New Zealand Division and 4th Light Armoured Brigade launched by Montgomery around his southern flank, Rommel felt he had little opportunity but to resume his retreat. When the Scots made their frontal attack, they found the Germans had gone.

FEEDING THE MEN on the move was a real task for the cooks

and quartermasters. Harold Harper found himself taken off the guns and given an onerous new responsibility.

> I was amazed when the battery commander told me that I was being taken off the guns and given the responsibility of battery quartermaster sergeant. I would be responsible for all equipment, ammunition, rations, water – everything which was needed to keep the battery in the field. I remember distinctly the words he said to me in his little bivouac, 'Up to now, you'll have been getting all the praise, everyone will have been saying well done, fantastic job, you've done this to the enemy and goodness knows what else! From now on, you're going to find that nobody is going to praise you. In fact the only thing you'll get will be brickbats!' I said, 'Thank you very much!' It was perfectly true of course![4]

Battery Quartermaster Sergeant Harold Harper, Headquarters, 107 Battery, 7th Medium RA

Where possible they provided hot meals at dawn and dusk and the men subsisted on cold tinned rations during the day. Harper's administrative torment did not last long, as he was promoted to troop sergeant major following the intervention of Captain Ivor Birkin, who was given command of B Troop on his return from sick leave in late December.

Birkin's return was widely welcomed. An 'original' South Notts Hussar officer, he had once been regarded as the 'weakest' of the Birkin clan, somewhat in the shadow of both Peter and Gerry Birkin. In their absence he started to come into his own. He had a curious unmilitary appearance and was not physically strong, the combined effect of his childhood polio and wounds having left him with a pronounced limp. Given the nature of soldiers, he was a figure of affectionate amusement to many, but overall he was well respected as a competent officer and a brave man who took everything in his stride. For the next two years he would be the man who carried the 'flame' of the 'old' South Notts Hussars, never ceasing in his efforts to get the regiment reformed.

The 7th Medium RA then moved forward to bivouac on 23 December, close to the imposing Marble Arch, built by Mussolini to celebrate his colonisation of Tripolitania. Here they would celebrate Christmas, before moving up to Sirte where they were assigned to support the 7th Armoured Division.

Colonel 'Toc' Elton was still experimenting with new artillery techniques, in particular one he christened 'snap monster'. He had realised that the maps of the area into which they were advancing were totally inaccurate, with an average error of several hundred yards. This made 'shooting off the map' impossible and other methods had to be devised to get both his batteries in action and on parallel lines as quickly as possible.

> Elton devised 'Snap Monster' himself, with the finishing touches supplied by Major Wainwright, second-in-command and a very expert gunner. The idea was that the regiment should be travelling along in open formation. The forward observing officer should shout into his wireless: 'Snap Monster'! Whereon everyone who heard it waved check-coloured flags, the guns dropped their trails where they were, the first into action fired two high airburst rounds, all the other troops took their locations from the bearings to these bursts, and within three minutes the regiment should be in action. All troops worked day in and day out perfecting the system and improving times.[5]
>
> Lieutenant Eric Dobson, Headquarters, 107 Battery, 7th Medium RA

The best time was achieved by Albert Swinton – his gun section managed to get a shell in the air just twenty seconds from the flag signal.

After this pause, they moved forward to fire a barrage in support of the assault on German defences at Wadi Zem Zem on 14 January. The advance continued the next day, but while the 51st Highland Division followed the coastal road, the 7th Armoured Division took the direct route, heading straight for Homs. That evening the Stukas duly arrived.

> Just before dark, a fierce Stuka raid which killed Gunner Shaw of B Troop. Lieutenant Westlake, who was sheltering under the same armoured car, and Captain Birkin, who was a few yards away, had lucky escapes. Just after nightfall in the middle of the battery leaguer the petrol lorry caught fire and there were heroic attempts to extinguish the flames before the Stukas should be invited to return and do even more damage. Somehow an echelon party, led by Captain Rickard and Battery Sergeant Major Beardall, managed to save everything except the lorry's canopy and superstructure. Woolford, Aitken and Bowler, among others, calmly stood on top of the blazing truck and threw off tins full of petrol.[6]
>
> Lieutenant Eric Dobson, Headquarters, 107 Battery, 7th Medium RA

Next, they drove across an unforgiving flinty stone-covered plain to Beni Ulid. The Matadors and lorries were beginning to suffer under the strain.

> Day after day we would be on the move. You just followed on the tracks of hundreds and thousands of vehicles that had gone before you without knowing exactly where you were going. Part of the country was absolutely frightful. For some days, we churned over areas of very, very rocky desert – great big rocks a foot to 18 inches across and you were bouncing from one to another. You couldn't do anything else but go on in bottom gear. All these vehicles, all of them loaded down to flat springs, they were grinding over this awful country. The whole vehicle was shaking all over the place, the engine was roaring away, the gears were screaming – and you kept on like this for hour after

hour after hour! Why all the vehicles didn't just fall into bits I don't know![7]

Second Lieutenant Charles Westlake, A Troop, 107 Battery, 7th Medium RA

On 18 January, a situation of frightful confusion developed as morning broke with the guns still close to a large concentration of 25-pounder guns and tanks from the 7th Armoured Division. Gunner Ernie Hurry had been away salvaging spares from an abandoned broken-down Matador and when he rejoined A Troop he was immediately deeply concerned.

It was almost light. All the advancing party were still in close laager – they hadn't opened out at all. I was a bit worried because we had been suffering from these dive-bomb attacks. I decided to dig a slit trench a little way from our vehicle. Somebody shouted, 'What's the matter Ernie, going for shit?' I said, 'No, you'll see in a bit when they come over!' I hadn't dug very far down, and these Stukas came from out of the sun. That's the idea so that when you look at them you can't see them through the sun! They came down, I dropped flat in this little hole that I'd dug, and I felt two more on the top of me! Not far from me there was an old tracked vehicle – and I heard two people scramble underneath that! There was a commotion, explosions all around us! When the Stukas had gone, I got up. One ammunition wagon had been blown sky-high. Bombardier Jackson was killed and a couple more wounded. When [Lieutenant] Westlake got from underneath the halftrack vehicle, he says to Sergeant Powell,[8] 'Come on, let's go!' And he never moved. They pushed the halftrack vehicle off him and then they realised he'd been killed by a piece of shrapnel.[9]

Gunner Ernie Hurry, A Troop, 107 Battery, 7th Medium RA

During the raid Albert Swinton got a slight head wound and

was evacuated back to hospital in Egypt. He soon walked out and made his own way back to rejoin his friends. Returning to 'their' unit was still very important to most of the men.

One of the real treats for the South Notts Hussars was the treasured moment when at last they drove out of the desert wastelands into 'the green fields and beyond' at Tarhuna in the approaches to Tripoli. Eric Dobson was entranced.

> It seemed that Utopia had been reached, for at Tarhuna, 20 miles south of Tripoli, there was the wonderful sight, after seven months of desert sand and scrub, of fields laid out in beautiful symmetry; from a ridge miles away one could see the green vegetable patches, the neat, orderly and trim white farmhouses. That night's gun position was in fact in an orchard.[10]
>
> Lieutenant Eric Dobson, Headquarters, 107 Battery, 7th Medium RA

On 23 January, Tripoli fell to the 7th Armoured Division. Yet the 'job' was only partly finished; North Africa had still not been cleared. Rommel had been placed in overall command of the Axis Army Group Africa: with the Fifth Panzer Army (General Hans-Jürgen von Arnim) facing the British First Army (Lieutenant General Kenneth Anderson); while the First (Italian) Army (General Giovanni Messe) faced the Eighth Army. It was evident that the Operation Torch invasion had been held up; the dash for Tunis had failed. Over the winter, Rommel's armies had been reinforced: plenty of hard fighting still lay ahead for the Eighth Army.

TRIPOLI HAD BEEN A GLITTERING PRIZE shimmering before the Eighth Army throughout the desert campaign. Now at last they were here. At first it was merely a staging post, as they accompanied the 7th Armoured Division in continuing to pursue and harass the retreating Germans. Then Montgomery decided it was time to rest his 'Desert Rats' and pulled the whole division back to Tripoli for a month out of the firing line. Disappointment would beset the South Notts Hussars as they found themselves bivouacked in a bare patch of ground well outside the city.

> We had a few days there in Tripoli. We were allowed to go into Tripoli itself. I went in by foot and I could see all these lovely big houses with iron balconies and there was a queue outside some of them! I thought there was some food or something – I was fond of my stomach those days! I joined a queue outside one of these big houses. I was standing in this queue for probably five to six minutes and I said to this bloke by me, 'What are we queuing up for here?' He looked at me and said, 'This is a brothel – we're queuing up for the brothel.' Then it dawned on me. I said, 'Oooh hell!' I was too innocent then – good God – I never dreamt of anything like that.[11]
>
> Gunner Frank Penlington, B Troop, 107 Battery, 7th Medium RA

During their stay, there was a joint parade with 64th Medium Regiment with a total of sixteen massive medium guns drawn up for inspection by a VIP visitor. Not everyone was pleased.

> The order came to 'bull' the wagons up, to clean the guns because Winston Churchill was going to inspect us! I thought, 'How ridiculous!' The guns and the wagons were cleaned with diesel oil and – Oooh – they shone like anything – they really were clean! The ends of the guns were burnished![12]
>
> Gunner Ernie Hurry, A Troop, 107 Battery, 7th Medium RA

Their resentment was ameliorated when Churchill made a real fuss of them, taking the time to talk to many of the men, while demonstrating that he had been well briefed.

He came in some sort of staff car, which he abandoned, and he walked round the whole of the parade. Up and down all the ranks, stopping on numerous occasions to talk to everyone: gunners, officers it made no odds. He gave us a little talk and a 'V-sign' at the end of it. He seemed very pale – as if he lived underground – against the tanned and almost blackened faces of all the troops on parade. He seemed a very pale figure – he certainly seemed a pugnacious one! He was popular.[13]

Second Lieutenant Bob Foulds, B Troop, 107 Battery, 7th Medium RA

Other inspections were held, with visits from several senior officers. By this time the South Notts Hussars had acquired a well-merited reputation for acquiring extra vehicles wherever possible – by fair means or foul. Spare lorries, jeeps, captured German vehicles, anything was grist to their mill. This was all well and good, but formal inspections by knowledgeable officers well aware of the 'tricks of the trade' were always testing.

Brigadier Dennis, he used to be adjutant of the South Notts at one time, so he came to see us. Unfortunately, we'd acquired a lot of trucks and we had to go and hide them – and a lot of other equipment that didn't tie up! We always had far more vehicles than the establishment. We always made sure we had enough cookhouses about – you never knew when a troop was detached from a regiment. And that meant trucks and cooking equipment – you just scrounge it. Go to various depots, you sign a sheet, you haven't got a clue what you're signing, just sign the perishing thing – and away you go! Our light aid detachment, the 'tiffies', if they see a [broken-down] vehicle around, they go and have a look at. Any bits and pieces they wanted, they would take! Or if they could get it going, they would take it![14]

Sergeant David Tickle, B Troop, 107 Battery, 7th Medium RA

The 'surplus' vehicles were driven away into the desert, out of sight and out of mind. There was considerable consternation when they saw Brigadier Meade Dennis approaching from that very direction. Somehow, he either did not notice, or more likely chose not to 'notice' the incriminating vehicles.

During the rest period, Colonel 'Toc' Elton left to take command of the newly formed 5th Army Group Royal Artillery (AGRA). This had been formed at least partially at his own instigation and banded together all the available medium regiments (including 7th Medium RA) ready to provide powerful support as and when needed on corps operations. On 19 February, his replacement, Colonel Miles Wood, arrived. Wood was by no means as abrasive as Elton, but he too was upset by the continued intransigence of the South Notts Hussars over the retention of their acorn badge.

> Everybody who came to the battery, no matter where they came from, lost no time in taking away their own artillery cap badge and were pleased and proud to wear the acorn. This regular soldier, Colonel Miles Wood, was given command of 7th Medium Regiment. One of his first things was he came to inspect his troops and introduce himself, and he gave instructions that the acorn cap badge was not an official badge and that it would be taken off! Everybody would wear the Royal Artillery cap badge! That caused real pain and agony! Nobody talked about anything else for day and days – but nobody took the cap badge off either! Wood didn't insist on his order – we weren't going to do it – the officers decided they weren't going to do it! He couldn't send us all back to base under arrest![15]

Lieutenant Ian Sinclair, Headquarters, 107 Battery, 7th Medium RA

THE HUSSARS RETURNED TO THE FRONT in the Mede-
nine Hills at the end of February. They were facing the former
French defensive positions, which had been expanded to create
the strong Mareth Line running along a ridge lying at right
angles to the coast. The ground in front was much lower but dis-
sected by a series of deep wadis. Towards the southern end there
was one distinctive hill, topped by an observatory, that bore a
marked resemblance to – and hence was quickly named – Edinburgh Castle. The British were gathering their strength ready
for an attack, but they were wary of a German spoiling attack
to disrupt their preparations. The South Notts Hussars took
up main battle positions by the road near Edinburgh Castle,
despatching forward a troop at a time to fire from close to the
front line, which in this sector was manned by three battalions
of the Queen's Royal Surrey Regiment. On the night of 5 March,
David Elliott was sent forward by Ivor Birkin to gain experience
of OP duties for B Troop. At first nothing happened.

> They'd taken a telephone cable up to the top of a small hill which
> looked out over the wadi. Then the ground rose up the other side
> and it went out into the shimmering desert towards where the
> Germans were supposed to be. You looked at nothing – nothing
> was moving! I went up that evening – there was a very, very
> small place that Ivor or somebody had scraped out – not more
> than 6 inches deep because it was so rocky You couldn't do more
> than lie down – if you stood up, you'd be on the skyline. Ivor
> told me we had a limited amount of ammunition and we were
> only to engage if we saw enough enemy movement. He wasn't
> anticipating anything; I didn't expect anything![16]
>
> Lieutenant David Elliott, B Troop, 107 Battery, 7th Medium RA

At 06.30 on 6 March the German bombardment commenced
and the Battle of Medenine began. Elliott told Lance Bombardier R. A. Clarke to contact the gun position by telephone.

I was very relieved a few moments later to hear Bob Foulds' voice. He reported they were having a hell of a time with shells falling all over the gun position – but that the gun pits were giving good cover to the men and there had been no casualties so far. I told him I would let him know what was happening as soon as I could see. It was 5.30a.m. by my watch and, although dawn was breaking, I still could not see clearly because of the dust thrown up by the bursting shells and a heavy mist which hung over the whole front. We could now hear the rattle of machine-gun fire and the sharp crack from what I thought was an anti-tank gun.[17]

Lieutenant David Elliott, B Troop, 107 Battery, 7th Medium RA

Shortly afterwards, Elliott could see that a full-scale attack was under way.

The sun came up and I could see trucks, a long way away, which I had to assume were German – you didn't know they were – so we opened fire on these trucks at a range of about 6,000 yards. It was terribly muddled because of the smoke. We hadn't been firing very long before the word came up that they were short of ammunition and would I be careful of it! I heard shuffling behind me and there was a major of the Queen's with a moustache and a walking stick! Climbing up behind me on his belly, he asked me, 'What's going on?' I said, 'Well, we seem to be under attack!'[18]

Lieutenant David Elliott, B Troop, 107 Battery, 7th Medium RA

A little later that morning the situation deteriorated still further.

We saw the first tanks through the smoke and heat haze on the far side of the wadi. That's when I realised that things were fairly bad. We called for fire and my one fear was then that I was shelling an area where our own troops had been – but I just had to presume they'd fallen back. The range was rapidly getting shorter and shorter. At one stage they came on the phone and told me I must stop firing so many shells – I told them I couldn't stop firing! For a while we fired one gun only.[19]

Lieutenant David Elliott, B Troop, 107 Battery, 7th Medium RA

Elliott was coming under increasingly heavy small arms fire.

I had my binoculars resting on this stone, watching this escarpment. I don't believe I could be seen at all. We had shells landing mostly behind us and machine-gun bullets – sprayed out from the tanks – going over the top, but I don't believe they were aimed. The line was cut and one of my assistants went back to mend it, which was very brave of him. I saw this large tank come out of the smoke on the other side and I called for fire on it and I had my glasses on it. Its barrel slewed round and was pointing over my head – I don't believe that it knew I was there! As I put my binoculars on it, it fired – and I saw the armour-piercing shot leave the barrel of the tank about 300–400 yards away. It came screaming over – I ducked down so quickly I lost my tin hat! At the same time our fire came down and it retreated – back out of sight. I'd survived and the tanks had not got over the edge of the wadi. Your adrenalin flows![20]

Lieutenant David Elliott, B Troop, 107 Battery, 7th Medium RA

It was estimated subsequently that his fire orders had disposed of five of the attacking tanks. Elliott would be awarded the Military Cross for his courage under fire.

Charles Westlake was also occupying an OP on the top of a ridge that day. He had a great view of what was going on, but in his sector any putative targets were all out of the range, even of the 5.5-inch guns. Never the less, he sent back detailed situation reports to the battery for dissemination to any local commanders.

Jerry sent over some Ju 87s – they'd obviously realised that there was somebody observing on top of this cliff. They stood on their noses straight above us and I was giving a running commentary over my telephone line to my gun position, 'This Ju 87 is standing up, its bombs have just gone, they're coming down now!' Then those at the other end heard an absolute silence – because the ruddy bombs had fallen just a few yards behind us and cut the telephone wire – they thought I'd gone![21]

Lieutenant Charles Westlake, A Troop, 107 Battery, 7th Medium RA

During the fighting the B Troop gun positions had come under fire from a new weapon – the nebelwerfer.

We found ourselves in a valley between two mountains – you'd have to be an idiot of a German general not to know where that artillery fire was coming from. Consequently, they brought into action, for the very first time, a mortar known as a nebelwerfer, which screamed as it came over, sounding like an organ grinding! That they used to great effect and plastered this valley – it was only about 500 yards across. There was no escaping it. We were stuck for about four or five days and had to take all that was thrown at us. We were shelled, and I dived into a shallow trench not a long way from the cookhouse to the rear of the guns. I laid myself flat in this shallow trench and suddenly felt this terrific burning sensation in my back. I felt this fluid trickling down my back – I thought this is it! I expected to find a hole in my back. It transpired that the shell had hit the cookhouse and the cook had got on a big dixie full of Maconochie's stew. He used to put the tins into boiling water. One of these tins had flown into the air and landed on my back – what was running down was Maconochie's stew – not blood.[22]

Troop Sergeant Major Harold Harper, B Troop, 107 Battery, 7th Medium RA

These multi-barrelled mortars were nicknamed the 'Moaning Minnie' and the men soon realised why.

> It was quite extraordinary. We hadn't heard them before – it sounded like a vast wailing. The noise was frightening, perhaps even more than the fall of shot when it arrived.[23]
>
> Second Lieutenant Bob Foulds, B Troop, 107 Battery, 7th Medium RA

The German attack had been thrown back but had achieved its primary aim in gaining time. During the interval the battery suffered a significant loss. On 10 March, Major Lewis-Jones, accompanied by the regimental second-in-command, Major John Wainwright, and their driver, Gunner Knott, went forward in a jeep on a recce and they had the misfortune to run over a mine. Both officers were badly injured and when they attempted to crawl back, the area was plastered by mortars and machine guns. Selflessly, Knott ran for assistance and managed to get an OP officer for a 25-pounder battery to drench the German positions with shells, allowing a Bren Carrier to rescue Lewis-Jones and Wainwright. Their wounds were such that neither ever returned. Wainwright was a large, heavy, slow-moving man with a pleasant manner and keen sense of humour who was always welcome when he dropped in on the South Notts Hussars messes, the gun pits or their cookhouse. As we have seen, Lewis-Jones was far less likeable and it is sad to say that for many the initial reaction to his departure was relief: David Elliott for one was convinced that he would never have been awarded the MC if Lewis-Jones had still been in a position of influence. Yet this is unfair: whatever his faults, Lewis-Jones had taken over the battery when it was in dire straits – all but useless in July 1942. He had driven them hard for a reason and he deserved much of the credit for the improvements achieved on 'his watch'. Harold Harper tracked their advance, measured against the regulars of 27/28 Battery.

At Alamein there was this great distinction between the two. We were a made-up battery; 27/28 Battery was a battery that had come out intact. We never felt we were 7th Medium Regiment, we still felt we were South Notts Hussars – we still kept our acorn cap badge. They were firing 4.5-inch guns, which they'd had for a number of years; we'd got equipment no one had ever fired. So, we were very much the inferior boys! After Alamein we were obviously on a par – and we were told so by various senior officers. By the end of the African campaign we'd passed them![24]

Troop Sergeant Major Harold Harper, B Troop, 107 Battery, 7th Medium RA

On the very same day, Colonel Miles Wood was urgently recalled to a staff post at General Alexander's headquarters. In his place arrived Lieutenant Colonel M. J. Stansfield, who proved an altogether milder and less forceful man than either of his daunting predecessors. Shortly afterwards, Major James Martin took over command of 107 Battery. Martin was a competent officer, but a kinder man, less aggressive and dogmatic, choosing to consult his officers and respecting their expertise as appropriate. Now that the battery was 'up and running' his gentler approach and concern for the welfare of his men was much appreciated.

Amid all the changes to the command structure of the 7th Medium Regiment there was one really significant change in the German High Command. After the failure of the Battle of Medenine, Rommel had returned to Germany, handing over the theatre command to General Hans-Jürgen von Arnim. The 'Desert Fox' had left the scene.

On 16 March 1943, the Battle of Mareth began. The whole of 7th Medium RA and several other artillery units had all been moved forward to a large wadi. Here they would fire a series of barrages in support of the attacks: first of the Guards Brigade on

Horseshoe Hill; then the main attack by the 50th Northumbrian Division, followed up by the 51st Highland Division and 4th Indian Division before the 7th Armoured Division exploited the anticipated success. Meanwhile the 2nd New Zealand Division was to make a wide sweep round to the south with the intention of outflanking the whole Mareth Line. The German defences proved to be far too strong and both the Guards and 50th Division assaults floundered and failed.

During the heavy firing, David Tickle suffered a potentially devastating misfire on his 5.5-inch gun after having fired all night – he estimated some 320 rounds.

> There was a very loud explosion, from right at the front of the gun pit. My first indications were that an enemy shell had landed right at the front of the gun pit. I looked at the gun and I saw the barrel was peeled back and I thought, 'Oh, crikey, yes!' Part of it finished up just missing the cookhouse which was 150 yards to the back of us! The first bloke into the gun pit was Bob Foulds. He fully expected to see people plastered about the place. But fortunately, nobody got hurt! We had a good gun pit – I think that probably accounted for it. But despite that you could find great chunks of the gun spread about the gun pit! I found a bit of shrapnel at the back of the gun pit and worked it out that it had travelled between one of my gun team and myself and we were 3 feet apart – so we were extremely lucky![25]
>
> Sergeant David Tickle, B Troop, 107 Battery, 7th Medium RA

Captain Alan Smith was far less fortunate.

> I was with my troop commander, Alan Smith, at a gun position. He'd been out doing OP work and he was immaculately dressed – he was that sort of man – always perfectly turned out even when he was dirty! We were stood on top of a very sandy escarpment – and suddenly were being shot at for no good

reason at all – the gun position was being shelled. We had to duck because there was one very, very near to us! I found out that Alan had been hit by a piece of shrapnel and he'd lost one of his testicles. That was the end of him – he had to go![26]

Lieutenant Ian Sinclair, Headquarters, 107 Battery, 7th Medium RA

Smith would return to the battery after a short period in hospital.

As the 50th Division withdrew to recuperate, Montgomery came up with a change of plan. The 4th Indian Division was now moved to the half left, passing through the Matmata Mountains, but inside the wider outflanking march of the 2nd New Zealand Division, whose strength was now to be bolstered by the addition of the 1st Armoured Division. Urgent orders were despatched that the South Notts Hussars were to supply a gun troop to support the Indian advance – and B Troop was selected for the task. They were hastily equipped with the best possible Matador gun towers and extra ammunition lorries to prepare for whatever they might encounter. One thing was apparent – the recce reports had indicated that driving conditions would be appalling in the mountains.

Our B Troop would go round and outflank them with the Gurkhas. At first, we were a little bit worried, we all started to fill in our paybooks with wills in case we didn't come back! We had to go so far up the mountains, and we came to this cart track which wound round and round. When you looked over the top you were talking about a 2,000-foot drop. The guns and the Matadors were so long and so big that going down, the corners were so acute – and the surface was all rubble – you could never get round with the vehicle and gun. You just had to put your brakes on and skid and the gun and everything would be over the top! I was getting a bit worried. I said to Harper, 'You'd better stop the troop and tell the commander, we'll have to let these guns down on a winch!' I practically took command of that operation because of all my experience in the quarry of all this kind of work. Each Matador went down on their own; every gun was unlimbered, and they were all individually let down on a Matador winch. Luckily, we did a good job, it took a long time, but we all got down safe and sound. After the operation the brigadier wanted to know how many guns we had lost, it was so delicate an operation. He got rather a surprise when he was told we were all standing limbered up waiting for fresh orders.[27]

Gunner Reg Cutter, B Troop, 107 Battery, 7th Medium RA

They had got through, but in the end they were not required: the combination of outflanking thrust by the 4th Indian Division and the wider manoeuvres of the 2nd New Zealand Division and the 1st Armoured Division had forced the Axis forces to retreat from their Mareth Line fastness.

The Germans took up one last defensive position in front of the Eighth Army. Just beyond the port of Gabes they occupied a range of hills overlooking the steep-sided Wadi Akarit, which formed a natural anti-tank ditch. The massed guns of the 5th AGRA moved forward ready to support the final assault by the 51st Highland Division. The 107 Battery thought themselves fortunate to be ordered to take up a gun position in a small olive grove.

It was surrounded by a stone wall. It was such a joy to find cover for the guns for the first time – and not have to dig in or pile stones round the wheels. We were able to take the guns right up against the wall. With the olive trees about 10 feet high and the camouflage net, it was very difficult for an aeroplane to see we were there – plus it gave shade to the troops! We'd already had orders from headquarters that there were booby traps about and nobody was to touch anything they didn't understand.[28]

Lieutenant David Elliott, B Troop, 107 Battery, 7th Medium RA

That afternoon they had a visit from Lieutenant Colonel Stansfield accompanied by Major James Martin.

They asked to be shown the four new gun pits and so we set off through the trees, each No. 1 calling his detachment to attention as we approached. Lance Sergeant McCall stood smartly to attention as the CO questioned him about his preparations. He was one of my best NCOs and ran a very efficient gun detachment. The colonel saluted the bronzed team of men standing in the sunlight in just their shorts and boots as we moved off towards the next gun pit. Hardly had we travelled 10 yards when there was an awful explosion behind us. I turned to see Sergeant McCall lying on the ground in obvious agony and the whole gun pit shrouded in smoke. One gunner ran past us in a panic clutching his stomach and everything was in confusion. I reached Sergeant McCall, knelt beside him and tried to ease his mangled hands away from his crutch where I could see a gaping wound through the tattered remnants of his shorts. Blood was spurting from his wrist into a discarded mess tin and my Field Ambulance training came back to me as I found the 'pressure point' in the crook of his elbow. Major Martin sent somebody off through the trees to locate the wounded man who had run away and, as we waited for a stretcher party, we questioned the remaining very dazed gun crew. It appeared that somebody had picked up a small brass cylinder in one of the dugouts. It had not been much larger in diameter than a shell case from a Spitfire machine gun but about twice as long and with a knurled end to unscrew. In spite of our warnings Sergeant McCall had been about to unscrew this 'thing' as we approached and had been holding it concealed in his hand as he stood to attention talking to the colonel. No sooner had we turned our backs on him then his curiosity got the better of him and he unscrewed the booby trap with the disastrous result.[29]

Lieutenant David Elliott, B Troop, 107 Battery, 7th Medium RA

The wounded were evacuated. Later Elliott visited Wallace McCall at a tented field hospital.

My sad memory is of him holding my hand and saying the words, very common among the men at that time, 'Fucking roll on! Fucking roll on!' He kept repeating it. He died next day.[30] A very good man lost for a very silly reason.[31]

Lieutenant David Elliott, B Troop, 107 Battery, 7th Medium RA

A heavy barrage was fired in support of the 51st Highland Division attack on the Djebel Roumana hill on 6 April and the Germans were once again forced to pull back. A hot pursuit began with the 107th Battery once again assigned to the 7th Armoured Division as it drove forward to the port of Sfax. The fall of Sfax allowed David Elliott to pay a visit on 11 April.

After travelling hundreds of miles and each success just gaining us another strip of desert and showing us a few knocked-out tanks and vehicles and several grinning Arabs – we now relieve a really large and friendly town for the first time. What a joy it was to be welcomed. The 'Frenchies' flocked out in their hundreds to cheer and wave to us. I wish I had gone in during the morning and seen Monty's triumphant entry with the Highland Division and their bagpipes etc. He was completely mobbed by the people and showered with flowers – the whole streets were strewn with flowers. As I drove in during the afternoon the streets were still full of people, everybody from the children to the Arabs were giving the 'V for Victory' sign and waving. I soon got in with a family who filled us with wine and gave us new loaves of bread to take away, even though they

were short. Everybody was smiling – never have I seen such a
happy town or so many happy faces. We were soon in a very
merry state ourselves![32]

Lieutenant David Elliott, B Troop, 107 Battery, 7th Medium RA

And so the North African campaign was over for the South
Notts Hussars.

The final stages of the campaign saw the Allied First and
Eighth Armies combine to smash the remaining shreds of
German resistance in Tunisia. Concentrated artillery fire was
again augmented by ground-strafing fighter bombers and heavy
bombing raids. Together they flayed the Axis positions, render-
ing them vulnerable to fast-moving assaults by armoured and
infantry units operating together in tandem. This, like the war-
winning methods of 1918 in the Great War, was an 'all arms
battle'. Axis attempts to launch counter-attacks were simply
shrugged off or eliminated. Sheer firepower won the day. In a
sense it was a shame that the 107 Battery were not there to see
the triumphant execution of the tactics learnt over the previous
three years. On 7 May the British raced into Tunis, while on the
same day Bizerte fell to the Americans. Six days later the Axis
forces surrendered, casting some 250,000 men into captivity.

THE SOUTH NOTTS HUSSARS MISSED this final battle for
Tunis. They had handed over their guns and moved to a concentration area in a small olive grove close to the small Arab
coastal village of Cheriba some 24 miles from Sfax. Here they
were to rest and recuperate; ready for whatever their next task
should be. It was a pleasant environment and many of the men
treasured their memories of this break in the horrors and discomforts of war. There may have been trouble still in store, more
tears to shed, but they were still alive and at last could relax. By

this time, Ken Giles had been promoted to bombardier and he was working as the B Troop clerk responsible for the guard rotas, fielding phone calls and general office duties. It did not stretch a man of his talents.

> I wrote a play, called 'Death in Daventry Square'. I did it for my own amusement to fill in my leisure time while I was in the troop office. Just wrote it out in an exercise book. Captain Birkin thought we ought to perform it. Then of course all the parts had to be copied out! It took quite a great deal of time. The idea was seized with some enthusiasm and we actually dug a deep and spacious theatre with a stage. Bombardier Halliwell had been a window dresser in civil life – he acquired long draperies, fixed them up and made a really good stage with curtains. He managed to acquire forms as seats, and we could put on the play. I took the chief part – and directed and produced the entire thing! To my chagrin I cannot remember what the plot was about, but it was a murder mystery! I was coming out of my shell by then and acquiring an independent personality: friendly with everybody![33]
>
> Bombardier Ken Giles, B Troop, 107 Battery, 7th Medium RA

David Tickle certainly enjoyed acting in the play.

> A detective story – and we all enjoyed taking part in it! We built our own little theatre in a tent. I was a detective, I think! I know I made the last comment of the whole play, 'What now, Sir?' It was a good little effort, very enjoyable – even for the people watching it! We took it to other regiments and put it on! We always used to have a collection and we made some money for the Red Cross![34]
>
> Sergeant David Tickle, B Troop, 107 Battery, 7th Medium RA

While at Cheriba they had considerable contact with the local

Arab civilians and there was a fair amount of bartering. Ernie Hurry remembered one dishonest trick employed by some of the less scrupulous men in their dealings with the locals.

> The Arabs used to come down asking for tea and they'd give us these eggs. What we did was we went to the cookhouse, where they'd got a load of old tea leaves that they were throwing away. We put them on a petrol can lid on top of a primus stove and we heated them up, sort of cooked them – it used to stink terrible! We'd got some proper tea bags and we put this tea in the teabags and – a bit of good tea on the top. When the Arabs came round, we gave them this packet of 'tea' and we'd get about twenty eggs for it![35]
>
> Gunner Ernie Hurry, A Troop, 107 Battery, 7th Medium RA

Reg McNish was aware of the horse-trading between the soldiers and the villagers. Many of the men participated in it and some were not even averse to 'selling' spare items of uniform and kit.

> We used to trade with the Arabs, tea or old shirts, cigarettes, all sort of things we'd trade with the Arabs and they'd give us eggs or anything they'd got! We actually marked out a place and called it the 'market' to try and control it a bit. We'd been trading with the Arabs for a week or so, so obviously they'd got khaki shirts and that sort of thing from us. Then someone complained about the Arabs stealing; they did use to pinch things if they could![36]
>
> Gunner Reg McNish, A Troop, 107 Battery, 7th Medium RA

There seems little doubt that some individual Arabs *were* stealing; but this picture was certainly muddied by the widespread unofficial bartering of kit by the soldiers – the loss of which could then be explained as 'stolen'. At the time it was widely assumed that many of the villagers were engaging in theft.

The thieving – the Arabs used to visit after dark when we were all asleep – despite our sentries. They were very adept – Fagin would have been delighted with them – they could whip things from under your pillow and you wouldn't even know they'd gone until you woke up in the morning! We caught one or two. We decided we wanted to get this nipped in the bud, so we went down to the village of Cheriba and met the local sheikh, an elderly man with a long white beard. We took our prisoners down – Captain Ivor Birkin went down with me and an escort. We would go into the local courthouse, a very ramshackle small building. The prisoner stood there in the dock as it were. The escort, Captain Birkin and I would sit cross-legged on the floor. I would do all the talking in a mixture of French and Arabic. We would state what had happened, we couldn't put up with this, we would have to take action, what would their punishment be? Every now and again the escort to the prisoner would whack him over the shoulders with a wooden cane, so that the poor chap received quite a lot of punishment before anything ever happened. They told us they would put him in prison. As we left, they tied him to a post outside. On one occasion, we crept back in about ten minutes, 'Let's see what they do to him!' He'd been released![37]

Bombardier Ken Giles, B Troop, 107 Battery, 7th Medium RA

Feeling that he ought to do something more, Ivor Birkin decided to launch a 'raid' on the Arab village in which David Elliott was one of those that participated.

We had great difficulty in talking to them – we didn't have interpreters. One Arab came out of a tent – I don't know why I was suspicious of him – but I touched his white clothing and could feel something underneath. I made him undo it and he had a gun! A very old revolver which I confiscated from him –

which I still have! I wouldn't like to shoot it; I don't think it's very safe.[38]

Lieutenant David Elliott, B Troop, 107 Battery, 7th Medium RA

In the course of the raid, not unsurprisingly, they found substantial amounts of army uniform and several arrests were made. Giles had not accompanied the raid, but he witnessed the harsh way in which the 'culprits' were treated in the aftermath.

I was in the troop office and the thieves were brought in. I was tearing them off a strip in French. Telling them what thieves they were, really putting it on! Gunner Fleming got a Bren gun out and trained it on them, obviously he had no intention of shooting them, but he made it look very real. I think they were scared to death. I don't know what became of them.[39]

Bombardier Ken Giles, B Troop, 107 Battery, 7th Medium RA

Reg McNish was outraged at the unfairness of what had happened. He and several of his friends were determined to complain on behalf of the accused villagers.

Ivor Birkin took a party with rifles along with him and went through this Arab settlement and fished out any khaki stuff he could find – he reckoned they'd stolen it. Well they hadn't stolen it, they'd traded it, but he thought he knew it all! Then of course this upset the Arabs, because we'd pinched back the things they'd paid for – he was too dim to realise this! One or two of us, there was Jack Sergeant and 'Wag' Westby, Dougy Truman, thought we'd better put this right, so we wrote him a letter pointing out the error of his ways, that this stuff had been bartered. He didn't like this much, but he didn't know who'd written the letter or we should have been for the high jump. Well he stuck this letter on the noticeboard and said, 'Somebody has sent this to me. I'm going to make another raid on the Arab village tonight!' I think he must have been advised by somebody, 'Better not do this!' What they did instead was have a debate! Got as many lads as they could and debated as to whether it was right – had we been mistreating the Arabs? It came out in favour that we had been wrong in doing this and we got an apology from him – and they did no more raiding of the Arabs! Which was a good thing![40]

Gunner Reg McNish, A Troop, 107 Battery, 7th Medium RA

Ivor Birkin was an unusual officer: having read the anonymous letter, he took it seriously and even organised a troop debate, with the 'professorial' Ken Giles in the 'chair'. Given the prevailing attitudes of the day it is not surprising that the discussion was polarised.

The letter said we should not treat the local people as we did. As a result, Captain Birkin suggested a debate. I believe I was in the chair. It wasn't a high-level thing. Lots of people spoke at once! People saying, 'Well, they're human beings like us! It's their way of life! A different culture! We should accept it! We're occupying their country! We should treat them with a certain amount of respect, even if we don't like the way they live!' There were also those who objected to them being called 'Wogs' – a derogatory term – that's an attitude I've always taken. The others were saying, 'They're just rogues and thieves! Anything they get is coming to them! They ought to be treated harshly – not leniently!' It was not acrimonious: I had to call 'Order!' once or twice, it was so informal. Then I had to make a summary at the end![41]

Bombardier Ken Giles, B Troop, 107 Battery, 7th Medium RA

As they rested by the sea, the powers that be had plans for the 7th Medium Regiment. Sicily beckoned.

16

SICILIAN SOJOURN

Whenever we had a successful shoot, I couldn't help thinking, 'There goes some mother's son, some girl's sweetheart, some wife's husband that I may have been instrumental in killing or maiming for life!' Those thoughts invariably passed through my mind, they never stayed there. I liked to think, 'Well it might be me in reverse!' I hate war; I always have. Even more than I did when I was young.[1]

Bombardier Ken Giles, B Troop, 107 Battery, 7th Medium RA

CHURCHILL'S OBSESSION with an imagined soft 'underbelly' to Germany had surfaced before. During the Great War he had been a key figure in launching the doomed Gallipoli campaign against the underestimated Ottoman Empire in 1915. Now Churchill thought an attack on Italy might open an easier route to Germany, a view he maintained despite the Alps barring the way. President Franklin D. Roosevelt and the American High Command had been grudgingly persuaded that it was a venture worth trying in advance of any attack on north-west Europe in 1944. Planning therefore began for an assault on Sicily, the necessary first step in any invasion of Italy from North Africa. American General Dwight Eisenhower was placed in supreme command, with Montgomery's Eighth Army assigned the responsibility for landings on south-east Sicily to seize key air-fields and the port of Syracuse, while the American Seventh Army (General George Patton) was to land in on the central Sicilian south coast, before moving inland to secure other vital airfields.

After the best part of two months' rest at Cheriba, the 7th Medium Regiment RA was moved to a transit camp at Sousse where they prepared once again for war. All excess vehicles and equipment were stripped away in preparation for a landing that could well face stiff resistance. They boarded the Landing Ship Tanks (LST) in the Sousse docks on 25 July. No one had any idea where they were going and there was much fevered speculation, until it was finally settled by the captain of the LST, who did after all know where he was going – it was Malta.

The voyage was uninterrupted, and on arrival at Valetta harbour they disembarked and then drove along the coast road to St Paul's Bay. Here there was much effort expended in lessons to ensure that every man could swim, which proved no hardship in the summer sunshine. Even better, the evenings were devoted by most men to visits to the bars back in the city. Early in July they moved into Pembroke Barracks in Valetta. While they were here, there were tests to ensure that all the vehicles and guns could be accommodated aboard the LST.

> We did a lot of practising loading guns and tractors on to LSTs: running off the quay, reversing the gun so the tractor pushed the gun into position in the hold of the ship. We had a brigadier come down to the dock to see us do this and he was going to give all the instructions as to how we approach the ramps and all this and that.[2]
>
> Troop Sergeant Major Harold Harper, B Troop, 107 Battery, 7th Medium RA

Reg Cutter was a superlative driver who had driven large vehicles for a living well before joining the army. For him this was a piece of cake.

> I jumped out of the cab and went over and said, 'Excuse me, Sir, do you want this gun placing on this Landing Ship?' He looked rather taken aback from the cheek of it! He said, 'That's the idea!' I said, 'Right!' I turned round, jumped in the cab. We didn't need to have practised because this was something we did every time you went into action. My No. 1, Harold Harper, and the gun crew knew exactly what to do. I just went round in a circle in front of the landing craft, the men unlimbered the gun, they held it, I went in a circle again, came round, nose on to the gun by the front bumper bar, nosed the gun straight into the position; there was men there telling me where they wanted it. The gunners walked alongside, lifted the gun up, dropped the trails and I reversed out in a circle, reversed straight back, no messing, straightened the gun, lifted it up and dropped it on – and it was all done in just under three minutes – and they were expecting it to be half an hour or so. With me driving was just a natural instinct – that's all I ever knew all my life.[3]

Gunner Reg Cutter, B Troop, 107 Battery, 7th Medium RA

They were also busy waterproofing the vehicles, which would allow them to land in up to 5 feet of water. A black sticky waterproof compound was moulded round the distributors and electrical fittings, while extension pipes were fitted to the top of the carburettor and the exhaust. After a final inspection by Montgomery on 9 July, the battery was ready for anything.

On 10 July, the invasion began with a series of successful landings by both British and American forces. The despatch of 7th Medium RA was slightly delayed by a gale, but eventually they sailed to land on Pachino beach unopposed on 12 July.

I've never seen so many ships – as far as the eye could see in both directions it was just solid shipping – and a great deal of aircraft activity, mostly ours. We landed right on the southern tip of the island at Cape Pachino. As a landing it was a doddle as the LST brought us right into the rocky shore and we hardly got the tyres of the vehicles wet. We were quickly whistled off the beach and up these narrow roads into a hide at Noto not very far inland. There we de-waterproofed the vehicles, having not needed it at all.[4]

Lieutenant Bob Foulds, B Troop, 107 Battery, 7th Medium RA

The process of getting ashore naturally took time to accomplish, and some of the men fell into temptation as they wandered off to explore their new surroundings.

There happened to be a village quite close to the assembly area. Lo and behold in the village they found some of these big casks of wine! They came back loaded with various items of dress, which were not actually military! They used to be stripped to the waist and you could see these old gunners, silk scarf over the shoulders, fancy hat on, umbrellas up![5]

Sergeant David Tickle, B Troop, 107 Battery, 7th Medium RA

Finally, they moved off.

The whole battery was now on a road moving roughly north and following the familiar 'HD' signs of the 51st Highland Division. The vehicles were kept well spaced out for fear of air attack and an officer or sergeant stood up in the cab keeping a sharp lookout all round. It was a very strange experience to be driving through an enemy country past empty white farmhouses and small Catholic shrines set in niches in the stone walls. Our troops must have been several miles ahead and a large bridgehead already safely established, because gunfire could only be heard in the distance and that only when our engines were turned off.[6]

Sergeant David Tickle, B Troop, 107 Battery, 7th Medium RA

Right from the start, Dave Tickle felt 'something' had changed when they got to Sicily. The scale of the war seemed to have got bigger; their own part in it somehow diminished.

> We started to lose the 'family' spirit side of the Eighth Army in North Africa. We'd got a number of divisions that had been brought into Sicily that hadn't been in North Africa – and of course you had got the advent of the Americans. You felt that things were changing! Whereas in North Africa we all felt that we were in the middle of what was happening – and playing an important part. We were known to all the divisions in North Africa, we knew them, and they knew us. Now it started widening out. You lost a sense of belonging.[7]

Sergeant David Tickle, B Troop, 107 Battery, 7th Medium RA

While Patton thrust up to the north-west of Sicily, Montgomery battered his way forward up the east coast towards Messina. By now the Italians had had enough. On 25 July, Mussolini was deposed and arrested, with the formation of a provisional government under Marshal Pietro Badoglio, who promptly began secretly to negotiate to secure an armistice with the Allies. As the Italian troops began to evacuate from Sicily, the Germans were ordered to fight on – and they did.

Sicily would also provide a very different fighting environment from North Africa. Perhaps it wasn't quite so hot, but there was a moist, 'sticky' heat that seemed to exhaust men engaged in physical exertion on the heavy guns. The terrain was also wildly different. The flat areas of southern Sicily had much of the ground under irrigation, with a myriad pattern of canals and ditches. At night the mosquitoes swarmed everywhere.

Every evening, just before dusk, the medical officer came round with a great can of ghastly ointment, which we had to smear on our wrists, hands, faces and necks. He used to dollop this out into the palm of one's hand – it was most unpleasant because when it was on your skin the perspiration could not evaporate. It was sealed into your skin. Also, we had to take mepacrine tablets to prevent the onset of malaria. I did manage to acquire a mosquito net so I was then able to sleep out in the open with this net tucked well in, but you could hear the mosquitoes buzzing around all through the night.[8]

Bombardier Ken Giles, B Troop, 107 Battery, 7th Medium RA

Even with all these precautions there were many cases of mild malaria.

The 7th Medium RA was tasked to support the 1st Canadian Division for the duration of the campaign. The Canadians were keen to get the 5.5-inch guns as far forward as possible to provide immediate close support whenever they made contact with the opposing Hermann Göring Panzer Division.

Our OP parties would be up almost along with the leading tanks and as soon as they bumped anything, we had targets come down and we dropped into action wherever we could. It was often very, very difficult to find a field to deploy in for four very large guns – if you think of these mountain roads and the rough country on either side. On one particular field, somewhere before Leonforte, because it was a large field by Sicilian standards there were sixteen medium guns and three regiments of 25-pounders and a Bofors troop. We fired like mad from that field – I've never heard such a din with all this stuff going off together.[9]

Lieutenant Bob Foulds, B Troop, 107 Battery, 7th Medium RA

There were sometimes problems in feeding the men with the

guns pushed right forward in the advance and Harold Harper came up with what he thought was the perfect solution.

> When we arrived in position, we had no hot drink or hot food, because we daren't light up stoves in the middle of the night. After two or three nights of this, I put forward a brilliant idea to the battery commander. 'If the observation post people plant out our new position for the night, what is wrong with me going up with the cookhouse truck, getting into position, cooking the food, putting it into the dixies and then when the lads arrive we'd be ready to serve it out!' He thought that was a very good idea! The cookhouse crew thought differently! We were going up this lane and suddenly saw infantrymen crouched in the hedge bottom. I jumped out of the truck and asked what was going off. They said, 'There are a couple of Tiger tanks, hull down over in the field to the right!' They were holding up the infantry. By the time I got back to the truck, the driver, having sensed that all was not well, had turned this 3-tonner round in the lane and we were going back, with all the pots and pans rattling like mad! With words coming from the driver saying, 'You medal-hunting bastard!' Looking at me![10]
>
> Troop Sergeant Major Harold Harper, B Troop, 107 Battery, 7th Medium RA

Albert Swinton encountered a rather more serious challenge to his authority as a gun sergeant when he returned from a recce to prepare a new position and found he had two new members added to his detachment. What he did not know was that they had recently been released from military prison!

> When I got back these two odd-bods were sat in my gun pit, who I didn't know. I must say here that I looked anything but a gun sergeant – all I'd got on was pair of shorts, a pair of socks and a pair of boots – and I was covered in black dust. I said

to these two chaps, 'Right, who are you?' I got a mouthful of abuse, asking, 'What the 'effing hell has it to do with you?' After a few words, I told them in no uncertain words that I was the gun sergeant and that I'd have a bit of respect from them – and if that's the way they wanted it, then, 'Stand to attention when I talk to you!' A thing that I had never done before! But their attitude warranted it! We had quite an argument and they decided they were better than me. They'd been turfed out of the military jails in the UK and a gang of them brought over to the combatant units and split out amongst them. For some reason we had two in our troop and I got both! We did not see eye to eye, so we finished up with me having to tell them who was boss and giving them a bit of a tawsing – we had a fight and I came off best. One at time – we had a gentlemen's agreement that we would sort it out between us man to man. I'll give them their due, it was a fair old tussle, but I was still sergeant at the end of it! I knocked a bit of sense into them.[11]

Sergeant Albert Swinton, B Troop, 107 Battery, 7th Medium RA

Later they all got on well together – one turned out to be a first-rate gunner, while his mate would prove a competent cook in the officers' mess – and would regularly give Albert Swinton an extra tray of food!

As they moved to the north the landscape changed as they encountered steep hills, dramatic ravines and narrow winding roads stretching up to villages and towns perched on the hilltops and ridges. It was very much a 'crowded' countryside.

There were fruit crops, olive groves, vineyards, very, very few fields of grass. Very difficult to get into action quickly, and on the road you felt very vulnerable to being attacked from the air, you were nose-to-tail moving up. The problem was the gates in the stone walls were too narrow to get through. It's all hills and mountains – and no way can you tell which road is going to which mountain. On top of these hills were the villages.[12]

Lieutenant David Elliott, B Troop, 107 Battery, 7th Medium RA

At times the fighting could be intense, particularly for the forward OP personnel. Bob Foulds remembered one dramatic incident at Nissoria.

They sent me out at first light to link up with the Canadian battalion, who were on top of the hill and attacking down a forward slope. I went up with a truck, a driver, OP ack and a signaller. We liaised with the Canadians, then went to make an OP which overlooked this forward slope. On the front corner of the rock was a Canadian OP which was busy shelling some targets. Their 25-pounders were in a wood to our right rear. We started to record some targets and did a couple of shoots, and then [the Germans] opened up on this OP with nebelwerfers. It gave us a fright as they dropped very well on target first time – and worse than that, we had been concealed in dry grass – and it set the grass on fire. It burnt the whole of the top of the hill off and we had to bail out. The nebelwerfer moved his range further back and he put them all around where our truck was parked at the back of the hill – and it knocked out a Canadian Bren gun carrier and set it on fire. Signaller Moore was the first on the scene to get the crew out. Fishing them out from this blazing Bren gun carrier. The whole place was a shambles: the nebelwerfers hit this 25-pounder troop squarely and turned some guns completely upside down. The attack failed and the whole situation quietened down.[13]

Lieutenant Bob Foulds, B Troop, 107 Battery, 7th Medium RA

The Germans were always dangerous opponents who could strike back hard at the slightest opportunity.

The South Notts Hussars were used to firing in the empty

wastes of the desert, but here they were sometimes fated to cause mayhem and slaughter among innocent civilians. There was no other way forward.

> By now we were shooting at occupied towns and villages which was pretty diabolical as far as we were concerned. We'd been used to four years of fighting with almost no civilians at all but the odd Bedouin. Now we were coming to villages which hadn't been evacuated – probably couldn't have been evacuated. Many were situated on the top of a hill from medieval times, so the roads themselves ran through the valley and over the top of the hill through the village. The only way to get through the mountains was to go through the town – and of course every town was made a strongpoint by the Germans and Italians. So, in turn they all got bombed and shelled by ourselves.[14]
>
> Lieutenant Bob Foulds, B Troop, 107 Battery, 7th Medium RA

Many of the men remembered the effects of their firing on the small town of Regalbuto. The Germans here occupied strong natural defences. The South Notts Hussars poured in shells, and air raids bombed the place flat before it was captured by 231 Brigade on 1 August. When the gunners eventually moved forward through the town they were shocked to see what they had done.

> In the square in the middle of the town there was this bonfire going, they were actually burning bodies as well. I can remember seeing a head on the side of the bonfire. The smell – stench – began to hit us. Nowhere in the desert war had we come across civilians being burnt and bombed. They were all quite helpless with no civilian administration to rescue them. There were still bodies in the rubble.[15]
>
> Lieutenant David Elliott, B Troop, 107 Battery, 7th Medium RA

Ken Giles, who had considered being a conscientious objector, was now faced with scenes of devastation for which he was partially responsible.

> This is one of my most disturbing memories. The enemy had been occupying this village perched on a kind of pinnacle. We had to fire in such a way that our fall of shot covered the German infantry, at the back of the village. Then we advanced towards the village. By this time our troops had captured it. There was a first aid post in the village, and we could see our troops being brought back on stretchers, all of them in gory bloody messes. The thing that really sticks in my mind to this very day and I find quite disturbing emotionally, we passed a row of shattered hovels, they had obviously been on fire, because they were still smoking. Now, whether it was our shells that had fallen on them – I had worked out the programme for that shoot – or whether it was enemy shells coming from the other side I didn't know. There were women leaning over the bodies of their babies and children, they seemed to have no clothes on, blackened skulls with all the flesh burnt off them – just skulls. And the women weeping over them looked badly burned as well. The sight was absolutely demoralising. As we passed through this place there was not a single sound from any person in that entire convoy.[16]

Bombardier Ken Giles, B Troop, 107 Battery, 7th Medium RA

As they moved forward, the bulk of Mount Etna began to loom over them.

> All the time the Germans were pulling further and further back on to the slopes of Mount Etna. Almost from the first few days we felt threatened by Etna: this massive lump of volcano, with its little cap of snow, smoking away, always higher than we were. We always felt that somebody was up there looking down.[17]

Lieutenant Bob Foulds, B Troop, 107 Battery, 7th Medium RA

In the event the campaign fizzled out for the South Notts Hussars as they were removed from the front line. The 5th AGRA, which had been split up for the duration of the campaign, was once more concentrated at a camp at Riposto some 25 miles north of Catania. Meanwhile, the Allied troops pressed forwards, although they were unable to prevent the bulk of the German forces from making their escape to the Italian mainland. When Patton's troops entered Messina on 17 August the city was empty.

The 5th AGRA was then moved forward to Messina, ready to take part in the support bombardments across the Straits for the landings on the Italian mainland. They embarked on the long drive round the west of Mount Etna, before taking up their initial gun positions on 26 August. Then, keen to maximise their range into Italy, they edged still further forward to positions behind the coastal road at Pistunina. At 03.45 on 3 September 1943 they began long-range counter-battery fire to support the landing of XIII Corps (Lieutenant General Miles Dempsey) in the Calabria area of the mainland. The bombardment and the invasion were a success, but there was a comical result.

> We dug in at the back of these rows of houses alongside the street. On our left front was the village church. Every time we fired, more slates came off the roof, we just blasted all the roof off – these houses really took a pounding. As for the church, every time we fired on a certain angle the church bell rang! We were only 200–300 feet away! When everything quietened down, the builders and their mates amongst us went and put these houses back into shape.[18]
>
> Sergeant Albert Swinton, B Troop, 107 Battery, 7th Medium RA

Not a single round came back at them from the Germans, despite the tempting vista of four medium regiments of the 5th AGRA in a straight line along the coast – sixty-four guns in all – with just 80 yards between each gun. Once ashore, the XIII Corps moved swiftly inland and the front line was soon placed well beyond the range of the 5.5-inch guns. The men of the South Notts Hussars did not know it, but their participation in the Italian campaign was at an end. On 8 September they heard the welcome news that Italy had unconditionally surrendered. The very next day came news of a second landing on the mainland, this time by the American Fifth Army at Salerno on the west coast. The German forces in Italy would fight on regardless for the best part of two years. The South Notts Hussars would not be involved.

WHILE THEIR FUTURE was being decided, the 107th RHA had a pleasant two-month interregnum in almost holiday conditions based at Pistunina. As the men relaxed, they were able once again to enjoy the funny side of life as revealed in several anecdotes from the period. One concerned Ted Holmes, who had recovered from his wounds and was acting as a sanitary corporal. This may have been a lowly task, but he showed considerable vision in his siting of one of their latrines.

> I made myself famous for building 'a loo with a view'. I dug a
> hole for a loo, got the thunderbox on, no canvas screen round
> it – you just sat there, and it overlooked the Straits of Messina –
> you could see right up the toe of Italy.[19]
>
> Gunner Ted Holmes, 107 Battery, 7th Medium RA

Equally ridiculous was the story of Albert Swinton and his peculiar preference for hair oil. This incident was so remarkable it even appeared in the regimental history![20]

> There was always a shortage of buffer oil, the oil used in
> the recuperator system of the gun, which is an air and oil

pneumatic system. Buffer oil consisted of glycerine and
vegetable oil, it wasn't any old rubbish; it was good stuff!
Captain Ivor Birkin was always shouting for buffer oil, he could
never get enough of it! This went on all the time. One day the
colonel came round to do an inspection and he obviously knew
me because he turned to me and said, 'How do you keep your
hair so immaculate, Sergeant?' I said, 'Well, buffer oil, Sir!'
It was the one and only time I remember Ivor Birkin being
embarrassed – he was always screaming for buffer oil – and
there was me wasting it on my hair! Just a little smear on your
hands, just enough to keep your hair down – like you did the
old Brylcreem![21]

Sergeant Albert Swinton, B Troop, 107 Battery, 7th Medium RA

As one might expect, Ken Giles engaged himself in more intellectual pursuits. He wrote and edited a newsletter for B Troop,
a mixture of salacious gossip and satire called 'The Acorn'
which was painstakingly typed up by Gunner 'Chaz' Winters.
However, this paled into insignificance compared to his composition and performance of a *tour de force* pianoforte piece for
B Troop.

I called it 'Island Rhapsody' because I planned it to reflect
the four guns of B Troop and it also reflected in my mind the
beauty of Sicily. The basic theme goes in beats of four so each
beat there represented one of the four guns; then I developed
the theme and tried to make it as romantic-sounding as
possible, but also with an element of underlying tragedy. There
are certain keys in my mind that have always been associated
with death. So, I introduced them and a slight, vague passage of
what we nowadays call atonality, since each hand is playing in a
different key, so there is a vague sense of not being connected –
I call it the churchyard effect! This 'Island Rhapsody' proved to

be very popular, mainly because it was a personal thing – I did it for B Troop![22]

Bombardier Ken Giles, B Troop, 107 Battery, 7th Medium RA

Several of the NCOs went as a party on local leave to Palermo. This was not in any way permitted – but they went anyway.

About four or five of us – Danny Lamb, Harold Harper, Ken Giles, a driver and myself, we commandeered one of our battery trucks, filled it with rations and petrol – and went off to Palermo – out of bounds! We had no trouble getting in; no one questioned us at all. We found a hotel that had one of its ends knocked out, but we got some bedrooms there. They couldn't supply us with food but that didn't bother us. We had a walk round Palermo, quite a pleasant place, and we bumped into about three or four of our officers, including David Elliott and Ivor Birkin. They said, 'Hello, what are you doing here?' We said, 'Well what the hell are you doing here!' We could talk to them like that! 'I suppose you realise it is out of bounds?' They said, 'Yes, do you?' We left them![23]

Battery Quartermaster Sergeant David Tickle, Headquarters, 107 Battery, 7th Medium RA

In Palermo, Giles caused quite a stir with his prodigious musical talents.

We came across a music shop. I wanted to get some music so I went in and the owner of the shop said that anything I wanted to buy I could try out on a quite beautiful grand piano – of course I jumped at the chance! Gradually a crowd gathered at the doorway and then a young lady placed a piece of music in front of me on the piano and it was entitled *Primo Vera*, which is Italian for spring. I started to play, she allowed me a few bars and then she stopped me. Then she clapped her hands and said, 'Encore! Encore!' I started off again and she sang – she sang

most beautifully! It turned out she was an opera singer. By the
time we had finished I was quite entranced with it. By this time
there was a great crowd outside and the police had to clear the
street![24]

Bombardier Ken Giles, B Troop, 107 Battery, 7th Medium RA

This, however, was not the end of the story.

The American military police had to come and move the crowd
along. We got invited to the family flat and they'd invited
one or two musicians along. What we were not aware of was
that the Americans had put a curfew of 9 o'clock at night of
everybody being off the streets! We left this flat at something
like 1 o'clock in the morning having had a musical evening –
and spent our time dodging back to the hotel – dodging the
military police.[25]

Troop Sergeant Major Harold Harper, B Troop, 107 Battery, 7th Medium
RA

IN OCTOBER 1943, A LARGE PARADE was called for all the
regiments in the 5th AGRA. It was evident that their fate had
been decided.

We were summoned into the square at Messina and addressed
by General Montgomery. We were all on parade in the correct
military fashion and he just drove into the middle and then
beckoned everybody round. He told us we were going home –
cheering – and that he was coming with us – because he might
be needing us in the invasion of Europe. Whereupon all the
men gave a loud boo! It was all good-humoured stuff.[26]

Troop Sergeant Major Harold Harper, B Troop, 107 Battery, 7th Medium
RA

Planning began at once for the return to the UK, as all the 107 Battery guns and equipment had to be handed in. This involved a tremendous amount of work, with the usual balancing act between the official record and the reality of all they had illicitly amassed in the course of the last couple of months. During these frantic preparations, one order was given that proved very upsetting to many of the gunners – and one in particular.

One of the gunners, an ex-lightweight boxer, 'Paddy' Swift, he was very fond of animals and had a habit of acquiring them if he could. Since we'd been in Sicily, he had rescued a little dog, something like a Jack Russell, from one of the bombed-out properties. He took very great care of this dog and managed to occupy a little room next to my office, where he and the dog always slept. Now the order had come round, knowing that we were going home to England, that anybody who had acquired pets, they could not be taken with us because of quarantine regulations and the general inconvenience. Since these dogs had become attached to their owners and they would only fret if left behind – they were not to be abandoned, they were to be destroyed. When Paddy heard this news, he went berserk. But unfortunately, he had to obey the order which came from quite high up I believe. The day duly arrived, Captain Birkin said to me, 'Will you take Paddy out with the dog and I'll lend you my revolver? I don't care who shoots the dog, Paddy or you, but unhappily this dog must be shot!' Knowing what was happening I had earlier got one of the gunners to dig a suitable grave in the orchard! I conducted a white-faced Paddy, carrying his dog, to this grave. I said to Paddy, 'Do you want to do it, or shall I?' He wouldn't answer. Paddy placed the revolver on the back of the dog's neck and fired. The dog seemed to give a little whimper and collapsed. I took the gun from him and

I remember Captain Birkin saying, 'I'm glad you took the revolver from him!' And I knew what he meant. Paddy might well have run amok with it or shot himself. I walked away with Paddy who was sobbing. I put my arm round him and tried to comfort him.[27]

Bombardier Ken Giles, B Troop, 107 Battery, 7th Medium RA

On their return to the billets, everyone was deadly silent. That night Paddy Swift got blind drunk to drown his sorrows. It was no surprise to any of them when he later deserted while on home leave back in Eire.

On 8 November, the 107 Regiment, along with the rest of 5 AGRA, embarked aboard a troopship and had a smooth passage to Algiers, where they disembarked. Here things started to go wrong. Most people presumed they were going to stay over-night in a transit camp before resuming their journey. That may be what they hoped would happen, but they would be sorely disappointed.

The first hint of something seriously wrong came in the length of the journey in the trucks. One had assumed the transit camp would be on the outskirts of the city, but the trucks went on and on and finally pulled up at the edge of a forest 25 miles or so outside Algiers. A lance corporal with a hurricane lamp appeared – by this time rain was pouring down – and announced that this was the Forest of Ferdinand and that this was the transit camp. Would we please follow him? A long string of 700 men, each carrying a haversack, pack and kitbag filed through the forest glades behind this one man with the lamp, for all the world like Snow White's dwarfs. About a mile in he stopped, swung his lamp to point out a few trees, and dropped the bombshell that this was the transit area. There was literally nothing there except six Soya stoves, a pipeline ending

in a tap, and thousands of trees. However, the battery was on
its way home, and that was great comfort to each man as he
unrolled his two blankets under a large tree and went to sleep,
impervious to the still pouring rain.[28]

Lieutenant Eric Dobson, Headquarters, 107 Battery, 7th Medium RA

They may have been cheerful enough at the start, but the stay
of 5th AGRA in these miserable conditions would drag on for
three weeks. Although a few tents eventually arrived, as if to
compensate, the water supply then failed, while just to torment
them the rain continued to pour down relentlessly. Somehow
the army then managed to find a way of making things even
worse.

There was a bit of a rumpus on! We'd no sooner got into this
camp and they started to come up with regimental discipline.
They wanted us same as in peacetime, polishing buttons, brasses
– and I think after all the fighting I think the men thought it
was a little bit stiff – a little bit hard. We didn't mind discipline.
It got the back up of some of the 7th Medium Regiment men.
They'd been abroad from 1932, they'd been in India six and half
years! The men started to moan and groan.[29]

Gunner Reg Cutter, B Troop, 107 Battery, 7th Medium RA

At last, on 3 December, the lorries arrived to take them back to
Algiers. Ian Sinclair was acting commander of A Troop and he
watched as his men endured further needless frustrations.

Trucks came to pick us up to take us to Algiers. They de-bussed
us lots of miles outside Algiers and we had to march with our
kitbags. We got into Algiers at about 11 o'clock in the morning
and – horror of horrors – we were told we weren't going to go
on the boat until 4 o'clock in the afternoon! What are we going
to do with these blokes who know they're going home – and

who are going to be let free in Algiers – which they'd been
desperate to get to! We gave them their orders that they mustn't
drink, that it was a dry boat they were going to get on to and
there was no question of anybody bringing any drink aboard.
Anybody who got drunk would be clapped in irons. We piled
all the kitbags and the rifles and told the men that they had to
be back at a certain time ready to march down to the ship – and
then they were on their own![30]

Lieutenant Ian Sinclair, A Troop, 107 Battery, 7th Medium RA

By then, Sinclair was an experienced officer, and he knew all too
well what was likely to happen, particularly as his new command
was the 'rogue troop' of the battery, with a large number of
known troublemakers.

Eventually we did round all my lot up and got them on parade,
but there was barely a man that hadn't got drunk. I hadn't
because I daren't, knowing this lot. I had to say to them, 'Right
there will be no drink – everybody who's got it, put it in the
gutter.' Not a move. I knew I'd got a mutiny on my hands! Oh,
dear oh dear – what are we going to do now? I decided to take
the bull by the horns! 'Right, if you don't put them down, I'm
going to come and get them – myself – and I'm going to start
with you!' He was a great big tall 'Scouser': McKay his name
was. Still not a move. So, I said, 'Right, I'm coming to get it!'
I went and took this thing off him. Smashed it in the gutter. I
said, 'Now then, do I have to take them all or are we going to
get rid of them?' There was still not a move. So, I went to the
next bloke and took his! Suddenly they all broke ranks. Christ,
what's happening? But they broke ranks to get rid of their
drinks – they broke their own bottles in the gutter – nobody
was going to have them if they didn't. Some remained trouble

and eventually we got on the boat with five of my men under close arrest and they spent the voyage home locked up.[31]

Lieutenant Ian Sinclair, A Troop, 107 Battery, 7th Medium RA

And so, they boarded the troopship *Franconia*. After almost four years, the South Notts Hussars were coming home.

17

BACK HOME

We'd been away for so long. Gone away as lads and come back as men. Very different sort of people. We'd lived a very strange life, knowing nothing about civilian life in England during the war – so we didn't really know what to expect. What's it going to be like? We were a little bit at a loss as to how we might be going to adjust. A little bit anxious.[1]

Lieutenant Ian Sinclair, A Troop, 107 Battery, 7th Medium RA

THE *FRANCONIA* DOCKED AT LIVERPOOL on the afternoon of 10 December. It had been an uneventful voyage, but to the men aboard seemed to last for ever. As the boat approached the harbour, they were made aware of stringent security precautions, presumably to hide the fact that the 5th AGRA had returned from foreign service and would soon be added to the order of battle for the upcoming invasion of Europe. Unit insignia was to be removed and the men were ordered not to speak to any Liverpudlians they encountered.

We didn't know what to expect. We were looking round expecting to see half of Liverpool shattered, buildings wrecked. It didn't strike us that way. Everybody came over to the port side and the old boat tilted. The 7th Medium Regiment people

had been out eleven years; they'd been to India. We hadn't seen
a WREN or an ATS lass for the whole of our trip. To see these
WRENS walking about on the quayside – it was eye popping!
People were whistling and shouting, we virtually drove them
off the quayside – these WRENS ran for it. When they'd gone
things quietened down a bit. Then we were told we were not
going to be allowed off the boat till midnight. We thought,
'What the hell! Why not? Let's get off!' But no way. They
marched us through Liverpool to the station; pitch-black –
nobody about![2]

Battery Quartermaster Sergeant David Tickle, Headquarters, 107 Battery,
7th Medium RA

However, some of the men managed to get the use of a telephone at the local post office. Dave Tickle rang his parents back
home in Birmingham.

I knew my mother would be on her own. I got through and
Mother answered the phone. She says, 'Hello?' I said, 'Hello,
Mum!' She said, 'What?' I said, 'Yes!' She said, 'Where are
you?' I said, 'I can't tell you where I am but I'm here. I'm
all right. Are you all right? What about Dad? Mum nearly
dropped through the floor. That was the first time I'd spoken to
them in nearly four years.[3]

Battery Quartermaster Sergeant David Tickle, Headquarters, 107 Battery,
7th Medium RA

Special troop trains took both the 7th and 64th Medium Regiments non-stop through to Felixstowe where the advance party
had sorted out their billets. But this was just a fleeing visit:
within forty-eight hours every man in the South Notts Hussars
was sent home on a month's leave. They had looked forward to
home for years – dreamt about it, fantasised about it – now they
were actually home.

We didn't know what to expect – what they were like. They didn't know what to expect – what I was going to be like! We made a practice of writing each week to each other, Joyce and I, and I wrote each month to my parents. But I didn't know what effects the bombing of Birmingham had had on them. They had no idea of the effect of four years out in the Middle East had had on me, what had changed. We pulled into Snow Street Station, and Father and Joyce were there. As soon as I saw them, I thought, 'All right! They're all right!'[4]

Battery Quartermaster Sergeant David Tickle, Headquarters, 107 Battery, 7th Medium RA

David Tickle was engaged to Joyce – they had decided not to get married before he went overseas in 1940 as he was unsure of the degree of danger he would be facing. Now they reckoned the time had come: as a battery quartermaster sergeant he thought he had a reasonable chance of surviving the war and would not leave Joyce as a war widow. During his long leave, in January 1944 they organised their wedding and honeymoon.

When Reg Cutter went back home to East Bolden on Tyneside he got quite a reception, but there was one thing he could not swallow.

Above the door was 'Welcome Home', there was a crowd round you, you feel embarrassed. When I eventually did get in the house, my mother was over the moon to see us, crying. I remember her first words, 'Thank God you're home safe, son! You'll never guess what I've kept for you over a number of years!' I said, 'What's that?' She says, 'A tin of corned beef!' For people at home it was a luxury! I says, 'Oh my God! Don't mention that stuff!' She thought she'd been doing good keeping it to one side for us all that time! I said, 'You eat that, we've had enough of that stuff up the desert!'[5]

Gunner Reg Cutter, B Troop, 107 Battery, 7th Medium RA

Ken Giles was an older man and he went back to a wife and son. He had been away for so long that it was a tremulous meeting for both him and his young boy.

> We went on leave – I had previously telephoned my wife to say that I would be home some time the following day. We were living in Stockwell at that time. When I got home, I knocked on the door and my son opened it. He would be 6 or 7 years old. He was obviously expecting me – I can still see his face – he blushed absolutely crimson. And he wouldn't say a word, he was clearly very embarrassed.[6]
>
> Bombardier Ken Giles, B Troop, 107 Battery, 7th Medium RA

During their leave, Ivor Birkin revitalised his dormant campaign to have the South Notts Hussars reinstated as a full regiment. He organised a dinner at the Mikado Café in Nottingham, attended by the great and good of the old 'county' set of officers, such as Lieutenant Colonels Jack Chaworth-Musters and Athole Holden. It was not a particularly inclusive meeting, as some of the younger officers, such as Ian Sinclair and Bob Foulds, were not invited. However, this was not the point; the intention was to mobilise all the political and social influence the regiment had at its disposal. In the event Colonel Holden was persuaded to make direct overtures to his friends at the War Office.

> Ivor Birkin of course was the instigator. Reformation was the only thing we ever thought of, talking about it! Although we *were* 7th Medium, we were always *apart* from 7th Medium! Never the twain shall meet unless it could be avoided. We were a cliquey lot! Thought we were better than the best! Probably were! We knew that if we'd got Ivor there was always the chance that we could possibly become the South Notts again, because of the strings he could pull.[7]
>
> Lieutenant Ian Sinclair, A Troop, 107 Battery, 7th Medium RA

After their leave, they returned to Felixstowe, where closer inspection revealed excellent billets with proper mess cooking, as opposed to the tinned rations they had become used to. Life was good.

News was received that the commander of 5th AGRA, Brigadier 'Toc' Elton[8], their old commanding officer at El Alamein, had been killed in a flying accident in the Middle East. He was replaced by Brigadier Reginald Morley, who had previously commanded the sister regiment of the South Notts Hussars, the 150th Regiment, RA. Morley soon made it clear that he sought to ensure that 5th AGRA gunnery standards did not in any way dip during this period away from the front line.

> There was great concentration on gun drill, with frequent snap inspections on the gun park by brigadier and colonel; and weekly formal inspections of the billets by the colonel. On the latter occasions, the men were supposed to be all on organised training and the area was to be clear of all except billet orderlies. Once Lieutenant Elliott, noticing two men hanging round the gun park when they should have been elsewhere, told them to disappear for a quarter of an hour. Inevitably, Colonel Stansfield saw them, asked where they were going and was told, 'Mr Elliott has told us to get out of the way!' More was heard of this![9]

Lieutenant Eric Dobson, Headquarters, 107 Battery, 7th Medium RA

New 5.5-inch guns had been issued and they were taken for a live firing at the Hunstanton ranges. It did not go terribly well.

> We suffered somewhat in our stay at Felixstowe inasmuch as the relaxation of being back in England, being amongst the beer and skittles, caused a certain lack of discipline when we came to go on the firing ranges again. In January, we went on a firing weekend near Hunstanton. Quite frankly, there were a number

of errors which ought not to have happened: people putting the wrong charge into the gun, firing short and all that sort of thing.[10]

Troop Sergeant Major Harold Harper, B Troop, 107 Battery, 7th Medium RA

As they prepared once more for war, many of the men were suffering from a sense of *déjà vu*, unable to accept that they would be placed back in the firing line quite so soon.

You'd rather not have gone to do any more soldiering! You'd done your fair share all right! Because we were some of the first in action and we'd been right through. There were people, lots and lots of people, who'd done nothing at all, who'd been stationed in England all the time for four years. No doubt they'd done training, but they'd not seen any action! There was a bit of feeling that it was time somebody else had a go.[11]

Gunner Reg McNish, A Troop, 107 Battery, 7th Medium RA

THE 5TH AGRA HAD RETURNED HOME FOR A REASON. At the behest of Stalin, planning for a Second Front invasion of 'Fortress Europe' had been under way for years, but Churchill had always hung back from a timed commitment. He preferred the classical maritime strategy of attacking an enemy indirectly, using naval power to concentrate on more isolated elements of the enemy forces and empire. The idea was to gradually erode the enemy strength and morale – and only then to join with coalition partners in the final continental assault. This had worked well in the Napoleonic Wars, but failed dreadfully in the Great War, with hundreds of thousands of men lost in campaigns in Gallipoli, Mesopotamia and Salonika. These 'Easterner' campaigns had sought a 'soft underbelly' and leached away strength fighting the Turks and Bulgarians rather than the 'main enemy'

– the Germans – on the Western Front, where the war would ultimately be decided. In 1943, Churchill had been allowed to launch the Italian campaign, but now he was sternly called to the task at hand. During the Tehran conference of November 1943, Roosevelt and Stalin had extracted a final commitment for the Operation Overlord direct assault across the English Channel[12] to be carried out by June 1944. There would be no more ducking and diving, the die was cast. General Dwight Eisenhower was appointed the commander of Supreme Headquarters Allied Expeditionary Force, while Montgomery was placed in command of 21st Army Group, responsible for the actual landings. Montgomery was acutely aware that the bulk of the British Army divisions had little or no experience of action. He sought the security of tried and tested units, of men who had proved themselves time and time again in action. The result was the recall to England of units like the 50th Division to be one of the assault divisions in the beach landings – trusted veterans of France in 1940, of slogging through the North African deserts in 1941–3, of enduring slaughter at Primisole Bridge in Sicily in 1943. It also meant the recall of 5th AGRA – and hence the South Notts Hussars, experienced men who could harness the massed power of the guns that would be needed in the bitter fighting to come in Normandy. Yet where once the presence of a couple of field artillery batteries could significantly influence the course of a battle, now there were whole mighty AGRAs of massed medium and heavy guns. Hundreds if not thousands of guns, their firepower augmented by massed bombing and strafing.

BUT FIRST A CHANGE IN STATUS that came as a surprise to many of the men serving in 107 Battery. On 27 February 1944, a letter was received confirming that Ivor Birkin and the 'old guard' of South Notts officers had won the day: the 107 Battery would be amalgamated with the 126 Battery from 16th Medium Regiment to form a new 107th Medium Regiment RA consisting of 425 and 426 Batteries. They would now be part of the 9th AGRA, commanded by Brigadier Walter Crosland. Most of the officers were delighted, but at a meeting of the sergeants' mess it soon became obvious that many of the senior NCOs were conflicted.

> I was torn with my loyalties. Obviously, I knew a lot of work had been done to getting our regiment back again, but on the other hand we'd made a lot of friends with members of the 7th Medium Regiment. It seemed a pity really to break that fighting unit up. In fact, quite a few resented the move, for the simple reason that the Nottingham contingent had disappeared at Knightsbridge anyway. By the time we came to February 1944, I would doubt if there were above fifty Nottingham people left! We got over it; we were all happy eventually![13]
>
> Troop Sergeant Major Harold Harper, B Troop, 107 Battery, 7th Medium RA

Similar views were expressed by another senior NCO, Dave Tickle.

> We were more than happy with the 7th, quite frankly – there's no two ways about it. As far as I was concerned, we were more sure of ourselves and what we were doing and contented when we were with the 7th Medium Regiment than we had been at any time with the old regiment. If it had stayed as it was, I would have been perfectly happy. I judged us to be a very good unit: we knew what we were doing, we knew where we were going, and the thing functioned like clockwork.[14]
>
> Battery Quartermaster Sergeant David Tickle, Headquarters, 107 Battery, 7th Medium RA

The 107 Battery left Felixstowe and the new 107th Medium Regiment RA gathered for the first time at Brighton on 19 March. The new colonel was a renowned gunner officer, Lieutenant Colonel Marshall St John Oswald, who had recently been employed as a staff officer at Tactical Headquarters, Eighth Army, during the Battle of Alamein and the subsequent advance to Tunis. Oswald made an immediate good impression when his first action on arriving was to request an acorn cap badge. Major James Martin was appointed to command 425 Battery (formed from A Troop, formerly C Troop, from 126 Battery and B Troop from 107 Battery), while Major Charles Rickard would command 426 Battery (C Troop, formerly A Troop, of 107 Battery and D Troop from 127 Battery). Different approaches were taken by the battery commanders. Major Martin decided to mix up his gun sections, transferring them between troops. His hope was that both the desert veterans and 'Blighty' men had something to offer and it could best be achieved by intermingling. 'Bonzo' Rickard took the opposite approach, leaving the two troops intact and seeking to set the 16th Medium troop 'something to aim at'.

As training began in earnest, they were issued with another set of 5.5-inch guns and American FWD petrol-engine gun towers which were similar to the Matadors but regarded as less reliable and slower. At first things seemed to go well.

> We were seasoned soldiers, having seen a lot of enemy action, whereas we were with a bunch of chaps who all they'd done was drill on the square. A bit of ribaldry went on, but I tried to make these people feel at home. They turned out to be a good bunch of lads. Their gun drill was very, very good, probably better than ours! We'd let a lot of things go 'by the board' in action. You learn certain thing on the square, they're always at the back of your mind, but when you get in action you do

things a little bit better. Our standards rose again – once we joined with 16th Medium we really had to show that we were a fighting unit![15]

Troop Sergeant Major Harold Harper, B Troop, 107 Battery, 7th Medium RA

On the other hand, some ingrained 'peacetime' habits could be prejudicial to efficiency on active service.

One of the first problems we had with these new gunners was they'd been trained for the last few years into a system which made them very, very slow to get into action and get the first shot on the ground. We had difficulty in breaking the habit they had when they went on to a gun position: the first thing they did was erect the camouflage nets – which was about the last thing we would do as we were always in a hurry to get into action![16]

Lieutenant David Elliott, Headquarters, 425 Battery, 107th Medium RA

Douglas Nicholls was one of the new arrivals. He had served on coastal artillery duties around Milford Haven, before serving as a bombardier on the 4.5-inch guns of 127 Battery since 1942. Now he was posted as a specialist command post assistant with A Troop. At first, he was a little overawed.

They'd been all together from the beginning of the war, a lot of them. They weren't unfriendly, but we'd always see them together. We were aware of the fact that they were Nottingham people and that we were a mixed bag from all over the country. We respected them because they'd been in action in the desert and they knew what they were doing! These are not novices; these men have actually been in action! When action came, they knew how to behave. To be quite honest they weren't as used to the discipline and the 'bull'. They felt that all the training that they had to do together with us was unnecessary

– they knew it all – and I don't mean that disrespectfully – but they'd actually done it in action – we hadn't! They used to get a bit fed up![17]

Bombardier Douglas Nicholls, A Troop, 425 Battery, 107th Medium RA

There is no doubt that the veterans chafed against the manifold restrictions of home service. Here rules were made to be adhered to, procedures to be followed.

Personal smartness and bullshit – smartening yourself up, making sure your belt was properly blancoed and your puttees properly done, the trousers beautifully creased, walking smartly, parades, that was not irksome. The irksome things were the things that we knew didn't matter. If it doesn't move, paint it. The way we were made to do silly little things that have got nothing to do with war – polishing vehicles underneath the wing mudguards. When it came to doing manoeuvres, having to blacken your faces, which we hadn't had to blacken our faces for four years at the wars! Having to go through things that we'd done for so long in the face of the enemy – to go back to a pretend – to learning how to do it from 'the book'. You'd learnt skills. You learn from the book to start with, but experience enables you to make innovations to do things more easily. We know this is how you should be doing it – but this is a better way of doing it.[18]

Lieutenant Ian Sinclair, Headquarters, 426 Battery, 107th Medium RA

He was not alone in his resentment at being taught how 'to suck eggs' on a series of exercises on the Downs.

Oh yes! To start off with when you went out on an exercise you were told to wear a tin hat! Well we hadn't worn tin hats for donkeys' years – they were bloody uncomfortable; they weren't particularly effective – and we never wore them. The amount of paint and signs – if you went out on an exercise you had to put a sign out to indicate where each troop was – an old petrol tank with holes punched in it to indicate C Troop. It was meant to hold a hurricane lamp, so it could be seen at night. As far as we were concerned this was a lot of nonsense! There was a lot of bull that we knew damn well would be forgotten as soon as you got into action.[19]

Lieutenant Charles Westlake, C Troop, 426 Battery, 107th Medium RA

On 29 April, the whole of 9th AGRA was posted to Yorkshire – an unpleasant surprise for many! The regiment was split between Baildon, a village on the outskirts of Shipley, and Guiseley. Here the training continued with exercises on the Ilkley Moors, although as steel helmets were still to be worn they were hardly 'On Ilkley Moor bah't hat'. While there, an old friend joined the regiment as second-in-command. Major Leonard Gibson had known the officers of the South Notts Hussars from their shared pre-war camps at Redesdale when he was serving with the 72nd Field RA. Since then his career had blossomed, serving as brigade major to the artillery units of 50th Northumbrian Division during the 1940 campaign in France. He had various senior staff postings on the home front, but he had recently refused promotion to be the lieutenant colonel responsible for planning ship movements in the Tilbury docks area.

It wasn't at all what I wanted! What I wanted was to go back to the battle and perhaps win a DSO or an MC and not to be killed outright by a 'doodlebug' in the middle of Tilbury Docks![20]

Major Leonard Gibson, Headquarters, 107th Medium RHA

As regimental second-in-command he had an administrative role in securing supplies of ammunition, stores and rations. His gunnery knowledge was no longer up to speed after years in staff positions – indeed his last technical gunnery course had been pre-war. Gibson's first impressions of his new regiment were positive.

> One found a tremendous mixture: the old desert veterans, who were real hard nuts and the other half were completely inexperienced – mostly Scots from the Scottish Horse I think it was. They all had to be married up! That was the task: I felt that on the one side I must bolster up the inexperienced, and rather sit on those war chaps who thought they were 'God's anointed' shall we say![21]
>
> Major Leonard Gibson, Headquarters, 107th Medium RHA

At well over 6 foot and not exactly thin, Gibson was a big man in every way; from head to foot a soldier's soldier. As an old territorial with active service experience, he was able to tactfully ensure that the regiment was collectively put through its paces without irritating either veterans or ingénues.

> One had to say they were still a bit rusty and weren't quite ready to go to war at that early stage – and that was our job to get them really cracking. Command-post teams, OP teams, they weren't teams – 'X' didn't know what 'Y' was doing! They had to get themselves practised. It was only by doing exercises – more and more and more – that you got them right. That was the colonel's job, but I was there to help in any way I could. The CRA, the brigadier, was a spit and polish chap and had not a great war experience. And so, he'd been brought up with a square-bashing, whitewashing, everything cut and dried – even unto the dustbins being painted! These desert warriors wouldn't have it, they couldn't be bothered! They reckoned they were training for war and dustbins they could throw down the road! There was quite a bit of a battle going on. That was one of the things I had to try and sort, because the colonel had

to say yes to the brigadier or he would have been thrown out and I had to put over to the chaps, 'Look here, we've got to try a little bit on this lark! Or there's going to be real trouble!' I had to support my colonel and try and soften up the orders from higher up. We got through. By the time we were ready to go we were quite a useful unit.[22]

Major Leonard Gibson, Headquarters, 107th Medium RHA

Gibson managed to bind the separate elements together, creating a sense of unity that would serve them well in the trials to come.

Major Gibson got everybody rallied round to pull themselves together and stop all the little bits of squibbling and squabbling with 16th Regiment and to work together as one unit. For a start the proportions of the man put the wind up you! A very big man! By the way he spoke, by the word of command, you knew you had to do it or else! It was as easy as that![23]

Lance Bombardier Reg Cutter, B Troop, 425 Battery, 107th Medium RA

On 13 May, there was a ceremonial parade in front of the people of Nottingham. At this stage, not many of the assembled South Notts Hussars were actually from Nottinghamshire, but it was still 'their' home town and they were made welcome by the teeming crowds – estimated to number well over 10,000. After riding through the town with all their guns and vehicles, they dismounted to be reviewed in the Old Market Square by the father of William Barber, the Honorary Colonel Philip Barber, who had replaced the sadly deceased Lancelot Rolleston. Also attending were Major William Barber and Peter Birkin, who had both been captured at Knightsbridge but managed to escape from Italy and regained the British lines.

On their return to Yorkshire, the pace of training increased exponentially with numerous special schemes, all culminating in a firing exercise on Grassington Ranges. Then, suddenly, they had orders to move south. At dawn on 4 June 1944, the convoy set off on the long journey to Dudsbury Camp, some 6 miles from Bournemouth. While they were there, they were relieved to have their FWD gun towers replaced with a set of the much-preferred Matadors for active service.

The 9th AGRA was not among the early units designated to follow up the D-Day landings on 6 June 1944. Everyone was all agog for news of the progress made, and Leonard Gibson proved invaluable in utilising his former staff contacts to find out exactly what was happening. The initial landings had managed to get ashore and establish tenable bridgeheads, but had failed to take their more ambitious targets – in particular the city of Caen, but also Carentan, Saint-Lô and Bayeux. As the Germans moved up their reserves the fighting was hard, as the Allies fought to advance against elite German troops, who were usually well concealed from air attack. Montgomery intended to engage the Germans in a dogfight for Caen, launching heavy attacks that would force the Germans to send in their armoured reserves. This would free the American forces to clear the Cotentin Peninsula, smash through to take the key port of Cherbourg, before exploiting out to the south and east. Cherbourg fell on 27 June, but Caen still held out.

As the weeks passed, the tension was mounting for the men of 107 Medium RA; when would it be their turn? Originally, they were intended to embark at Southampton docks, but instead they were designated for Tilbury Docks in East London. The long drive passed without incident, and on 9 July the men were moved into tents on an area previously flattened by German air raids during the Blitz. Here they were held back for another three days due to storms in the Channel, which delayed the return of their designated transport. This was unfortunate, as an hour after they arrived the first of a series of V1 flying bombs crashed down nearby. As they waited, not unnaturally the Londoners among their ranks were keen to take the opportunity to visit their families.

> Sergeant Fred Taylor's home was very adjacent to the initial staging area. He asked permission to leave the convoy to go and see if his home was OK, because while we were going down there, 'doodlebugs' were going over at a fair rate of knots. Well it transpired that when he got there his house had just been destroyed. He gleaned that from the family point of view things were all right, but he hadn't got the time to do anything further.[24]
>
> Battery Quartermaster Sergeant David Tickle, Headquarters, 425 Battery, 107th Medium RA

Reg Cutter summed up the view of many of the men as they prepared once again to go to war. They may have moaned about regiments who had served nowhere but the UK, they may have been personally afraid, but in the end they would see it through.

> Montgomery wanted experienced men – and he could rely on the men that had proved themselves up in the desert. We were saying to ourselves, 'It's the same people doing the same job over and over again! What the hell are they doing in Blighty!' But you couldn't expect these people in Blighty to do it because they'd never had any experience. Actually, to tell you the truth, I would have hated to be stationed in this country – a 'Blighty Waller' – polish this, polish that, painting lumps of coal white and all that! I joined the army to fight! And that's what I did! We'd made a name for ourselves and we were going to make sure we kept it up![25]
>
> Lance Bombardier Reg Cutter, B Troop, 425 Battery, 107th Medium Regiment

18

NORMANDY ATTRITION

Flames were shooting up yards into the air, many of the fruit trees had caught fire; cartridges were bursting, comet-like, through the darker patches; bullets from burning magazines sprayed around dangerously, and the muffled explosion of burning petrol cans made the night hideous with sound. Our own truck was now blazing fiercely, a yard or so from our shelter.[1]

Signaller Ronald Paisley, D Troop, 426 Battery, 107th Medium RA

ON 13 JULY 1944, THE SOUTH NOTTS HUSSARS boarded their American Liberty ships and set off across the English Channel: 425 Battery aboard the *Fort La Joie* and 426 Battery ensconced on the *Fort Livingston*. Among them was Ronald Paisley, whose memories are preserved in his excellent book *From Normandy to Victory with the South Notts Hussars*.[2] Pre-war he had been a grocery shop assistant in Carlisle; now he was a signaller in the Royal Artillery and off to war. Just as in January 1940, when the regiment first left for Palestine, there were many young men aboard the ships wondering what their future held.

We boarded the boat on a warm July morning; I recall vividly with what misgivings I viewed the khaki-clad men climbing the gangway. What lay before us over that strip of water? How long would it be before we docked once more with the war behind us? It was my turn to tender up the embarkation ticket; to alight on the slippery deck. I'd stepped off English soil; the adventure had begun. I remember the busy scene on board; vehicles and guns being loaded and lowered by crane into the hold; men's voices raised in nautical and other language; the creaking of chains and whine of motors; the chatter and laughter of the boys as they hunted a bed space in our sleeping quarters, the upper half of the hold; some, relying on the old adage, 'When in Rome', were already adjusting hammocks; it was a rowdy scene, but underneath was a very real air of depression; men were killed in war; not all of us would return.[3]

Signaller Ronald Paisley, D Troop, 426 Battery, 107th Medium RA

As they approached Arromanches they could see there were still hundreds of the ships there that had been involved in the Operation Neptune D-Day landings. Ships of all shapes and sizes: mighty battleships, monitors, cruisers, destroyers, various landing craft and the humble minesweepers. Once they landed in Normandy, the South Notts Hussars' story was all but subsumed within the overall narrative of complex operations involving millions of men fighting in the common cause. Their actions no longer determined the outcome of battles. The war had changed. They were now a very small cog in a very big wheel. No simple survey can paint the wider picture of what was going on around them. But their story still counts; they still represent all the thousands of gunners playing their part in the war against fascism.

As they landed, they were grateful to see there was no sign of the Luftwaffe, but the skies were filled with Allied aircraft. Although there were some delays, by 15 July they were all ashore.

Once again, their hard work in waterproofing the vehicles had been redundant, as they landed in just a few inches of seawater. By the time they cleared the beaches, the South Notts Hussars had already demonstrated that their ability to 'win' extra vehicles had not deserted them during their stay back in England.

> Both batteries were a number of vehicles 'over strength', shall we say. I've officially no idea at all, but I know full well that if there was any vehicle about, someone would jump in if it was driveable and add it to our strength – thinking of when anything went wrong, we'd have an extra vehicle. Some of those could have been on the beaches. By this time replacement vehicles were all being landed, and they were lying about on the beach. If the staff there couldn't cope with the amount of vehicles then it was up to anyone quick to nick one – the odd jeep![4]
>
> Major Leonard Gibson, Headquarters, 107th Medium RHA

On 17 July, Leonard Gibson and his recce parties were sent ahead to locate suitable gun positions in the village of Le Mesnil, which was a mile to the east of the original glider landing site at Ranville and some 5 miles south-west of Caen.

> A regimental recce party was myself in charge, with the regimental survey officer and sergeant with me. Each battery had its command post and gun position officer and a minimum of two or three would be handy – the rest would be behind. I would go forward with the survey officer, scratch about, crawl, looking for gun positions to get the guns into action as quickly as possible. As soon as I was happy, I would call up the two battery representatives with a hunting horn! I would blow it 'Brrrrr!'; they were only half a mile away and they would know that I wanted them. I had different signals. One toot or two toots – a simple code so the Hun wouldn't know! I love my

hunting horn! There was only about one possible gun position which I found for all sixteen guns – that was just to blast away at the Germans still holding Caen.[5]

Major Leonard Gibson, Headquarters, 107th Medium RHA

As the main body followed them inland, Ronald Paisley was taking in every moment of this exhilarating new experience.

To look at the convoy did present rather a thrill – the powerful appearance of the guns with muzzles sniffing the air like hounds eager for the kill; the squat armoured halftracks; the swaying aerials of the radio vehicles with the South Notts Hussars pennant fluttering in the slight breeze and the gallant Bren-gun carrier leading the way; a sinister yet imposing column. Bayeux was gay with bunting and the French tricolour flew side by side with the Union Jack. My impression was that most of the people had recovered from their delight at being freed and were taking military convoys more or less for granted.[6]

Signaller Ronald Paisley, D Troop, 426 Battery, 107th Medium RA

With his knowledge of the collateral casualties suffered during the fighting by many villages in Sicily, Ken Giles had rather more understanding of the less than enthusiastic reception.

We realised there had been plenty of action because villages we went through were virtually non-existent. I don't think the French people were terribly pleased to see us. After all we'd knocked their world to hell – smithereens! Although we might have been liberators, I think they were on the fringe of occupation and I don't suppose they had suffered too badly. They looked rather fed up with the whole thing and I don't wonder, because they were trying to get their lives together again.[7]

Bombardier Ken Giles, B Troop, 425 Battery, 107th Medium RA

And already the desert warriors were looking round in concern. The Normandy countryside was a whole new environment within which to wage war.

> The French countryside was vastly different from anything we'd been accustomed to previously. Such close country with high hedges, woods, cottages, fairly intensively occupied and cultivated. You couldn't see what the devil was going on! Despite Sicily, we'd really been used to desert warfare where you could see for miles in every direction. In this country you couldn't see a damn thing! It took a bit of getting used to! You always felt you might be surprised – shells would arrive – and you couldn't see where the hell they were coming from.[8]
>
> Lieutenant Charles Westlake, C Troop, 426 Battery, 107th Medium RA

Ronald Paisley left a detailed account of their daily iron rations at this stage of the war. It makes interesting reading and although it was hardly appetising, it was enough to keep body and soul aligned.

Most of us then prepared a meal from the mysterious contents of our twenty-four-hour ration pack. It was rather a neat job and may interest the reader as to the contents:

- One square 2in. × 2in. dehydrated meat (with water makes quite a substantial quantity of a mince-like substance which is quite good).
- One square 2in. × 2in. oatmeal (not quite like mother makes, but not a bad substitute).
- Eight small cubes of tea (these dissolve into a remarkable substance in which milk and sugar are self-contained. Hot and wet are its main features.)
- Three bars of chocolate, one with fruit (always acceptable).
- About 4 oz of sweets.
- A quantity of matches.

- One Tommy cooker. A small ingenious device for use in emergency. Fuel for same with spares.
- Four fairly substantial biscuits.

On the whole one can at least satisfy the inner man for the time stated.[9]

Signaller Ronald Paisley, D Troop, 426 Battery, 107th Medium RA

As they tried to grab some sleep prior to the barrage they would be firing next morning, one of the gunners had a terrifying shock.

Our artificer had rather an alarming experience when, after finding a spare and well-protected slit trench, he deposited his bed therein. Returning after supper – it was quite dark – he dived in this hole and to his horror found it already occupied by a German corpse. He left that hole like a human rocket and spent that night sleeping on the surface. I expect his dreams were none too pleasant.[10]

Signaller Ronald Paisley, D Troop, 426 Battery, 107th Medium RA

THEY WERE NOW UNDER THE OPERATIONAL COMMAND of the headquarters of the Canadian Corps, which was about to launch Operation Goodwood finally to complete the long-delayed capture of Caen. On 18 July, the attack was to go in, assisted by a huge bombing raid on Caen, while the 107 Regiment RA were to attempt to destroy or suppress the fire of all identified German anti-aircraft batteries in order to give the bombers a clear run on to their targets. They then moved forward to new gun positions in the suburbs of Caen, looking to provide close artillery support to the advancing infantry. Here they were to the left of a main road, with a railway embankment just behind them close to the River Orne, just a few hundred yards from the German positions on the south bank. That night they heard an approaching German aircraft.

> We took little notice at first but dived for cover when the anti-aircraft opened up and squeezed into a cut-out part of the railway embankment. It was terrifying crouching there – and then suddenly the plane dived low over the line of the railway and roared only a few hundred feet overhead. Then in the midst of the anti-aircraft barrage of sound we had our first sensation of those deadly anti-personnel bombs which burst about 8 feet high and shoot out steel in all directions. We held our breath: it is an awful sensation, not improved by the noise, and we expected a packet any moment. He was over now – and the drone began to recede. We were just congratulating ourselves when the urgent call for stretcher-bearers echoed out in the darkness.[11]

> Signaller Ronald Paisley, D Troop, 426 Battery, 107th Medium RA

Lance Bombardier Raymond Whittington[12] was killed and four other men wounded. Whittington was their first fatality since they had landed in France. Another period of stalemate then commenced as the Canadians fought to expand their tenuous bridgehead over the Orne.

Meanwhile Major William Barber returned to the regiment and immediately took over his old command of 426 Battery. Around the same time Harold Harper had been promoted to act as his battery sergeant major. Initially, he was not happy with the situation.

> Some senior ranks from 16th Medium buckled under. A battery sergeant major and two sergeants found it too much. As a result, I was moved to be battery sergeant major of 426 Battery. A majority of my chaps were then from 16th Medium. I despaired, quite frankly, because I found the sergeant major was operating as if he was still on Salisbury Plain. He had about fifteen rounds

of ammunition per gun – the battery I'd just left I had 250 rounds per gun! It was a lack of fighting experience. Within about ten minutes of looking at the situation, I'd got the complete echelon ammunition trucks to go back 5–6 miles in the middle of the night to the ammunition depot to load up – I think they were quite shaken actually. They dumped all the rounds early the following morning and from then on we were all right.[13]

Battery Sergeant Major Harold Harper, Headquarters, 426 Battery, 107th Medium Regiment

As an experienced long-standing NCO, Harper was confident to make his own mind up on the relative competence – or otherwise – of his officers. At times he had to metaphorically 'bite his lip' as he encountered evidence of their inexperience and lack of basic command skills.

The officers were pleased to see someone with some battle experience in a fairly vital position. But in all fairness, they gave the instructions, they made the final decisions. But they weren't afraid occasionally to come and ask the sergeant major's opinion and I wasn't afraid at times to voice my opinion if I thought something was wrong. I did one or two things off my own bat which nobody seemed to disapprove of! I had a battery captain to whom I was mainly responsible, a Captain Lees Smith. He was by profession a vicar; he was not the easiest chap to get along with, not because he was offensive, but because he dithered, he dithered too much for me! When you were used to certain officers who you'd been with for a number of years, you were able to judge them and see their value. Then you find yourself with a bunch of chaps who hadn't any experience. If you weren't careful you were drawing comparisons and I think that was unfair.[14]

Battery Sergeant Major Harold Harper, Headquarters, 426 Battery, 107th Medium Regiment

At last the German resistance in Caen crumbled, and on 21 July the South Notts moved forward. They were astounded at the scale of the damage the Allies had inflicted on the town.

> No earthquake could have created more havoc in such a large town than the perpetual bombing and shelling Caen had experienced over the last few days. The whole centre was one huge mass of fallen masonry, brickwork, buckled and twisted steel girders and charred woodwork. Roads were torn open and pitted with bomb craters in which the rain was settling in dull red pools. Complete carnage was visible on every hand as we passed through the streets, or rather valleys forced through the debris. It was impossible to distinguish any particular building, though to our left a mass of barely recognisable railway coaches and locomotives marked the site of the station. In that depressing drizzle the sight presented a truly grotesque picture. Absolutely unforgettable.[15]
>
> Signaller Ronald Paisley, D Troop, 426 Battery, 107th Medium RA

Pressing forward in front of them were their recce parties, led by the irrepressible Leonard Gibson.

> Caen fell and I was very fortunate in that I was right on the ball and wide awake in the move forward to Démouville – I got my recce parties through Caen before anyone else did. You see there was always a scramble for gun positions and first there, first served. You just had to stake your claim on the ground for where you wanted to put your guns. Then armour might want to come through where you were – infantry didn't matter, but armour was a bit of a problem – as you can imagine if you're just sighting your gun positions and a whole tank battalion arrives![16]
>
> Major Leonard Gibson, Headquarters, 107th Medium RHA

The only feasible gun positions he could find in these highly pressurised circumstances were in the tiny village of Démouville some 3 miles east of Caen. They were facing south, with 425 Battery on the left, 426 Battery to their right and the regimental headquarters in a chateau showing considerable signs of the bombing it had previously suffered. It proved a horrendous spot, as the ground was boggy and they couldn't dig out proper deep gun pits and had to improvise protective 'walls'. It was soon evident that they were located in a bulge in the British line and hence vulnerable to shellfire from both flanks as well as from the front. Soon German shells began to pour down on them, but, strangely, this resulted in a couple of funny stories.

> One of us found three or four little round boxes of Camembert cheese. That to us was an absolute luxury having not seen it for years. We handed this cheese in to Bombardier Platt in the officers' truck, with instructions that we were to have it that night on our biscuits for dinner. But during this artillery attack, one shell, fortunately a dud, went through the side of the lorry at head height, and out through the other side. When night came, we expected our Camembert for dinner, when with an absolutely bland face Bombardier Platt said, 'No, sorry, it was destroyed by the shell!' Later we heard that the staff were so put off by the smell of this cheese, not knowing what Camembert should smell like, that they couldn't bear the smell in the truck and decided to bury it – and blame it on the shell![17]
>
> Captain David Elliott, Headquarters, 425 Battery, 107th Medium RA

Albert Swinton also remembered a funny side to the shelling.

> There was a wall round this orchard, and I said to the gun sergeants, 'To save filling sandbags and messing about, knock holes in this wall so that you have enough room to swing your gun round!' Which they did! Things were pretty quiet and

that evening I went across to the other troop to see old 'Andy' Drewett. He was in this barn with a big jar of jellied eels; he'd found them in the house. We sat there and scoffed all these and drank a bottle of whisky between us. I went back to my gun and I must have flaked out! I woke up next morning and there was shell holes all round the place, half this wall was missing and there was me laid out on the deck. I looked round and a head peered out of a hole in the ground, 'Are you all right, Sarge?' I said. 'Yes, what's been going off!' 'Well we didn't want to wake you in case you got up and got killed. You were all right flat out on the deck!' Apparently old Jerry knocked hell out of us during the night, there were shells flying about all over the place – and there was me sleeping it off![18]

Sergeant Albert Swinton, B Troop, 425 Battery, 107th Medium RA

Doug Nicholls was not so amused by the German shellfire.

The arc of fire seemed to be about 180 degrees; wherever you looked there were enemies. We had a very difficult time there. It was the first time I had ever seen any real heavy fire. I was scared stiff! You just tried to concentrate on the job you were doing but it was difficult at times. On one occasion it got so heavy we were sent into the slit trenches. I left my boots on the top and when it eased off a bit my boots were holed with shrapnel![19]

Bombardier Douglas Nicholls, A Troop, 425 Battery, 107th Medium RA

The Luftwaffe also paid them far too much close attention.

At dusk every night we invariably had an exciting hour due to enemy air activity. I'd a splendid view one night of an ME109 as he dived low to strafe the position; a snub-nosed, black, sinister-looking object streaked across the sky flying very low. The brilliant red of his tracer bullets as he opened up. Just then the awful ripping sound of his bomb load as they struck earth between the wood and the village pinned me to the earth – thick black smoke curled skywards – that was enough for me. I flew, reaching the shelter of the trench without mishap.[20]

Signaller Ronald Paisley, D Troop, 426 Battery, 107th Medium RA

Yet to Paisley there was a pest that seemed far worse than the German aircraft.

One of our chief discomforts at Démouville were the swarms of mosquitoes. They appeared chiefly at dusk and made the narrow confines of trenches a veritable breeding ground. Night after night their sharp whine was a constant nuisance and oft times the result of night operations was visible next morning on the facial contours of all concerned. It was amusing sometimes when all was quiet about 1 a.m. to hear the muttered curses of their victims as they smote the air, right and left, usually with little or no effect. I've spoken to one or two of the chaps for their opinions of mosquitoes and they all say unhesitatingly that of mosquitoes and bombs they prefer the latter.[21]

Signaller Ronald Paisley, D Troop, 426 Battery, 107th Medium RA

However, one night they came under a concentrated night artillery bombardment. They had been shelled before; but this time the Germans clearly meant business.

I was awakened by a loud crump, sounding dangerously near, followed by another also in close proximity. The others were awake now, and five rather startled people looked fearfully at each other. In their sleepy state the effect might have been comical, but for the sense of impending danger. A loud explosion and a sound like a draught playing on a furnace reached our ears; the opening into our dugout reflected a flickering red glow; something was on fire. Heavy explosions were still in evidence and the roaring of flames becoming louder, intermingled with a peculiar hissing sound, occurring at intervals. Finally, Paddy, always curious, could curb his patience no longer and made for the entrance, raising his head through the narrow aperture. I heard him give vent to an alarmed exclamation, 'The Matador's on fire!' He was soon back in the safety of the dugout – and with good reason; the Matador was not more than 10 yards from our dugout and contained quite a large supply of high-explosive shells, cartridges and small arms ammunition. The hissing sound we could hear was due to the burning cartridges as they were flung through the air. Evidently the tractor had received a direct hit by a heavy shell. I looked out now – and just then another truck burst into flames. The orchard resembled a scene from Dante's *Inferno*.[22]

Signaller Ronald Paisley, D Troop, 426 Battery, 107th Medium RA

Next morning there was a scene of devastation, with the charred remnants of burnt-out Matadors and lorries. The exploding shells and cordite had devastated the gun position, with many of the gunners losing nearly all their personal kit. They were fortunate that they had suffered relatively few casualties in D Troop, but Gunners Henry Beardsworth[23] and Ernest Donaldson[24] had both been killed when the trench in which they were sleeping was hit by a heavy shell.

Our two unfortunate comrades were buried during the morning by the Roman Catholic padre. The whole troop was present – it was a very moving scene and still stands out vividly in my mind. As we listened to the last rites performed, my thoughts were rather bitter. It seemed hard that two chaps so young had to pay the supreme sacrifice and in such a violent manner. Only yesterday they had been laughing and joking with the rest; today two lifeless and broken forms, their part in the hubbub of war ended.[25]

Signaller Ronald Paisley, D Troop, 426 Battery, 107th Medium RA

The position was clearly no longer tenable. On 31 July, they moved to the nearby village of Mondeville, on the reverse slope of a hilly wood close to the eastern outskirts of Caen. This was an immeasurably better site for the guns, and they were barely disturbed throughout their stay there by either shells or bombs. This does not mean that the men were inactive. Perhaps it is inevitable that stories concern the incoming shells, but already the regiment had fired over 20,000 shells into the German lines. Although a signaller, Ronald Paisley helped on the guns during a night bombardment. The sheer power of the guns made a big impression on him.

> Our team was ready, 'Stand by!' 'Fire!' A terrific boom for the moment stunned the senses. The vivid flash at night necessitates the turning away of the head to save the eyes. The gun had barely ceased rocking when the next 100lb of metal was thrust into the breech and from then onwards all other sense was lost in the thunder of cannon. The earth shook as barrel after barrel probed the darkness with vicious sheets of flame. Time was forgotten. The prancing gun, the sweating gunners, the rhythm of a team in action, all added zest and excitement to the moment.[26]

Signaller Ronald Paisley, D Troop, 426 Battery, 107th Medium RA

The next large attack was Operation Totalise, to be launched by the Canadian Corps on 7 August. The intention was to advance towards Falaise covered by massed artillery and bombing raids. One of the bombers, hit by anti-aircraft fire, was forced to jettison its bombs, which unfortunately fell on the headquarters of the 9th AGRA located in a chateau – and also on a large ammunition dump nearby. The result was utter chaos. Charles Westlake had been detached as liaison officer to the 9th AGRA, where he was on wireless duties responsible for deciding whether targets justified a concentration of fire from more than one regiment.

> The brigadier had found himself some quite pleasant headquarters in a largish manor house. We were just having lunch in the officers' mess there. We'd just got as far as the dessert stage – prunes and custard! We'd heard planes going over, which nobody paid any attention to because there was wave after wave of American bombers going over. One of them started dropping their bombs round us! Which was most upsetting to put it mildly! It brought the ceiling down in the mess – shattered the windows. Everything was covered in plaster and people instinctively took cover, diving to the ground. The brigadier got up with prunes and custard, plaster and God knows what all over him! It wasn't really funny because the officer sitting opposite me at the table was killed – a bomb splinter went through him. One of the mess waiters was walking round with a long piece of bomb splinter straight through his calf – sticking out both sides. Quite a few were injured in the initial explosion. We were all ushered down into the cellars and going down there some more bombs exploded – and I got shot down these steps by the blast. My elbow hit a step on the way down and I dislocated my shoulder. The wounded were gathered together, but we couldn't be evacuated because they'd set on fire an ammunition dump just the other side of the track – and this was exploding all over the place. Nobody could get anywhere near us for quite some time.[27]

Lieutenant Charles Westlake, C Troop, 426 Battery, 107th Medium RA

Leonard Gibson was not that far away at his own headquarters when he heard the tremendous explosions.

I said to the adjutant, 'Look, I'd better go over and see if we can help in any way!' This young captain from one of the batteries rushed me over. We arrived to see our own brigadier, Brigadier Crosland, coming down the steps of the house in which they were billeted, covered with custard from head to foot! The young officer alongside him had been killed outright and Charles Westlake – our liaison officer with him – had been wounded. We were able to call up an ambulance and help.[28]

Major Leonard Gibson, Headquarters, 107th Medium RHA

Eventually ambulances got through and Westlake was safely evacuated to a field hospital. Here his shoulder was reset, but the ligament damage meant he was airlifted back to Britain to regain full use of his arm. Postings to various training regiments followed and he never got back to the South Notts Hussars.

THE NEXT STAGE IN THE ATTACK was a requirement from the Canadian Corps for close support for another attack to be carried out by the 3rd Canadian Division and the Polish Armoured Division on Quesnay Woods, which had hitherto been holding up the assault with an effective combination of well-dug-in panzers and a covering screen of 88mm guns in the trees. As a recognition of the seriousness of the resistance, a 1,000 RAF bomber raid had been arranged on the wood. The South Notts' role was to fire a preparatory programme from a position close by village of Cintheaux, then move forward to provide the closest possible support. This was a constant refrain from the Canadians.

We kept on moving forward and bringing the guns forward.
The Canadians reckoned they wanted our 100lb shells
being delivered as far forward as could be – rather than the
25-pounder landing. They pressed us all the time to be – really

– too far forward! There were no signs of infantry quite often – they hadn't come up – nothing to defend us – or our OP parties. We just had rifles and a revolver. It was a very fast-moving battle.[29]

Major Leonard Gibson, Headquarters, 107th Medium RHA

The guns moved forward to take up positions just to the right of the road near the village of Langannerie. Bob Foulds remembered organising the move.

We were to move to a position which was quite near to Quesnay Wood. I went out in the morning to recce this gun position on a reverse slope in a little valley. We got the director up and gun positions marked and so forth. I borrowed a motorbike to go back to bring the troop forward. As I went back, I passed a quarry and a lot of RAF top brass were sitting on the top edge of this quarry, with staff cars, binoculars and map board. They had a grandstand view of where these 1,000 bombers were going to come over and pulverise Quesnay Wood. Before I got to the old troop position to meet the guns coming out on to the Falaise road, further back than that, I could see marker bombs dropping, a sort of white phosphorous type of bomb which gave a huge spray. I was terribly apprehensive from that moment on![30]

Lieutenant Bob Foulds, B Troop, 425 Battery, 107th Medium RA

His worries were more than justified: it was soon evident that everything had gone wrong.

We'd no sooner got these guns in place when the bombers came over. For the first twenty minutes, it all came down on Quesnay Wood: tremendous bombing, clouds of smoke, dust and everything going up from these woods. Cheers all round, 'This'll show 'em!' All of a sudden, some bombs dropped behind us! Obviously back towards where these markers had fallen. From then on, they started bombing between Quesnay Wood and our old positions at Cintheaux! We had a very frightening afternoon – these bombs were just being dropped at random into the smoke that the previous ones had created. Once the target had been obscured they weren't navigating on to the target; they were bombing where the previous bombers had been.[31]

Lieutenant Bob Foulds, B Troop, 425 Battery, 107th Medium RA

The bombs crashed down all around him, stretching back all the way from Langannerie to Cintheaux. The 426 Battery had not yet moved forward, and hence were partially protected by their existing gun pits and dugouts. Never the less, Ronald Paisley was shaken by the earth-shattering detonations of bombs close by. It seemed they could not survive.

Cruuuuump! Debris and stones hurled against the trees above our shelter with the sound of a rainstorm. Cruuuuump! It was terrifying, the ground shook! Cruuuuump! Cruuuuump! Couldn't someone give warning or in some way make them understand. We hugged the earth. Cruuuuump![32]

Signaller Ronald Paisley, D Troop, 426 Battery, 107th Medium RA

Battery Sergeant Major Harold Harper was watching in horror and noticed a courageous air observation pilot in an Auster light aircraft, desperately trying to attract the attention of the bombers, flying in and out of the formation while firing Very signal lights.

Waves and waves of Lancasters – they were opening their bomb doors and they were raining down. It seemed ages before one of the little Auster aircraft went flying amongst them waggling his wings as much as to say something was wrong and directed them farther forward. As soldiers we were expected to be killed by the enemy, but one didn't fancy being killed by one's own air force.[33]

Battery Sergeant Major Harold Harper, Headquarters, 426 Battery, 107th Medium RA

Eventually, the bombers corrected their aim back to Quesnay Woods. At first it seemed likely that 426 Battery had been destroyed.

A final roar overhead and the sounds receded. We began to breathe again – bombs were still falling in the distance. Some of us ventured out. Thick black smoke blotted out entirely the sky-like smoke from burning oil. What of the guns? A huge crater showed about 10 yards from the nearest gun; there was no sign of the gunners. We learned later that they had fled at the sound of the first bomb. Examination of the position disclosed that five bombs had fallen between four guns; these were all miraculously enough unharmed; the craters were tremendous and how they survived remains a mystery. The tannoy lines of communications between guns and command post were broken and buried. An ack-ack officer on our position had been killed outright; one of our drivers had received injuries to the ear and forearm, and though a hospital case, was not seriously injured. He was our only casualty.[34]

Signaller Ronald Paisley, D Troop, 426 Battery, 107th Medium RA

It was a miraculous escape, especially as 425 Battery also had only a couple of casualties. The Poles were not so fortunate. The surrounding fields were littered with their corpses.

The Polish Division formed up on the road had taken the full brunt of this. They scattered into the fields alongside and done all they could to try and get out of the direct line of these

bombers. Many of the troops were just lying in the cornfields
days and weeks later.[35]

Lieutenant Bob Foulds, B Troop, 425 Battery, 107th Medium RA

Quesnay Woods were abandoned by the Germans next day and
so the advance to Falaise continued. The British and American
forces were acting in tandem, with the Americans speeding to
close the Falaise Gap from the direction of Argentan with the
intention of cutting off and trapping the bulk of the German
units engaged in facing the British.

On 16 August, the advance began to take on aspects of a
pursuit. The forward observation officers pressed against the
front lines, to such an extent that they even took prisoners, as
Leonard Gibson recalled.

> They were walking back, just giving themselves up and they
> came back through my OP post where I was watching all this.
> There was no one with them – they could have run away or
> done anything! The thing that struck me was that a lot of these
> so-called top German Army soldiers were nothing more than
> poor little schoolboys. It was quite extraordinary that they
> should have been there in the Panzer regiments at the forefront
> of battle. I reported this back and the adjutant's assistant
> answered me back when I told him that they were young and
> small – and that it might be of interest to High Command.
> This is the joke: I'm big – 6 foot 3: and he said, 'It's not fair, you
> should take someone on of your own height and weight!' He
> was quite a humourist, that boy![36]

Major Leonard Gibson, Headquarters, 107th Medium RHA

Next they approached the town of Trun. The Canadians were
still exerting great pressure on the gunners to get the guns as
far forward as possible. On 18 August this led to disaster, when
Colonel Oswald was taking a turn in looking for forward gun

positions on the high ground near Le Mesnil – an area which had supposedly been cleared of Germans.

> The Canadian Army wanted us forward, and more forward and more forward! One had to try and check that the area was clear of enemy, then move the guns up there – and then start firing on targets that their armour, or recce regiments, were sending down. The pace was so hot – they were so keen to cut off the whole of the German Fourteenth Army that were approaching Falaise. Colonel Oswald got his orders from the CRA, Fourth Canadian Armoured, and, as the recce was obviously going to be rather more dangerous, he was given a tank with a second tank to cover him. So he came up to me and said, 'Now you wait there and I'll have a look into this forward position here – and see if we can get the guns into that area that looks rather nice.' He was so fed up doing nothing, I think. Bit of bravado – I've got a tank – this is fun. He drove straight into a strongly held enemy position and he was bazookered and his tank put out of action – I think they were both put on fire. He jumped out of it, he got shot and they got hold of him. The Canadians weren't very happy about this – and I was the chap who had to go and tell them. My colonel has disappeared – I know he's been shot up. Whether he's alive or dead I don't know![37]

Major Leonard Gibson, Headquarters, 107th Medium RHA

In the confusion of orders and counter-orders that ensued they failed to find a suitable position from which to fire that day, during an otherwise successful Canadian attack that captured Trun.

On 19 August, however, the South Notts Hussars came into their deadly own. Gibson had moved the batteries forward to gun positions near Trun, and here they suddenly received reports that a large number of German troops were trying to break through all that was left of the Falaise Gap. They were not surveyed in and had no zero lines established so they used the airburst ranging method.

> I had to get my guns into action and start firing – that was quite a tricky thing – but our young officers were up to it. With no survey at all they would fire an airburst, by which the OP officer could get his bearings. Then they would fire a second one and then he could order them on to these various targets. We pumped 100lb shells into that area right through the day. The very second-rate German Army that had been in occupation in France since 1940 – really completely out of date. Horses – poor things. Later on, as we moved forwards, I saw all the damage we had caused, and it was heartbreaking – particularly when you see animals still alive – they hadn't been put out of their misery. By this time, I was hardened – you had to close your eyes and just get on. What our young unblooded men felt I don't know.[38]

Major Leonard Gibson, Headquarters, 107th Medium RHA

However, despite their success, it also became apparent that their gun positions were under serious threat as the Germans counter-attacked – from less than quarter of a mile away – with only a few infantry holding a line along the River Dives. With mortar and nebelwerfer shells falling close by, there were then reports of Tiger tanks rumbling forward. Gibson realised the great danger his men faced and took immediate action.

> It was far too far forward. We could have done better if we were 5,000 yards from our target; we got ourselves right up there where targets were as close as 2,000 yards. Now if we'd been field guns, we could have used ourselves as anti-tank guns and that would have been all right. It was reported that panzer tanks were within a very short distance of us, so all I could do was to move back to another position I had already reccied. It

was this Canadian brigadier had made us go so far forwards. I'd argued with him, and then I just took it into my own hands. We pulled out – we might have stayed – we might have been written off – we might have been heroes – I don't know! But I had the regiment and the men to think about and so I pulled them back about a mile and then we got into action again.[39]

Major Leonard Gibson, Headquarters, 107th Medium RHA

It was subsequently accepted that Gibson had done the right thing.

At this point Leonard Gibson was appointed to command the 107 Medium Regiment RA, with Major William Barber acting as his second-in-command, and Major Peter Birkin returning to take over command of 426 Battery. For a while, it seemed to be back to the future for the South Notts Hussars. Almost immediately this was overturned with the news that on 23 August, Colonel Oswald had managed to escape from the Germans. He had disguised his rank by removing his collar and tie, duping his captors into believing he was a lance bombardier, so he was not sent off with the other officer prisoners and managed to escape from the prisoner of war cage. He returned to the command but was promptly sent home on leave and Gibson remained in acting command.

The Falaise battles had ended with most of the German Seventh Army having been destroyed or in captivity. Many of the Canadian and British units, including the South Notts Hussars, were then given a precious period of respite. The regiment later made several short moves well behind the lines, staying at various French villages before ending up in the Rouen area.

Civilian life seemed to be restoring gradually to normal and we were encouraged by hand-waving and the appearance of the British flag with the French tricolour in the most odd places. It was obvious that the tempo of our advance was quickening. Buildings and villages presented themselves almost unmarked save for an odd gap torn in the brickwork by a tank or 88mm gun. Wreckage on the verges, of enemy tanks and lorries, was plentiful, with here and there the lone muzzle of an abandoned enemy gun thrusting its nose aggressively, but uselessly, Falaise-wards. Unused ammunition was strewn everywhere at random, together with numerous Bosche steel helmets and a number of potato-masher grenades. The enemy's flight had been one of complete confusion and indiscretion; it was a good sign.[40]

Signaller Ronald Paisley, D Troop, 426 Battery, 107th Medium RA

As they moved into areas that had not been devastated by the fighting they began to meet a more welcoming response from the French civilians.

One of the chief occupations was that of barter with the French people, cigarettes and soap being offered to them in exchange for butter and eggs. This was becoming almost an obsession now as we approached the farm districts, and the phrase, '*Avez vous des oeufs, s'il vous plait, pour cigarette?*' came into constant use. This opening phrase led the farm wife to believe that we could converse fluently in French and the result was a rapid counter-attack in that language. A shamefaced, '*Pardon?*' was all we could muster in reply! However, by making up various words from our limited vocabulary and by using signs, we found we could manage to understand fairly well, though with considerable laughter.[41]

Signaller Ronald Paisley, D Troop, 426 Battery, 107th Medium RA

In late August, Leonard Gibson took the opportunity to allow his men to go on unofficial leave sessions to Paris. A lorry load was despatched from each troop and most who fancied the trip were able to go. Ian Sinclair was one who went. The city had only just been relieved.

> We ran into gunfire, fighting on the outskirts. We could see the Eiffel Tower, so we had to do a quick detour. We drove up to the Arc de Triomphe and parked our wagon in the Place de la Concorde. Everybody was told they could go and please themselves. One of the unfortunate things was we had no money! So, there wasn't much we could do if we weren't getting hospitality! Other than go and look round. We kept very much out of the way of anybody who looked like they might be important, because we weren't there officially! It turned out to be a little bit of an anti-climax for a lot of people.[42]
>
> Lieutenant Ian Sinclair, Headquarters, 426 Battery, 107th Medium RA

Harold Harper certainly ran into trouble, being present during a famous dramatic incident.

> We were on the Place de la Concorde when General de Gaulle marched down there. We saw everything that was going off – and then suddenly somebody from the top window of a hotel[43] opened up with a machine gun. There we were lying on the Place de la Concorde with machine-gun bullets flying around us! We were cursing each other for whose idea it was to come to Paris![44]
>
> Battery Sergeant Major Harold Harper, Headquarters, 426 Battery, 107th Medium RA

Leonard Gibson took a party of officers with him and was determined to treat them to the best the city had to offer.

> Paris was still in the dark – there was no electricity. There was still a little bit of spasmodic fighting, but everyone was out in the streets celebrating and one could have drunk oneself stupid – as soon as they saw we were English – and we were the very

first English to be seen in Paris. I went into the famous Ritz Hotel, and took the adjutant and intelligence officer who were with me in my jeep. My driver and batman went off on their own – they were told to report back at 8 o'clock in the morning. The hotel had been taken over by General Eisenhower and his headquarters, so we were only allowed into some of the minor rooms. The one that I felt I really would have liked was a French dry martini! This I ordered and we all had one! It was so good we all had another. I said, 'Look, we'd better pay for this, how much is it?' It was an assistant manager – and whatever it was we had nothing like the amount of money required to pay for these drinks! So, I said, 'I'm awfully sorry about this, but I am a good customer of the Ritz in London. You are the same company, I will have to make some arrangement for paying the bill with the manager. The manager arrived and was so thrilled to see us and he said, 'Sir, don't bother about that, in fact, these are American prices you've been charged – if we'd known you were English! Well you are going to have not only those drinks with me on the hotel, but we'd be very pleased if you would now sit down and have dinner with us as well!'[45]

Major Leonard Gibson, Headquarters, 107th Medium RA

Ian Sinclair and his friends also found that they fell on their feet despite their lack of funds.

It caused great amusement and attracted a huge crowd of people in the Champs-Élysées when we got out our petrol brew cans and our kettles and made tea. Some chaps drank from their mess tins. The crowd grew and grew and grew at somebody lighting a fire in the Champs-Élysées – and even more exciting – we'd got tea. They'd never seen tea for years. So, we became everybody's friend very quickly. We had a very pleasant time just off the Champs-Élysées, where there were some celebrations going on – and there was lots of wine flowing![46]

Lieutenant Ian Sinclair, Headquarters, 426 Battery, 107th Medium RA

Ronald Paisley had not gone to Paris, but he wryly observed what most people remembered on their return.

They came back bursting with enthusiasm, mainly on the smart appearance of the mademoiselles with their almost consistent good looks, this naturally being the most striking impression they had had. Oh, yes, they'd noticed the Arc de Triomphe; no, they didn't remember seeing the Louvre – but the women! They waxed almost incoherent.[47]

Signaller Ronald Paisley, D Troop, 426 Battery, 107th Medium RA

With the fall of Paris many of the men may have thought the worst of the fighting was over, but although struggling, the German Army was by no means defeated. The war hadn't finished with the South Notts Hussars.

19

END GAME IN EUROPE

It's all very well in theory to 'give them stick' and 500 rounds of gunfire, but when you saw the damage that had been done, the corpses on the ground, it wasn't a very thrilling sight. On the other hand, they were there to do the same thing to us – so it couldn't be total remorse. It's just a messy horrid business. The more I think about it afterwards, the more messy and horrible I realise it all was.[1]

Lieutenant Bob Foulds, B Troop, 425 Battery, 107th Medium RA

THE EBULLIANT FIGURE OF MAJOR LEONARD GIBSON was determined to enjoy his periods in acting command of the 107 Medium Regiment while Colonel Oswald was absent, first as a prisoner, then in hospital and finally on leave. Gibson was the type of officer who always wanted to be involved in whatever was happening.

I could then go round the gun positions. If Gunner Bloggs said, 'Sir, do you see my boots! I've put in for new ones weeks ago and nothing's happened!' I would deal with that and he would get his boots. I helped everyone that I could. There were home problems and one wrote letters to families. That was a matter of shaking up the chain of command. I gather they all got to know me – rather Monty-like – it was a good thing! They couldn't really miss me at 6 foot 3, walking round. I wore rather a special battledress – tailored – smart – properly cut with lapels. I always wore a yellow tie, cream shirt. I don't think I ever wore a tin hat – it wasn't comfortable! Style and turnout are extremely important.[2]

Major Leonard Gibson, Headquarters, 107th Medium RHA

The relationship between Oswald and Gibson was of a professional nature, rather than any kind of warm friendship. Gibson privately believed that Oswald was somewhat bad-tempered and drank too much out of the line; but also thought that he was more concerned with his own career development, seeing the regiment as just a stepping-stone and a means of securing a Distinguished Service Order (DSO). In turn, it might be considered that Gibson was a little jealous: after all he had craved command of an artillery regiment and had turned down a staff promotion to lieutenant colonel to achieve it. Also Gibson was a self-confessed 'medal hunter' obsessed with 'winning' honours and decorations. This can be a reprehensible trait, but he also took care that his men got what he considered their proper reward for brave or dedicated actions. His experience from within the staff hierarchy meant he knew that a simple unvarnished account of 'duty done' got nowhere in the administrative labyrinth above them.

I think the regiment earned more honours and awards during the short time I was commanding than at any other time. When you decide someone had done a very good job, it was no good writing the job that they'd done; you had to write it up and double it, treble it and make it as good as you could – then you knew that officer would get his reward. You exaggerated; but absolutely merited![3]

Major Leonard Gibson, Headquarters, 107th Medium RHA

All told, both Oswald and Gibson had their merits and would provide good service to the regiment during their periods of interchanging command.

Alongside these mighty affairs of war, those of David Elliott may seem to be of little consequence, but he told a sad little story that demonstrates the sufferings of the French civilian population under German occupation. This was no cheery *'Allo 'Allo!* with its Café René setting, full of friendly Germans, cheery sex-workers and compliant proprietors. In the real world unbearable pressures were placed on individuals that forced them to act as collaborators just to stay alive. Elliott had served in France before as a stretcher-bearer with the 141st Field Ambulance, RAMC. As he passed through northern France, Elliott decided he wanted to pay a visit to one of his old haunts.

> I was near to Lens and Lille where I'd last been in May 1940. I immediately thought of the girl in the café at Halluin, whose name was Giselle, the café owner's daughter. She was a very popular girl in 1939, but however much we tried to take her out, none of us could get anywhere at all with her – all she was interested in was us soldiers spending their money and enjoying ourselves in the café. For sentimental reasons – and every other reason I thought, 'Well, I'll go and see if I can find her!' I had no difficulty in finding the café and I had an extraordinary welcome. When I went in there was quite a lot of noise and soldiers drinking. Behind the till in her usual place was Giselle. I like to think she recognised me because she called out, 'Monsieur David!', came through this crowd of soldiers and threw her arms round my neck. It did a lot for my morale! It certainly surprised the soldiers because I was then an officer. We had some soup and food – and of course my one desire – she was a very attractive girl – was to get her away and possibly find somewhere and spend the night with her! Remembering how

difficult it had been four years before, I found a very different
reaction. I said, 'Would you like to come down to Lille for
the evening?' 'Yes.' We got to this hotel in Lille, not a very
expensive hotel, had a meal and went to bed. Next morning,
I found when I woke up, she had her hair shaved off and her
hairpiece was lying by the side of the bed! She was in tears that
I'd found out. We found as we went through France this awful
business of old scores being paid off. She and other café owners
who had served Germans during the occupation in the course
of their job had had their hair shaved off as collaborators.[4]

Captain David Elliott, A Troop, 425 Battery, 107th Medium RA

AFTER THEIR REST and recuperation, the South Notts
Hussars were assigned to support the 3rd Canadian Division.
The Germans were intending to fall back on a defensive line
based on the River Meuse to defend the homeland, but still
sought to deny from the Allies the logistical benefits of posses-
sion of the Channel ports of Calais and Boulogne for as long
as possible. On 4 September, the regiment moved off towards
the Cap Gris Nez sector and by 10 September were in gun positions at Rinxent, just outside the town of Marquise. Here they
had batteries at both Cap de Gris and Calais well within their
range. The gun positions soon came under fire from one of the
heavy German coastal guns contained within the Cap Griz Nez
garrison.

At 4 a.m. on the morning of 14 September we were aroused
from slumber by an unholy crash near at hand, followed by
a rapid whirring over our tent. Shells, and big ones at that,
were bursting very close to the position. We remained in bed,
but rather anxiously awaited further explosions. Ten minutes
elapsed and all seemed quiet when, 'Crraaaash!' another one

struck the earth. A further 'Woo-Wwooing!' of metal flew through the air while we crouched flat. Heavens! They were big, much bigger than an ordinary field gun. We were wide awake now. From then on at ten-minute intervals others struck home and always the threatening sound of those chunks of jagged metal which could behead a man in an instant. Another violent explosion brought forth the comment, 'That one's nearer!' but we had escaped again. The suspense lasted until about 6 a.m. In all, fourteen super-heavy shells were fired, the nearer one being actually on the position, not many yards from our No. 1 gun. One chap had a narrow escape when shrapnel cut through the box on which his head was resting, as clean as a whistle.[5]

Signaller Ronald Paisley, D Troop, 426 Battery, 107th Medium RA

While the Canadians were preparing an assault, David Elliott, who had been promoted to command A Troop, went on a mission in a halftrack, seeking to establish an OP on a hill over-looking Cap Griz Nez.

I'd been told to go forward and get an observation post overlooking the Channel guns, which we'd heard firing the day before. The Canadians pointed out this hill which they said would give us a very good view. There was a track leading up and it was a dark night. It seemed fairly straightforward to drive up to the top – everything was very quiet. In the armoured halftrack, I had Ken Madden driving and myself in front, and Bombardier Shepherd and one or two signallers in the back manning the radio sets. As we approached the top of this hill we were shaken by this colossal explosion! I thought we'd been hit and were on fire because the whole of the cab filled with smoke. My immediate reaction was we were going to 'brew up', so I ran round the back to open the back of the halftrack to get my chaps out from inside. They were very stunned, and they came tumbling out. I then went on round the other side thinking that as we were all alive and kicking, poor Ken Madden most have copped it – I couldn't believe with a direct hit like that one of us wouldn't have been killed or injured. To my horror when I got to the front there was nobody there! I went on round the front of the vehicle, the smoke was blowing away – and I fell in the crater – by which time I realised we'd gone over a mine! Ken Madden came back from round my side and in broad Scotch he was asking me if I was all right. He'd bailed out of his side and gone round the front to get me out as I was going round the back – we were both all right! The front wheel and axle of the halftrack had been completely blown off![6]

Captain David Elliott, A Troop, 425 Battery, 107th Medium RA

The pair of them pushed on and managed to establish an OP up on the hill, from which they could direct fire right on to the German cross-Channel guns.

It was getting light, about 5 o'clock in the morning, a lovely summer's morning. The cliffs of Dover were very clear indeed. One of the cross-Channel guns opened fire and it was an extraordinary sight. I got my binoculars on the cliffs of Dover and I was able to see the smoke of the shell exploding behind Dover. We decided to open fire to try and stop these two German guns firing. We ordered the troop into action and as soon as Jack Attewell reported they were ready, we ordered one gun to fire a ranging shot. I put my binoculars on this colossal gun emplacement and waited for our shell to land. I didn't see anything at all. We repeated the exercise and I didn't use my binoculars – and to my surprise and amusement there was a great plume of water out in the Channel – we were very, very far off target. Much of it due to my own error in map reading and calculation, but the guns had by this time fired thousands and thousands of shells and we did begin to wonder! We gave corrections and very soon had a shell land on the top of this bunker. We ordered the troop to fire. I don't remember whether it had anything to do with stopping the Channel guns firing, but it certainly didn't have any impression on the concrete. When we went down two days later the area was like a lunar landscape. There were bomb craters inside other bomb craters – very big 'blockbuster' craters had smaller bomb craters in them – but it hadn't made any difference.[7]

Captain David Elliott, A Troop, 425 Battery, 107th Medium RA

The Canadian assault with Operation Undergo to capture Cap Gris Nez and Calais began on 25 September. That day, Douglas Nicholls, who had reverted to Gunner after being hospitalised with gastroenteritis, suffered a terrible leg wound.

We were firing at the German anti-aircraft guns. It was early in the morning and I was setting fuses; we were firing airburst. You have a key with numbers on it and you were given a setting and you had to bend down and set the fuse to the setting required. That's when I got hit – a piece of shrapnel hit me in the leg – the top of my left thigh. It was like a dull thud – a numbing pain – and suddenly my leg went weak. I remember sitting down. One chap on the gun, his name was Jack Pettitt and he looked a bit sick when he saw it. He pulled out some field dressing and put it on. A piece of shrapnel about 2 inches by 1 inch had shattered the bone into a lot of little pieces – it smashed the thigh. Our medical orderly, Tom Madeley, came and put me on a stretcher. They put a Thomas Splint on my leg. I can remember Tom putting a pad on my face – and he was dropping chloroform on to put me out of it. I came round when we were going over a ploughed field in a jeep, bumping up and down – I was in a lot of pain then because the sensation was beginning to come back.[8]

Gunner Douglas Nicholls, A Troop, 425 Battery, 107th Medium RA

Nicholls was evacuated to hospital in St Omer, where they put on a temporary plaster to immobilise his shattered leg.

> I had an idea it was pretty bad. I thought to myself, 'That's the end of my football career!' It was touch and go – they told me later I might have lost my leg. I'd always thought to myself, 'If ever I do get wounded, I hope it's not in the stomach or the head – I hope it's in the leg!' And it was; so I was pleased about that![9]

Gunner Douglas Nicholls, A Troop, 425 Battery, 107th Medium RA

Behind him the Canadian assault had been successful with the capture of Cap Gris Nez on 29 September, followed by the fall of Calais the next day. The Battle for France was over.

THE NEXT MAJOR OBJECTIVE was to secure unimpeded sea access to Antwerp, which had been captured on 3 September but which was not yet 'open' as the Germans still controlled the Scheldt estuary. The massive Allied armies in North-west Europe were voracious for stores, supplies and munitions and, even augmented by the Channel ports, there was still insufficient capacity. It was essential that the massive port facilities of Antwerp be captured, repaired and utilised as soon as possible. The South Notts Hussars initially moved to the area of the Leopold Canal in north-west Belgium. Their role was to support the crossing of the well-defended Leopold Canal Line, which was to be carried out by the 3rd Canadian Division. Gun positions were established behind the village of St Laurent, close to two farmhouses on either side of the road, just 300 yards from the canal bank. As soon as they started firing the preparatory bombardment, the Germans retaliated with everything they had.

Heavy concentrations of mortars pounded the near bank of the canal daily. Nights were exceptionally noisy with the din of our own guns blending with the shell bursts of the enemy. Light, medium and heavy guns hurled over shell after shell and the night was rarely dark for long. Flashes played like lightning over wrecked buildings – tracers criss-crossed the sky in pencils of red. Heavy shells began dropping behind us and lighter stuff to our flanks. The ripping sound of an occasional air burst kept heads down. Slit trenches are of little use against the latter unless amply covered with timber and earth. By day it was quieter, but none the less consistent, and we had an excellent view of the Typhoons as they cut up the far bank of the canal.[10]

Signaller Ronald Paisley, D Troop, 426 Battery, 107th Medium RA

Albert Swinton was shocked by the German use of flamethrowers.

I thought flamethrowers were the most diabolical weapon I'd ever seen in my life. We were one side of the canal and the Germans were the other side – it was so close. You could see these things. I couldn't put up with that – just burning people alive – it didn't seem right somehow! It's not a gentleman's fight! The fact that I was blowing them to bits didn't matter![11]

Troop Sergeant Major Albert Swinton, B Troop, 425 Battery, 107th RHA

The Germans fought hard, but the concentration of artillery fire and the ceaseless air attacks were too much for them; eventually they began to fall back northwards towards the town of Oostburg. The 107th Medium RA began to follow up the advance to the north, dropping into action as required to assist the Canadians. The Germans were desperate to deny Antwerp to the Allies and although the south bank of the Scheldt estuary was eventually cleared, they still retained a firm grip on the islands of Walcheren and South Beveland which together formed the north bank.

The first task was South Beveland. The plan was bold: while the 2nd Canadian Division launched a desperate attack pushing westwards on to the island along the 2-mile-wide narrow causeway, the 156 Brigade of the 52nd (Lowland) Division, accompanied by a squadron of the Staffordshire Yeomanry in amphibious DD Sherman tanks, would launch a seaborne landing on the south-east corner of the island. On 23 October, the whole of the 9th AGRA was concentrated on the headland directly opposite the island ready for the attack, with the South Notts Hussars clustered round the village of Groenendijk. The dank, cold, miserable weather marked the imminent onset of winter.

> There were the usual discomforts – repairing line to guns at night in pitch darkness, mud and rain, doing odd jobs with the aid of a broken hurricane lamp – dismal meals with numb hands and the usual anticipation of enemy shelling which, like the sword of Damocles, was always suspended over our heads. However, most of us kept fairly cheerful and good humoured and often laughed at our own misfortunes – a British trait.[12]
>
> Signaller Ronald Paisley, D Troop, 426 Battery, 107th Medium RA

In the wet, low-lying ground of Belgium and the Netherlands, it was often necessary to build gun platforms.

> We had a great deal of problems with the heavy guns – as soon as you fired them, they started to dig into the ground. The softer the ground, the further they went in, until it became impossible to move the trails round. So, we became engineers, we constructed platforms of railway sleepers and goodness knows what to park these guns on, so that we could keep them firing.[13]
>
> Lieutenant Bob Foulds, Headquarters, 425 Battery, 107th Medium RA

The attack was launched at 05:45 on 26 October. The South Notts Hussars forward observation officers would accompany the infantry and tanks as they crossed the Scheldt. The 425 Battery would supply two forward observation officers to the 52nd (Lowland) Division: Major James Martin would be one, but David Elliott realised that either he or his friend Eric Dobson would have to be the other; he did not relish the prospect. The Scheldt was a veritable sea and at the other side were the entrenched Germans.

> Eric immediately said it was his turn to go, but James replied that this was something quite different from the skirmishes we had been taking part in lately and that we should toss for it. I could hardly believe my ears, but he was already taking a coin out of his pocket! I had a foreboding that my luck was running out and I certainly did not relish any mock heroics of winning the toss and volunteering to go! I put my hand on his arm just in time to stop him tossing the coin and said, 'You say: "heads" David goes and "tails" Eric goes!' Of course, it came down heads and with a horrible empty feeling in my stomach I knew I had to do the seaborne crossing. I met Ian Sinclair, recently promoted to Troop Commander of C Troop, and learnt that he was to travel in an amphibious Sherman tank (a DD tank) belonging to the Staffordshire Yeomanry – I do not think he was any happier about the plan and his brief than I was.[14]
>
> Captain David Elliott, A Troop, 425 Battery, 107th Medium RA

He was assigned to the 6th Cameronian Highlanders as they crossed the Scheldt in their Buffalo assault craft. He had been allotted a M29 Weasel, a small tracked vehicle capable of dealing with rough ground and with a very limited amphibious capacity, which – just about – fitted inside one of the Buffalo troop-carrying amphibious craft. Elliott took the precaution of taking with him a beer bottle filled with rum.

There was just room for Bombardier Shepherd and my signaller to stand with me by one side of the Weasel and peer out at the rapidly approaching sea, which appeared wet and cold and horribly choppy in the morning mist. With a sudden lurch which threw us all together we were in the water and floating. The tracks churned madly, and we started to follow the bobbing rear lights in front. I felt that our successful launching called for a nip of rum and passed the bottle round. We were soon out of sight of land and everything was quiet except the low pop-popping of our engines and the slap of small waves against the side of our craft.[15]

Captain David Elliott, A Troop, 425 Battery, 107th Medium RA

As the barrage opened up, the skyline behind them was lit up with gun flashes. They had lost their way and a green light ahead told them that they were approaching the wrong beach.

The noise of the shells screaming overhead was very frightening and the sudden feeling of being lost and absolutely alone most unnerving. I passed the rum bottle around again and stood up front next to the driver. Dawn was coming fast and there – looming out of the mist – was the sea wall. As suddenly as it had started the barrage stopped, and I realised that the assault troops would be going ashore without us. Before I could encourage the marine to make greater speed, a machine gun opened up on us from the shore. Fortunately, the gunner's aim was faulty at first and we all dropped to the bottom of our craft and watched the tracer bullets passing overhead. It was too good to last. The semi-darkness was lit by a flare and the bullets began to clatter on the small part of the armour-plated side of the Buffalo which was above the waterline. We were safe enough lying in the bottom. The rum bottle went round again – and this time was quickly finished. During these few minutes the Buffalo had ploughed its way on south and, as the flare dropped into the sea and went out, the machine gun stopped firing.[16]

Captain David Elliott, A Troop, 425 Battery, 107th Medium RA

To his great relief, they then spotted the amber light which indicated the correct beach.

As we approached the shore there was an explosion and an amphibious vehicle of some sort burst into flames on top of the sea wall – the landing was certainly not unopposed and from the crack it sounded as though we were up against 88mm guns again. The garish light of the brew-up helped our approach run but, to my consternation, I could see a line of wooden stakes sticking out of the water at the foot of the sea wall. Nobody had warned us of this – or the aerial photographs had failed to spot this extra hazard. The marine's instructions had been to take us over the wall before unloading, but he took one look at the height of the barrier and at the water lapping the bottom of the stakes and lowered his ramp. He said words to the effect that he was: 'Buggered if he was going over the top!' All four of us were now standing in water up to our knees wrestling with the stakes. Fortunately, it did not take much to work them loose from the mud, though there is no doubt they would have wrecked the tracks of our small Weasel had we tried to drive over them. Shepherd now climbed into his cramped driving seat, let off the brakes – and our vehicle rolled out of the Buffalo into the muddy surf.[17]

Captain David Elliott, A Troop, 425 Battery, 107th Medium RA

There was still the sea wall towering above them.

I told Shepherd he was to drive our vehicle over the wall as fast as he could and that in order to decrease the chance of casualties the signaller and I would crawl over the top. Imagine my surprise when I saw as much water in front of us as we had left in the Scheldt behind us! The Germans had flooded all the land, the only dry parts being the road and verges running inland. Before I could go back and warn him – Shepherd was over the top. For a moment the vehicle hovered on the brow and then – seemingly out of control – it crashed down 20 feet on to the perimeter road which ran round inside the sea wall, bounced once, skidded off into the flooded area with a great splash and floated. Bombardier Shepherd was soon in control again and thankfully there was now no doubt that the vehicle was amphibious.[18]

Captain David Elliott, A Troop, 425 Battery, 107th Medium RA

They had completely lost touch with the Cameronians, for whom they were meant to be providing fire support. Elliott moved inland along the road, passing wrecked German vehicles that marked the passage of the Scots. Eventually he located the battalion headquarters.

A tin-hatted Scotsman waved us down and told us Battalion HQ was round the next bend and that the CO was enquiring for us. I found the colonel and his adjutant sitting on the grassy bank eating a sandwich of bully beef and dry biscuit. He immediately asked if I was ready to engage a target – no questions as to where we had been or any recriminations at all – which was a relief! I told Bombardier Shepherd to contact the regiment and give the orders 'Take Post' whilst I obtained particulars of the target. It transpired that the Germans had at least two 88s in front of us and that they were giving each other covering fire as they retreated inland. At the moment, they were thought to be in some farm buildings about half a mile ahead which was also defended by machine guns. Our maps were accurate, and we were able to identify the buildings and pass the map reference to the guns. In an impressively short time I had a gun ready, was able to range on to the target and then give five rounds of gunfire.[19]

Captain David Elliott, A Troop, 425 Battery, 107th Medium RA

More targets were identified and engaged as they began to carry out their allotted role. During the afternoon they were held up half a mile short of a village.

I found the colonel lying on the bank peering across the fields at the outskirts of the village and the row of Dutch houses which were concealing the machine gunners and goodness knows what else. There was very little cover for the Scotsmen to advance across and just at that moment we saw three grey-clad men crouching down and hurrying behind a hedge in the distance. The CO gave the command for a platoon to open up with rifles on the bushes behind which the men had vanished. It was then that I borrowed a rifle from a nearby man who was helping set up a 3-inch mortar. I did not fire many rounds and have no idea whether any found their target – but I did have a feeling of satisfaction – that in some way I had got some of my own back.[20]

Captain David Elliott, A Troop, 425 Battery, 107th Medium RA

When asked by the colonel if he could supply an artillery support for an attack on the village, Elliott called up the massed fire of the whole of 9th AGRA to provide a creeping barrage moving slowly forward in front of them.

I gave the order, 'Fire!' from the safety of the roadside bank and with my head just over the edge of the road I watched these brave Scotsmen advance across the field towards the smoke of our bursting shells. The noise was indescribable. Every half-minute the barrage lifted 50 yards towards the village and, as the men vanished into the smoke by the hedge, I realised the predicament of those men who had to keep close to our bursting shells so as to reach the enemy before they had a chance to recover and, at the same time, if they got too close there was the very real danger of being hit by a fragment of our own shells. I am very thankful to be able to say that the Cameronians reached the village almost unopposed – the enemy had done another withdrawal.[21]

Captain David Elliott, A Troop, 425 Battery, 107th Medium RA

As night fell, Elliott made his way back to the brigade headquarters.

A cheerful voice called me out of the darkness – it was Lance Bombardier Ward, our battery commander's very experienced signaller. James Martin had posted him outside to meet us. Jimmy Ward told Shepherd where to take the Weasel and how to find the cookhouse and then said he would take me to the battery commander. I walked by the side of this man in the pitch black of that never to be forgotten night – because the next thing I knew was a flash and an explosion and I was blown off the road into the ditch at the side. My head hurt, but otherwise I seemed to be all in one piece and so I pulled myself back on to the road on my stomach feeling sure somebody would come hurrying to see what had happened and the nightmare would soon be over – but not a sound of anybody. I called the bombardier's name but still silence and then I reached him lying in the middle of the road. I could not feel any sign of life and when my hand reached the back of his head my fingers could tell that Jimmy Ward[22] was indeed dead. I got to my feet covered in mud and blood. The explosion had been a mortar shell which had passed close by my head before exploding on the road on the other side of my companion and his body had shielded me by taking the full blast. My luck had not run out after all.[23]

Captain David Elliott, A Troop, 425 Battery, 107th Medium RA

The mortar shell had been fired by an isolated group of Germans that had been missed in the day's frenetic fighting. All Elliott had suffered was a cut on the cheek caused by a flying stone.

MEANWHILE CAPTAIN IAN SINCLAIR was suffering a no less dramatic and stressful time as he accompanied Sherman tanks of the Staffordshire Yeomanry across the Scheldt. As an exceptionally poor sailor he would have far preferred to stay on dry land.

> I went to report to this brigade headquarters and was shattered
> to find out that I was going in one of these wretched Sherman
> DD tanks with the Staffordshires! We weren't using our own
> signalling; we were using the tank radio back to brigade,
> who were in touch with the gun positions, relaying targets.
> Remembering my propensity for being seasick – that alone was
> enough to make me feel that I'd rather be anywhere else! It was
> quite an experience when you knew you were no longer on dry
> land – driving into the sea! Standing on the outside of the tank
> and you've got canvas wall around. It propelled itself very, very
> slowly towards the enemy. It wasn't very far – 2,000 to 3,000
> yards. I wasn't seasick on this occasion![24]
>
> Captain Ian Sinclair, C Troop, 426 Battery, 107th Medium RA

The crossing seemed to take for ever and for most of that time Sinclair felt incredibly vulnerable.

> Anybody seeing you would have no trouble picking you
> off! But we'd got everybody's heads down with all the firing
> we'd been doing from the mainland. Before we got onshore,
> we were in all sorts of trouble. Considerable gunfire against
> the attacking force; more than anybody had appreciated.
> My tank did not get ashore, it was hit in the tracks at water-

level – the shell didn't come inside the canvas wall. The tank was immobilised, and we were on the sea bottom – beached about 100 yards off. Everybody except me bailed out! We were beaching at low tide and they could just walk holding their equipment and rifles up before they got on to the beach.[25]

Captain Ian Sinclair, C Troop, 426 Battery, 107th Medium RA

Sinclair had no alternative but to stay where he was.

I was in touch by radio with the brigade – having to tell them what had happened. You could see over the top of the canvas screen stood on the turret, with a microphone down to the radio inside the tank relaying information. I was also in touch with the people who had landed, found by a map reference where they needed help, then able to tell brigade where our gunfire was needed. They decided which guns were going to fire. It might not have been my guns at all. I became a vital link for infantrymen, tank men and other gunners who had managed to get ashore. I was also very frightened – I didn't think I was ever going to get out. I spent a day and a whole night there.[26]

Captain Ian Sinclair, C Troop, 426 Battery, 107th Medium RA

At night, the tide came in. It's easy to appreciate the horror of his situation: under heavy fire, all alone, aground in a tank with only the turret poking above the waves.

That was very frightening – I thought I might be swamped. The thing didn't float, it was bogged down. I got inside the tank, pulled the lid down and told them what the situation was. Water was coming in! When the tide went out again, I went back outside again and was able to get out. Other forward observation officers had come across and had got on to the island.[27]

Captain Ian Sinclair, C Troop, 426 Battery, 107th Medium RA

Sinclair was eventually awarded the Military Cross for his courage.

For two days the 5.5-inch guns supported the 51st Division and 2nd Canadian Division in the bitter fighting raging on South Beveland. At last the German resistance broke.

The 9th AGRA were now required to supply the artillery support for the assault on Walcheren. This time they moved round the southern bank of the Scheldt to take up gun positions underneath the sea wall at Breskins.

> Guns were lined up facing over the dykes and sea to where the Walcheren port of Flushing reared its cranes and warehouses, just then invisible in the November murk. To our right front was the hamlet of Hoofdplatte, huddled under one of the dykes – elsewhere was flat uninteresting marshland.[28]

Signaller Ronald Paisley, D Troop, 426 Battery, 107th Medium RA

It seemed likely that Walcheren would be even more of a problem as it was almost completely an island, connected to South Beveland only by a very narrow causeway. On 1 November, the seaborne assault by the Buffalos of the 51st Division was augmented by a Commando assault on the docks of the port of Flushing. Eric Dobson had been promoted to command B Troop and he remembered their role in assisting the attack.

> After a heavy fire programme, the Commandos, followed by 4th King's Own Scottish Borderers and a mountain battery, landed safely, though a few craft were lost. From the sea wall in front of B Troop, a German coast defence gun could be seen firing at the landing craft. It was quickly registered by B Troop through several temporarily unemployed members of the battery; a signaller was posted with a telephone in an attic window and every time he saw a flash from the gun he ordered, 'Target B.1: one round gunfire!' The coastal gun was

almost certainly in a concrete emplacement and even a direct
hit might not have knocked it out; but four medium rounds
falling every time it fired must have been disturbing for the gun
detachment.[29]

Captain Eric Dobson, B Troop, 425 Battery, 107th Medium RA

The island finally fell on 4 November. The entrance to Antwerp
was now free and once the German minefields blocking the
Scheldt were cleared, then the logistical situation would be
transformed for the Allies.

After calibrating the guns over the Scheldt, the 107th
Medium RA moved on 7 November on the long journey to
the eastern Netherlands. Driving conditions were awful, with
a combination of unmetalled roads, deep dykes lurking for the
unwary and traffic jams from the press of military traffic to the
front. They eventually took up firing positions at Tunglerooi,
some 3 miles south of the town of Weert.

On 13 November, they and the rest of the 9th AGRA joined
a mass artillery barrage in support of a successful XII Corps
assault across the Canal du Nord and River Meuse towards
Roermond. This was another world from the situation earlier
in the war; now the rear areas were so crowded with guns that it
was difficult to find any feasible unoccupied gun positions. The
barrages generated were destructive maelstroms which blasted
apart the German defences and shell-shocked their infantry.

The 107 Medium RA then moved forward to gun positions
in Roggel, just a couple of miles from the Meuse. This proved a
dangerous salient and that night, shell and mortar fire poured
down upon them. As a signaller, it was part of Ronald Paisley's
job to keep the telephone lines repaired.

Our lines were cut by close mortar fire, the six- barrelled
nebelwerfer – the scream as they hurtled over was unnerving.
Our position was, I think, known to the enemy. The nights and

early mornings we lay listening to the crump of violent shell bursts were rather terrifying. It was quieter during the day, but the position was often threatened even then. One night a string of anti-personnel bombs from an enemy plane burst around our billet. Going up the line was common to do a repair, and as it was usually night it was an unenviable job.[30]

Signaller Ronald Paisley, D Troop, 426 Battery, 107th Medium RA

Strive as they might, the German gunners were hopelessly out-numbered, and the massed guns of the Allies forced them to either pull back – or be destroyed. The superiority was such that even a piece of personal vanity from the 9th AGRA commander, Brigadier Walter Crosland, could be accommodated.

On 20 November, the brigadier celebrated his birthday by firing the whole AGRA on to a target in Germany for the first time. There had been keen rivalry between the regiments to have the honour of being the first, but the brigadier's shoot meant that all the sixty-four guns in the four regiments did it within the space of one second. There was no question of being the first gun to have fired into Germany, for already XXX Corps further south had crossed the River Meuse with the Americans and most of the targets were in the Fatherland.[31]

Captain Eric Dobson, B Troop, 425 Battery, 107th Medium RA

The infantry pushed forward and soon the west bank of the Meuse was cleared.

On 25 November, the recce parties were preparing the gun positions for the next move to the village of Maasbree, just 5 miles short of Venlo. Here they encountered another threat: Bombardier Beaumont was setting up a survey point when he detonated a mine and had his foot blow off. Seeing what had happened, Gunner Harry Barnes went into the minefield to try to rescue his friend – an act of supreme courage. Sadly, he too trod on a mine and had his own leg blown off just under the knee. Somehow, Barnes managed to drag both himself and Beaumont out of the minefield. Gibson went to visit them afterwards in hospital.

> Those two poor chaps were carted off to hospital. As soon as I heard I went to see them. Here they were with amputated limbs behind a shield. They said, 'We knew, Sir, you wouldn't be long in coming to see us!' They were smoking! Cheerful as anything and saying, 'Do you know it's a wonderful feeling being able to waggle your toes!' And there they were with no legs.[32]

Major Leonard Gibson, Headquarters, 107th Medium RHA

Once the gun positions had been established, it soon became apparent that the whole area was infested with German anti-personnel mines. This rather played on the nerves of Ken Giles.

> This business of the mines was rather terrifying. I had to take the director out each morning to put the guns on line. By now snow was falling and a lot of the ground had ceased to become waterlogged but was just frozen. We knew that beneath the ground were – possibly – anti-personnel mines. I chose a path that looked pretty clear to me from what I could see of the remains of white tape. I used to take my director along this path about 200 yards and set it up there. As I did so I had to pass by a half-ploughed field and in this field were two shire-like horses who had obviously trodden on a mine and their bellies had been disembowelled – and there they lay. Magnificent animals. They didn't smell because the weather was so cold – I guess their entrails were just frozen. But the sight was dreadful. I would get my director legs, the tripod, on to the position I chose – and then you had to ram the sharp points home with your heel! You have no idea with what trepidation I did that! Then with a thankful prayer in your heart you would walk

quietly and gently, as though walking on a tightrope, back to the command post.[33]

Bombardier Ken Giles, B Troop, 425 Battery, 107th Medium RA

That night, the Luftwaffe also made an unwelcome reappearance.

We were all seated around the hurricane lamp, having a kind of general discussion when the screaming of the fuselage wires of a plane neared the billet, then a series of sharp explosions burst out. There was a general panic for the slit trenches, some of us hit the deck quickly and waited rather fearfully. Heavy ack-ack opened up as the plane swooped in again – 'Great Scott!' – more violent explosions, the impact of a heavier bomb, and we breathed again. We were rather glad when the time came for us to leave Maasbree.[34]

Signaller Ronald Paisley, D Troop, 426 Battery, 107th Medium RA

After a brief move south on 28 November, to the village of Eigenlines near Maastricht, they moved on 3 December to the town of Sittard. Their arrival was not propitious. As the recce parties tried to identify suitable gun positions, a high-flying German jet bomber dropped its bombs apparently at random. The effects were devastating. Bob Foulds was in charge of the recce parties as the command post officer of 425 Battery.

I went in with a recce party and we'd staked out gun positions for A and B Troops on the right-hand side of a reverse slope hill, on the outskirts of this small town. Then I went back across the road and I told two signallers, Sergeant Miles and Gunner Annan, to go down to make a temporary command post in a sort of pavilion the other side of a little park on the left-hand side of the road. They'd no sooner moved off and there was a terrible scream, a German plane diving and it put a stick of bombs across the park. It killed Miles[35] and Annan[36] outright.

We went rushing down to see what was left of them: the bomb burst right alongside them, and they were both very dead when we got down there. Annan lying on his face and Miles lying on his back. We sent for some stretchers. One or two Dutch civilians had turned up by that time. We lifted Annan on to a stretcher. As I helped lift Miles on the stretcher, he was lying on his back and his face looked undamaged, but when we picked him up, his brain fell out of the back of his head on to the floor. I had the job whipping off to get a spade and bury this before a gawping crowd of Dutch civilians. I always have it on my conscience that I sent them there to their deaths: there's no reason at all why I should, because I was just doing what I had to do, but I was very upset at the time. And certainly, when I wrote to their two families, I was very moved by that.[37]

Captain Bob Foulds, Headquarters, 425 Battery, 107th Medium RA

The South Notts Hussars were still at Sittard on 14 December, when the Germans launched their last-gasp offensive in the Ardennes with the 'Battle of the Bulge'.

We gathered there was no way that the Germans were going to win this war. That it was inevitable, just a question of time, how quick, or how long! It changed the attitude of both sides. You realised that things were coming to a finish, therefore you were a trifle more careful in what you did and where you went – not nervous! You kept your ears and eyes open that little bit extra! Whereas the Jerries realised that this was the end for them, and it was a question of keeping us out of Germany.[38]

Battery Quartermaster Sergeant David Tickle, Headquarters, 425 Battery, 107th Medium RA

The German Ardennes offensive caused a massive redeployment of British artillery, armour and infantry divisions in their ulti-mately successful attempt to help the Americans in stemming the German tide. However, throughout all this panic and frenetic activity, the South Notts Hussars stayed in place at Sittard. Their problems were more local. On 20 December, giant shells began to fall around the gun positions.

> We came under shellfire from heavy guns, 210mm, terrifying speed and burst; one heard the boom of the guns and almost instantaneously an unholy crash and telltale whine of hot, jagged metal. It was dangerous to be above ground at all and, if on guard, one's position was unenviable. C Troop suffered with the first onslaught and had a number of casualties, some fatal, in their gun pits. The second night they opened up again and we had an alarming three hours in the cellar. They fell quite near, but just off the position; they struck earth with the sound of a bomb rather than a shell, and the guns were evidently ranging on our own gun flashes. The tension was such that the commanding officer thought it advisable to move into an alternative position, as not only our own men and equipment, but the civilians looked like suffering – their houses being in direct line of fire.[39]

Signaller Ronald Paisley, D Troop, 426 Battery, 107th Medium RA

Eric Dobson noticed the pronounced effect the German shells, dropping as regularly as clockwork, had on the morale of his men.

> The gun firing on to Sittard produced a state of nervousness in the regiment that almost nothing throughout the war had been able to produce. One felt so helpless. Fortunately, the gun never fired in daylight, thereby confirming the theory that it was a railway gun, kept in a tunnel to be screened from air observation. On 23 December Colonel Oswald decided to pull his batteries back to Geleen, from where they could still cover their defensive commitments. Regimental headquarters

remained where it was, 425 Battery moved to the east side of the road on the forward edge of the town, and 426 Battery to the west side of the road and slightly further back. Everything possible was done to avoid firing from these positions at night, and from the outset each troop went out in turn to a position of its own choosing to spend the night firing harassing programmes and to return before dawn. The monster gun never got the range of Geleen, but the move from Sittard had been particularly well timed; within a few hours of the regiment's departure shells fell full on to three of 425 Battery's now empty gun pits.[40]

Captain Eric Dobson, B Troop, 425 Battery, 107th Medium RA

Although Geleen was only 4 miles further back, it provided a relative rest cure for the somewhat shaken gunners. Indeed, they found comfortable billets and were even able to celebrate Christmas.

Marie, a very genial and friendly young woman, took us into her custody and made us at home with little ceremony. Geleen, I think, was the best and quietest position we ever had in action. For three weeks, including Christmas and New Year, we enjoyed a life of comfort almost amounting to luxury. [We] had the use of a sitting room and bedroom. Coffee suppers, presided over by the pleasant, smiling face of our hostess, were an order of the day each evening. It seemed to be such a pleasure to her to do every job for us.[41]

Signaller Ronald Paisley, D Troop, 426 Battery, 107th Medium RA

The only problem at Geleen was the severe snowfalls. Ted Holmes was working with a troop on ammunition resupply and he well remembered the effects.

It was ever so cold. It was so cold that any metal, the shells, or the side of the gun, your fingers stuck to it with the intense cold. If you had any gloves it just pulled the fingers off the glove – metal when it gets real freezing – it's like a glue. When you picked a shell up you had to sort of peel your fingers off it one by one. It was the coldest I've ever known it. Fortunately, near there was Sittard, a big coal-mining area and you could get coal easily. We had accumulated a few bits of old doors and things and we used to dig holes in the ground and put these boards to make a roof. We'd make a little stove and a chimney, and you could get a little fire going.[42]

Gunner Ted Holmes, 425 Battery, 107th Medium RA

Ken Giles suffered a severe attack of Raynaud's circulatory disease due to these excessive cold conditions.

The weather was so cold that drivers had to turn the engines of their vehicles over about once an hour in order to keep the things going. The guns had to be fired during the day, even if there were no targets to fire upon, fired at random, in order to keep the mechanism worn so that the buffer oil should not freeze. My own troubles were due to this Raynaud's circulatory condition. I was beginning to feel the effects of the very cold weather. On one occasion the temperature was down to minus 7 degrees Fahrenheit. It was cold! I was on an errand from the command post to one of the gun pits, and upon my return I came over quite ill. If one's fingers go numb and white, that is a great inconvenience, but they don't really stop you doing things. But if they start to go very, very red, almost vermillion, they hurt. There comes a point when the pain reaches an intensity and you pass out – as I did that night. When you come to, you feel very, very ill indeed, as white as a ghost and bathed in gallons of perspiration.[43]

Bombardier Ken Giles, B Troop, 425 Battery, 107th Medium RA

As a result of his collapse Giles was given a period of temporary light duties at the 425 Battery office. He then triggered a further relapse by engaging in a snowball fight; which demonstrates once again that there is often nothing quite as stupid as an intelligent man!

The war became a relentless progression of moves to new gun positions, firing bombardments and the resumption of the advance. The cold, the wet, the mud, seemed almost – not quite – as much their enemies as the Germans. Men like Ronald Paisley recognised that whatever privations and dangers the gunners had to endure, they were dwarfed by those inflicted on the 'poor bloody infantry'.

> The sufferings of the fighting infantryman are many: he footslogs all the time, does the bulk of the fighting, gets a minimum of food and rest, for very little appreciation, and those chaps didn't grumble, but laughingly and cheerfully belted on their kit and took the road.[44]
>
> Signaller Ronald Paisley, D Troop, 426 Battery, 107th Medium RA

The 107th Medium RA arrived at Susteren on 17 January 1945. There a bleak vista stretched out before them.

> In front of the guns was a No Man's Land outlook. Here and there was the grotesque shape of a disabled tank or gun – a ruin of a building or farm, a blighted tree, a wrecked airplane showing black in the half-light against the dirty white background of churned-up snow. The Bosche was retreating slowly. His fire was therefore constant, but not furious.[45]
>
> Signaller Ronald Paisley, D Troop, 426 Battery, 107th Medium RA

One more move to gun positions at Koningsbosch near the German border saw this phase of the operations come to an end.

THE GERMANS WERE BEATEN. The failure of their Ardennes offensive had been the last nail in a coffin already hammered full of nails. Montgomery, in command of 21st Army Group, was determined to attack while the Germans were still reeling from their latest defeat. His answer was Operation Veritable. The plans are beyond the remit of this book, but in outline: the First Canadian Army would drive eastwards from Nijmegen, the Second Army would assist and hold the line of the River Meuse, while to the south the attached American Ninth Army attacked across the Roer to the Rhine. These would be the last great battles before the crossing of the Rhine. They would not repeat the mistakes of the Great War. There would be no armistice until the Germans were utterly defeated.

By 6 February, the South Notts Hussars were moved north to gun positions on the west bank of the Meuse opposite the town of Gennep, some 15 miles south of Nijmegen. Leonard Gibson had struggled to get a decent position for the guns.

> Everything had to be tremendously camouflaged and movement was only at night without lights. We had to dig our guns in, cover up all the spoil. Hide ourselves from the face of the earth. I had already reconnoitred the positions allotted to us – it was the worst gun position I'd ever come across. There was practically nothing in the way of buildings, so we would just have to exist on our vehicles – and most of those would have to be taken away and hidden well away from the gun positions.[46]

Major Leonard Gibson, Headquarters, 107th Medium RHA

They also had extreme difficulties with the deep, unyielding mud, with each gun needing the combined efforts of two Matadors and a bulldozer to get it safely into its gun pit, where a platform of logs was required to stabilise it during firing. Despite all the difficulties, preparations were well under way for the attack, which was scheduled to start on 8 February.

The morning outlook was grey and showery. To our left a misty rise in the ground denoted the first defences of the Siegfried Line east of the winding length of the Meuse. Artillery were in front as well as on both flanks and the whole area was bristling with guns – 1,500 of various calibre and type. The battle would be at any rate noisy. The troop's guns were camouflaged some distance apart in the shelter of wrecked houses and haystacks. Ammunition was piled in numerous places and spattered with mud and water. Gun platforms were made, as pits in that soft ground would have been useless. As we worked mortar barrages could be heard on the Meuse banks. Though the enemy certainly had wind of something, they had no idea of the Allied strength in the area.[47]

Signaller Ronald Paisley, D Troop, 426 Battery, 107th Medium RA

The 107 Medium RA were attached to XXX Corps (Lieutenant General Brian Horrocks) who was throwing five divisions (2nd Canadian, 3rd Canadian, 15th Scottish, 53rd Welsh and 51st Highland) into the attack with the intention of sweeping the Germans out of the whole area stretching from Nijmegen to Geldern and Xanten, while trying to secure a bridgehead over the River Rhine at Wesel. At 05.00 on 8 February the great barrage began.

Over the Meuse arcs of tracer bullets were forming a continual fire display in the still dark sky. The guns around us then woke to the fray with the sound of a thousand drums. From every field, every farmyard, every haystack, flash after flash illuminated the sky. As our jeep nosed through our own gun lines the silhouettes of the gunners working furiously, but silently, showed dark in the flame from their guns. We passed a troop of heavies, trails on the road itself, the whole massive weight of each devastating weapon bounding like a barking mastiff as each 100lb of metal was unleashed. From away over the Reichswald came the swishing roar of the Typhoons as they hurled in their deadly rockets, merging with the rumble of Jerry mortars, desperately trying to ward off and break up our advancing infantry.[48]

Signaller Ronald Paisley, D Troop, 426 Battery, 107th Medium RA

Just after 07.30 the infantry would go in behind a creeping barrage, sweeping the ground just ahead of the attacking troops and edging forwards at the rate of some 100 yards per minute. Then tragedy struck, when a stricken Allied bomber jettisoned its bombs in trying to reach its own lines.

It was close on midday then and the advancing drone of aircraft heralded the arrival of the bombers. This sound had grown to a crescendo as they began to pass overhead, when suddenly two terrific explosions uprooted the ground out on the position – a shudder shook the building, and splinters of glass sprayed into the room. The troop commander, the gun position officer, his assistant and myself flung ourselves to the floor as another grinding roar struck fear into the very being. What on earth was happening? Were we being shelled or bombed? I heard the skipper yell out as he cautiously peered through the window opening, 'They've hit E Sub![49] Pass that to the battery command post!' I grabbed the phone and, trying to keep the voice steady, reported 'E Sub and H Sub out of action. Have casualties. Can we stand down?' 'Oh, hell! Yes!' came the groaning answer. We were then ordered to take shelter and found a small group in the water-filled cellar, white with anticipation and fear. As yet no one knew what had actually happened. Harry Ball came racing in, his voice an octave higher with the strain of nerves. He reported all E Sub casualties but himself – most of them apparently dead. He had escaped himself by nothing short of a miracle, the bomb burst 5 yards away from him. A number of H Sub too were badly mauled, some killed. Ammunition stacks were still going sky-high, it was dangerous to be in the open.[50]

Signaller Ronald Paisley, D Troop, 426 Battery, 107th Medium RA

They were ordered to take shelter and did so in the water-filled cellar. Still no one knew what had happened. Leonard Gibson was at regimental headquarters when he heard the explosions.

> With 400 rounds per gun and all the charges – that was a bit of a target. So, when four bombs landed on four guns – the explosions – what must have happened to the gun teams is beyond belief. I ordered the adjutant to ring up for all the medical aid that could be sent. I ran from RHQ over to this stricken troop, and there was a terrible scene of chaos, with the gun position officer in charge, trying to pull out the wounded and sort out the wounded from the dead. The captain commanding the troop arrived about the same time and he and I – with these explosions going on all the time – helped in that with stretchers coming forward.[51]

Major Leonard Gibson, Headquarters, 107th Medium RHA

Albert Swinton arrived in time to see his old friend Andy Drewett, the troop sergeant major of D Troop, desperately trying to rescue his men.

> I dived across there to see what I could do to help out, because there was old Andy dragging bodies out. I can see Andy now: he'd got this body over him in a fireman's lift. He dived round this wall just as a load of ammunition went off and a lump of shell went through this wall and into Andy's right shoulder. As he went away, I said, 'Well you're a right bugger, your mum told you to look after me! Now what are you going to do, who's going to look after me now?'[52]

Troop Sergeant Major Albert Swinton, B Troop, 425 Battery, 107th Medium RA

Paisley saw the wounded – including Andy Drewett – being brought in for treatment.

> Many were beyond all aid. Tiffy (Frank) Phillips had been killed outright, 'Taffy' Young, a Welshman, and a signaller, Sergeant Mills, Sergeant Perry, Lance Bombardier Tatham, Gunners Charlton, Hales, Rushton and Necchi. Gunner Smith died in hospital, having lost both legs, Gunner Elliott too died some weeks later. Among the wounded were Lance Bombardier Harvey, a Dumfries Scot, he had severe chest wounds; Lance Bombardier Iliffe, who I believe has since lost his sight; Sergeant Major Drewett, who received shrapnel in the shoulder, whilst trying to help the others. It was indeed a sad day for the troop.[53]
>
> Signaller Ronald Paisley, D Troop, 426 Battery, 107th Medium RA

The loss of so many men from just one troop was a terrible blow and cast a gloomy cloud over the men for several days afterwards.

> It was hard to believe that those prominent personalities would never again appear on this earth. Their death was ironic, having escaped enemy bombing and shelling from time to time only to be killed by a British action. The funeral service took place on a dismal, wet morning in the rickety shed near the scene of the tragedy and where the ten bodies[54] awaited burial. The mud was too deep to allow transport to reach the spot and the remains had to be carried by stretcher to the road.[55]
>
> Signaller Ronald Paisley, D Troop, 426 Battery, 107th Medium RA

Gibson realised that his men had been hard hit and tried as best he could to raise the mood, whilst carrying out his duties to the dead and their grieving families.

I sat down and wrote out an order of the day saying that we must battle on, the war was nearly over, and how tragic this was that this should have happened to us when victory was obviously so close. I was now sitting down and writing to the parents and relations of those who had been killed, but I was not going to tell them exactly what had happened, just that they had been killed in action, that they were very brave and had given up their lives for the regiment.[56]

Major Leonard Gibson, Headquarters, 107th Medium RHA

Within three days, two new guns and a batch of replacement gunners had arrived. The war went on.

This tragedy aside, the attack had indeed gone well. On the left flank, the assaulting troops were advancing deep into the natural fortress of the fearsome Reichswald Forest, but despite that, by 10 February they had reached Kleve. On the right the fighting was exceedingly hard: the 51st Highland faced violent German opposition founded on the solid rock of the Siegfried Line defences, coupled with the appalling mud which was still clogging up the whole battlefield. On 13 February, more barrages were fired to assist the Scots in their attack on Goch, the keystone of the German defence. By the time the Scots had cleared the ground on the other side of the Meuse, the South Notts had fired an estimated total of 14,000 rounds, around 830 per gun. This was sheer hard graft, the gunners driving themselves well beyond the normal limits imposed by fatigue. They knew that they could not let down the infantry that depended for their lives on the 5.5-inch shells smashing down to crack open the German strongpoints.

They were then ordered across the Meuse, moving all the way to the north to cross near Nijmegen, then 15 miles back to the south, to take up positions on the eastern outskirts of Gennep. At last the fighting died down. As the Canadians made progress on the left flank and the American Ninth Army surged forward on the right, the Germans in the centre were forced to fall back or be cut off.

On 1 March they moved forward across the border into Germany. At least one senor warrant officer reacted with rather more levity than perhaps the situation warranted.

> Couldn't see a thing except white, all over, not a building anywhere. It was really bitterly cold. Another sergeant major came walking down, I can see him now with his balaclava on and his mittens, wafting his arms to keep warm. He said, 'Now, come on Harold, when do we start the atrocities!'[57]
>
> Battery Sergeant Major Harold Harper, Headquarters, 426 Battery, 107th Medium RA

To everyone's relief they now had a period of rest before the final effort – the Rhine crossing still lay ahead of them.

THE RHINE WAS A SERIOUS OBSTACLE. Behind this the German defenders may have been outnumbered, battered and bedraggled, but they were defending the inner sanctum of their homeland. There was still plenty of potential for things to go seriously wrong and for massive casualties to be incurred. The South Notts Hussars moved up to the main British concentration area near the town of Xanten. As ever, Leonard Gibson was industrious, with an estate agent's eye for the best possible 'property' to set up his command observation post. This time he seems to have rather overdone it!

> I had found a wonderful place on this wooded hillside where the whole operation could be seen from. Eventually, the colonel and those who were directing – if any special direction was wanted – would order it from that point. After we'd been

there about half a day, some very senior gunner arrived and said, 'You seem to have got the spot here!' I said, 'Yes, Sir!' He said, 'Well now, could you possibly move about 30–40 yards away because I'd like to take this area over; we have some VIPs coming!' We moved along and it turned out that that was the point to which they were bringing the Prime Minister, Winston Churchill, Field Marshal Alanbrooke and everyone that mattered – stood in the very spot that I had previously chosen for myself![58]

Major Leonard Gibson, Headquarters, 107th Medium RHA

The crossing was planned for 23 March. From 18.00 to 20.15, the South Notts Hussars were just part of a concentration of hundreds of medium and heavy guns firing a preliminary heavy counter-battery barrage to silence as many as possible of the identified German batteries. They would then switch to direct their fire in support of the initial assault by the 1st Commando Brigade, before finally firing at the behest of the 15th Scottish Division as they moved across to develop and expand the bridge-head. Everything went well, but the most spectacular part of the operation was the huge airborne fleet depositing hordes of glider-borne troops and parachutists behind the German lines. Soon the guns were edged forward, closer to the Rhine, a sure sign that the bridgehead was expanding ahead of them. By 30 March, the fighting had moved well out of the range of the 5.5-inch guns.

The 107th Medium RA were then selected for one last task, being detached to support the operations of the Canadian Corps in their efforts to clear the 'island' formed between the River Waal and the Rhine close to Arnhem. They moved up and were soon busy firing in support of the 49th Division as they cleared the 'island'. Next, at 22.40 on 12 April, came their assault across the River IJssel on Arnhem itself. Ronald Paisley watched the barrage as every type of artillery and support weapon peppered the town.

> As dusk was merging into the dark, we let fly with the artillery barrage and soon the night was shattered by the tornado of sound. Tanks hurled rockets over the river, thin red streams of fire arched upwards. Heavy and light guns swung in from every direction. Explosions and bursts of fire rocked the town. All through the night the grim carnage went on. Back came 88mm and heavier shells from Bosche positions, mortars thundered into a nearby copse, the sharp sound of machine-gun bullets clipped the air. Thick smoke enveloped the town. The terrifying hiss of the rockets as they swept in made us wince. Jerry would never hold Arnhem under such fire.[59]
>
> Signaller Ronald Paisley, D Troop, 426 Battery, 107th Medium RA

The town was taken and a couple of days later Paisley had the chance to examine the terrible damage they had caused.

> The town was deserted. Not a soul was visible in the ravaged streets save an occasional MP diverting traffic. Once fashionable hotels and tea gardens scowled shabbily with torn facades. Rubble was in heaps everywhere. Shops pulled asunder and empty. Electric trams in ribbons, entangled in coils of wire – electric lamp standards bowed drunkenly in every direction. The 'mailed fist' had delivered the once obviously lovely town of Arnhem a crushing blow.[60]
>
> Signaller Ronald Paisley, D Troop, 426 Battery, 107th Medium RA

Still the Germans fought on. Among the South Notts Hussars, many of the men realised that the end of the war must be coming soon, but the Germans were still fighting; still killing. And so the war continued.

We knew that it was 'in the bag' so to speak. The nerves started to creep in a bit then, you thought, well, having survived six years of war you get a bit on edge in case anything should happen.[61]

Battery Sergeant Major Harold Harper, Headquarters, 426 Battery, 107th Medium RA

They would not have been human had they not had the imminent peace in mind. Frank Penlington was determined to take extra care – as best he could – to ensure he survived.

There was something in the air. I know it did make me think, 'Well look after yourself, Frank! Don't go putting yourself in any precarious situations in case you get killed!' It made me hang back, I was afraid of getting killed then! I was saying to the lads, 'We don't want to bloody well get killed in the last minute! Now the war's coming to an end!'[62]

Gunner Frank Penlington, Headquarters, 425 Battery, 107th Medium RA

One figure who had played such an important role in the last year of the regiment's history left in April in rather unfortunate circumstances. After various periods of leave, Colonel Oswald had resumed his command, whereupon Major Leonard Gibson had been despatched for a refresher course at the School of Artillery at Larkhill, back in England. He would have been the first to admit his gunnery was rusty, but he had other leadership and administrative skills, combined with an unparalleled ability to recce the best-possible gun positions. Despite his protest, Gibson had to go. Much to his chagrin, when he returned he found that his departure had been ill-timed, as Oswald had finally left the unit and a new colonel had been appointed in the form of regular soldier Colonel T. H. Hardy. Shortly afterwards Gibson was promoted to lieutenant colonel and given a staff posting. He would much rather have stayed with 'his' regiment.

Given his liking for medals and decorations he was subsequently furious that *all* the commanding officers of the South Notts Hussars between 1944 and 1946 were awarded Distinguished Service Orders – except Gibson. This I think we might concur was unfair in view of his substantial contribution.

The Allies were now advancing rapidly beyond the town of Ede. On 24 April, the whole regiment was ordered to fire one last valedictory round for each gun. It could have proved fatal.

> We got this order to find a one-round salvo. They all fired all right, bar one and he got a premature – the shell burst in the barrel. The barrel peeled back like a banana and one of the chaps got a piece of barrel in his foot. As it turned out it was the last round we fired in the war.[63]

Troop Sergeant Major Albert Swinton, B Troop, 425 Battery, 107th Medium RA

Harold Harper had his own amusing perspective on what happened that day.

> Sensing the war was coming to a close, I was in charge of the battery rum ration, so I hadn't issued any rum out for about a fortnight. I kept it all in my jeep, I'd got about four 2-gallon stone jars ready for the big night when peace was declared. When we were firing one of our guns had a premature; the shell exploded in the barrel. Having had the experience of knowing what happens in a gun pit when a premature goes off, I drove hell for leather across this field, bouncing hither and thither, smashed all the jars of rum – and when I got to the gun found that no one was injured – and everybody was quite OK! Nobody believed me about the rum rations! It took until about the end of June before I got the smell out of my kit and the jeep itself.[64]

Battery Sergeant Major Harold Harper, Headquarters, 426 Battery, 107th Medium RA

There was no more fighting, but still they pressed on, until finally they were settled in village billets near the town of Coesfeld: 425 Battery at Gescher and 436 Battery at Ramsdorf. It was here that the war ended for the South Notts Hussars on 8 May 1945 – Victory in Europe (VE) Day. David Elliott decided that the best way to celebrate would be build a massive bonfire with an effigy of Hitler to burn on top. He then managed to put himself in surrealistic danger on that day of peace.

> We all drank too much and at what stage we decided to have the bonfire I don't know! We had to walk quite a long way down from the men's mess down to the field. We were all mixed up, the officers and the ranks, all terrifically friendly and all very inebriated! I was very worried because it had been raining and everything was wet. It was 8–10 feet high and fairly large, with this dummy of Hitler on the top. I'd kept a can of petrol to make sure the bonfire went well. I climbed up on top of this bonfire, the men were all surrounding it – and a lot of them had got lighted brands! I started pouring this petrol down from the top, a good 10 or 12 feet up in the air, and I had this horrible feeling that somebody was going to throw the lighted brand on the fire – and here was I stupidly pouring a can of petrol! I don't know whether I could make myself heard but shouted to the men to 'Hold on till I get down!' I suddenly thought, 'To get right through to the end of the war to go and incinerate myself on VE Day was the height of stupidity!' But I got down and with a great cheer they threw the lighted brands on the fire and it went up in a great 'Whoosh' and everyone was madly cheering![65]
>
> Captain David Elliott, A Troop, 425 Battery, 107th Medium RA

Many of the men had drunk far too much and some began to get a little 'out of hand' towards the end of the party, as Ian Sinclair recalled. Tensions sublimated by the grim requirements of war began to resurface.

Bombardier Monteith, who'd been with us all the war, a Nottingham High School man, he'd never been anything more than a specialist bombardier – never made sergeant – and he was very resentful because most of his schoolfriends had gone on to commissions. He started shouting the odds – about me in particular! That I was no bloody good – a drunken tongue speaking a sober mind! Everything he said was nonsense – real venom that had built up not particularly against me, but against the whole system. I said, 'Come on Monty, I'm taking you home!' I got him into the jeep, and he was still being very abusive, and he said, 'If you weren't an officer I should hit you!' I stopped the jeep, got out and said, 'Good! C'mon Monty forget that I'm an officer – hit me!' He did and broke a tooth! So, I then roughed him up in no uncertain manner – I really thrashed him![66]

Captain Ian Sinclair, C Troop, 426 Battery, 107th Medium RA

Sinclair carried the near-unconscious Monteith him back to his billet and cleaned him up. Monteith knew what had happened, but he maintained a discreet silence. A few may have squabbled among themselves when drunk; but at last peace had come to the South Notts Hussars. The war was over.

20

GERMANY

They used to taunt us. One of the guard posts was right next door to a house and the girls used to be up on the top floor and they used to taunt the lads on guard. We had one lad by the name of Moss – they were really 'working him', shouting at him, laughing at him, egging him on![1]

Battery Quartermaster Sergeant David Tickle, Headquarters, 425 Battery, 107th Medium RA

AT LAST THE WAR IN EUROPE was over and the South Notts Hussars were given the responsibility by the Military Government for the administration of the whole of the Coesfeld area in Westphalia – about 55 square miles in total. The regimental headquarters were housed at Lette. The 425 Battery was located at Gescher, with the men in a school, the messes in large houses and the battery office in a factory premises. The 426 Battery was somewhat more geographically scattered, with C Troop in Schloss Romberg at Buldern, while D Troop was at Dulmen. All told, most of the men were accommodated in reasonable comfort.

Their first task was to clear the whole area of munitions, battlefield debris and equipment, which was a danger to both the army and the local German civilians. Recce teams were sent out to identify wartime ammunition dumps, which were then moved by lorry to central dumps, or blown up *in situ* by the Royal Engineers. This did not always go according to plan, as Frank Penlington discovered.

> They came round in the morning and they said, 'The engineers are going to blow the ammunition up today! Don't really know what time!' Out of the blue it blew up! Most of the windows in the mess and the village blew out! Unfortunately, I received a piece in the upper arm! They thought, 'Oh, God, Penny's had his chips at last! He survived all these years and he's got something!' It wasn't as bad as it looked – Sergeant Swinton pulled it out. It just had a dressing on it, and it healed itself![2]
>
> Gunner Frank Penlington, Headquarters, 425 Battery, 107th Medium RA

Clearing munitions is always a dangerous task, but they luckily managed to avoid any 'real' casualties. Many units were not so fortunate in the weeks following VE Day.

Of course, the war with Japan was still raging in the Far East, where the British forces prepared to launch the invasion of Malaya and Singapore, while the Americans slogged their way across the island of Okinawa. But for most of the men of the South Notts Hussars that seemed a world away. Surely their war was over. However, Albert Swinton had a bolt from the blue that shook him to the very core.

> It was a Sunday morning; I'd got the troop on church parade and I was on the square of this school building. A window opened and it was Major Birkin. He shouts, 'Sergeant Major, I want to see you – now!' He says, 'There you go!' and presented me with a message from the War Office, saying that 912374 WO2 A. H. Swinton was posted to the Far East. He said, 'What do you think of that?' I said, 'Not a lot! As a matter of fact, I'm damned annoyed! I think I've done more than my

share of this war! What can I do about it?' 'Nothing, it's a War Office posting!'[3]

Troop Sergeant Major Albert Swinton, B Troop, 425 Battery, 107th Medium RA

Dave Tickle was also amazed at the news of Swinton's posting.

We were absolutely staggered when Albert announced that he had been posted to the Far East. We were as shocked as Albert. It was a bit shattering to see a lad like Albert break down and shed a few tears. He said, 'Look, haven't I done enough? How can they post me out to the Far East when I've been through all I've been through? I can't understand it!' We were all of the same mind.[4]

Battery Quartermaster Sergeant David Tickle, Headquarters, 425 Battery, 107th Medium RA

Swinton determined to fight his fate as best he could, but it seemed hopeless: a posting was a posting and that was that. He was left in utter despair: he had gone to the well too often and could face no more war.

I saw the colonel, I saw the brigadier, I finished up at Army Group Headquarters – all they said was it's come from the War Office! I couldn't get this thing stopped so I eventually finished up back at the Royal Artillery Depot Woolwich. I was very much anti-army at the time because of the way they had treated me. I was very much a 'Bolshie type' – I lost all interest in what I was doing. I couldn't care less. They could have put me against a wall and shot me as far as I was concerned. I was really annoyed and felt let down. I met up with four other WO2s and two WO1s, all on the same business. I went home on embarkation leave for a fortnight. My stepfather said, 'I am going to get in touch with my MP!' I said, 'Well don't quote me, because it's strictly not on – we're not supposed to

approach MPs on these sort of things!' 'Never mind about you
– I'm doing this!' He got it stopped![5]

Troop Sergeant Major Albert Swinton, B Troop, 425 Battery, 107th
Medium RA

Swinton was instead posted to an anti-aircraft unit in Holzmin-
den, Germany; but with the help of Ian Sinclair, who 'pulled a
few strings', he managed to get himself returned 'home' to the
South Notts Hussars.

At first their lives in Germany were governed by strict non-
fraternisation rules which had been issued by Montgomery back
in March 1945. These looked to 'punish' all Germans, treating
them as all equally responsible for the crimes committed under
the Nazi regime.

> In streets, houses, cafés, cinemas etc., you must keep clear of
> Germans, man, woman and child, unless you meet them in the
> course of your duty. You must not walk out with them, or shake
> hands, or visit their homes, or make them gifts, or take gifts
> from them. You must not play games with them or share any
> social event with them. In short you must not fraternise with
> Germans at all.[6]

Field Marshal Bernard Montgomery, Headquarters, 21st Army Group,

This did not prevent the men from carrying out their administrative role in trying to restore some normality to that region of
Germany. The Matador gun towers and lorries were emptied out
and used to ferry fuel.

> The Germans had no transport and we were on details, taking
> coal and coke to local hospitals, schools and places where they
> needed help. We had two or three Germans with us for loading
> and unloading – it was all done by shovel.[7]

Lance Bombardier Reg Cutter, B Troop, 425 Battery, 107th Medium RA

The ludicrous strictures of non-fraternisation were obviously unenforceable, and by June the policy was relaxed to allow soldiers to talk to small children. The political climate gradually changed, and punishment of Germans ceased to be the 'prime objective'. After all, it was evident that if the priority was a re-education programme to create a new Germany, then that could hardly be achieved without talking to them. By September the British administration abandoned the policy .

There was a serious point to the desire to 'change' the very character of Germany in the postwar years. Some of the men had seen the evidence of the Nazi atrocities with their own eyes. Bob Foulds was one who saw a deeply disturbing sight shortly after he entered the country.

> It was afternoon and somebody from the hedge by the road shouted, 'Good God, what's this?' We ran over to this hedge and on a series of lorries there came a whole succession of incredible people: they were living skeletons, completely emaciated, in extraordinary striped clothes and little striped caps. We couldn't understand what these people were. We didn't associate it with rumours we'd heard of concentration camps. They went past – a dozen lorries with these terrible-looking people. The penny didn't drop as to who they could possibly be. Very shortly afterwards we began to hear about Belsen – they'd come from some concentration camp.[8]
>
> Captain Bob Foulds, D Troop, 426 Battery, 107th Medium RA

The British government was aware of the horrors of the concentration camps and took film footage on the liberation of many of the camps. Sidney Bernstein was commissioned as the producer of a propaganda film designed to show the Germans what they as a nation had done, or rather allowed to happen. Alfred Hitchcock was involved in editing the film to ensure the maximum emotional impact of the graphic scenes. Although the film was ultimately shelved as being too politically sensitive, some of the footage from Belsen was sent to Germany for compulsory viewing. David Elliott helped organise these screenings in the Coesfeld area.

> The order came down that this film of Belsen concentration camp, which had been taken by the Army Film Unit, was to be shown to all the civilian population over 16 years of age. We had a cinema in the village, and it was fairly straightforward to go along and tell the burgomaster what we wanted. He did protest to start with, said it couldn't be done, and one had to say, 'Of course it can be done! We had an ex-inmate of a concentration camp, I think he was a German Jew: a very, very gaunt figure and most of his teeth had been broken. The dialogue was in English, so we showed it without the dialogue and this chap was on the stage talking about what was being shown on the screen. It affected the Germans very deeply indeed. As they came out there was a mixture: the younger women and girls in tears, the men shaking their heads in disbelief. We had a general impression that they didn't realise it had been going on. I don't think they wanted to know.[9]

Captain David Elliott, A Troop, 425 Battery, 107th Medium RA

There is a cynical view that everyone in Germany denied responsibility for the concentration camps once the war was lost, but Albert Swinton had some sympathy for the shocked villagers.

> We had to round up all the civilian population, push them in this room and say, 'Right, you will watch this!' And we showed this film of Belsen. It was rather horrendous. This was a very rural area and I don't think a lot of people knew anything about this, I honestly don't – they came out in tears. It really upset

them. I wouldn't have thought it possible for any human being
to treat another human being like it![10]

Troop Sergeant Major Albert Swinton, B Troop, 425 Battery, 107th
Medium RA

ONE OF THE MOST SERIOUS RESPONSIBILITIES of the
British units stationed in Germany was the administration and
control of the various displaced persons and POW camps. In
all, the South Notts Hussars were made responsible for seven
camps of varied nationalities. This was an extremely problematic assignment: no one spoke the languages, so communication
was difficult; and the inmates had suffered a hell on earth for
years and were not in the mood to compromise now they were
'free'.

We had to look after the displaced persona that came into our
sector. All over Germany there had been gathered together
groups of people who had been taken there as slave labour. They
were divided up in six or seven camps under the jurisdiction
of the South Notts. D Troop had one camp – Russians and
Slavs in this camp. There must have been about 300 of them,
in a wired-off section of houses alongside the railway track in
Dulmen. They were a very unlikeable lot; we never had any sort
of rapport with them unfortunately. They were very primitive
types: big stolid people who stood round you and just looked
blankly at you whenever you went in the compound – and they
weren't easy to deal with. They had terrible grudges against the
Germans, and they used to go out at night raiding German
farms for food, women and everything else. We finished up in
the stupid, ironic position of trying to protect the Germans
against the displaced persons – it was sad but that was how it
worked out. We were there to maintain some law and order and

they were a very lawless bunch. We did our best to look after them, control them and feed them.[11]

Captain Bob Foulds, D Troop, 426 Battery, 107th Medium RA

An NCO and a few guards were assigned to each camp, but there was no way they could stop some of the inmates breaking out to extract a terrible revenge on the Germans.

Every night we were called out by the local population because the Russians were going round looting and raping and God knows what. We saw some terrible instances of rape. I once had the job of taking a young girl who had been raped to hospital. I never found out if she lived or not, but she was in a terrible state. Then we went into this barn and there was this young girl lying there – the grandparents in the corner had obviously gone to her protection – and they'd been shot. There was a fair amount of antagonism between the troops and the Russian prisoners – they were taking out their revenge on the German people for what had happened to them.[12]

Battery Sergeant Major Harold Harper, Headquarters, 426 Battery, 107th Medium RA

As the months wore on, it was ironic that the South Notts Hussars, who had fought so hard against fascism, should find themselves – all unknowing – complicit in a war crime as they obeyed orders.

Eventually towards the end of the summer orders came through that they were going to be repatriated. In our innocence, we thought, 'Well, they'll enjoy going home!' We got them on to lorries with not a great deal of trouble and started off going east towards the Russian zone. Then we couldn't understand why they kept on jumping off the lorries – we had to stop and fix bayonets, get them back on again. We got them to the frontier with a great deal of difficulty. They were terribly apprehensive about going home – which was something we didn't understand because we knew nothing of the Russian internal set-up at that time. They were deloused – sprayed with DDT powder and whipped away – and that was the last we saw of them. We began to understand later on that forced repatriation was a terribly cruel and unkind thing – in our innocence it hadn't occurred to us that we'd sent all these Russians back to a very uncertain future – to put it mildly.[13]

Captain Bob Foulds, D Troop, 426 Battery, 107th Medium RA

David Elliott had a very similar experience with the Russian inmates at a camp in his sector.

The camp was controlled by a sergeant and two gunners and I think there were about 700 inmates, all Russian POWs. We were told that they were being repatriated – and our reaction was, 'Lucky them!' We were all waiting for news of our demobilisation! Word came down that lorries would be arriving at the camp and we went down and made it quite clear that they were being repatriated and would they have their gear and kit packed next day when the lorries were turning up. It seemed a perfectly natural and straightforward thing to do. Word came back next day from my sergeant to say that the lorries had arrived, but the camp was empty – 700 Russians had vanished into the countryside.[14]

Captain David Elliott, A Troop, 425 Battery, 107th Medium RA

Over the next few days, the 'Russians' filtered back to the camp. It turned out they weren't Russian at all – they were Ukrainians who certainly did *not* want to be repatriated to the Russians. On their inner arms they all had a tattoo which indicted they had been forced to work for the Germans whilst they were POWs. This to the Soviets would be perceived as 'collaboration' and merit a death sentence.

Then we got this extraordinary order saying that the transport was being laid on again, but this time we weren't to tell the Russian commandant. They arrived at 6 o'clock in the morning and I think they had machine guns mounted on the 3-ton lorries. The men were loaded into the lorries and driven off. We in our ignorance were instrumental in sending men back to their deaths[15]

Captain David Elliott, A Troop, 425 Battery, 107th Medium RA

SLOWLY THE SITUATION NORMALISED, and the soldiers began to enjoy themselves and make genuine efforts to establish friendly contacts with the Germans. A mutual interest in sport was one obvious point of contact.

After the fraternisation ban was off, we decided to try and get on with the local population. We organised this football match – what we didn't realise was that this team was playing in the second division of the German league. They'd raked in one or two 40-year-olds who had been ex-professionals, and they'd labelled it as 'Stadtlohn versus the British Army' – and all it was, was against our battery! We lost seven-nil. The only bloke that came out with any sort of credit in our crowd was the poor old goalkeeper who let seven in but nevertheless made about twenty marvellous saves![16]

Battery Sergeant Major Harold Harper, Headquarters, 426 Battery, 107th Medium RA

The Germans also watched in astonishment as the soldiers attempted to introduce them to the national sport of England – cricket.

One or two blokes came to me and they said, 'What about a game of cricket!' I said, 'Good heavens above – they don't play cricket in Germany!' Everywhere we went there were goalposts – no cricket! About 5 to 6 miles away we found this lovely flat meadow. We acquired a roller off a farm and we rolled this pitch meticulously for about a fortnight. Eventually we had this game. I bowled the first over and my friend was batting. I'm no bowler! I just took two paces, brought my arm over and the ball reared up and hit him on the head – off two paces! I thought it must have been a freak. Next one hit him on the shoulder, so we decided to pack it in – the wicket wasn't good enough. The funny thing about it was all the German village had turned out to see this freak match and they thought it was rather funny to see the British soldiers knocking hell out of each other![17]

Battery Sergeant Major Harold Harper, Headquarters, 426 Battery, 107th Medium RA

They had to keep the men amused: there were regular ENSA shows, cinemas were set up running British films, regular football matches were organised in a league with neighbouring units. Ken Giles occupied himself in his 'secret' capacity as 'The Nark', writing a scandalous gossip column for the new regimental magazine.

Regimental headquarters started their own newspaper which they called *The Oak Leaves*. I think Sergeant Angus Bell was particularly involved – I believe he was the editor. This was done on a much grander scale than I had ever been able to attain with *The Acorn*. A German printing firm was engaged, and the production was quite professional. I confess now for the first time in my life that I wrote a weekly column under the pseudonym of 'The Nark'. I tried my best to dig up any scandal about anybody – in a nice way of course – printing little anecdotes of various members in the battery. On one occasion Captain Elliott went on a trip into the Moselle looking for wine for the officers' mess. I turned it into a kind of almost criminal-like journey and christened him '*Papa L'Elliot*'. I think these things were taken in good part – sometimes a little bit piqued perhaps – 'Where did you hear of this!' Perhaps my style of writing gave me away, most people said, 'Are you "The Nark"?' I always denied it![18]

Lance Sergeant Ken Giles, B Troop, 425 Battery, 107th Medium RA

Black-market activities were prevalent, although not usually on a 'grand' scale. It was not always pretty, as unprincipled soldiers would exchange their rations with German civilians, seeking and gaining rewards that were disproportionate in value. Watches, jewellery, silverware, clocks and various family heirlooms were all 'fair game'. Some traded for sexual favours, capitalising on the destitution of German women. Such things rarely appear in oral history, but they did happen. Others formed 'genuine' relationships with German women, although in retrospect we might be suspicious as to the underlying motives of women offered the possibility of an escape from war-ravaged reality.

In the end it was all an anti-climax. For soldiers surviving a war, there is always a prolonged time of waiting – an interregnum when nothing really matters to them but demobilisation and a return to civilian life. For any regiment there is the same impact as the core of the unit begin to drift away. Men were posted to other units, sent away on courses or, best of all, from the autumn onwards one by one they were demobbed.

The first chap to be demobbed, we had a party and it turned out disastrous. We were drinking German schnapps and that's terrible stuff. It wasn't matured – we were getting it from a local still. We had at the foot of the stairs a marble statue of a girl and a couple of sergeants decided that they'd put this statue in the commanding officer's bed! It was only about 2-foot high, but when they tried to take it off the pedestal, then they realised how heavy it was – and it crashed down. The chap who was about to be demobilised was underneath – he broke all his teeth and his demob got put back about six weeks.[19]

Battery Sergeant Major Harold Harper, Headquarters, 426 Battery, 107th Medium RA

The men were demobilised by an age group system, which reflected accurately when they had volunteered, or been called up for war service. It was a conscious effort to avoid the confusions and unfairness of the system at the end of the Great War. By and large it succeeded.

The various groups went off in numbers: we'd lose two blokes on this group, and four blokes on that group. If any of my blokes were going away, I always made a point of grabbing a couple of bottles out of the sergeants' mess and go down to the men's billets, get the blokes who were being demobbed and their particular friends – and we'd all sit down and have a drink! It got a bit hectic I must say![20]

Troop Sergeant Major Albert Swinton, B Troop, 425 Battery, 107th Medium RA

Most of the 'original' serving members of the regiment on mobilisation on 1 September 1939 were already back home when the regimental adjutant, one Captain Ian Sinclair, received notice of the official disbandment of the regiment on 28 February 1946. The few remaining soldiers left were dispersed around other artillery regiments in Germany. The South Notts were no more.

21

APRÈS LA GUERRE

We all got on very well. We were all just brothers in arms the whole lot of us.[1]

Reg Cutter

HOME. ONE WORD THAT MEANT EVERYTHING. The hopes, the dreams, the emotional investment of six long, painful years at war. Six years of risking everything in the cause of their country, facing the bursting shells, the hissing bullets, the rolling tanks. Six years of physical punishment: the terrible wounds, the injuries, aches and pains, the hunger, the endless thirst. The mortifying humiliations inflicted by dysentery, the pustulating desert sores, the piles, scabies and fleas. For some, a couple of years deprived of their liberty as prisoners of war. Six years of seeing comrades killed before their eyes – a fate they could have shared at any moment. Six years separated from their families, not knowing whether they would ever see them again.

When at last it was all over, the men of the South Notts Hussars returned home to no great homecoming, no civic receptions. Most went in dribs and drabs as their demob number came up. Some were back a little earlier, although often because they had been wounded or imprisoned. For most it would be a bit of an anti-climax. Just as there was no common response to war, so there was no common response to the return to civilian life. Most realised that whatever the promises of politicians, there were far too many people in the armed services to allow any 'special' care to be taken of them. True, they could have their old job back and the new Labour government was prioritising house-building, but this was against the backdrop of a near-bankrupt economy. There would be no homes fit for heroes, no brave new world for these men. They were also losing something that had become very important to them – the comradeship of their mates that had fought alongside them. This was a special bond that was never really available or understood in civilian life.

> One always thought the day you got demobbed was going to be fantastic, you'd jump for joy. As I left Münster and left all the chaps behind who I'd been with – some for many years – there was a touch of sadness. One felt quite cut off from something that had been part of your life. Even if I was going home to a new bride.[2]
>
> Harold Harper

These men had gone to war as little more than boys and come back as men. Six years may not seem much to a man in his sixties, it can pass in a blink of an eye, but for a 20-year-old it was a life-time. A lifetime that could never really be regained.

> I went to war at 20 years of age and came back at 25. Those of us that had been NCOs and then officers, there had never been a time within those five or six years where you had not got responsibilities to other people – looking after other people. What should have been your youthful years of most fun – your early twenties – they'd been past and you'd *always* had responsibilities. I won't say you didn't enjoy yourself, you did of course, but your most youthful years had been taken away from you.[3]
>
> George Pearson

They had also changed. The polite young boys had been exposed to some of the most dreadful things imaginable, lost some of their best friends in a split-second of mayhem, with no chance to say goodbye or even grieve in the heat of the moment.

> I'd had a fairly sheltered sort of life before I went in the army –
> I'd lived with my grandma, pretty spoilt, never drank, smoked
> or went out with young ladies! I learnt a few facts of life while I
> was in the army and that hardened me up, made me much more
> self-confident and taught me how to get on with people.[4]
>
> Jack Sykes

Now they were ordinary civilians. Everyone around them had been through the war in one way or another. People on the home front had suffered their own privations, risked death from bombs and V weapons, had worked long shifts in the coalmines or munitions factories. They too had lived on restricted rations. Many did not have the empathy to understand the 'extra mile' walked by the soldiers at the front. When Ted Whittaker was demobilised after returning from being a POW, he went back to see about returning to his old job as a clerk at a light engineering factory. The reception he received was appalling.

> I was not exactly made welcome. The chap who'd taken charge
> came to see me. The first thing he said was, 'Can't spare long,
> we're so ever so busy! You've no idea what it's been like while
> you've been away!' I thought, 'This is really promising!' A
> friend of mine rang me up and said, 'This job they've put you
> on – they are just going to give you the minimum they're
> required to do! It's sorting out stuff we've got in stock from
> government contracts – and when that's finished, you're
> finished!' I think they had to take you on for a year.[5]
>
> Ted Whittaker

Forewarned by his friend, Whittaker did not pursue the job, but attended a government-sponsored business studies course, before pursuing a career as a clerk with Nottingham City Treasurer's Department.

David Elliott returned home to take up a lifelong career on the family 300-acre farm at Whipley Manor in Surrey. It was as idyllic as anyone might have wished.

> My first day of freedom dawned bright and sunny and after breakfast I decided to walk round the whole farm, something I had probably not done since I was a boy. I found myself walking through Hoop Copse alongside the old disused Wey-Arun canal and, as I paused to listen to the cooing of a wood pigeon, I suddenly heard the joyous trilling of a skylark over the spring barley in West Park field. I was, and still am, a very lucky man.[6]
>
> David Elliott

Less fortunate men found that their ranks and achievements in the army counted for little or nothing in civilian life. Albert Swinton returned to his old job at the Players Cigarette Factory.

> No bother; no bother at all. As far as I was concerned the war was finished and I was civilian, and the fact that I'd been a sergeant major didn't count for anything. Our warrant officer Danny Lamb he worked at Players; he was only on a machine same as me! My machine was at the end of the row, nearest the window. I used to stand there with these two windows open and my head stuck out – the number of times the foreman came along and caught me was nobody's business! Having spent the last six years living in a hole in the ground – and to then get stuck in an air-conditioned factory – it didn't go down very well.[7]
>
> Albert Swinton

He stuck it for nearly a year but eventually he looked elsewhere for the sort of outdoor life he craved. He was married with a family by then, so he couldn't join the regular army; instead he became a policeman.

Ray Ellis had no settled job before the war having worked as junior clerk, a trainee engineer and furniture salesman. On his return from German POW camps, it initially looked as if he would fall apart. He had become very bitter and disillusioned; indeed, he went absent without leave from the army. However, he got over the worst of his depression and began to look for something worthwhile to do with his life. Eventually he trained under the government Emergency Teacher Training Scheme.

> I was overjoyed – I really was thrilled to think that now, instead of spending my life killing, I was going to be able to do some good with things I loved – children. I really did – it wasn't a phoney thing, it wasn't silly. I was a very serious-minded person and I really was sincere about wanting to do good and be good to children. I'd got through the hatred and was coming through to a more positive way of thought and thinking of what I could do. I became a teacher and my love of children and wanting to help them was there the day I started teaching and it was there the day I retired.[8]
>
> Ray Ellis

He would blossom in his new vocation as a teacher, rising to become a much-loved headmaster.

George Pearson could sense that the war had changed him; he could see it in the way he now looked at the whole world differently from those who had stayed at home.

> When I came back home, I met a very old friend of mine who had been in electronics, a reserved occupation. I found that though you knew the same people, you didn't share the same

stupid little jokes, you weren't somehow speaking the same
language any longer. That's all.[9]

George Pearson

It was extremely difficult for war veterans not to look down on
their contemporaries who had found reasons – genuine or otherwise – for staying out of the services. But, at the same time, the
veterans had lost six years of their life. Men with whom they had
stood on an equal footing back in 1939 were now streets ahead in
terms of their careers. This led to conflicted emotions.

> The beneficial effect was that when you came back – it
> sounds smug – but you could hold your head high! People –
> particularly accountants who had managed to stay at home – it
> sounds a bit childish now – but you did feel you'd done your
> bit. You were resentful that you'd lost six years against people
> who were competing with you and you'd got to catch up six
> years, which is quite a long time in an accountant's life![10]

Charles Ward

Ward proved to be a very special case – he treated his wartime-
induced disadvantages as a challenge. He had already completed
his accountancy exams whilst incarcerated as a POW. Then,
after an initial difficulty in acclimatising again to civilian life,
he had a successful career in business, rising to be chairman of
Dobson Park Industries. His lifelong interest in cricket also
developed and he ultimately became chairman of Nottinghamshire County Cricket Club.

Some men, such as Dennis Middleton, believed that they
had changed for the better due to their time in the forces.

> Mentally, I gained a great deal in self-confidence. I had acquired
> the philosophy not to bother about what everybody else thinks!
> You know the expressions, 'You can't do that!' or 'You can't

wear that!' 'What will people think?' I couldn't care less what
people will think! If you're fortunate enough to come through
it and not have too many bad experiences, there are a lot of
things worse than a war![11]

Dennis Middleton

However, many suffered from what we would now diagnose as
Post-traumatic Stress Disorder (PTSD), although many would
argue that the 'disorder' was an entirely natural reaction to the
stresses they had endured. Many of the men seemed to cope perfectly well during the fighting, or as a POW, but encountered
terrible problems when they returned home.

It was like taking a splint off a fracture. While the splint was
'on' – while you were in situations of stress and fear you were
all right – you could combat it – because you'd become used to
combatting it. When you got home the 'splint' fell off! I could
not go into a public house on my own! A train letting off steam
was like a bomb and I would drop to the ground in those early
days. For years that is how we kept ourselves alive. It wore off –
altogether it took about a year. My local doctor said 'As much
sport as you can manage!' That was great – I loved sport![12]

Harry Day

Some had developed signs of increasing nerves during their war
service. Ted Homes found that as the war went on, the stress
got worse. Each incident survived just seemed to stoke up the
mental pressure. This then carried on into his civilian life.

I think you got more nervous. It was what I used to call 'bomb
happy'. If you heard an aeroplane coming, you were looking
round and sometimes if there was a noise sounding like a
bomb you'd drop on the floor – even today, after all these
years, if a low-flying plane comes over I'm nearly down flat on

the floor – I can't help it, it's just a reaction. We used to call it 'bomb happy'. It doesn't affect you very much, but you still felt nervous.[13]

Ted Holmes

Many never really recovered. Their ingrained wartime reactions to danger could not be suppressed.

I still suffer from bad nerves. I was always listening for things happening – I'd had that all the way through. Any movements, wherever I went, approaching a house, or anywhere, I'd be always listening and ready to jump at the first sign of anything. It never leaves you; you've still got that intuition – any sound, you jump! Sometimes I'd be working and some of the people they drop something behind me for a joke – I'd jump a mile startled – and they'd think it was funny. I still have it today! It's a thing I live with.[14]

Ernie Hurry

This was emphatically not weakness. Take the case of Harold Harper, an unflinching and superlatively competent soldier: he is perhaps the best example of what could happen when the pressure was released.

I was the type of soldier that went in to do a job and having done the job was quite happy to get back to civilian life. I went back to Boots Accounting Department. I went in as a boy and came out as very much a man! I was very worn out. The stress of getting back into civilian life: because you realise how much you'd lost when you pitted yourself against the blokes at work who hadn't left the company – they knew everything that was going off – and you didn't. The reaction set in after I got home – about six months after I had ulcers and goodness knows what. You tense yourself up during the war and now you weren't so

tense the thing was backfiring on you. I didn't have a nervous
breakdown, but I was very close to it – I was scared to cross
the road, scared to sit on the top of a double-decker bus. That
started about a year after I was demobbed. My father was very
blunt, and he told me in no uncertain manner what to do! 'Pull
yourself together!' When the Territorial Army reformed in
1947, I had a fair amount of persuasion to join – but I wouldn't.
I just didn't feel as if I wanted to get involved again. I suppose
war weariness – and the nerve had gone a little bit.[15]

Harold Harper

Frank Penlington summed up the effect on him, and indirectly
illustrates the problems of wives and children who had to cope
with the mental trauma inflicted on husbands and fathers by
the war.

The war wasn't reality was it? After the war you come out to
reality and I've never accepted that. Although I say it myself,
I've never been normal since I left the army – and the wife will
tell you![16]

Frank Penlington

Peter Birkin was one of the most tragic cases. Throughout the
war, he had proved himself an inspiring leader and courageous
soldier who had served his country with exceptional fortitude.
His sexual preferences were generally accepted by the men that
fought with him, but he was brought down in the postwar years,
at least in part by the fact that his country was still riddled with
prejudice – and homosexuality was illegal until 1967. We know
little about his later years, but his heavy drinking declined into a
sad alcoholism, and a very public court case marked his downfall
in the public eye. He died relatively young in 1971 at just 61 years
old. One hopes this book will help secure an unreserved and
unstinting recognition for Peter Birkin – a man his comrades

considered as one of the true heroes and an inspiration to all the South Notts Hussars.

Of course, some of the men had to suffer the after-effects of their physical wounds. Bobby Feakins had been invalided out of the army after being wounded in the armoured car alongside Major Gerry Birkin on 27 May 1942. He was still suffering from the physical effects when I interviewed him more than fifty years later. Many men in his situation sought to overcome, or disguise, their disabilities in the postwar years, but the effects often returned to haunt their old age. By the time he was in his eighties he could hardly walk.

> I received a disability pension of 20 per cent for my legs. I still limped and in those days somebody that limped was known as 'Gimpy'. I was determined to get rid of the limp! I struggled and struggled, and the pain was pretty bad, but I eventually did. It took me eighteen months to get rid of the limp. I hadn't got a job to go to. No counselling or training whatsoever. I was no different from anybody else. We were all returning from overseas – the jobs having been done by young women in our absence that had to be scaled down to allow those coming home to take jobs. We gradually got back on our feet. I'd always been very interested in motor cars and I got a job with a second-hand car company. I had become of a nervous disposition and I always felt that I was unequal to an awful lot of people. That has never left me. I always feel that I should have done an awful lot more with my life.[17]
>
> Bobby Feakins

Another severely wounded veteran was Harry Barnes, who had been awarded a well-merited George Medal for his actions in dragging Bombardier Beaumont to safety from a minefield at Maasbree in November 1944. Whilst carrying out the rescue, Barnes had his own leg blown off just under the knee, and in view of his courageous self-sacrifice it is somehow sad to learn that all his medals were sold in 2001 for £1,250. Did our country really do enough to look after the veterans and their families in the years after the war?

Douglas Nicholls had also been badly wounded in the leg back in September 1944. Flown back to England, he was hospitalised for months with special *hip spica* plasters to immobilise the limb. For a while he needed callipers to walk, with perhaps the only consolation that he managed to marry one of his nurses. He left the hospital with a new wife – and his left leg some 1½ inches shorter than other. Even after he was demobilised, he would still limp very badly. Nicholls was awarded a disability pension for injuries and overcame any disadvantage in civilian life to enjoy a successful career as a teacher. When asked whether it was all worth it, he had a wonderful reply that sums up the drive and commitment of these men.

> I felt that Hitler was somebody that had to be stopped. He was stopped – and that gave me great satisfaction![18]
>
> Douglas Nicholls

Let the last words lie with Bill Adams. After a relatively light wound on 27 May 1942, he had resumed his service, only to be eventually medically downgraded out of the army. After the war he had severe anxiety dreams that plagued him for many years.

> I still do think about things that happened then – you still do. It's all right these in the Gulf talking about their six weeks 'do', but ours was nearly six years! You don't get over that in a hurry. Especially when you see the bombs blowing round you, the men being killed and things like that – you never forget it.[19]
>
> Bill Adams

Many of the men I interviewed told me of the dreams they

suffered in the nights immediately preceding or following our recording sessions; nightmares where they relived their former terrors. The interviews may have awakened demons, but most of the men were nonetheless still keen to record their memories so that people might understand what it was *really* like. Not the gung-ho imaginings of journalists, or the fantasies of war films, but the nitty-gritty reality of life at war. Of the unstinting comradeship of their fellows. Most of all to remember and pay tribute to the friends they had lost in battle; the friends left buried beneath the sands or mud of far-off lands. Now that almost all the South Notts Hussars I interviewed are dead, it is time to remember and pay due homage to them all. But most of all to say thank you.

FIFTY SOUTH NOTTS HUSSARS
INTERVIEWS TOTALLING 356 HOURS
HELD AT SOUND ARCHIVE, IWM

Adams, William 14791/13

Barber, William 14230/4

Bonnello, Herbert William
11959/16

Brookes, Frederick 14730/10

Coup, Wilfred Edward 12411/6

Cutter, Reginald 13125/10

Daniell, Robert B T 14761/11

Day, Joseph Harry Woodhouse
12412/13

Elliott, David Scotchford 16706/30

Ellis, Ray Knight 12660/50

Feakins, Eric 'Bobby' 15607/7

Foulds, Robert Leslie 12715/24

Gibson, Leonard 12183/22

Giles, Kenneth 14728/29

Harper, Harold 10923/17

Harrold, Victor George 12682/5

Hayward, Leslie Edward 'Ted'
14727/14

Hingston, Bob 14789/22

Holmes, Edward 11958/16

Hurry, Ernie 14729/18

Hutton, William Allan 11957/13

Knowles, Frank Roland 11465/12

Laborde, Charles 15103/21

Langford, Frederick Coombes
12240/10

Loyley, George Frederick 16351/4

Mayoh, Dennis 16280/8

McNish, Reginald 12435/15

Middleton, Dennis 14986/11

Morley, Erik 16281/6

Nicholls, Douglas 14731/7

Parker, Albert 14788/15

Peachment, Donald 12917/5

Pearson, George 10912/14

Penlington, Frank 16085/14

Pringle, William 14790/11

Scott, Alan 15322/4

Shipley, Ted 14719/3

Sinclair, Ian 11468/25

Swinton, Albert 15104/19

Sykes, Jack 11960/12

Tebbett, Norman 12410/14

Tew, Ken 11956/6

Thompson, Harold 12242/17

Tickle, David 14794/21

Walker, John Ralph 11464/17
Ward, Albert 15321/6
Ward, Charles 14897/15

Westlake, Charles 11048/14
Whitehorn, John Edward 11466/13
Whittaker, Edward 12409/30

NOTES

1. As Bad as It Gets

1. IWM SOUND: AC 12660, Ray Ellis, Reel 31.
2. IWM SOUND: AC 12660, Ray Ellis, Reel 29.
3. IWM SOUND: AC 12660, Ray Ellis, Reel 31.
4. IWM SOUND: AC 12660, Ray Ellis, Reel 31.
5. IWM SOUND: AC 12660, Ray Ellis, Reel 31.
6. IWM SOUND: AC 12660, Ray Ellis, Reel 32.
7. IWM SOUND: AC 12660, Ray Ellis, Reel 32.
8. IWM SOUND: AC 12660, Ray Ellis, Reel 32.

2. Growing Pains

1. IWM SOUND: AC 11048, Charles Westlake, Reels 1 & 2.
2. IWM SOUND: AC 14230, William Barber, Reels 3 & 4.
3. IWM SOUND: AC 14789, Bob Hingston, Reel 2.
4. IWM SOUND: AC 15103, Charles Laborde, Reel 2.
5. IWM SOUND: AC 14790, William Pringle, Reel 1.
6. Sadly, the story of 150th Regiment, RA is not part of either the original IWM oral history project or this book. For more information see Eric Dobson, *History of the South Nottinghamshire Hussars, 1924–1948* (York & London: Herald Printing Works, 1948).
7. IWM SOUND: AC 11048, Charles Westlake, Reels 1 & 2.
8. IWM SOUND: AC 12660, Ray Ellis, Reel 1.
9. IWM SOUND: AC 11959, Herbert Bonnello, Reel 1.
10. IWM SOUND: AC 14788, Albert Parker, Reel 1.
11. IWM SOUND: AC 12715, Robert Foulds, Reel 1.
12. IWM SOUND: AC 11957, Bill Hutton, Reel 1.

13. IWM SOUND: AC 11468, Ian Sinclair, Reel 1.
14. IWM SOUND: AC 10912, George Pearson, Reel 2.
15. IWM SOUND: AC 12410, Norman Tebbett, Reels 1 & 2.

3. The Basics

1. IWM SOUND: AC 14789, Bob Hingston, Reel 4.
2. IWM SOUND: AC 12410, Norman Tebbett, Reel 1.
3. IWM SOUND: AC 12660, Ray Ellis, Reel 1.
4. IWM SOUND: AC 12715, Robert Foulds, Reel 1.
5. IWM SOUND: AC 12660, Ray Ellis, Reel 1.
6. IWM SOUND: AC 11466, John Whitehorn, Reel 2.
7. IWM SOUND: AC 14794, David Tickle, Reel 1.
8. IWM SOUND: AC 10912, George Pearson, Reel 2.
9. IWM SOUND: AC 10912, George Pearson, Reel 1.
10. IWM SOUND: AC 15103, Charles Laborde, Reel 2.
11. IWM SOUND: AC 10912, George Pearson, Reel 1.
12. IWM SOUND: AC 11048, Charles Westlake, Reel 2.
13. IWM SOUND: AC 10912, George Pearson, Reels 1 & 2.
14. IWM SOUND: AC 11960, Jack Sykes, Reel 1.
15. IWM SOUND: AC 12660, Ray Ellis, Reel 2.
16. IWM SOUND: AC 12240, Fred Langford, Reel 1.
17. IWM SOUND: AC 11464, John Walker, Reel 2.
18. IWM SOUND: AC 12715, Robert Foulds, Reel 2.
19. IWM SOUND: AC 14897, Charles Ward, Reel 1.
20. IWM SOUND: AC 10923, Harold Harper, Reel 1.
21. IWM SOUND: AC 14789, Bob Hingston, Reel 2.
22. IWM SOUND: AC 11959, Herbert Bonnello, Reel 2.
23. IWM SOUND: AC 11468, Ian Sinclair, Reels 2 & 3.
24. IWM SOUND: AC 12660, Ray Ellis, Reel 2.
25. IWM SOUND: AC 12660, Ray Ellis, Reel 2.
26. IWM SOUND: AC 12183, Leonard Gibson, Reel 4.
27. IWM SOUND: AC 14789, Bob Hingston, Reel 4.

4. Mobilisation

1. IWM SOUND: AC 12412, Harry Day, Reel 1.
2. IWM SOUND: AC 14790, William Pringle, Reel 1.
3. IWM SOUND: AC 10912, George Pearson, Reel 3.

4. IWM SOUND: AC 14986, Dennis Middleton, Reel 2.
5. IWM SOUND: AC 11960, Jack Sykes, Reel 1.
6. IWM SOUND: AC 14791, William Adams, Reel 2.
7. IWM SOUND: AC 10923, Harold Harper, Reel 1.
8. IWM SOUND: AC 12412, Harry Day, Reel 1.
9. IWM SOUND: AC 12409, Ted Whittaker, Reel 3.
10. IWM SOUND: AC 11465, Frank Knowles, Reel 1.
11. IWM SOUND: AC 11468, Ian Sinclair, Reel 3.
12. IWM SOUND: AC 11468, Ian Sinclair, Reel 3.
13. IWM SOUND: AC 12660, Ray Ellis, Reel 3.
14. IWM SOUND: AC 12409, Ted Whittaker, Reel 3.
15. IWM SOUND: AC 12409, Ted Whittaker, Reel 3.
16. IWM SOUND: AC 11957, Bill Hutton, Reel 1.

5. Getting Ready

1. IWM SOUND: AC 12660, Ray Ellis, Reel 3.
2. IWM SOUND: AC 12240, Fred Langford, Reel 2.
3. IWM SOUND: AC 12660, Ray Ellis, Reel 3.
4. IWM SOUND: AC 12715, Robert Foulds, Reel 3.
5. IWM SOUND: AC 14790, William Pringle, Reel 2.
6. INTERNET SOURCE: Ronald Miles Autobiography (Copyright Paul Miles), http://ronaldmiles.blogspot.com/
7. IWM SOUND: AC 12411, Edward Coup, Reel 2.
8. IWM SOUND: AC 11466, John Whitehorn, Reel 3.
9. IWM SOUND: AC 14897, Charles Ward, Reel 2.
10. IWM SOUND: AC 11465, Frank Knowles, Reel 2.
11. IWM SOUND: AC 12715, Robert Foulds, Reel 3.
12. IWM SOUND: AC 11958, Ted Holmes, Reel 2.
13. IWM SOUND: AC 11465, Frank Knowles, Reel 2.
14. IWM SOUND: AC 11048, Charles Westlake, Reel 3.
15. IWM SOUND: AC 11957, Bill Hutton, Reel 2.
16. IWM SOUND: AC 14897, Charles Ward, Reel 2.
17. IWM SOUND: AC 14727, Ted Hayward, Reel 2.
18. IWM SOUND: AC 14727, Ted Hayward, Reel 2.
19. IWM SOUND: AC 14727, Ted Hayward, Reel 3.
20. IWM SOUND: AC 10923, Harold Harper, Reel 2.
21. IWM SOUND: AC 14897, Charles Ward, Reel 3.

22. Colonel Lancelot Rolleston was born in 1847. Served in the Boer War with 3rd Imperial Yeomanry; he was badly wounded and mentioned in despatches. He died in 1941.
23. IWM SOUND: AC 12660, Ray Ellis, Reel 4.
24. IWM SOUND: AC 12660, Ray Ellis, Reel 4.

6. Phoney War in Palestine

1. IWM SOUND: AC 14729, Ernie Hurry, Reel 2.
2. IWM SOUND: AC 11958, Ted Holmes, Reel 3.
3. IWM SOUND: AC 11958, Ted Holmes, Reel 3.
4. IWM SOUND: AC 14730, Frederick Brookes, Reel 3.
5. IWM SOUND: AC 14729, Ernie Hurry, Reel 2.
6. IWM SOUND: AC 12660, Ray Ellis, Reel 4.
7. IWM SOUND: AC 14729, Ernie Hurry, Reel 2.
8. IWM SOUND: AC 12660, Ray Ellis, Reel 4.
9. IWM SOUND: AC 12435, Reg McNish, Reel 3.
10. IWM SOUND: AC 14729, Ernie Hurry, Reel 3.
11. IWM SOUND: AC 14789, Bob Hingston, Reel 6.
12. IWM SOUND: AC 14729, Ernie Hurry, Reel 3.
13. IWM SOUND: AC 12660, Ray Ellis, Reel 5.
14. IWM SOUND: AC 10912, George Pearson, Reel 4.
15. IWM SOUND: AC 14789, Bob Hingston, Reels 6 & 7.
16. IWM SOUND: AC 14897, Charles Ward, Reel 3.
17. IWM SOUND: AC 11465, Frank Knowles, Reel 2.
18. IWM SOUND: AC 12242, Harold Thompson, Reel 6.
19. IWM SOUND: AC 15104, Albert Swinton, Reel 3.
20. IWM SOUND: AC 14789, Bob Hingston, Reel 7.
21. IWM SOUND: AC 15103, Charles Laborde, Reel 4.
22. IWM SOUND: AC 12660, Ray Ellis, Reel 6.
23. IWM SOUND: AC 15103, Charles Laborde, Reel 4.
24. IWM SOUND: AC 15103, Charles Laborde, Reel 4.
25. IWM SOUND: AC 14789, Bob Hingston, Reel 8.
26. IWM SOUND: AC 12412, Harry Day, Reel 3.
27. IWM SOUND: AC 12412, Harry Day, Reel 3.
28. IWM SOUND: AC 12242, Harold Thompson, Reel 5.
29. IWM SOUND: AC 14727, Ted Hayward, Reel 4.
30. IWM SOUND: AC 14727, Ted Hayward, Reel 4.

31. IWM SOUND: AC 14727, Ted Hayward, Reels 3 & 4.
32. IWM SOUND: AC 11468, Ian Sinclair, Reel 5.
33. IWM SOUND: AC 14729, Ernie Hurry, Reel 4.
34. IWM SOUND: AC 12715, Robert Foulds, Reel 4.
35. IWM SOUND: AC 12660, Ray Ellis, Reel 6.
36. Robert Paulson died on 16 May 1940 at the age of 19. He is buried in Ramleh War Cemetery.
37. IWM SOUND: AC 12660, Ray Ellis, Reel 6.
38. IWM SOUND: AC 14729, Ernie Hurry, Reel 8.
39. IWM SOUND: AC 12409, Ted Whittaker, Reel 6.
40. IWM SOUND: AC 15103, Charles Laborde, Reel 5.
41. IWM SOUND: AC 14897, Charles Ward, Reel 4.

7. Mersa Matruh

1. IWM SOUND: AC 12660, Ray Ellis, Reel 6.
2. IWM SOUND: AC 15103, Charles Laborde, Reel 5.
3. IWM SOUND: AC 12660, Ray Ellis, Reel 6.
4. IWM SOUND: AC 12660, Ray Ellis, Reels 6 & 7.
5. IWM SOUND: AC 15103, Charles Laborde, Reel 5.
6. IWM SOUND: AC 12660, Ray Ellis, Reel 7.
7. IWM SOUND: AC 15103, Charles Laborde, Reel 5.
8. IWM SOUND: AC 10923, Harold Harper, Reel 3.
9. IWM SOUND: AC 10923, Harold Harper, Reel 3.
10. IWM SOUND: AC 12660, Ray Ellis, Reels 7 & 8.
11. IWM SOUND: AC 12412, Harry Day, Reel 4.
12. IWM SOUND: AC 11466, John Whitehorn, Reel 6.
13. IWM SOUND: AC 10912, George Pearson, Reel 5.
14. IWM SOUND: AC 12242, Harold Thompson, Reel 6.
15. IWM SOUND: AC 14794, David Tickle, Reel 3.
16. IWM SOUND: AC 14789, Bob Hingston, Reel 9.
17. IWM SOUND: AC 11464, John Walker, Reels 5 & 6.
18. IWM SOUND: AC 10912, George Pearson, Reel 5.
19. IWM SOUND: AC 11466, John Whitehorn, Reel 6.
20. IWM SOUND: AC 14791, William Adams, Reel 4.
21. IWM SOUND: AC 12660, Ray Ellis, Reel 7.
22. IWM SOUND: AC 12410, Norman Tebbett, Reel 5.
23. IWM SOUND: AC 14789, Bob Hingston, Reel 9.

24. IWM SOUND: AC 15103, Charles Laborde, Reel 5.

25. IWM SOUND: AC 11468, Ian Sinclair, Reel 5.

26. IWM SOUND: AC 11956, Ken Tew, Reel 2.

27. IWM SOUND: AC 12412, Harry Day, Reel 5.

28. IWM SOUND: AC 10912, George Pearson, Reel 5.

29. IWM SOUND: AC 10912, George Pearson, Reel 5.

30. IWM SOUND: AC 12412, Harry Day, Reel 5.

31. IWM SOUND: AC 11466, John Whitehorn, Reel 5.

32. IWM SOUND: AC 11464, John Walker, Reel 5.

33. IWM SOUND: AC 12660, Ray Ellis, Reel

34. IWM SOUND: AC 12660, Ray Ellis, Reel 9.

35. IWM SOUND: AC 12409, Ted Whittaker, Reel 7.

36. IWM SOUND: AC 11468, Ian Sinclair, Reel 6.

37. IWM SOUND: AC 15103, Charles Laborde, Reel 6.

38. IWM SOUND: AC 14789, Bob Hingston, Reel 12.

39. Lieutenant Harry Clark died on 26 August 1940. He is buried in the Cairo War Memorial Cemetery.

40. IWM SOUND: AC 14986, Dennis Middleton, Reel 4.

41. IWM SOUND: AC 12660, Ray Ellis, Reel 12.

42. IWM SOUND: AC 15104, Albert Swinton, Reels 14 & 15.

43. IWM SOUND: AC 10912, George Pearson, Reel 6.

44. IWM SOUND: AC 10912, George Pearson, Reel 6.

45. IWM SOUND: AC 11959, Herbert Bonnello, Reel 5.

46. Also known as F Troop in some accounts. Most SNH accounts use X Troop and I have followed that convention.

47. IWM SOUND: AC 11466, John Whitehorn, Reel 6.

48. IWM SOUND: AC 16280, Dennis Mayoh, Reel 2.

49. IWM SOUND: AC 14986, Dennis Middleton, Reel 4.

50. IWM SOUND: AC 14789, Bob Hingston, Reel 10.

51. IWM SOUND: AC 14789, Bob Hingston, Reel 10.

52. IWM SOUND: AC 14789, Bob Hingston, Reel 11.

53. IWM SOUND: AC 14789, Bob Hingston, Reel 11.

54. IWM SOUND: AC 14789, Bob Hingston, Reel 11.

55. IWM SOUND: AC 11468, Ian Sinclair, Reel 6.

56. Gerry Birkin quoted by Eric Dobson, *History of the South Nottinghamshire Hussars, 1924–1948* (York & London: Herald Printing Works, 1948), p. 53.

57. IWM SOUND: AC 11466, John Whitehorn, Reel 6.

58. IWM SOUND: AC 11466, John Whitehorn, Reel 7.

59. IWM SOUND: AC 12660, Ray Ellis, Reel 11.

60. IWM SOUND: AC 11959, Herbert Bonnello, Reel 4.

61. IWM SOUND: AC 11958, Ted Holmes, Reel 4.

62. IWM SOUND: AC 11959, Herbert Bonnello, Reel 6.

63. IWM SOUND: AC 14730, Frederick Brookes, Reel 5.

64. IWM SOUND: AC 12660, Ray Ellis, Reel 12.

65. IWM SOUND: AC 12715, Robert Foulds, Reel 7.

66. IWM SOUND: AC 12660, Ray Ellis, Reel 13.

67. IWM SOUND: AC 12715, Robert Foulds, Reel 7.

68. IWM SOUND: AC 12660, Ray Ellis, Reel 13.

69. IWM SOUND: AC 12409, Ted Whittaker, Reel 9.

70. IWM SOUND: AC 14897, Charles Ward, Reel 7.

71. IWM SOUND: AC 10912, George Pearson, Reel 7.

72. IWM SOUND: AC 14788, Albert Parker, Reel 4.

73. IWM SOUND: AC 14788, Albert Parker, Reel 4.

8. Siege of Tobruk

1. IWM SOUND: AC 11957, Bill Hutton, Reel 5.

2. IWM SOUND: AC 15104, Albert Swinton, Reel 5.

3. IWM SOUND: AC 12715, Robert Foulds, Reel 7.

4. IWM SOUND: AC 12409, Ted Whittaker, Reel 9.

5. IWM SOUND: AC 12660, Ray Ellis, Reel 14.

6. IWM SOUND: AC 16281, Erik Morley, Reel 2.

7. IWM SOUND: AC 10912, George Pearson, Reel 7.

8. IWM SOUND: AC 14897, Charles Ward, Reel 4.

9. IWM SOUND: AC 12660, Ray Ellis, Reel 14.

10. IWM SOUND: AC 11957, Bill Hutton, Reel 5.

11. IWM SOUND: AC 12715, Robert Foulds, Reel 7.

12. IWM SOUND: AC 14986, Dennis Middleton, Reel 5.

13. IWM SOUND: AC 14729, Ernie Hurry, Reel 9.

14. IWM SOUND: AC 12660, Ray Ellis, Reel 14.

15. IWM SOUND: AC 14794, David Tickle, Reel 4.

16. IWM SOUND: AC 14789, Bob Hingston, Reel 13.

17. IWM SOUND: AC 14789, Bob Hingston, Reel 13.

18. IWM SOUND: AC 10912, George Pearson, Reel 9.

19. IWM SOUND: AC 11468, Ian Sinclair, Reel 7.

20. IWM SOUND: AC 10923, Harold Harper, Reel 5.

21. IWM SOUND: AC 12660, Ray Ellis, Reel 16.

22. IWM SOUND: AC 11957, Bill Hutton, Reel 5.

23. IWM SOUND: AC 12409, Ted Whittaker, Reel 9.

24. IWM SOUND: AC 14897, Charles Ward, Reel 5.

25. IWM SOUND: AC 10912, George Pearson, Reel 7.

26. IWM SOUND: AC 12660, Ray Ellis, Reel 15.

27. IWM SOUND: AC 12660, Ray Ellis, Reel 15.

28. IWM SOUND: AC 14794, David Tickle, Reel 5.

29. IWM SOUND: AC 14761, Robert Daniell, Reel 7.

30. Corporal Jack Edmondson died aged 26 on 14 April 1941. He is buried in Tobruk War Cemetery, Libya.

31. John Murray, *I Confess: A Memoir of the Siege of Tobruk* (Newport, NSW: Big Sky Publishing, 2011), p. 73.

32. IWM SOUND: AC 15104, Albert Swinton, Reel 5.

33. Eric Dobson, *History of the South Nottinghamshire Hussars, 1924–1948* (York & London: Herald Printing Works, 1948), p. 71.

34. IWM SOUND: AC 14789, Bob Hingston, Reel 14.

35. IWM SOUND: AC 14730, Frederick Brookes, Reel 6.

36. IWM SOUND: AC 11048, Charles Westlake, Reel 6.

37. IWM SOUND: AC 11468, Ian Sinclair, Reel 8.

38. IWM SOUND: AC 12660, Ray Ellis, Reel 20.

39. IWM SOUND: AC 12715, Robert Foulds, Reel 8.

40. IWM SOUND: AC 11958, Ted Holmes, Reel 5.

41. Lance Sergeant Philip Collihole died aged 28 on 1 May 1941. He is buried in Tobruk War Cemetery, Libya.

42. IWM SOUND: AC 10912, George Pearson, Reels 7 & 8.

43. Battery Sergeant Major Clifford Smedley died aged 21 on 1 May 1941. He is buried in Tobruk War Cemetery, Libya.

44. IWM SOUND: AC 10912, George Pearson, Reel 7.

45. IWM SOUND: AC 11959, Herbert Bonnello, Reel 7.

46. IWM SOUND: AC 14790, William Pringle, Reel 4.

47. IWM SOUND: AC 14729, Ernie Hurry, Reel 7.

48. IWM SOUND: AC 12715, Robert Foulds, Reel 8.

49. IWM SOUND: AC 11048, Charles Westlake, Reel 7.

50. IWM SOUND: AC 12409, Ted Whittaker, Reel 13.

51. IWM SOUND: AC 12409, Ted Whittaker, Reel 13.
52. IWM SOUND: AC 12660, Ray Ellis, Reel 21.
53. IWM SOUND: AC 10923, Harold Harper, Reel 6.
54. IWM SOUND: AC 10923, Harold Harper, Reel 7.
55. IWM SOUND: AC 15104, Albert Swinton, Reel 5.
56. IWM SOUND: AC 12660, Ray Ellis, Reel 21.
57. IWM SOUND: AC 12409, Ted Whittaker, Reel 13.
58. IWM SOUND: AC 12660, Ray Ellis, Reels 9 & 22.
59. IWM SOUND: AC 15103, Charles Laborde, Reel 8.
60. IWM SOUND: AC 11959, Herbert Bonnello, Reel 7.
61. IWM SOUND: AC 12409, Ted Whittaker, Reel 13.
62. IWM SOUND: AC 14790, William Pringle, Reel 6.
63. IWM SOUND: AC 10912, George Pearson, Reel 10.
64. IWM SOUND: AC 15103, Charles Laborde, Reel 9.
65. IWM SOUND: AC 15104, Albert Swinton, Reel 7.
66. IWM SOUND: AC 14791, William Adams, Reel 7.

9. A Way of Life

1. IWM SOUND: AC 12240 Fred Langford, Reel 5.
2. IWM SOUND: AC 14790, William Pringle, Reel 4.
3. IWM SOUND: AC 12715, Robert Foulds, Reel 8.
4. IWM SOUND: AC 14897, Charles Ward, Reel 8.
5. IWM SOUND: AC 14790, William Pringle, Reel 5.
6. IWM SOUND: AC 14727, Ted Hayward, Reels 6 & 7.
7. IWM SOUND: AC 14789, Bob Hingston, Reel 16.
8. IWM SOUND: AC 14897, Charles Ward, Reel 6.
9. IWM SOUND: AC 11958, Ted Holmes, Reels 6 & 7.
10. IWM SOUND: AC 15104, Albert Swinton, Reel 7.
11. IWM SOUND: AC 11465, Frank Knowles, Reels 2 & 5.
12. IWM SOUND: AC 10923, Harold Harper, Reel 6.
13. IWM SOUND: AC 15104, Albert Swinton, Reel 7.
14. IWM SOUND: AC 14986, Dennis Middleton, Reel 6.
15. IWM SOUND: AC 12411, Edward Coup, Reel 5.
16. IWM SOUND: AC 12409, Ted Whittaker, Reel 11.
17. Ted Whittaker's cartoon 'The Beer Ships Here Again'.
18. A pith helmet.
19. Major General Leslie Morshead commanding 9th Australian Division at Tobruk.

20. IWM SOUND: AC 12409, Ted Whittaker, Reel 11.
21. IWM SOUND: AC 11957, Bill Hutton, Reels 3 & 6.
22. IWM SOUND: AC 14729, Ernie Hurry, Reel 8.
23. IWM SOUND: AC 10912, George Pearson, Reel 9.
24. IWM SOUND: AC 10923, Harold Harper, Reel 6.
25. IWM SOUND: AC 12240, Fred Langford, Reel 6.
26. IWM SOUD: AC 11958, Ted Holmes, Reel 7.
27. IWM SOUND: AC 11468, Ian Sinclair, Reel 8.
28. IWM SOUND: AC 10923, Harold Harper, Reels 4 & 8.
29. IWM SOUD: AC 11958, Ted Holmes, Reel 7.
30. IWM SOUND: AC 12660, Ray Ellis, Reel 19.
31. IWM SOUND: AC 11957, Bill Hutton, Reel 7.
32. IWM SOUND: AC 14789, Bob Hingston, Reel 17.
33. IWM SOUND: AC 11464, John Walker, Reel 9.
34. IWM SOUND: AC 15103, Charles Laborde, Reel 11.
35. IWM SOUND: AC 14790, William Pringle, Reel 6.
36. IWM SOUND: AC 12409, Ted Whittaker, Reel 11.
37. IWM SOUND: AC 15104, Albert Swinton, Reel 7.
38. IWM DOCS: Robert Daniell unpublished typescript memoir.
39. IWM SOUND: AC 12409, Ted Whittaker, Reel 11.
40. IWM SOUND: AC 16280, Dennis Mayoh, Reel 4.
41. Presumably Lale Andersen, who recorded 'Lili Marlene' in German in 1939. It became very popular with soldiers on both sides in the Western Desert.
42. IWM SOUND: AC 10923, Harold Harper, Reel 7.
43. IWM SOUND: AC 14761, Robert Daniell, Reel 8.
44. IWM SOUND: AC 12660, Ray Ellis, Reel 17.
45. IWM SOUND: AC 11464, John Walker, Reel 9.
46. IWM SOUND: AC 11464, John Walker, Reel 9.
47. IWM SOUND: AC 15104, Albert Swinton, Reel 7.
48. IWM SOUND: AC 12660, Ray Ellis, Reel 17.
49. IWM SOUND: AC 12660, Ray Ellis, Reel 17.
50. IWM SOUND: AC 15104, Albert Swinton, Reel 7.
51. IWM SOUND: AC 16351, George Loyley, Reel 3.
52. IWM SOUND: AC 14897, Charles Ward, Reel 8.
53. IWM SOUND: AC 11468, Ian Sinclair, Reel 10.
54. IWM SOUND: AC 10912, George Pearson, Reel 11.

55. IWM SOUND: AC 14789, Bob Hingston, Reel 14.

56. IWM SOUND: AC 12660, Ray Ellis, Reel 22.

57. IWM SOUND: AC 12660, Ray Ellis, Reel 17.

58. IWM SOUND: AC 10912, George Pearson, Reel 9.

10. Breakout from Tobruk

1. IWM SOUND: AC 15103, Charles Laborde, Reel 11.

2. IWM SOUND: AC 11468, Ian Sinclair, Reel 9.

3. Lieutenant Michael Weaver of the 1st King's Dragoon Guards, Royal Armoured Corps died 17 October 1941. He is buried in Tobruk War Cemetery.

4. IWM SOUND: AC 14789, Bob Hingston, Reels 17 & 18.

5. IWM SOUND: AC 14789, Bob Hingston, Reel 18.

6. IWM SOUND: AC 14761, Robert Daniell, Reel 8.

7. IWM SOUND: AC 14789, Bob Hingston, Reel 18.

8. IWM SOUND: AC 11960, Jack Sykes, Reel 4.

9. IWM SOUND: AC 12409, Ted Whittaker, Reel 14.

10. IWM SOUND: AC 14986, Dennis Middleton, Reel 7.

11. IWM SOUND: AC 10912, George Pearson, Reel 4.

12. IWM SOUND: AC 12660, Ray Ellis, Reel 23.

13. IWM SOUND: AC 12715, Robert Foulds, Reel 10.

14. IWM SOUND: AC 14794, David Tickle, Reel 7.

15. IWM SOUND: AC 12409, Ted Whittaker, Reel 14.

16. IWM SOUND: AC 16085, Frank Penlington, Reels 5–6.

17. IWM SOUND: AC 12409, Ted Whittaker, Reel 14.

18. IWM SOUND: AC 12409, Ted Whittaker, Reel 15.

19. IWM SOUND: AC 12409, Ted Whittaker, Reel 15.

20. IWM SOUND: AC 12409, Ted Whittaker, Reel 15.

21. IWM SOUND: AC 14729, Ernie Hurry, Reel 9.

22. IWM SOUND: AC 15104, Albert Swinton, Reel 9.

23. IWM SOUND: AC 15104, Albert Swinton, Reel 9.

24. IWM SOUND: AC 10923, Harold Harper, Reel 8.

25. IWM SOUND: AC 15104, Albert Swinton, Reel 9.

26. IWM SOUND: AC 10912, George Pearson, Reel 8.

27. IWM SOUND: AC 12715, Robert Foulds, Reels 8 & 10.

28. IWM SOUND: AC 11468, Ian Sinclair, Reel 11.

29. Ian Playfair, *History of the Second World War, United Kingdom,*

Military Series, The Mediterranean and the Middle East, Vol. 3
(London: HMSO, 1960), p. 46.

30. IWM SOUND: AC 12715, Robert Foulds, Reel 10.
31. IWM SOUND: AC 12660, Ray Ellis, Reel 24.
32. IWM SOUND: AC 15104, Albert Swinton, Reel 9.
33. IWM SOUND: AC 10912, George Pearson, Reel 11.
34. IWM SOUND: AC 12715, Robert Foulds, Reel 11.
35. IWM SOUND: AC 14788, Albert Parker, Reel 7.
36. IWM SOUND: AC 12660, Ray Ellis, Reel 25.
37. IWM SOUND: AC 12660, Ray Ellis, Reel 25.
38. IWM SOUND: AC 10912, George Pearson, Reel 11.

11. Battle of Knightsbridge, 27 May 1942

1. IWM SOUND: AC 12660, Ray Ellis, Reel 30.
2. IWM SOUND: AC 12660, Ray Ellis, Reel 26.
3. IWM SOUND: AC 12660, Ray Ellis, Reel 13.
4. IWM SOUND: AC 12409, Ted Whittaker, Reel 16.
5. IWM SOUND: AC 15607, Bobby Feakins, Reel 3.
6. IWM SOUND: AC 11465, Frank Knowles, Reel 6.
7. IWM SOUD: AC 11959, Herbert Bonnello, Reel 9.
8. IWM SOUND: AC 12660, Ray Ellis, Reel 27.
9. IWM SOUND: AC 12660, Ray Ellis, Reel 27.
10. IWM SOUND: AC 10923, Harold Harper, Reel 9.
11. IWM SOUND: AC 16706, David Elliott, Reel 10.
12. IWM SOUND: AC 10923, Harold Harper, Reel 9.
13. IWM SOUND: AC 11959, Herbert Bonnello, Reel 9.
14. IWM SOUND: AC 11957, Bill Hutton, Reel 8.
15. IWM SOUND: AC 10923, Harold Harper, Reel 9.
16. Sergeant Patrick Bland died aged 22 on 27 May 1942. He is commemorated on the Alamein Memorial, Egypt.
17. IWM SOUND: AC 10923, Harold Harper, Reel 9.
18. Major Gerry Birkin died on 27 May 1942.
19. IWM SOUND: AC 15607, Bobby Feakins, Reel 4.
20. Gunner Walter White died on 27 May 1942. There is a discrepancy in date of death between the CWGC and the SNH records.
21. Gunner William Lloyd died on 27 May 1942. He is buried in Knightsbridge War Cemetery, Acroma, Libya.

22. IWM SOUND: AC 15607, Bobby Feakins, Reel 4.

23. IWM SOUND: AC 10923, Harold Harper, Reel 9.

24. IWM SOUND: AC 10923, Harold Harper, Reel 9.

25. Major Philip Gervais Birkin died aged 33 on 27 May 1942. He is buried in Knightsbridge War Cemetery, Acroma, Libya.

26. IWM SOUND: AC 10923, Harold Harper, Reel 9.

27. Stuart Pitman, *Second Royal Gloucestershire Hussars, Libya–Egypt, 1941–1942* (London: The Saint Catherine Press Ltd, 1950), p. 57.

28. George Buxton died aged 21 on 27 May 1942. He is buried in Knightsbridge War Cemetery, Acroma, Libya.

29. Lance Corporal John Chamberlain died aged 22 on 27 May 1942. He is buried in Knightsbridge War Cemetery, Acroma, Libya.

30. Victor Bridle quoted by Stuart Pitman, *Second Royal Gloucestershire Hussars*, p. 57.

31. Lieutenant Edmond Ades died aged 24 on 27 May 1942. He is buried in Knightsbridge War Cemetery, Acroma, Libya.

32. Victor Bridle quoted by Stuart Pitman, *Second Royal Gloucestershire Hussars, Libya–Egypt, 1941–1942* (London: The Saint Catherine Press Ltd, 1950), p. 57.

33. IWM SOUND: AC 10923, Harold Harper, Reel 9.

34. IWM SOUND: AC 15607, Bobby Feakins, Reel 5.

35. IWM SOUND: AC 15607, Bobby Feakins, Reel 5.

36. IWM SOUND: AC 15607, Bobby Feakins, Reel 5.

37. IWM SOUND: AC 15607, Bobby Feakins, Reel 5.

38. IWM SOUND: AC 15607, Bobby Feakins, Reels 5 & 6.

39. IWM SOUND: AC 10923, Harold Harper, Reel 9.

40. IWM SOUND: AC 10923, Harold Harper, Reel 10.

41. IWM SOUND: AC 14729, Ernie Hurry, Reel 10.

42. IWM SOUND: AC 11957, Bill Hutton, Reel 8.

43. IWM SOUND: AC 14729, Ernie Hurry, Reel 10.

44. IWM SOUND: AC 14794, David Tickle, Reel 8.

45. IWM SOUND AC 11959, Herbert Bonnello, Reel 10.

46. Eric Dobson, *History of the South Nottinghamshire Hussars, 1924–1948* (York & London: Herald Printing Works, 1948), p. 123.

47. IWM SOUND: AC 11957, Bill Hutton, Reel 9.

48. IWM SOUND AC 11959, Herbert Bonnello, Reel 10.

49. IWM SOUND: AC 14729, Ernie Hurry, Reel 10.

50. IWM DOCS: Robert Daniell, typescript memoir, p. 78.

51. IWM SOUND: AC 12412, Harry Day, Reel 7.

52. IWM SOUND: AC 11959, Herbert Bonnello, Reel 10.

53. IWM SOUND: AC 11957, Bill Hutton, Reel 8.

54. IWM SOUND: AC 11464, John Walker, Reel 11.

55. IWM SOUND: AC 11464, John Walker, Reel 11.

56. IWM SOUND: AC 14790, William Pringle, Reels 7 & 8.

57. IWM SOUND: AC 11958, Ted Holmes, Reel 8.

58. IWM SOUND: AC 11464, John Walker, Reel 11.

59. IWM SOUND: AC 11464, John Walker, Reel 11.

60. IWM SOUND: AC 11958, Ted Holmes, Reel 8.

61. IWM SOUND: AC 12242, Harold Thompson, Reel 11.

62. IWM SOUND: AC 12409, Ted Whittaker, Reel 18.

63. IWM SOUND: AC 12409, Ted Whittaker, Reel 19.

64. The value of oral history can be explained when comparing Ted Whittaker's account with the heroic version promulgated by the regimental history: 'One of the tyres on the exposed side of Major Peter Birkin's armoured car had been punctured by a machine-gun bullet. Though the car drew intense enemy fire Gunner Worley coolly changed the wheel under a hail of small arms fire.' Eric Dobson, *History of the South Nottinghamshire Hussars, 1924–1948* (York & London: Herald Printing Works, 1948), p. 124.

12. The Last Round, 6 June 1942

1. IWM SOUND: AC 12660, Ray Ellis, Reel 29.

2. IWM SOUND: AC 12409, Ted Whittaker, Reel 19.

3. IWM SOUND: AC 12660, Ray Ellis, Reel 30.

4. IWM SOUND: AC 12660, Ray Ellis, Reel 30.

5. IWM SOUND: AC 12409, Ted Whittaker, Reel 19.

6. IWM SOUND: AC 14790, William Pringle, Reels 7 & 8.

7. Bernard Fletcher quoted by Anthony Brett-James, *Ball of Fire: The Fifth Indian Division in the Second World War* (Aldershot: Gale & Polden Ltd, 1951).

8. IWM SOUND: AC 14790, William Pringle, Reels 7 & 8.

9. IWM SOUND: AC 14761, Robert Daniell, Reel 10.

10. IWM SOUND: AC 16706, David Elliott, Reel 10.

11. IWM SOUND: AC 14788, Albert Parker, Reel 8.

12. IWM SOUND: AC 12660, Ray Ellis, Reel 31.
13. IWM SOUND: AC 14897, Charles Ward, Reel 10.
14. IWM SOUND: AC 12409, Ted Whittaker, Reel 19.
15. INTERNET SOURCE: Ronald Miles Autobiography (Copyright Paul Miles), http://ronaldmiles.blogspot.com/
16. IWM SOUND: AC 14790, William Pringle, Reel 8.
17. IWM SOUND: AC 12660, Ray Ellis, Reel 31.
18. IWM SOUND: AC 16280, Dennis Mayoh, Reel 5.
19. IWM SOUND: AC 11960, Jack Sykes, Reel 6.
20. IWM SOUND: AC 11960, Jack Sykes, Reel 6.
21. IWM SOUND: AC 14897, Charles Ward, Reel 10.
22. IWM SOUND: AC 14897, Charles Ward, Reel 10.
23. IWM SOUND: AC 12409, Ted Whittaker, Reel 20.
24. IWM SOUND: AC 12409, Ted Whittaker, Reel 20.
25. IWM SOUND: AC 14788, Albert Parker, Reel 8.
26. IWM SOUND: AC 11465, Frank Knowles, Reels 6 & 7.
27. IWM SOUND: AC 12412, Harry Day, Reel 8.
28. IWM SOUND: AC 12412, Harry Day, Reel 8.
29. IWM SOUND: AC 12412, Harry Day, Reel 8.
30. IWM SOUND: AC 11465, Frank Knowles, Reel 6.
31. IWM SOUND: AC 12412, Harry Day, Reels 5 & 8. Captain Graham Slinn died aged 25 on 6 June 1942. He is buried in Knightsbridge War Cemetery, Acroma, Libya. Lieutenant Jeffrey Timms died aged 29 on 11 June 1942. He is buried in Benghazi War Cemetery, Libya. There is an inconsistency in the date of death in Day's account.
32. IWM SOUND: AC 12412, Harry Day, Reel 8.
33. Sergeant William Lake died aged 34 on 6 June 1942. He is commemorated on the Alamein Memorial, Egypt.
34. IWM SOUND: AC 14897, Charles Ward, Reel 10.
35. IWM SOUND: AC 14897, Charles Ward, Reel 10.
36. IWM SOUND: AC 12660, Ray Ellis, Reel 32.
37. Lieutenant Colonel William Seely died aged 39 on 6 June 1942. He is commemorated on the Alamein Memorial, Egypt.
38. Captain Henry Peal died aged 30 on 7 June 1942. He is buried in Knightsbridge War Cemetery, Acroma, Libya.
39. IWM SOUND: AC 14788, Albert Parker, Reel 8.
40. IWM SOUND: AC 12409, Ted Whittaker, Reel 20.

41. IWM SOUND: AC 14761, Robert Daniell, Reel 10.

42. IWM SOUND: AC 14761, Robert Daniell, Reel 10.

43. IWM SOUND: AC 11464, John Walker, Reel 12.

44. Lance Bombardier Albert Harrison died aged 33 on 6 June 1942. He is buried in Knightsbridge War Cemetery, Acroma, Libya.

45. Gunner George Stevenson died aged 21 on 6 June 1942. He is buried in Knightsbridge War Cemetery, Acroma, Libya.

46. IWM SOUND: AC 12409, Ted Whittaker, Reels 20 & 21.

47. IWM SOUND: AC 14790, William Pringle, Reel 8.

48. IWM SOUND: AC 14761, Robert Daniell, Reel 10.

49. IWM SOUND: AC 14790, William Pringle, Reel 9.

50. Captain Alan Chadburn died aged 25 on 6 June 1942. He is buried in Knightsbridge War Cemetery, Acroma, Libya.

51. IWM SOUND: AC 14790, William Pringle, Reels 8 & 9.

52. IWM SOUND: AC 12412, Harry Day, Reel 8.

53. IWM SOUND: AC 12240 Fred Langford, Reel 7.

54. IWM SOUND: AC 11465, Frank Knowles, Reel 7.

55. IWM SOUND: AC 12409, Ted Whittaker, Reel 21.

56. IWM SOUND: AC 12660, Ray Ellis, Reel 32.

57. IWM SOUND: AC 14897, Charles Ward, Reel 10.

58. IWM SOUND: AC 12660, Ray Ellis, Reel 32. Captain Colin Barber died aged 29 on 6 June 1942. Buried in Benghazi War Cemetery, Libya.

59. IWM SOUND: AC 14897, Charles Ward, Reel 11.

60. Lance Bombardier Frederick Charles died aged 21 on 7 June 1942. He is buried in Knightsbridge War Cemetery, Acroma, Libya.

61. IWM SOUND: AC 11465, Frank Knowles, Reel 7.

62. IWM SOUND: AC 12660, Ray Ellis, Reels 32 & 33.

63. IWM SOUND: AC 14761, Robert Daniell, Reel 10.

64. Eric Dobson, *History of the South Nottinghamshire Hussars, 1924–1948* (York & London: Herald Printing Works, 1948), pp. 135–6.

13. Rebuilding

1. IWM SOUND: AC 10923, Harold Harper, Reel 10.

2. IWM SOUND: AC 12435, Reg McNish, Reel 10.

3. IWM SOUND: AC 14794, David Tickle, Reel 9.

4. IWM SOUND: AC 16706, David Elliott, Reel 11.

5. IWM SOUND: AC 15104, Albert Swinton, Reel 9.
6. IWM SOUND: AC 16706, David Elliott, Reel 11.
7. Erwin Rommel quoted by Ian Beckett, *Rommel Reconsidered* (Mechanicsburg, Pennsylvania: Stackpole Books, 2014), p. 89.
8. Claude Auchinleck quoted by Bryn Hammond, *El Alamein: The Battle that Turned the Tide of the Second World War* (Oxford: Osprey Publishing, 2012), p. 49.
9. Erwin Rommel quoted by Bryn Hammond, *El Alamein*, p. 52.
10. It was briefly known as 426 Battery but soon changed to 107 Battery. I have used that throughout to avoid confusion.
11. IWM SOUND: AC 13125, Reg Cutter, Reel 4.
12. IWM SOUND: AC 14729, Ernie Hurry, Reel 13.
13. IWM SOUND: AC 10923, Harold Harper, Reel 10.
14. IWM SOUND: AC 10923, Harold Harper, Reel 10.
15. IWM SOUND: AC 14728, Ken Giles, Reel 5.
16. IWM SOUND: AC 14728, Ken Giles, Reel 8.
17. Eric Dobson, *History of the South Nottinghamshire Hussars, 1924–1948* (York & London: Herald Printing Works, 1948), p. 144.

14. Battle of El Alamein

1. IWM SOUND: AC 14729, Ernie Hurry, Reel 11.
2. Bernard Montgomery quoted by Bryn Hammond, *El Alamein: The Battle that Turned the Tide of the Second World War* (Oxford: Osprey Publishing, 2012), p. 107.
3. Bernard Montgomery memo 14/9/1942.
4. IWM SOUND: AC 11048, Charles Westlake, Reel 10.
5. IWM SOUND: AC 12715, Robert Foulds, Reel 12.
6. IWM SOUND: AC 11048, Charles Westlake, Reel 10.
7. IWM SOUND: AC 14728, Ken Giles, Reel 6.
8. Eric Dobson, *History of the South Nottinghamshire Hussars, 1924–1948* (York & London: Herald Printing Works, 1948), p. 144.
9. IWM SOUND: AC 15104, Albert Swinton, Reel 10.
10. IWM SOUND: AC 16706, David Elliott, Reel 12.
11. IWM SOUND: AC 16706, David Elliott, Reel 12.
12. IWM SOUND: AC 15103, Charles Laborde, Reel 14.
13. Eric Dobson, *History of the South Nottinghamshire Hussars*, pp. 147–8.

14. IWM SOUND: AC 14728, Ken Giles, Reel 6.

15. IWM SOUND: AC 12715, Robert Foulds, Reel 12.

16. IWM SOUND: AC 15103, Charles Laborde, Reel 15.

17. Eric Dobson, *History of the South Nottinghamshire Hussars, 1924–1948* (York & London: Herald Printing Works, 1948), p. 153.

18. IWM SOUND: AC 15103, Charles Laborde, Reel 15.

19. Gunner Alfred Brownlow died aged 22 on 19 September 1942. He is buried in Alexandria War Memorial Cemetery.

20. Gunner William Becks died aged 33 on 5 September 1942. He is buried in El Alamein War Cemetery.

21. Eric Dobson, *History of the South Nottinghamshire Hussars, 1924–1948* (York & London: Herald Printing Works, 1948), pp. 154–5.

22. IWM SOUND: AC 11468, Ian Sinclair, Reel 12.

23. I am indebted to the work of Stig Moberg and his brilliant book, *Gunfire: British Artillery in World War II* (Barnsley: Frontline Books, 2017), pp. 354–5.

24. IWM SOUND: AC 12715, Robert Foulds, Reel 13.

25. IWM SOUND: AC 11468, Ian Sinclair, Reel 13.

26. IWM SOUND: AC 15103, Charles Laborde, Reel 14.

27. IWM SOUND: AC 10923, Harold Harper, Reel 10.

28. IWM SOUND: AC 12715, Robert Foulds, Reels 12 & 13.

29. IWM SOUND: AC 15104, Albert Swinton, Reel 11.

30. IWM SOUND: AC 12715, Robert Foulds, Reels 12 & 13.

31. IWM SOUND: AC 15103, Charles Laborde, Reel 15.

32. IWM SOUND: AC 15104, Albert Swinton, Reel 11.

33. Eric Dobson, *History of the South Nottinghamshire Hussars*, p. 158.

34. IWM SOUND: AC 12715, Robert Foulds, Reel 14.

35. IWM SOUND: AC 11048, Charles Westlake, Reel 11.

36. IWM SOUND: AC 15103, Charles Laborde, Reels 15 & 16.

37. IWM SOUND: AC 12715, Robert Foulds, Reel 14.

38. IWM SOUND:, AC 10923, Harold Harper Reel 12.

39. IWM SOUND: AC 14728, Ken Giles, Reel 8.

40. IWM SOUND: AC 11048, Charles Westlake, Reel 11.

41. IWM SOUND: AC 14729, Ernie Hurry, Reels 11 & 12.

42. IWM SOUND: AC 10923, Harold Harper, Reel 12.

43. IWM SOUND: AC 10923, Harold Harper, Reel 12.

44. IWM SOUND: AC 15103, Charles Laborde, Reel 16.

45. IWM SOUND: AC 15103, Charles Laborde, Reel 16.
46. IWM SOUND: AC 15103, Charles Laborde, Reels 16 & 17.
47. IWM SOUND: AC 15103, Charles Laborde, Reels 16 & 17.
48. IWM SOUND: AC 15103, Charles Laborde, Reels 16 & 17.
49. IWM SOUND: AC 15103, Charles Laborde, Reel 17.
50. Erwin Rommel quoted in Bryn Hammond, *El Alamein*, p. 52.
51. IWM SOUND: AC 14728, Ken Giles, Reel 8.

15. Advance to Victory in North Africa

1. IWM SOUND: AC 11048, Charles Westlake, Reel 11.
2. IWM SOUND: AC 12715, Robert Foulds, Reel 14.
3. Eric Dobson, *History of the South Nottinghamshire Hussars, 1924–1948* (York & London: Herald Printing Works, 1948), p. 162.
4. IWM SOUND: AC 10923, Harold Harper, Reel 13.
5. Eric Dobson, *History of the South Nottinghamshire Hussars, 1924–1948* (York & London: Herald Printing Works, 1948), p. 162.
6. Eric Dobson, *History of the South Nottinghamshire Hussars, 1924–1948* (York & London: Herald Printing Works, 1948), p. 167.
7. IWM SOUND: AC 11048, Charles Westlake, Reel 12.
8. Sergeant Percy Powell died aged 24 on 18 January 1943. He is commemorated on the Alamein Memorial, Egypt.
9. IWM SOUND: AC 14729, Ernie Hurry, Reel 12.
10. Eric Dobson, *History of the South Nottinghamshire Hussars, 1924–1948* (York & London: Herald Printing Works, 1948), p. 167.
11. IWM SOUND: AC 16085, Frank Penlington, Reels 5 & 6.
12. IWM SOUND: AC 14729, Ernie Hurry, Reel 12.
13. IWM SOUND: AC 12715, Robert Foulds, Reel 15.
14. IWM SOUND: AC 14794, David Tickle, Reel 11.
15. IWM SOUND: AC 11468, Ian Sinclair, Reel 14.
16. IWM SOUND: AC 16706, David Elliott, Reel 15.
17. SNH MUSEUM: David Elliott typescript memoir, 'Our Mothers Knew Your Grandfathers', pp. 157–8.
18. IWM SOUND: AC 16706, David Elliott, Reel 15.
19. IWM SOUND: AC 16706, David Elliott, Reel 15.
20. IWM SOUND: AC 16706, David Elliott, Reel 15.
21. IWM SOUND: AC 11048, Charles Westlake, Reel 11.
22. IWM SOUND: AC 10923, Harold Harper, Reel 13.

23. IWM SOUND: AC 12715, Robert Foulds, Reel 16.
24. IWM SOUND: AC 10923, Harold Harper, Reel 13.
25. IWM SOUND: AC 14794, David Tickle, Reel 12.
26. IWM SOUND: AC 11468, Ian Sinclair, Reel 14.
27. IWM SOUND: AC 13125, Reg Cutter, Reel 5.
28. IWM SOUND: AC 16706, David Elliott, Reel 16.
29. SNH MUSEUM: David Elliott typescript memoir, 'Our Mothers Knew Your Grandfathers', p. 168.
30. Lance Sergeant Wallace McCall died aged 29 on 3 April 1943. He is buried Enfidaville War Cemetery, Tunisia.
31. IWM SOUND: AC 16706, David Elliott, Reel 16.
32. SNH MUSEUM: David Elliott typescript memoir, 'Our Mothers Knew Your Grandfathers', p. 181.
33. IWM SOUND: AC 14728, Ken Giles, Reel 11.
34. IWM SOUND: AC 14794, David Tickle, Reel 12.
35. IWM SOUND: AC 14729, Ernie Hurry, Reel 13.
36. IWM SOUND: AC 12435, Reg McNish, Reel 12.
37. IWM SOUND: AC 14728, Ken Giles, Reel 12.
38. IWM SOUND: AC 16706, David Elliott, Reel 16.
39. IWM SOUND: AC 14728, Ken Giles, Reel 12.
40. IWM SOUND: AC 12435, Reg McNish, Reel 12.
41. IWM SOUND: AC 14728, Ken Giles, Reel 12.

16. Sicilian Sojourn

1. IWM SOUND: AC 14728, Ken Giles, Reel 10.
2. IWM SOUND: AC 10923, Harold Harper, Reel 14.
3. IWM SOUND: AC 13125, Reg Cutter, Reel 7.
4. IWM SOUND: AC 12715, Robert Foulds, Reel 18.
5. IWM SOUND: AC 14794, David Tickle, Reel 13.
6. IWM SOUND: AC 14794, David Tickle, Reel 14.
7. IWM SOUND: AC 14794, David Tickle, Reel 14.
8. IWM SOUND: AC 14728, Ken Giles, Reel 14.
9. IWM SOUND: AC 12715, Robert Foulds, Reel 18.
10. IWM SOUND: AC 10923, Harold Harper, Reel 14.
11. IWM SOUND: AC 15104, Albert Swinton, Reel 13.
12. IWM SOUND: AC 16706, David Elliott, Reel 17.
13. IWM SOUND: AC 12715, Robert Foulds, Reel 18.

14. IWM SOUND: AC 12715, Robert Foulds, Reel 18.
15. IWM SOUND: AC 16706, David Elliott, Reel 17.
16. IWM SOUND: AC 14728, Ken Giles, Reel 14.
17. IWM SOUND: AC 12715, Robert Foulds, Reel 18.
18. IWM SOUND: AC 15104, Albert Swinton, Reel 14.
19. IWM SOUND: AC 11958, Ted Holmes, Reel 10.
20. Eric Dobson, *History of the South Nottinghamshire Hussars, 1924–1948* (York & London: Herald Printing Works, 1948), p. 213.
21. IWM SOUND: AC 15104, Albert Swinton, Reel 14.
22. IWM SOUND: AC 14728, Ken Giles, Reel 15.
23. IWM SOUND: AC 14794, David Tickle, Reel 15.
24. IWM SOUND: AC 14728, Ken Giles, Reel 15.
25. IWM SOUND: AC 10923, Harold Harper, Reel 14.
26. IWM SOUND: AC 10923, Harold Harper, Reel 14.
27. IWM SOUND: AC 14728, Ken Giles, Reel 16.
28. Eric Dobson, *History of the South Nottinghamshire Hussars*, p. 214.
29. IWM SOUND: AC 13125, Reg Cutter, Reel 8.
30. IWM SOUND: AC 11468, Ian Sinclair, Reel 17.
31. IWM SOUND: AC 11468, Ian Sinclair, Reel 17.

17. Back Home

1. IWM SOUND: AC 11468, Ian Sinclair, Reel 18.
2. IWM SOUND: AC 14794, David Tickle, Reel 16.
3. IWM SOUND: AC 14794, David Tickle, Reel 16.
4. IWM SOUND: AC 14794, David Tickle, Reel 16.
5. IWM SOUND: AC 13125, Reg Cutter, Reel 8.
6. IWM SOUND: AC 14728, Ken Giles, Reel 17.
7. IWM SOUND: AC 11468, Ian Sinclair, Reel 18.
8. Brigadier Horace Elton died aged 44 on 5 November 1943. Buried at Halfaya Sollum War Cemetery, Egypt.
9. Eric Dobson, *History of the South Nottinghamshire Hussars, 1924–1948* (York & London: Herald Printing Works, 1948), pp. 219–20.
10. IWM SOUND: AC 10923, Harold Harper, Reel 15.
11. IWM SOUND: AC 12435, Reg McNish, Reel 13.
12. The actual landing and naval elements were codenamed Operation Neptune.
13. IWM SOUND: AC 10923, Harold Harper, Reel 15.

14. IWM SOUND: AC 14794, David Tickle, Reel 16.
15. IWM SOUND: AC 10923, Harold Harper, Reel 15.
16. IWM SOUND: AC 16706, David Elliott, Reel 20.
17. IWM SOUND: AC 14731, Douglas Nicholls, Reel 4.
18. IWM SOUND: AC 11468, Ian Sinclair, Reel 18.
19. IWM SOUND: AC 11048, Charles Westlake, Reel 13.
20. IWM SOUND: AC 12183, Leonard Gibson, Reel 16.
21. IWM SOUND: AC 12183, Leonard Gibson, Reel 16.
22. IWM SOUND: AC 12183, Leonard Gibson, Reel 17.
23. IWM SOUND: AC 13125, Reg Cutter, Reel 8.
24. IWM SOUND: AC 14794, David Tickle, Reel 18.
25. IWM SOUND: AC 13125, Reg Cutter, Reel 8.

18. Normandy Attrition

1. Ronald Paisley, *From Normandy to Victory with the South Notts Hussars* (Carlisle: R. G. Paisley, 1945), pp. 15–16.
2. Ronald Paisley, *From Normandy to Victory with the South Notts Hussars*, pp. 15–16.
3. Ronald Paisley, *From Normandy to Victory with the South Notts Hussars*, p. 1.
4. IWM SOUND: AC 12183, Leonard Gibson, Reel 17.
5. IWM SOUND: AC 12183, Leonard Gibson, Reels 17 & 18.
6. Ronald Paisley, *From Normandy to Victory with the South Notts Hussars*, p. 7.
7. IWM SOUND: AC 14728, Ken Giles, Reel 19.
8. IWM SOUND: AC 11048, Charles Westlake, Reel 13.
9. Ronald Paisley, *From Normandy to Victory with the South Notts Hussars*, p. 6.
10. Ronald Paisley, *From Normandy to Victory with the South Notts Hussars*, pp. 8–9.
11. Ronald Paisley, *From Normandy to Victory with the South Notts Hussars*, p. 10.
12. Lance Bombardier Raymond Whittington died aged 33 on 19 July 1944. He is buried in Bayeux War Cemetery.
13. IWM SOUND: AC 10923, Harold Harper, Reel 15.
14. IWM SOUND: AC 10923, Harold Harper, Reel 15.

15. Ronald Paisley, *From Normandy to Victory with the South Notts Hussars*, p. 12.

16. IWM SOUND: AC 12183, Leonard Gibson, Reel 18.

17. IWM SOUND: AC 16706, David Elliott, Reel 20.

18. IWM SOUND: AC 15104, Albert Swinton, Reel 15.

19. IWM SOUND: AC 14731, Douglas Nicholls, Reel 5.

20. Ronald Paisley, *From Normandy to Victory with the South Notts Hussars*, pp. 13–14.

21. Ronald Paisley, *From Normandy to Victory with the South Notts Hussars*, p. 14.

22. Ronald Paisley, *From Normandy to Victory with the South Notts Hussars*, pp. 15–16.

23. Gunner Henry Beardsworth died aged 20 on 31 July 1944. He is buried in Ranville War Cemetery.

24. Gunner Ernest Donaldson died aged 24 on 31 July 1944. He is buried in Ranville War Cemetery.

25. Ronald Paisley, *From Normandy to Victory with the South Notts Hussars*, p. 18.

26. Ronald Paisley, *From Normandy to Victory with the South Notts Hussars*, pp. 20–21.

27. IWM SOUND: AC 11048, Charles Westlake, Reel 14.

28. IWM SOUND: AC 12183, Leonard Gibson, Reel 18.

29. IWM SOUND: AC 12183, Leonard Gibson, Reel 18.

30. IWM SOUND: AC 12715, Robert Foulds, Reel 21.

31. IWM SOUND: AC 12715, Robert Foulds, Reel 21.

32. Ronald Paisley, *From Normandy to Victory with the South Notts Hussars*, pp. 24–5.

33. IWM SOUND: AC 10923, Harold Harper, Reel 16.

34. Ronald Paisley, *From Normandy to Victory with the South Notts Hussars*, p. 25.

35. IWM SOUND: AC 12715, Robert Foulds, Reel 21.

36. IWM SOUND: AC 12183, Leonard Gibson, Reel 18.

37. IWM SOUND: AC 12183, Leonard Gibson, Reel 18.

38. IWM SOUND: AC 12183, Leonard Gibson, Reel 19.

39. IWM SOUND: AC 12183, Leonard Gibson, Reel 19.

40. Ronald Paisley, *From Normandy to Victory with the South Notts Hussars*, p. 30.

41. Ronald Paisley, *From Normandy to Victory with the South Notts Hussars*, p. 36.

42. IWM SOUND: AC 11468, Ian Sinclair, Reel 20.

43. This seems to be the incident of firing from Hôtel Crillon during de Gaulle's official entry to the city in the Place de la Concorde, 26 August 1944.

44. IWM SOUND: AC 10923, Harold Harper, Reel 16.

45. IWM SOUND: AC 12183, Leonard Gibson, Reel 20.

46. IWM SOUND: AC 11468, Ian Sinclair, Reel 20.

47. Ronald Paisley, *From Normandy to Victory with the South Notts Hussars*, p. 36.

19. End Game in Europe

1. IWM SOUND: AC 12715, Robert Foulds, Reel 21.

2. IWM SOUND: AC 12183, Leonard Gibson, Reel 19.

3. IWM SOUND: AC 12183, Leonard Gibson, Reel 19.

4. IWM SOUND: AC 16706, David Elliott, Reels 22 & 23.

5. Ronald Paisley, *From Normandy to Victory with the South Notts Hussars* (Carlisle: R. G. Paisley, 1945), p. 43.

6. IWM SOUND: AC 16706, David Elliott, Reel 22.

7. IWM SOUND: AC 16706, David Elliott, Reel 22.

8. IWM SOUND: AC 14731, Douglas Nicholls, Reel 6.

9. IWM SOUND: AC 14731, Douglas Nicholls, Reel 6.

10. Ronald Paisley, *From Normandy to Victory with the South Notts Hussars*, p. 48.

11. IWM SOUND: AC 15104, Albert Swinton, Reel 16.

12. Ronald Paisley, *From Normandy to Victory with the South Notts Hussars*, p. 50.

13. IWM SOUND: AC 12715, Robert Foulds, Reel 22.

14. SNH MUSEUM: David Elliott typescript memoir, 'Our Mothers Knew Your Grandfathers', p. 297.

15. SNH MUSEUM: David Elliott typescript memoir, 'Our Mothers Knew Your Grandfathers', p. 301.

16. SNH MUSEUM: David Elliott typescript memoir, 'Our Mothers Knew Your Grandfathers', p. 302.

17. SNH MUSEUM: David Elliott typescript memoir, 'Our Mothers Knew Your Grandfathers', pp. 302–3.

18. SNH MUSEUM: David Elliott typescript memoir, 'Our Mothers Knew Your Grandfathers', p. 303.

19. SNH MUSEUM: David Elliott typescript memoir, 'Our Mothers Knew Your Grandfathers', p. 304.

20. SNH MUSEUM: David Elliott typescript memoir, 'Our Mothers Knew Your Grandfathers', p. 305.

21. SNH MUSEUM: David Elliott typescript memoir, 'Our Mothers Knew Your Grandfathers', p. 306.

22. Lance Bombardier James Ward died aged 25 on 26 October 1944. He is buried at Bergen op Zoom War Cemetery.

23. SNH MUSEUM: David Elliott typescript memoir, 'Our Mothers Knew Your Grandfathers', pp. 307–8.

24. IWM SOUND: AC 11468, Ian Sinclair, Reel 22.

25. IWM SOUND: AC 11468, Ian Sinclair, Reel 22.

26. IWM SOUND: AC 11468, Ian Sinclair, Reel 22.

27. IWM SOUND: AC 11468, Ian Sinclair, Reel 22.

28. Ronald Paisley, *From Normandy to Victory with the South Notts Hussars*, p. 51.

29. Eric Dobson, *History of the South Nottinghamshire Hussars, 1924–1948* (York & London: Herald Printing Works, 1948), p. 323.

30. Ronald Paisley, *From Normandy to Victory with the South Notts Hussars*, p. 54.

31. Eric Dobson, *History of the South Nottinghamshire Hussars*, p. 329.

32. IWM SOUND: AC 12183, Leonard Gibson, Reel 19.

33. IWM SOUND: AC 14728, Ken Giles, Reel 21.

34. Ronald Paisley, *From Normandy to Victory with the South Notts Hussars*, p. 55.

35. Bombardier William Miles died aged 24 on 3 December 1944. He is buried in Sittard War Cemetery.

36. Gunner Kenneth Annan died aged 33 on 3 December 1944. He is buried in Sittard War Cemetery.

37. IWM SOUND: AC 12715, Robert Foulds, Reel 22.

38. IWM SOUND: AC 14794, David Tickle, Reel 19.

39. Ronald Paisley, *From Normandy to Victory with the South Notts Hussars*, p. 59.

40. Eric Dobson, *History of the South Nottinghamshire Hussars, 1924–1948*, p. 329.

41. Ronald Paisley, *From Normandy to Victory with the South Notts Hussars*, pp. 59–60.

42. IWM SOUND: AC 11958, Ted Holmes, Reel 12.

43. IWM SOUND: AC 14728, Ken Giles, Reel 21.

44. Ronald Paisley, *From Normandy to Victory with the South Notts Hussars*, p. 62.

45. Ronald Paisley, *From Normandy to Victory with the South Notts Hussars*, p. 62.

46. IWM SOUND: AC 12183, Leonard Gibson, Reels 20 & 21.

47. Ronald Paisley, *From Normandy to Victory with the South Notts Hussars*, pp. 68–9.

48. Ronald Paisley, *From Normandy to Victory with the South Notts Hussars*, p. 69.

49. Gun detachment.

50. Ronald Paisley, *From Normandy to Victory with the South Notts Hussars*, p. 70.

51. IWM SOUND: AC 12183, Leonard Gibson, Reels 20 & 21.

52. IWM SOUND: AC 15104, Albert Swinton, Reel 17.

53. Ronald Paisley, *From Normandy to Victory with the South Notts Hussars*, pp. 70–71.

54. Gunner Thomas Charlton died aged 34 on 8 February 1945. Gunner John Elliott died aged 19 on 14 February 1945. Gunner William Hales died aged 25 on 8 February 1945. Sergeant Ernest Mills died aged 29 on 8 February 1945. Gunner Edward Necchi died aged 27 on 8 February 1945. Sergeant John Perry died aged 27 on 8 February 1945. Gunner Frank Phillips died aged 20 on 8 February 1945. Gunner William Rushton died aged 31 on 8 February 1945. Gunner William Smith died aged 32 on 8 February 1945. Lance Bombardier Walter Tatham died aged 26 on 8 February 1945. Gunner Geoffrey Young died aged 19 on 8 February 1945. All are buried in Uden War Cemetery.

55. Ronald Paisley, *From Normandy to Victory with the South Notts Hussars* (Carlisle: R. G. Paisley, 1945), p. 71.

56. IWM SOUND: AC 12183, Leonard Gibson, Reel 21.

57. IWM SOUND: AC 10923, Harold Harper, Reel 16.

58. IWM SOUND: AC 12183, Leonard Gibson, Reel 21.

59. Ronald Paisley, *From Normandy to Victory with the South Notts Hussars* (Carlisle: R. G. Paisley, 1945), p. 77.
60. Ronald Paisley, *From Normandy to Victory with the South Notts Hussars* (Carlisle: R. G. Paisley, 1945), p. 78.
61. IWM SOUND: AC 10923, Harold Harper, Reel 16.
62. IWM SOUND: AC 16085, Frank Penlington, Reels 5 & 6.
63. IWM SOUND: AC 15104, Albert Swinton, Reel 17.
64. IWM SOUND: AC 10923, Harold Harper, Reel 16.
65. IWM SOUND: AC 16706, David Elliott, Reel 27.
66. IWM SOUND: AC 11468, Ian Sinclair, Reel 24.

20. Germany

1. IWM SOUND: AC 14794, David Tickle, Reel 21.
2. IWM SOUND: AC 16085, Frank Penlington, Reels 5 & 6.
3. IWM SOUND: AC 14794, David Tickle, Reel 21.
4. IWM SOUND: AC 14794, David Tickle, Reel 21.
5. IWM SOUND: AC 15104, Albert Swinton, Reel 18.
6. B. Montgomery (Letter by the Commander-in-Chief on Non-fraternisation, March 1945), Germany, 21st Army Group, 1945.
7. IWM SOUND: AC 13125, Reg Cutter, Reel 12.
8. IWM SOUND: AC 12715, Robert Foulds, Reel 23.
9. IWM SOUND: AC 16706, David Elliott, Reel 28.
10. IWM SOUND: AC 15104, Albert Swinton, Reel 18.
11. IWM SOUND: AC 12715, Robert Foulds, Reel 24.
12. IWM SOUND: AC 10923, Harold Harper, Reel 16.
13. IWM SOUND: AC 12715, Robert Foulds, Reel 24.
14. IWM SOUND: AC 16706, David Elliott, Reel 29.
15. IWM SOUND: AC 16706, David Elliott, Reel 29.
16. IWM SOUND: AC 10923, Harold Harper, Reel 17.
17. IWM SOUND: AC 10923, Harold Harper, Reel 17.
18. IWM SOUND: AC 14728, Ken Giles, Reel 25.
19. IWM SOUND: AC 10923, Harold Harper, Reel 16.
20. IWM SOUND: AC 15104, Albert Swinton, Reel 18.

21. Après la Guerre

1. IWM SOUND: AC 13125, Reg Cutter, Reel 7.
2. IWM SOUND: AC 10923, Harold Harper, Reel 17.

3. IWM SOUND: AC 10912, George Pearson, Reel 11.
4. IWM SOUND: AC 11960, Jack Sykes, Reel 12.
5. IWM SOUND: AC 12409, Ted Whittaker, Reel 21.
6. SNH MUSEUM: David Elliott typescript memoir, 'Our Mothers Knew Your Grandfathers', p. 421.
7. IWM SOUND: AC 15104, Albert Swinton, Reel 19.
8. IWM SOUND: AC 12660, Ray Ellis, Reel 50.
9. IWM SOUND: AC 10912, George Pearson, Reel 11.
10. IWM SOUND: AC 14897, Charles Ward, Reel 15.
11. IWM SOUND: AC 14986, Dennis Middleton, Reel 11.
12. IWM SOUND: AC 12412, Harry Day, Reel 12.
13. IWM SOUND: AC 11958, Ted Holmes, Reel 12.
14. IWM SOUND: AC 14729, Ernie Hurry, Reel 18.
15. IWM SOUND: AC 10923, Harold Harper, Reel 17.
16. IWM SOUND: AC 16085, Frank Penlington, Reels 5 & 6.
17. IWM SOUND: AC 15607, Bobby Feakins, Reel 6 & 7.
18. IWM SOUND: AC 14731, Douglas Nicholls, Reel 7.
19. IWM SOUND: AC 14791, William Adams, Reel 13.

ACKNOWLEDGEMENTS

First of all, I would like to thank the men of the South Notts Hussars who were interviewed for the IWM Sound Archive Project. For historians the IWM is the repository of the most amazing collections of valuable archive material. As my retirement approaches, I would offer my appreciation of my long-suffering heads of department: David Lance, Margaret Brooks, Tony Richards and Carl Warner. Not forgetting my chum Bryn Hammond, the head of collections, who has always supported my efforts inside and outside of the museum. Second, my thanks to the Trustees of the South Notts Hussars Museum who allowed me to use their photographs and the memoirs of David Elliott. Thanks also to Sally Bailey, the daughter of Bob Foulds, who supplied several photos. Paul Miles supplied a memoir and photos of his father Ron Miles. Without the generosity of these people there would have been no book.

I would offer my appreciation of my editor Nathanial McKenzie and my lovely copy-editor Penny Gardiner, who have both been patience personified. My two chums John Paylor and Phil Wood both read an early copy of the script and made many helpful comments that I think have greatly improved the text. They also made unhelpful negative comments on my overall intelligence and personality; I have put those aside, washed away in a surge of gratitude for all they have done. Grateful thanks also to Ian Drury, my agent, a man who would bring a touch of style to the Brigade of Guards, who provided much-needed advice on some tricky points of historical interpretation.

The world of the internet has rendered a bibliography little more than a prolonged boasting session, but the following books were utterly invaluable:

Eric Dobson, *History of the South Nottinghamshire Hussars, 1924–1948* (York & London: Herald Printing Works, 1948)

Stig Moberg, *Gunfire: British Artillery in World War II* (Barnsley: Frontline Books, 2017)

J. A. C. Monk, *The History of the 7th Medium Regiment Royal Artillery during World War II, 1939–1945* (London: Loxley Brothers, 1951)

Stuart Pitman, *Second Royal Gloucestershire Hussars, Libya–Egypt, 1941–1942* (London: The Saint Catherine Press Ltd, 1950)

PICTURE CREDITS

The author and publisher would like to extend their thanks for the kind cooperation and generosity in reproducing the photographs displayed in this book. Our thanks to the following:

South Notts Association Museum: 1, 2, 3, 4, 5, 6, 7, 8, 9, 10, 11 12, 14, 15, 16, 17, 18, 19, 20, 21, 22, 23, 24, 25, 31
Sally Bailey: 26, 27, 28, 29, 30, 32
Paul Miles: 13
Edward Whittaker: cartoon on p. 169

While every effort has been made to contact copyright-holders of illustrations, the author and publishers would be grateful for information about any illustrations where they have been unable to trace them, and would be glad to make amendments in further editions.

INDEX

Page references in *italics* indicate images.

Index

Index